P9-DNG-966

ALSO BY BERNARD GLADSTONE

THE COMPLETE BOOK OF GARDEN AND OUTDOOR LIGHTING, 1956

HINTS AND TIPS FOR THE HANDYMAN, 1960

THE HOW-TO BOOK OF PLUMBING AND HEATING, 1964

THE NEW YORK TIMES COMPLETE MANUAL OF HOME REPAIR, 1966

THE NEW YORK TIMES GUIDE TO FURNITURE FINISHING, 1969

THE NEW YORK TIMES GUIDE TO HOME REPAIRS WITHOUT A MAN, 1973

THE NEW YORK TIMES COMPLETE GUIDE TO HOME REPAIR, 1976

THE COMPLETE GUIDE TO FURNITURE FINISHING & REFINISHING, 1981

THE SIMON & SCHUSTER COMPLETE GUIDE TO HOME REPAIR AND MAINTENANCE, 1984

BOATKEEPER: THE BOAT OWNER'S GUIDE TO MAINTENANCE, REPAIR
      AND IMPROVEMENT, 1984

MORE BOATKEEPER: ALL-NEW GUIDE TO BOAT MAINTENANCE, REPAIR
      AND IMPROVEMENT, 1988

The Condo, Co-op, and Apartment Dweller's Guide to

REPAIRS AND

· ·

IMPROVEMENTS

· ·

BERNARD GLADSTONE

SIMON & SCHUSTER

NEW YORK   LONDON   TORONTO   SYDNEY   TOKYO   SINGAPORE

SIMON & SCHUSTER
Simon & Schuster Building
Rockefeller Center
1230 Avenue of the Americas
New York, New York 10020
Copyright © 1993 by Bernard Gladstone
All rights reserved
including the right of reproduction
in whole or in part in any form.
SIMON & SCHUSTER and colophon are registered trademarks of Simon & Schuster Inc.
Designed by Karolina Harris
Layout by Barbara Marks
Manufactured in the United States of America
10   9   8   7   6   5   4   3   2   1
Library of Congress Cataloging-in-Publication Data
Gladstone, Bernard.
    The condo, co-op, and apartment dweller's guide to repairs and
improvements / Bernard Gladstone.
        p.   cm.
    Includes index.
    1. Condominiums—Maintenance and repair—Amateurs' manuals.
    2. Apartments—Maintenance and repair—Amateurs' manuals.
    3. Apartment houses, Cooperative—Maintenance and repair—Amateurs'
    manuals. I. Title.
TH4817.3.G547 1993
643'.7—dc20   92-34107
                                                            CIP

ISBN: 0-671-55670-3

C O N T E N T S

INTRODUCTION

When most people think of a person they can describe as an enthusiastic "do-it-yourselfer" or a typical "home handyman," chances are that person lives in a conventional private house with a workshop set up in the garage or basement. Usually that homeowner is solely responsible for all the repairs and maintenance of his house—inside and outside—and normally does a great deal of that kind of work himself.

This picture, however, has changed considerably in recent years because of the steadily increasing number of people who now own and live in condominiums and cooperative apartments. Many of these people have also become avid do-it-yourselfers—sometimes by choice, and sometimes out of economic necessity. In fact, they probably have discovered that doing their own repair work is the only

way to get the job done in a reasonable amount of time—particularly when it's a small one.

Why the huge increase in people who live in condos and co-ops? There are many reasons, but certainly one leading cause is that condominiums and co-ops generally cost less to buy and maintain than conventional private houses in a similar location—especially if a housing shortage exists in that community. For many, buying a condo or co-op is the only affordable way to live in a location convenient to their places of employment, schools, shopping, and various cultural attractions.

Condominiums and co-ops also appeal both to young couples who are just starting out and to older people and "empty nesters" who no longer want the hassle and the expense of maintaining a large house. Many retired people—so-called senior citizens—have also sold their too-large houses for the more casual life-style of a condo or co-op where they no longer have to worry about maintaining the exterior of the building or grounds, which is usually taken care of by a superintendent, service manager, or management company of some kind.

Of course, individual owners of co-ops and condo units are still responsible for interior maintenance and repair of their own apartments—and that can sometimes pose a problem. Although there was a time when they could expect reasonably prompt and efficient repair service simply by calling the building superintendent or manager, that is, unfortunately, no longer always true. Service personnel are seldom as reliable as they should be, and are frequently reluctant to respond promptly to requests for small, minor repairs. As a result, residents are sometimes forced to face days, weeks, or months of frustrating delays and postponements. And when help does finally arrive, it is often neither as competent nor as efficient as the resident hoped it would be.

These are just some reasons why so many co-op and condominium owners today are interested in learning how to repair and maintain their own apartments. They are eager to learn all they can about the newest, simplest repair techniques and the materials they need to get the job done quickly and inexpensively. And while saving time and money may be their fundamental motives, many first-time do-it-yourselfers discover that they also derive a great deal of satisfaction and a feeling of accomplishment from doing much of their own work.

Even those who claim they're "all thumbs" find it necessary—and enjoy-

able—to do simple repairs themselves when they cannot find a professional to do the work for them. And when they do hire a professional, they are particularly interested to learn just how a job *should* be done, even if they aren't doing it themselves.

The Condo, Co-op, and Apartment Dweller's Guide to Repairs and Improvements is a comprehensive, up-to-date source of all the information they need to know, featuring detailed "how-to" instructions and step-by-step directions for every kind of interior home repair and maintenance chore. It will enable any reader—regardless of previous "how-to" experience—to tackle any household job safely, and the easy-to-follow text is illustrated by detailed drawings that fully explain every step involved.

This book is based on the wealth of information and experience I acquired while serving as Home Improvement editor of *The New York Times* for more than thirty years, writing two columns a week on home repair and improvement, one of which is still being nationally syndicated. It is also based on my almost fifty years of practical experience in the field of home repair, maintenance, and improvement—as a professional contractor, a distributor of home improvement products, a consultant to various manufacturers, an editor and writer of hundreds of magazine articles and newspaper columns in this field, and the author of numerous books—including *The Simon & Schuster Complete Guide to Home Repair and Maintenance*.

That comprehensive volume covers all phases of home repair and maintenance—from simple techniques that even a neophyte can easily follow to major exterior and interior projects that only an experienced do-it-yourselfer would be likely to tackle. But like all other home repair books, it is directed primarily at those who own conventional private houses, so it includes detailed information on all kinds of exterior maintenance and repair projects—information that most condo and co-op owners aren't concerned with.

It's true that owners of condos and co-ops are still responsible for fixing their own leaky faucets, replacing faulty light switches, repairing doors that stick or won't close properly, and doing all their own interior painting and decorating. However, they usually have only a limited amount of space available for storing tools and materials, so they want to learn how to handle these chores with fewer tools and less equipment. They also do not have the space needed to set up a well-equipped home workshop—or, in many cases, any kind of workshop at all.

Since exterior maintenance problems are not normally their responsibility, individual condo and co-op owners are not particularly interested in learning about the techniques involved in repairing stucco or siding, roofs and gutters, exterior painting, or keeping sidewalks, driveways, and other outside components clean and safe. They are, however, often faced with a number of problems that are not as common among homeowners. For example, what can they do to improve poorly designed or inadequate storage space? What can they do about a noisy next-door neighbor, or with noisy children in adjoining rooms in the same apartment? And how do they select—and then deal with—a contractor in those rare cases when it is necessary to hire professionals to get the job done?

These are only some of the specialized concerns that are covered in this new book. Bearing in mind that most co-op and condo owners are not as likely to own power tools or to have a fully equipped workshop or tool chest, I describe the simplest and least expensive ways to complete each type of repair and improvement project successfully. The text is comprehensive, and words and terms that may be unfamiliar are clearly defined. This guide contains *no* technical jargon that a novice might have trouble understanding. In addition, the book provides a wealth of valuable information and guidance that will prove helpful to the most experienced do-it-yourselfers, including many "tricks of the trade" that even a veteran handyman might find surprising. *The Condo, Co-op, and Apartment Dweller's Guide to Repairs and Improvements* is chock-full of shortcuts and solutions to all common (and not so common) problems that co-op and condo owners and apartment dwellers can solve for themselves. If you are one of them, it will save you time and money, and give you the great satisfaction of a job well done.

Bernard Gladstone

*T*ools and Materials

Even those who live in a small one-room rented apartment will have occasional need for a hammer, a screwdriver, or a pair of pliers—whether it be to hang up a picture, make needed repairs to a wobbly chair, or simply to tighten a loose screw on a pot handle. This doesn't mean that everyone needs to own a complete collection of tools equal to that of a professional—but it is a good idea to keep at least a basic assortment of tools and repair materials on hand to take care of day-to-day home maintenance chores and the inevitable simple repairs that almost everyone has to attend to themselves when there is no one else around (or available) to do the job.

THE TOOLS YOU WILL NEED

When shopping for tools—even when you are looking for a single screwdriver—always remember one important rule: Don't look for "bargains." Buy only top-quality, name brand tools and stay away from unknown brands or imports that are priced well below those of the recognized brands.

Not only will good-quality tools last longer than cheap ones (which means they will always cost you less in the long run), they will also save time and effort by making most jobs faster, easier, and less frustrating to complete. In addition, good-quality tools, when properly handled and maintained, are also much safer to work with—there is less chance of a blade slipping or a handle breaking while you are working.

When you get all your tools together, keep them together. Whether you want simply to store them all in an empty drawer or keep them in a well-organized toolbox, keep them all in one place where they can be found quickly when needed—and get in the habit of putting each tool back in its place as soon as the job is done. There are all kinds of toolboxes you can buy, some with trays and drawers, but don't get one so large that you won't be able to lift it when it is full. Two small or medium-size boxes are preferable to one large bulky one.

You don't have to store your tools in a box; there are also a wide variety of bags and pouches that you can buy that can be even more convenient than a rigid box. Or you can put racks up on the inside of a closet door or a cabinet door—or put up a panel of perforated hardboard and then hang your tools on hooks that are sold specifically for this. (See pages 250–51 for more information on installing such storage panels.)

What tools do you actually need? This will, of course, vary with individual requirements and with how much of your work you intend doing yourself—and you will undoubtedly acquire additional tools as knowledge and confidence grows. But here is a good basic list of tools that will be useful for most apartment dwellers and condominium owners, along with some pointers on how and where to use each of these tools.

HAMMERS

The most popular type of hammer, and probably the only one most beginners will need, is a conventional carpenter's claw hammer. Designed both for driving nails and for pulling them out, claw hammers come in various sizes, with heads that weigh from about 8 to 20 ounces. Generally speaking, a medium-weight hammer with a 12-ounce or 16-ounce head will be right for most home jobs. The claws on the hammer may be either straight or curved, but you'll probably find curved claws more useful for pulling nails (straight-claw hammers are preferred by professional carpenters for ripping joints apart).

Regardless of weight, the hammer should be well balanced, with a nice "feel" when you lift it. The hammer head should be made of polished steel and have a slightly crowned or bell-shaped face. The handle should be securely fastened to the head with wedges to keep it from slipping off, and it should provide a firm but comfortable grip.

When using a hammer for driving nails, you should hold it near the end (not up near the head) and swing the hammer with your forearm, not just by flexing your wrist. Try to aim your blows so that the face of the hammer always comes down squarely on the head of the nail, and concentrate on driving the nail in with a number of medium to light blows, rather than one or two very hard blows.

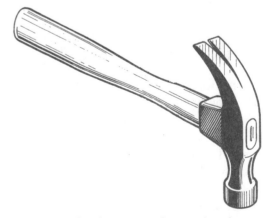

Carpenter's claw hammer with curved jaws.

Mallet with hard plastic face.

When using a claw hammer to pull nails, it's often advisable to put a small block of wood under the head of the hammer after you have pulled the nail partway out—especially if it is a long nail. The block of wood provides extra leverage so that the claws will continue to pull straight up instead of sideways. The nail will then come out more easily, without bending, and there will be less chance that the hammer head will mar the surface of the wood.

Although an ordinary claw hammer is probably all you will need for most jobs, you may eventually find it worthwhile to buy a mallet with a head made of wood or hard plastic. This will come in handy for pounding on the handle of a wood chisel, for assembling pieces of furniture when joints are tight, or for driving wood dowels into snug-fitting holes without smashing or distorting them.

SCREWDRIVERS

Screwdrivers can be bought with various types of blades, depending on the types of screw head they are designed to fit. There

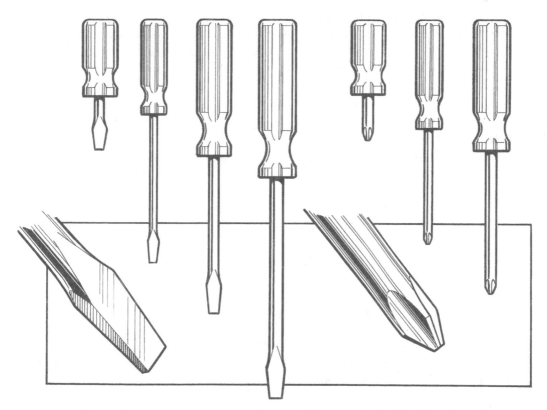

Assortment of screwdrivers in various sizes and in two different styles: flat blade for slotted screws (left) and Phillips-type blade for Phillips head screws (right).

are specialized variations that are widely used in industry, but for home use you are likely to need only two basic blade types—the conventional flat-blade or straight-blade screwdriver that fits ordinary slotted screws, and the Phillips-type screwdriver that has an X-shaped blade to fit into Phillips-head screws (cross-slotted screws that are widely used in furniture, appliances, and other such manufactured equipment).

Screwdrivers also come in a wide range of sizes that vary both in the length of the blade and in the width of the blade's tip. You don't have to start out with one of every size and style, but you should begin with the following:

1. Two flat-blade screwdrivers of medium length, one with a blade about ¼ inch wide, and another with a blade about ³⁄₁₆ inch wide.

2. A very small "jeweler's-type" screwdriver with a small flat blade to loosen or tighten the very small screws that are often found on instrument panels, electrical appliances, and similar items. These screwdrivers can be purchased individually or in small compact sets in a handy plastic pouch.

3. Two Phillips-type screwdrivers, one with a medium-size blade and one with a smaller blade.

4. Two "stubby" screwdrivers with very short handles and blades—one with a flat blade of medium width and the other with a Phillips-type blade of medium size. No more than 2 or 3 inches long overall, these screwdrivers are often essential for reaching into narrow spaces or tight corners where no ordinary-size screwdriver will fit. You won't need them every day, or necessarily on every project, but when you do need them nothing else will do.

Some Tips on Using Screwdrivers

Screwdrivers come in many different sizes to fit the many sizes of screw heads. For maximum driving power the blade should fill the slot in the head of the screws as snugly as possible—especially with conventional flat-blade screwdrivers. (Phillips-type drivers have a bit more room for error.)

The blade should fill the slot of the screw in width as well as in thickness. If you select a blade that is wider than the head of the screw, it is likely to gouge or scratch the surface of the wood when the screw is driven home. If, on the other hand, you use a blade that is too narrow, you won't be able to apply the leverage needed to drive the screw down tight (or to free it up if you are trying to loosen it). You are also very likely to damage the screwdriver blade or the screw head, even both.

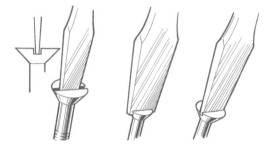

To avoid slipping, blade should be a snug fit inside screw slot and should be as close to the same width as possible.

It is important to remember that screwdrivers are designed only for removing screws or driving them home. They should not be used as pry bars, chisels, scrapers, or punches. Such use will invariably damage the blade and could render it almost useless for turning screws. When a blade does get nicked or worn, touching it up with a file will often restore its square edge.

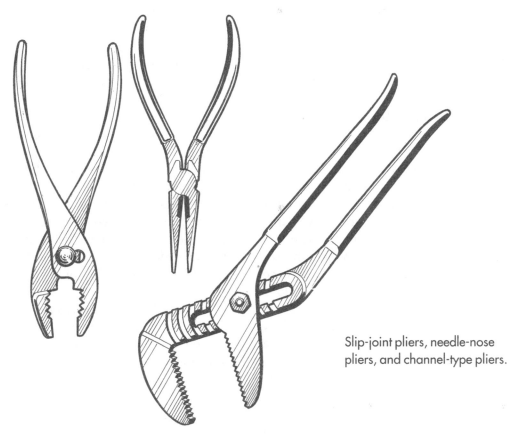

Slip-joint pliers, needle-nose pliers, and channel-type pliers.

PLIERS

Like screwdrivers, pliers come in a great many sizes and styles. You won't need all of them, but you cannot get by for long with just a single pair of all-purpose pliers. Every toolbox will need at least two or three pairs for a variety of different purposes. Here are the most widely used versions around the home, as well as some pointers on when and where each will be most handy.

Slip-joint pliers are probably the most useful and are the first ones most people acquire. The jaws are serrated and are curved, with the tips slightly rounded. The pivot bolt is of slip-joint construction so that you can set the handles in two posi-

tions: a standard position for gripping average-size objects, and another that allows the jaws to open much wider so they can grip wider objects. The handles in this position are much closer together, so you cannot apply as much pressure and the grip won't be quite as strong as in the "normal" position.

Channel-type pliers are sometimes referred to as water-pump pliers or mechanics pliers. These versatile models have angled jaws and are equipped with a series of grooves at the pivot point that permit the jaws to be set for a range of different-size openings. Available in various sizes from 6 to 18 inches in length, they are most generally useful in the

8-inch or 10-inch lengths. The angled jaws make them especially handy in plumbing work, to reach in to grab pipes and packing nuts where ordinary pliers would not fit. The handles are designed to apply greater leverage and turning power than is possible with an ordinary pair of straight slip-joint pliers.

Needle-nose pliers, as the name implies, have long tapered jaws that are ideal for reaching into tight corners or for handling small-diameter objects and tiny parts. Some models also have built-in wire cutters in the jaws—a handy feature for electrical jobs (and indeed needle-nose pliers are often required when working with wires, to bend loops at the ends and to pull wires around terminals). They come in various sizes or lengths, but as a rule you will find a pair 5 to 6 inches in length most useful, especially with built-in wire cutters.

Locking pliers, often referred to as a plier-wrench because it can perform many of the functions of a wrench as well as those of pliers. A pair of locking pliers is an extremely versatile tool. Although some may not consider this an essential tool that needs to be included in a beginner's "basic" tool kit, it is an extremely versatile and useful tool that once tried becomes almost indispensable to most do-it-yourselfers as well as pros. Its uses overlap those of an adjustable wrench, slip-joint pliers, and heavy-duty cutting pliers, although unlike ordinary pliers, the

jaws on this tool can be locked or clamped firmly onto the work to grip securely until manually released. The amount of tension applied to the jaws can be adjusted by turning a knurled screw or knob in the end of the handle.

The compound lever action used for clamping pressure permits you to apply tremendous force to the jaws—for cutting as well as for gripping—and the locking action makes it practical to use this tool as a small portable vise, as well as an efficient clamp. The type with curved serrated jaws can also be used as a pipe wrench or for grasping round objects that an ordinary wrench could not grasp tightly.

Locking pliers come with either straight or curved jaws and with or without built-in wire cutters near the pivot joint. They also come in various lengths and sizes.

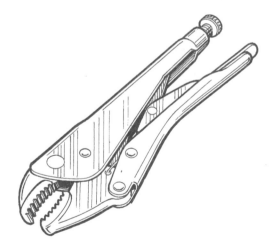

Versatile locking pliers can be used as wrench, pliers, or small clamp.

MEASURING AND LEVELING TOOLS

RULERS

For measuring, you will need some type of fairly accurate ruler. The most convenient for the average do-it-yourselfer is a flexible steel tape that rolls in and out of a case. Such tapes come in sizes that extend anywhere from 6 to 50 feet, but an 8-foot or 10-foot tape should prove adequate for most projects. The best ones have extra-wide blades that make it easy to keep them extended, vertically or horizontally, when working alone. Any such tape can be used for inside measurements between surfaces by adding the case's width (usually 2 inches) to the measured reading when the back of the case is butted against one surface and the hook end is pressed against the other surface.

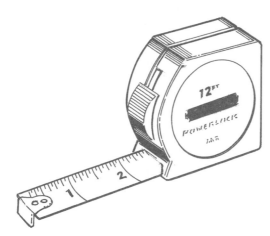

Flexible steel ruler, 8 to 10 feet in length, is useful for many jobs.

SQUARES

These are used to insure that pieces form an exact right angle or 90-degree joint when assembling or repairing projects, as well as for measuring and leveling (the blade of the square has inches and frac-

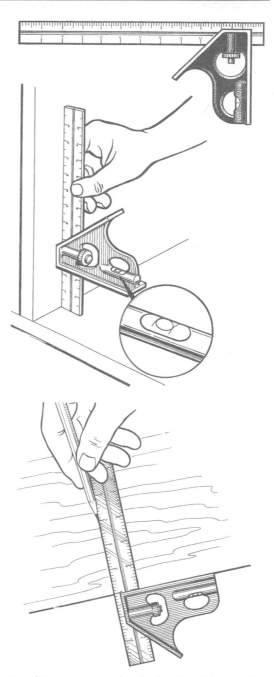

Combination square has built-in level that can be used to check plumb of vertical surfaces (middle), as well as for scribing for square cut (bottom).

tions of inches marked along both edges).

Probably the most versatile and most useful type of square for the apartment dweller or condominium owner is a combination square similar to the one illustrated here. Useful for leveling and checking to see if something is plumb (truly vertical), combination squares have a small spirit level built into the handle (as shown). When the flat side of this handle is placed against a surface, it will indicate if that surface is level, and to check if a vertical surface is plumb (vertical), you hold the blade against that surface as shown and read the level on the handle. Since the handle is at 90 degrees to the blade, you know that when the handle is level the blade is plumb.

The steel blade is usually 10 or 12 inches in length and is adjustable—that is, you can slide it in or out past the edge of the handle. This enables the tool to be used as a depth gauge, as well as a square, or for marking lines parallel to the edge of a straight surface. In addition to measuring or marking off 90-degree angles, the beveled or angled edge of the handle enables this square to be used for drawing and measuring 45-degree angles.

LEVELS

Spirit Levels (also called bubble levels) may be made of wood, metal, or plastic and come in various lengths—from pocket-size models only a few inches long to professional models that may be 4 to 6 feet in length. As a rule, a 24-inch carpenter's level, equipped with two or three sets of bubbles, will be adequate for most home jobs. One set of bubbles is used for checking the level of horizontal surfaces, while another set at right angles to the first checks vertical edges to make certain they are plumb. Some models have a third set of bubble vials for measuring 45-degree angles.

WRENCHES

Wrenches come in a tremendous variety of sizes, styles, and shapes—as a glance into any professional automobile mechanic's toolbox will indicate. However, most home repair and improvement projects require only a few basic types for tightening and loosening common-size nuts and bolts and for gripping pipes and other round objects.

The adjustable open-end wrench is usually the first wrench most people acquire. It has one movable jaw and one fixed jaw

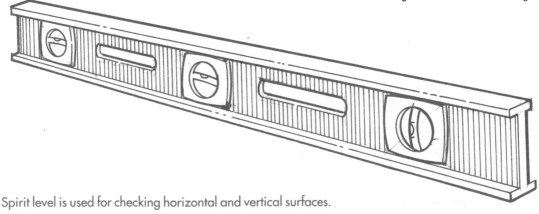

Spirit level is used for checking horizontal and vertical surfaces.

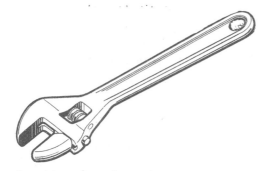

Adjustable open-end wrench.

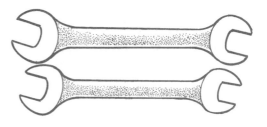

Fixed open-end wrenches.

and comes in various sizes—from as short as 6 inches to as long as 18 to 24 inches. The most useful sizes for home use would be one small model, 6 to 8 inches long, and a larger one, 10 to 12 inches long. These have worm-screw adjustments that enable you to set the size of the opening between the jaws. When setting the opening it is best to place the wrench over the nut or bolt head, then turn the screw until a snug fit is obtained. Adjustable wrenches do not grip as firmly as fixed wrenches, so you have to be more careful to avoid slipping. Make sure you check the adjustment periodically to see if it has loosened.

Open-end wrenches, which are nonadjustable, are a good investment for those who plan to do even a moderate amount of mechanical work. Although these may be considered as "optional" tools for most apartment dwellers, they are quite useful for many jobs because they do provide a stronger grip than adjustable wrenches. Also, since they are less bulky they will fit into tight places where an adjustable wrench will not. Open-end wrenches can be purchased individually or in sets, and they have a different-size opening at each end so that one wrench will fit two different sizes of nuts or bolts.

Allen wrenches should be in almost every home tool kit. Unlike conventional wrenches, these do not have jaws that lock on to the outside of the fastener— they fit inside a hollow in the head of the screw or bolt. An Allen wrench is actually a hexagonal length of steel rod bent into an L shape so that you can use either end while the other end serves as a handle to provide leverage for turning. They come in various sizes or diameters to fit hex-shaped recesses in setscrews and locking screws on tools, appliances, toys, and other household items. You probably won't need these wrenches very often, but

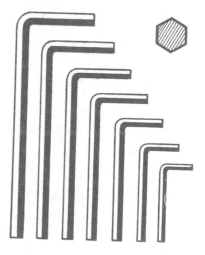

Allen wrenches, also called hex wrenches.

they're indispensable when you're making repairs or adjustments on appliances or tools, because manufacturers make wide use of Allen-head setscrews in assembling their equipment.

Some Pointers on Using Wrenches

With any type of wrench—fixed or adjustable—always make sure the head of the bolt or nut is clean and dry and that there is no grease or oil on the jaws of the wrench. The jaws should fit snugly with a minimum amount of play.

Always position the wrench so that you will be pushing the handle in the direction of the open jaws. Try not to push or pull the wrench handle in the opposite direction, since this will often result in the jaws slipping off the work or sliding open when a great deal of pressure must be applied. Repeated slipping will not only round off and eventually ruin the nut or bolt head (thus making it almost impossible to get a firm grip), it can also cause skinned knuckles or other injuries.

Pipe wrenches (also called Stillson wrenches) are adjustable wrenches with serrated, slightly curved jaws, one movable and one fixed. These wrenches will seldom be needed by most condominium owners and apartment dwellers, except for more ambitious do-it-yourselfers who live in older buildings that have plumbing systems that consist of threaded steel pipe and fittings. They come in various lengths or sizes and are designed so that the more force you apply on the handle, the more pressure the jaws will apply. For most plumbing jobs, especially when dealing with threaded pipe and fittings, you'll need two pipe wrenches. The reason for two wrenches is that you'll almost always need one to turn the pipe and another to hold the fitting or coupling into which it fits. As a rule, one 10-inch and one 12-inch model will be adequate for most work.

HANDSAWS

The first handsaw most people will buy is a conventional carpenter's crosscut saw 24 to 26 inches in length. These vary in coarseness depending on the number of teeth (points) per inch. Most have from 7 to 12 teeth per inch. A 7-point saw (7 teeth per inch) will cut faster than a 10- or 12-point saw, but it will also leave a rougher edge; 10- or 12-point saws give a finer cut but are slower-working. Generally speaking, blades with 8 to 10 points per inch are about right for most home jobs.

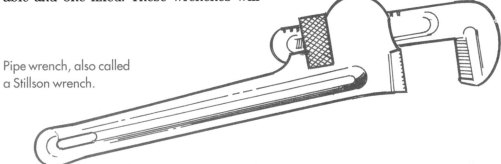

Pipe wrench, also called a Stillson wrench.

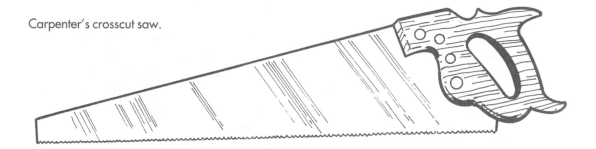

Carpenter's crosscut saw.

Crosscut saws, as the name implies, are designed primarily for cutting across the grain, although they can also be used for ripping (cutting parallel to the grain) if you don't mind working a little harder. Professional carpenters and serious woodworkers usually keep both a crosscut and a ripsaw in their boxes, but most people can get by easily with just a good crosscut saw. This is also the saw to use when cutting sheets of plywood, particle board, hardboard, and similar wood panel materials.

A keyhole saw (also called a compass saw) is often used for cutting in tight places where an ordinary crosscut saw will not fit, or for cutting openings in the middle of a panel. Its narrow, tapered blade can fit through a small starting hole drilled beforehand, and it can also cut curves. Some models come with only one blade, but others, often referred to as a utility saw set, come with three or four interchangeable blades in different sizes and types, one of which is usually a metal cutting blade.

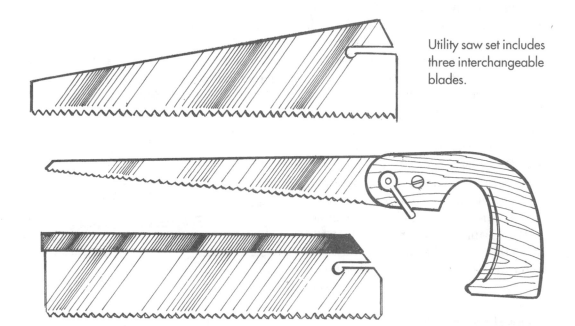

Utility saw set includes three interchangeable blades.

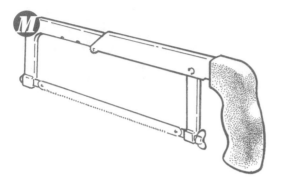

Hacksaw is used for cutting metal.

A hacksaw cuts metal, and in addition to saws for cutting wood, every tool kit will need at least one metal-cutting saw. The hacksaw has a steel frame that accepts replaceable blades that are available in a range of coarse and fine teeth. Equipped with the right blade, a hacksaw can cut almost any of the metals normally encountered around the house. It is also handy for cutting pipe and tubing when doing plumbing work. A blade with fine teeth is used for cutting light-gauge, thin stock such as sheet metal or thin-wall tubing. A blade with coarser teeth is better for cutting thicker metal, including rods, bolts, and angle iron. Like the woodworking saws, hacksaws do their cutting on the forward stroke, so you should get in the habit of lifting up slightly on the backward stroke. Otherwise the teeth will dull very rapidly. For maximum efficiency and accuracy, a hacksaw should be operated with two hands—one holding the handle, the other gripping the front end of the frame. Make sure the blade is fully tensioned by tightening the wing nut as much as you can by hand (using pliers on this wing nut can exert too much pressure, for the blades break easily).

CHISELS

Most wood chisels nowadays come with tough plastic handles that no longer split or "mushroom" when struck with a hammer or mallet, but it's still a good idea to use a plastic-, wood-, or rubber-faced mallet instead of a conventional steel hammer to pound on the chisel handle.

For fine trimming, a well-sharpened wood chisel can serve without a hammer—one hand guides the front end of the blade while the other pushes on the handle to force the blade along. The chisel should cut with a paring action, rather than the chopping or splitting action imparted by a hammer or mallet. On most jobs, such as when cutting mortises (recesses in the wood) while installing or resetting door hinges, you will use both methods—first hammering on the chisel handle for the preliminary roughing out, then switching to hand chiseling for the final trimming.

Most wood chisels are from 8 to 10 inches in length and have a blade that is beveled along the sides as well as on the cutting edge. For use in tight places, butt chisels are a couple of inches shorter, but only the larger hardware stores that cater to professional carpenters normally stock them.

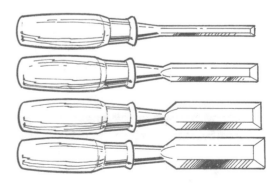

Set of wood chisels.

You'll want two or three wood chisels, from ½ inch to 1 inch in width. You can buy these in sets (½ inch, ¾ inch, and 1 inch), which are packed in a handy plastic pouch, or separately as needed.

• •

Pointers on Using Wood Chisels

Generally speaking, a chisel is used with the beveled side of the blade up (facing the part to be trimmed off or removed), but it can also be used with the beveled side down, for thin paring cuts or fine trimming where you don't want the blade to dig in too deep.

Whether you're working the chisel with your hands or tapping on the handle with a hammer, try to remove wood in small amounts and not dig too deep.

When you're cutting parallel to the grain, be careful that the blade doesn't try to follow the grain if it slopes away from you—this can cause it to dig in much deeper than you want it to and leads to splitting. When cutting recesses or mortises, always do the job in stages, making a series of shallow cuts rather than trying to cut the full depth at one time.

• •

WOOD PLANES

A wood plane is used to shape, trim, or smooth wood. It is most widely used for trimming to precise dimensions when necessary to ensure a close fit, as well as for final smoothing after cutting to size. All planes consist basically of a sharp, chisel-like blade that is held at an acute angle to the plane's base—usually anywhere from a 20- to 45-degree angle (depending on the type of plane). The cutting edge of this blade sticks down through a slot in the base, and the depth of cut is controlled by how much this blade projects down below

Small, one-hand block plane.

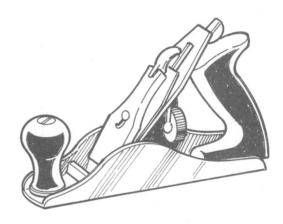

Bench plane is larger and is held with two hands.

the base. This amount of projection is precisely controlled by a depth-adjustment knob on the top or front of the tool.

Although wood planes come in a very wide range of sizes and styles, most do-it-yourselfers who live in apartments will need only one style—a small block plane about 6 inches long that can easily be used with one hand. Ideal for trimming moldings, drawers, shelf edges, and similar small surfaces, a block plane could also be used for trimming a sticking door, but you must handle it carefully since the short base will tend to follow curves or waves in the edge of the door without actually straightening them out.

Later on, if you decide to tackle more ambitious woodworking projects that involve trimming longer pieces of wood—or you have some doors to hang—then there is an "optional" tool you may want to add: a larger two-handled jack plane or

Pointers on Using Wood Planes

When using any wood plane, it is important that you adjust the depth of cut carefully before starting, preferably by experimenting on some scrap pieces of wood to see if the blade digs in. Also, make sure the blade is sharp and free of nicks. With a properly sharpened blade the shavings should come out in long continuous spirals (except when trimming end grain) and should be of relatively uniform thickness.

Hold the plane at a slight angle to the direction of travel, and try to work with the grain—that is, with any angle in the grain running up and away from you. There will be less likelihood then of the blade digging in or snagging as it tries to follow the grain down into the wood—you'll feel the difference quickly if you merely reverse the direction of travel and plane from the other end.

As you begin each stroke, apply more pressure to the knob at the front end of the plane to keep the back end from dipping. As the back end comes onto the surface, gradually shift pressure so that you are bearing down harder on the handle at the back end. Be careful to avoid dipping the front end of the plane as it goes out past the edge of the board. If you are planing end grain, work from either side toward the middle to avoid splitting off or splintering the edge of the wood. If you must plane past an edge, clamp a piece of scrap wood snug against that edge; splintering will then occur on the scrap piece rather than on the piece you are working on.

bench plane. These have two handles, one on the front end and another at the back. Usually 7 to 10 inches in length, these wood planes make it easier to do a smooth and accurate job of planing on long straight edges such as a door because the plane's base is less likely to follow dips or hollows in the surface of the wood as it rides over it.

FILES

Files come in an almost unlimited range of different sizes, styles, and shapes, but most are specialized models that are of interest only to serious craftsmen and professional mechanics. They are classified according to shape (flat, round, half-round, triangular, and so on), coarseness of cut (single-cut and double-cut), and size. Single-cut files give the smoothest finish, but they are also the slowest cutting. Double-cut files remove stock faster, but they leave a rougher finish.

Most home handymen or handywomen will find they can get by with just two files: an 8-inch combination flat file that has single-cut teeth on one side and double-cut teeth on the other, and a 5- or 6-inch triangular file that will be used for notching and trimming of inside corner joints, as well as

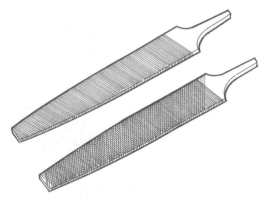

Single-cut file (top) and double-cut file (bottom).

for scratching a starting mark on tile and similar hard materials prior to drilling.

SURFORM TOOLS

These tools are sort of a cross between a wood rasp (a coarse file for use on wood) and a wood plane with a multitude of tiny blades. (Surform is a brand name for the ones made by Stanley Works, which introduced these tools originally.) Suitable for use on wood, hard plastics, and soft metals, the Surform tool has a replaceable sheet metal blade with many small teeth cut into the face of the metal—something like that of an old-fashioned potato grater. It comes in a variety of sizes and shapes— some for one-handed use and some for two-handed use. It is ideal for trimming the edges of a sticking door, drawer, or window, as well as for shaping or smoothing rough edges on shelves and moldings.

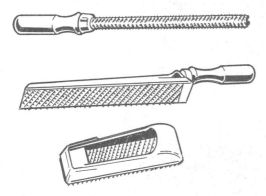

Surform-type tools come in various sizes, shapes, and styles.

CLAMPS

Although you won't need them very often, a couple of C-clamps will come in handy for many repair jobs where parts must be clamped together while gluing or where two or more pieces must be held together while they are being drilled or cut. As the

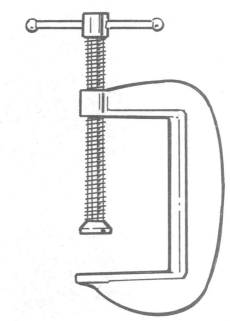

C-clamp.

name implies, the clamps are shaped like a capital C with a fixed jaw at one end of the C and a movable jaw at the end of a threaded shaft that goes across the open end (as shown in the drawing). These clamps come in various sizes, but as a rule a pair of clamps that open to 4 inches will be adequate for most home needs.

OTHER MISCELLANEOUS HAND TOOLS

Although you will undoubtedly keep adding new tools as you need them, here are a few miscellaneous tools that most will find useful.

For countersinking nails when you want to set the head of the nail below the surface of the wood, you will need a nail set similar to the one shown on page 26. In addition to setting or recessing nail heads, this tool is also handy as a small punch and for driving nails in tight corners where the hammer head won't fit.

Nail set.

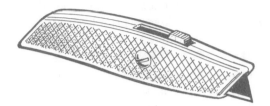

Utility knife has replaceable blades.

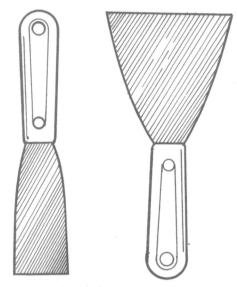

Large and small putty knives.

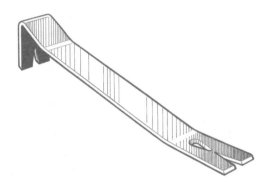

Pry bar.

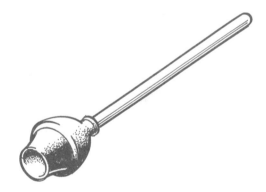

Rubber force cup for clogged drains, also called a "plumber's helper."

Putty knives are used for patching walls and ceilings, as well as for scraping off peeling paint, old wallpaper, and the like. It's a good idea to own two—one about 1½ inches in width and another about 4 or 5 inches wide. Both should have flexible steel blades for easy smoothing of patching materials.

Every toolbox should also include a utility knife that accepts disposable, razor-sharp blades, plus a small pry bar similar to the one illustrated. The pry bar comes in handy for prying off moldings without splitting them (as would happen if you used a claw hammer for this purpose), as well as for scraping off tiles and prying open stuck windows.

The utility knife is useful for cutting floor tiles, sheet plastics, gypsum board, and similar materials, as well as for scoring plastics and thin wood panels prior to cutting.

Since plumbers can never be located on weekends and holidays when an emergency arises, every home or apartment should have a "plumber's helper"—a rubber force cup or plunger that can be used to free up clogged drains. It's best to buy the combination type that can be used on either toilets or sink drains (these have a fold-out flap at the bottom that provides a better seal when used on the inside of a toilet bowl).

ELECTRIC DRILLS

Although a small hand drill could probably take care of most needs around the home, portable electric drills have now all but replaced them. They cost only a little more than a hand drill, and they are much easier and faster to use, plus a lot more versatile. In addition to drilling holes, with proper accessories an electric drill can be used for sanding, grinding, polishing, and even driving or removing screws (if you buy one of the variable-speed models that are also reversible).

Electric drills are sized according to the maximum-size drill bit that the chuck will accept. Models sold for home use are either ¼ inch, ⅜ inch, or ½ inch in size, but the ¼-inch and ⅜-inch models are by far the most popular. Since ⅜-inch drills cost only slightly more than equal-quality ¼-inch models, and often are only slightly larger or heavier than their smaller cousins, it's generally wiser to buy a ⅜-inch model. They have more torque and power than the smaller ones and thus can take larger bits with ease.

A ¼-inch drill or a ⅜-inch drill can be used to drill larger holes by using larger drill bits that are made with smaller (¼-inch) shanks, because then they can be chucked into a ¼-inch (or ⅜-inch) drill chuck. The most widely used type of bit is the twist drill, which can be used in both wood or metal and comes in sizes up to ½ inch in diameter (those designed for use in metal must be made of high-speed steel). In addition, you can also buy larger-

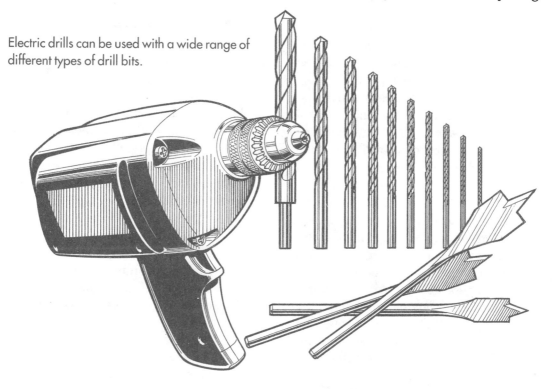

Electric drills can be used with a wide range of different types of drill bits.

diameter spade bits that go up to 1 inch in diameter (for wood only) and hole saws that will cut holes up to about 3 inches in diameter. Just remember that drilling with larger bits and hole saws should be limited to wood, plastic, and similar soft materials—unless you are using a heavy-duty ½-inch professional-quality drill.

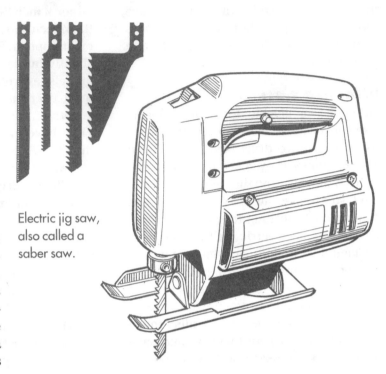

Electric jig saw, also called a saber saw.

Other features should be considered when shopping for an electric drill. For safety's sake, always buy a drill that is "double-insulated"—these come with a two-prong plug (a three-prong plug requires grounding). This type protects the user against shock if a short develops in the cord or the motor—a particularly important consideration when working outdoors or in damp locations.

It's also a good idea to select a drill that is reversible (handy for backing out drill bits that stick or bind) and one that also has a variable-speed control (rather than merely a single speed). On these the speed is controlled by the pressure on the trigger switch—the harder you pull on the switch, the faster the motor goes. Slower speeds are needed when working with large-diameter bits or when starting a hole on a very slick surface (starting slow makes it easier to keep the bit from skidding around on the surface before it bites in). When equipped with a screwdriver bit instead of a drill bit, variable-speed drills are also handy for driving and removing screws.

PORTABLE ELECTRIC SAWS

Most do-it-yourselfers who live in an apartment or condominium are interested only in taking care of essential home repairs and maintenance, so they can probably get by without a power saw. However, those who enjoy tackling more ambitious projects (such as the addition of some built-ins) may find that a portable electric saw will come in handy (these can be rented if needed only rarely). There are two types that may be of interest: portable circular saws and jig saws.

The circular saw is only for straight cutting, and it also cuts much faster—at least when working with thick lumber such as 2×4 studs and heavy joists. It is also useful for cutting up large sheets of thick plywood or particle board (more than ¼ inch in thickness).

Since most apartment dwellers and condominium owners seldom have occasion to tackle projects of this kind, a portable jig saw will probably be more useful and more versatile. It can be used to cut curves as well as straight lines and is lighter in weight (and thus easier to handle, especially when working overhead or on vertical surfaces). When using a jig saw to cut long straight lines, a straightedge should always be used as a guide.

Most jig saws have a base that can be tilted to one side for bevel cutting, and all will accept a wide choice of blades in different grades of coarseness for cutting through metal and plastics as well as wood. There are fine-tooth blades that cut so smoothly that no sanding of the cut edge is required, and there are special blades that allow you to cut flush into a corner or right up to a vertical surface—something that no circular saw can do.

PORTABLE ELECTRIC SANDERS

You won't really need one of these power tools for any of your home maintenance chores, so an electric sander can be truly considered an "optional" tool for all but the most serious do-it-yourself enthusiasts. However, there are some jobs where a portable electric sander can save lots of time, effort, and hard work—for example, when refinishing kitchen cabinets and furniture or when smoothing down rough patches on plastered walls. It's true that these jobs will come up rarely for most apartment dwellers and condominium owners, so buying one may not be sensible—but they can be rented from local dealers when needed, so it would be wise to know something about them.

Three different types of portable electric sanders are available: disk sanders,

Pointers on Working with a Portable Power Saw

Portable power saws cut either on the upstroke of the blade (in the case of a saber saw) or from the bottom up (in the case of a circular saw), so any splintering that does occur will take place on the top side, the side you are working from. This means that you should place the panel or piece of lumber with the good side *down,* so that you cut from the back side, the side that won't show when the job is done.

In the interests of safe and accurate cutting, the work should be solidly supported for minimal vibration. If the cut-off piece is sizable, it too should be supported to prevent binding as it begins to fall free. The idea is to support the work on both sides of the cut—or have a helper hold one half for you—so that the saw will not tend to bind as the wood sags or twists.

When cutting with a circular saw, adjust the depth of cut so that the blade protrudes only slightly through the wood.

With any saw make sure you cut on the waste side of the penciled line if accuracy is important. Start the machine with the foot or base of the tool just resting on the work, with the blade not yet in contact with it. Advance slowly, watching carefully to see where the cut will actually be made. That way you can still correct a slight misalignment before much damage is done.

Portable power saws can make "blind" pocket cuts (openings in the middle of a panel or board), as well as crosscuts from one edge to the other. Rest the toe (front end) of the base plate on the work, with the saw tilted forward enough so the blade is not in contact with the surface. Start the saw, and gradually lower the blade into the work until the base is flat against the surface—then continue to cut in the usual manner.

finishing sanders, and belt sanders. Of these, only the finishing sander will probably be of interest to most condo owners.

The most common type of disk sander is the kind that is used as an accessory with an electric drill. It consists of a flexible disk or pad faced with abrasive paper and mounted on an arbor that is inserted into the drill chuck. Unfortunately, sanding with one of these will leave gouges and swirl marks on the surface, so it is of little practical use for most sanding jobs.

Belt sanders are heavy-duty, fast-working machines that are of interest only to serious woodworking enthusiasts or those who tackle large remodeling projects. They are seldom if ever used for ordinary furniture finishing jobs or for other sanding jobs around the inside.

Finishing sanders (technically referred to as orbital sanders because they have a flat sanding pad that moves in an oval or orbital path) can be useful time-savers on many painting and finishing jobs (they can also be rented when needed). They come in a number of different sizes and styles, but the easiest ones to work with are the so-called palm-type sanders similar to the one illustrated. Not only are these "palm sanders" lighter in weight and more compact (you can hold them in one hand), they also run at a higher speed than most other finishing sanders, so they leave a finer finish with fewer scratch marks on the surface.

When you are using an electric sander, never press down hard in the mistaken notion that this will help the tool cut deeper or faster. Bear down with only enough pressure to maintain firm and constant contact with the surface. Pressing harder serves only to slow the machine—and the cutting action—down. Too much pressure can cause overheating and clogging of the abrasive paper and can possibly result in overheating and damage to the motor.

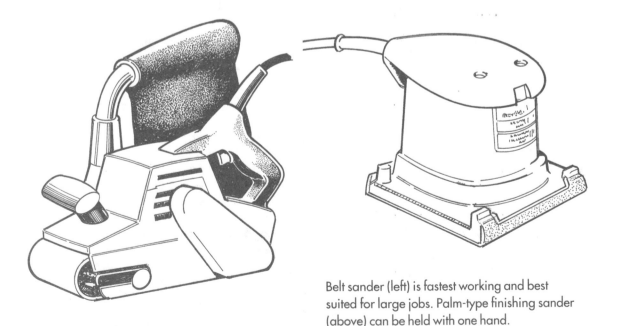

Belt sander (left) is fastest working and best suited for large jobs. Palm-type finishing sander (above) can be held with one hand.

FASTENERS

It's rare that you will tackle a repair or improvement job around the house without using fasteners—nails, screws, hollow wall anchors, adhesives, and so forth—the list is almost endless, and every hardware store carries a very wide variety of these fasteners in all sizes and styles. As a do-it-yourselfer you won't necessarily need to know about all of these, nor do you have to keep a huge assortment on hand, but it does help to stock some of the more popular sizes and styles so that you will have them available for emergencies, even if you keep them all jumbled together in a large jar or coffee can.

What follows is a brief description of the most widely used types of fasteners that apartment dwellers and condo owners will find useful, as well as some suggestions as to where and when each of these is likely to be used.

CHOOSING AND USING NAILS

Nails come in hundreds of different sizes and styles and may be made of steel (plain or galvanized), aluminum, copper, or brass. Few hardware stores or lumberyards stock more than a handful of basic types, each in a normal range of sizes, but you are likely to need only a few types to do practically any job around the house. These will generally include the following: common nails, box nails, finishing nails, roofing nails, and spiral threaded or ring-shank nails.

Although most nails nowadays are sized by their length in inches, many still carry the old-fashioned "penny" designation (6-penny, 10-penny, and so on). This goes back to the days when nails were priced in pennies per hundred (the larger and heavier the nail, the more pennies it cost per hundred); nowadays nails are sold by the pound, but the old designation has persisted to some extent.

Common nails have regular-size heads and a shank with slight grooves directly under the head to increase holding power. They are used in ordinary construction when framing or building homes and in general wherever you don't mind seeing nail heads.

Box nails are similar to common nails in that they also have a large head with grooves on the shank, but they are usually of lighter gauge for an equivalent length and thus are more suitable for use with thin, easily split lumber or when holding power is not as important.

Finishing nails have very small, scarcely noticeable heads that can be easily countersunk (recessed below the surface) to leave a small hole that is then easy to fill in. A very similar type of nail, called a casing nail, is of slightly heavier gauge (for the same length) in order to provide increasing holding power when securing moldings and narrow strips that might be split if too many ordinary finishing nails were used.

Brads are very small finishing nails, 1 inch or less in length. They often have a slightly rounded finishing head instead of the usual blunt head of a regular finishing nail. When these small, light-gauge nails have a conventional head (like a common nail), they are referred to as wire nails.

Ringed or **"threaded" nails,** often referred to as drywall nails, are used where extra holding power is required—some have almost as much holding power as a wood screw, even though you drive them in with a hammer in the usual way. Ringed nails have rings around the shank, and "threaded" nails have spiral-threaded shanks, but because of their great holding power both types should be used only where you want a really permanent joint—they are extremely difficult to pull out once you have driven them home.

Masonry nails are made of specially hardened steel and often have flutes or spiral grooves in the shank to increase holding power. As their name implies, they are used for fastening to masonry or brick—for example, when nailing furring strips or other lumber to concrete walls or floors. Masonry nails must be driven straight home with heavy blows from a large hammer or small sledgehammer, and you have to hit them square on the head with each

Pointers on Using Nails

• When you are using nails to assemble simple joints that involve driving nails through the end of one board and into the end grain of another, a stronger joint will result if you drive the nails in so they slant slightly at opposing angles as shown in the drawing, rather than driving them straight in as is normally done. Don't use this method for joints that you intend to pull apart later on.

• To minimize splitting when driving nails near the edge or end of a board, it is a good idea to drill a small pilot hole first, using a drill bit that is about half the diameter of the nail.

• Another "trick" that will help minimize splitting when driving nails near the edge, particularly with soft woods, is to first turn the nail over and set its head down on a hard surface (metal or stone) so that the point is sticking straight up. Then use a hammer to tap the nail sharply, thus dulling the point slightly. Now drive it into the wood in the usual manner (a sharp point splits wood more readily than a dull point).

• When driving nails in, always keep your eye on the nail head and swing the hammer with your forearm, not with your wrist. Also, keep the wrist fairly straight and firm to avoid bending the nail.

• If you have trouble getting a nail started in a tight corner where you cannot reach with your fingers, use a wad of modeling clay or chewing gum to hold the nail in position until you get it started with one or two blows of the hammer. Then remove the wad before you finish driving the nail all the way in.

Nails grip better if they are driven in at opposing angles.

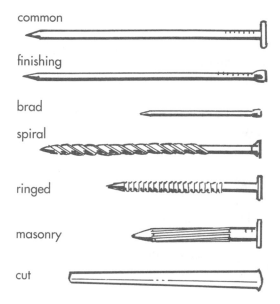

common

finishing

brad

spiral

ringed

masonry

cut

Nails most often used for home repairs.

blow. Striking them even slightly off center will cause them to break or snap. So it is very important when using masonry nails to wear safety goggles to protect your eyes—flying chips could be dangerous.

If you have a job that involves driving in many masonry nails, it may pay to buy one of the special hammer-in masonry anchoring tools. These consist of a rubber- or plastic-covered cylindrical tool that accepts specially hardened masonry fasteners (nails or threaded studs) in its hollow center with the point of the nail sticking out through the bottom end. An anvil, or driving head, slides down on top of the nail head and protrudes from the top of the tool for easy striking with a hammer. You position the point of the nail over the masonry at the spot where you want it to go, then pound on the anvil to drive in the nail. The tool's hollow center keeps the nail from bending, and the anvil

makes sure that all blows are concentrated squarely on the head of the nail-like fastener.

CHOOSING AND USING WOOD SCREWS

Wood screws not only have much greater holding power than nails, they are also much less likely to cause splitting of the wood (assuming a pilot hole is drilled first). In addition, screws can be removed more easily when you want to take a joint apart.

Wood screws may be made of steel (plain, cadmium-plated, or galvanized) or of brass, bronze, aluminum, or stainless steel. They can be as small as ⅜ inch in length or as long as 6 inches, and each length is available in different gauges (diameter). The smaller the gauge number, the smaller the diameter or thickness of the screw.

Another important respect in which wood screws differ is in the shape of the head. There are three styles—flat, half-round, or oval (see illustration). Each may have either a straight slot that accepts a standard flat-blade screwdriver or a cross-slot that takes a Phillips-type screwdriver. Phillips-head screws are preferred by most cabinet makers and experienced

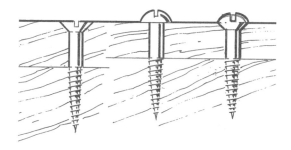

Wood screws are available with flat, round, or oval heads.

woodworkers because they are less likely to slip or gouge the wood, especially when working with an electric screwdriver or driver-drill.

Flat-head screws have heads that are flat on top. They are used when the head will be countersunk—that is, recessed flush with the surface or below the surface of the wood. When these heads are set below the surface of the wood, the hole is usually filled in and the head covered with some type of wood plastic, or the head may be concealed by driving in a snug-fitting matching wood plug as shown in the illustration.

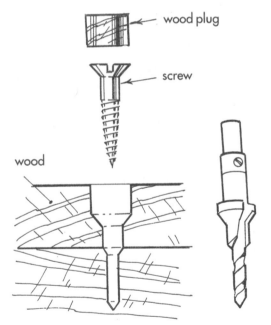

Combination drill bit (right) drills pilot hole, clearance hole, and hole for countersinking screw head all at the same time.

Oval-head screws are used when the head is to be partially recessed or countersunk so that only the top half of the head sticks up (as shown in the drawing). The lower part of the head is recessed into the wood by tightening the screw. These are used where the head will be visible because oval heads look neater than exposed flathead or round-head screws. Also, for joints that must be taken apart occasionally, these screws are easier than flat-head screws to remove without damaging the surrounding wood surface.

Round-head screws are used when the head will not be countersunk or recessed at all; the underside of the head is flat so that it presses against the surface of the wood or other material being fastened down. They are used where appearance is not of primary consideration or where the screws will have to be removed periodically. They are also used for when the material being joined to the wood is so thin that countersinking or recessing the screw head would cause damage (a flat washer is often placed under the head in these circumstances to keep the head from pinching through the thin material as the screw is tightened).

CHOOSING AND USING WALL ANCHORS FOR HOLLOW WALLS

When you want to fasten something to a hollow inside wall of plaster or gypsum board, there are two possibilities:

1. You can position the object you are hanging so that it is directly over one of the 2×4 studs in the wall and then use nails or wood screws to secure it, driving them into the studs.

2. You can use one of the various types of widely available hollow-wall anchors. They can be found in almost any hardware store or lumberyard. Some are made of metal and some of plastic, but all work on

•••

*P*ointers on Driving Wood Screws

When selecting wood screws, pick a size that is long enough to grip properly. When you are joining or assembling two pieces of wood, the unthreaded shank of the screw should go completely through the first piece and the threaded portion should penetrate far enough into the second piece so that at least two-thirds of its length is buried.

It is essential that a pilot hole always be drilled into the second piece with a larger clearance hole being bored through the first piece of wood. To make sure your pilot hole is the correct diameter, hold the screw, point up, in front of a bright light; then hold the drill bit directly in front of the screw and aligned with it. If the bit is the right size, you should just see the threads of the screw projecting out past each side of the bit while the solid core of the screw is covered by the drill bit.

If you want to be professional about it, the clearance hole that goes through the first layer of wood should be just large enough to let the thickest part of the screw's shank (under the head) pass through without binding.

To simplify the task of boring three different-sized holes for each screw—a pilot hole, a clearance hole, and in many cases a hole for countersinking or recessing the head of the screw—there are special combination pilot hole bits that you can buy similar to the one in the illustration. These drill all three holes at one time, including a hole for countersinking the head (if you intend covering it with a wood plug afterward). If the head is not to be countersunk, then the same type of bit can still be used—you just stop drilling after the bit has gone in far enough to make the clearance hole but before the bit penetrates enough to make the largest of the three holes (the one for the screw head).

••

the same basic principle—the anchor or fastening device goes through a small hole in the plaster or gypsum board, and a screw or bolt goes through the device so that when tightened it causes the fastener to expand or spread open inside the wall and lock firmly against the back side of the plaster or gypsum board.

Although there are many different brands and variations of wall anchors on the market, most fall into one of three overall categories: plastic anchors, expansion anchors, and toggle bolts.

Plastic anchors are the least expensive of all and are the easiest to use—but they can be used only for comparatively light loads. They consist of tapered plastic sleeves that are serrated along the outside and

accept wood screws or special threaded nails in the center. After pushing a plastic anchor into a hole drilled in the plaster, you drive a screw into the center. The anchor then splits or expands to lock itself tightly and permanently in place, as shown on page 36.

Expansion anchors usually consist of a hollow metal sleeve or shield that is slotted so that it will split open and mushroom out when a threaded bolt is inserted in the center and then tightened (the end of the bolt goes through a threaded nut on the inside end of the sleeve).

These metal anchors will hold heavier loads than the plastic ones, depending on the strength and condition of the wall material. Like the plastic anchor, the expansion anchor is inserted through a hole of the right size drilled in the wall beforehand. The bolt that will hold the fixture in place is then inserted and tightened, causing the anchor to spread out and lock into place. Molly is the best-known brand of this type.

With either a plastic anchor or a metal expansion anchor, after you drill the hole in the wall, insert the anchor, and then tighten the screw or bolt that goes in the center, you will be able to remove the screw or bolt and the anchor will stay in place in the wall. This allows you to position and secure the anchor in the wall without having to hold up the fixture or

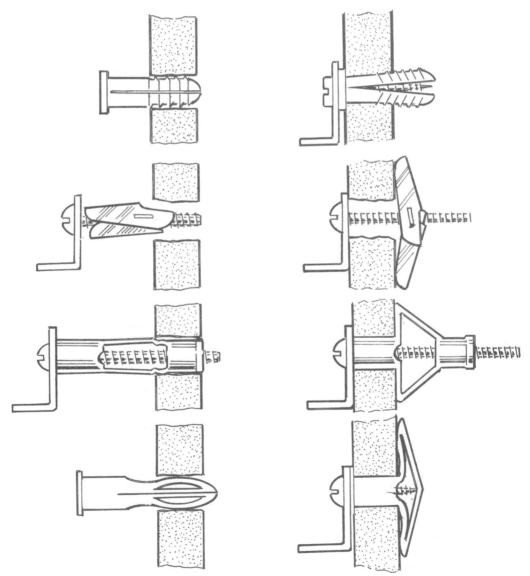

Common types of hollow wall anchors for use in either plaster or drywall. Each is pushed into hole (left) and then spreads or expands as it is tightened (right).

appliance being installed. You simply remove the bolt or screw and, after securing the anchor, use it to mount the fixture or appliance.

Toggle bolts generally hold heavier loads than metal or plastic expansion anchors, but they require larger holes. They consist of a long threaded bolt whose front end goes through a nut attached to folding metal wings, and the hole drilled has to be large enough to accept the folded wings and the nut. You insert them by holding the wings folded tightly against the shank of the bolt and pushing them through the hole until they protrude into the hollow space inside the wall. Built-in springs then cause the wings to snap open. As you tighten the bolt, the wings are drawn up tightly against the back side of the wall.

This creates an exceptionally strong support, but once a toggle bolt is installed the screw cannot be removed without losing the wings inside the wall. This means that when you are installing a shelf bracket or cabinet, for example, the fixture being installed must be held up and positioned at the same time that you press the toggle through the hole in the wall. You then have to hold the whole thing in place while you tighten the toggle. The procedure is more demanding than for expansion anchors, which can be installed in the wall ahead of time, then the bolt removed for putting up the fixture or bracket.

Combination toggle bolt/expansion anchors that are made of plastic, rather than metal, eliminate this handicap. These work like a toggle bolt in that they have wings that spring open behind the wall surface. But they also have a collar or

neck on the inside end that serves to lock them in place once installed. After you push the folded toggle/anchor through the hole in the wall, the wings are popped open on the inside by pushing a small plastic pin in through the center (a nail could also be used).

The pin is then removed, leaving the fastener locked permanently in place without the wings dropping down into the wall (as happens with an ordinary metal toggle bolt). You can then drive a screw through the center to secure the fixture or bracket you want to fasten in place. This means you can install this type of toggle ahead of time, just as you would an expansion anchor, and you can remove the fixture or bracket at any time without losing the anchor inside the wall. In addition, the anchor can be used in solid walls of masonry or brick—in this case the wings do not get fully opened, they merely expand to lock the anchor firmly in place when a regular screw is driven in through the center.

ANCHORS FOR SOLID MASONRY WALLS

Although you can use masonry nails (see illustration, page 33) to fasten wood strips and 2×4 studs to a concrete wall or floor, such nails are really not designed to take much of a load or resist a great deal of stress. Nor are they suitable for use in brick or cement block. For such jobs, and indeed for any occasion when maximum holding strength is required for fastening to a solid masonry wall—for example, when hanging heavy objects or securing fixtures and appliances that are subject to vibration—there are various types of masonry anchors designed specifically for use in solid walls. Such anchors enable you to bolt down large appliances, metal railings, and similar fixtures, as well as hang heavy signs, lighting fixtures, shelves, and other heavy loads.

All anchors designed for use in solid masonry walls work on the same principle—a plug, shield, or hollow insert is tapped into a hole previously drilled in the masonry, then a screw or bolt of suitable size is threaded into the hollow center of the insert. The screw or bolt splits or expands the anchor so that it locks firmly against the sides of the hole inside the masonry, gripping with tremendous strength.

The most common types of wall anchors for use in solid concrete or masonry are illustrated. Some are made of plastic, some of a reinforced fiber, and some of lead or other soft metal. They range from small plastic anchors measuring only

plastic anchor

fiber anchor

lead anchor

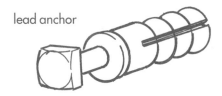

Masonry anchors for use in solid walls of brick or masonry.

about ⅛ inch in diameter (very similar to those designed for use in hollow walls) to heavy lead-and-steel anchors into which large-diameter steel bolts can be inserted. When you are installing such anchors in a brick wall, it is better to locate the plugs or anchors in the mortar joint rather than in the brick itself—an expansion anchor in brick will often split or crack the brick and will not hold as securely as when set into one of the mortar joints.

All masonry-wall anchors require a hole predrilled in the masonry, so you'll need either a carbide-tipped masonry bit for your electric drill or a type of hammer-in hand drill known as a star drill.

Carbide-tipped masonry drill bits are available in sizes up to ½ inch in diameter. They can be used with almost any electric drill, but a variable-speed drill is best. You want to run the carbide bit at a slower speed than you would use to drill into wood or soft metal. Make sure you maintain a steady pressure on the drill while it is turning so that the bit doesn't slip inside the hole; otherwise it will dull rapidly.

A star drill is more like a cold chisel that you hammer in manually. To make a hole of a particular size, you will want a star drill of the same size, plus a small sledge or heavy hammer. Made of one piece of steel, and resembling a cold chisel, a star drill has two cutting edges at the tip at right angles to each other (forming a star-like pattern), rather than the single cutting edge of an ordinary cold chisel.

To use one of these, position the tip against the masonry and hit the head of the star drill repeatedly with a heavy hammer while rotating the drill about a quarter turn after each blow. Periodically pull the drill out and blow out the dust, then continue hammering and rotating until the hole is as deep as required. After blowing out the last of the dust, insert the metal or plastic anchor, then pass the bolt or screw through the fixture or bracket and thread it into the center of the anchor. Tighten securely, being careful not to overtighten to a point where you could actually pull the plug back out of the wall.

MISCELLANEOUS FASTENERS

When you are assembling pieces of wood or sheets of plywood and particle board where nailing and/or screwing is not strong enough, and where appearance is not the paramount consideration, most joints can be greatly reinforced by using one of the various metal braces and metal

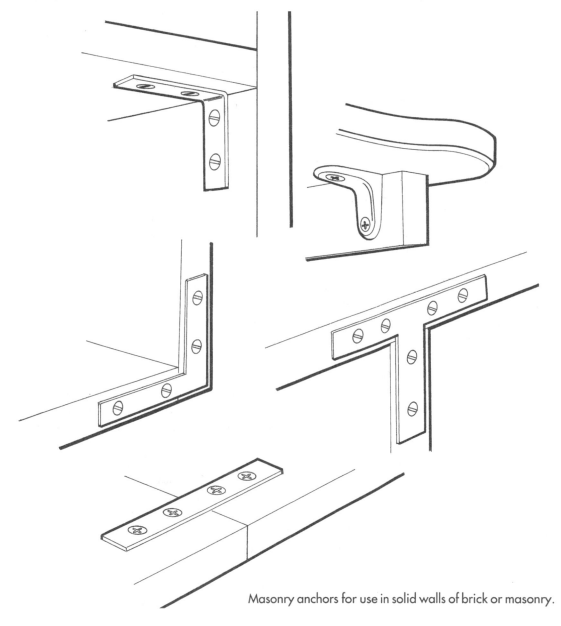

Masonry anchors for use in solid walls of brick or masonry.

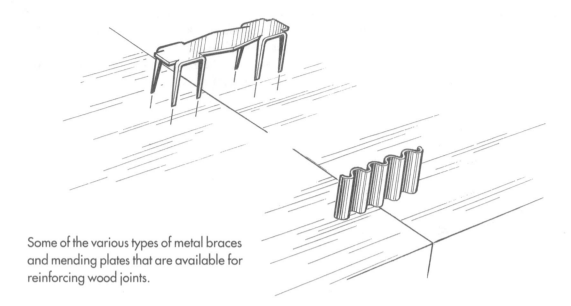

Some of the various types of metal braces and mending plates that are available for reinforcing wood joints.

"mending plates" that are widely sold in all hardware stores and home centers.

As shown in the illustrations, these are fastened to the pieces of wood being joined together with wood screws driven into the face or the edge of each piece. For reinforcing corner joints, inside corner braces usually make neater and stronger joints than do the flat T-shaped braces that fit against the outside edges of the wood, but make sure you use screws that are short enough to not go clear through the wood.

An even faster way to assemble simple joints—or to join boards edge to edge when you want to create a wider board out of two narrow ones—is to use either corrugated fasteners or Skotch fasteners similar to the ones shown here. Both have sharp spurs that make it easy to drive them into place with a hammer, much as nails are hammered in. They are designed to bring pieces together as you hammer them into place but will generally not form as strong a joint as will metal mending plates or braces.

CHOOSING AND USING ADHESIVES

Visit any well-stocked hardware store or home center and you will see dozens of different types of glues and adhesives on display, many of which claim to be the answer to all bonding problems. Unfortunately, these claims are just not true. There is no one glue or adhesive (the terms are used almost interchangeably these days) that can be used to join all materials under all kinds of conditions—in many cases you still have to match the adhesive to the particular job at hand.

Although even an enthusiastic do-it-yourself homeowner would not be expected to stock all of the adhesives that are available at local hardware stores and home centers, most will find it useful to know something about the various types on the market. That way they will know what to ask for when a job comes up where a particular adhesive may be needed. Also, as you see various glues and/or adhesives advertised, or on display at your dealer, you may wonder what some of them are actually good for—a little advance knowledge will help you decide whether or not this is the one you need for a particular repair problem you are facing (unfortunately you can't always trust the advertising claims made, nor can you believe all store clerks these days).

Most adhesives can be used on a wide variety of different materials, so chances are that most condominium owners will need to stock only the first two or three types that are described below. These should take care of most of your home repair problems.

White glues. Probably the most widely sold of all adhesives, these usually have an emulsion base, which means they can be dissolved or washed away with water. White in color, they dry clear and come packaged in a plastic squeeze bottle or tube. They are most suitable for use on paper, cardboard, wood, cork, fabric, and foamed plastic, and do not form a very strong joint. However, they also do not leave stains or visible glue joints when dry, and they are widely used in crafts projects.

Carpenter's glue. Similar to the white glues mentioned above, these are much stronger glues that are designed specifically for wood. They are darker than the white glues, varying from a light tan to a muddy yellow, and although not waterproof, they are more resistant to moisture than the white glues. They are excellent for woodworking and furniture repair, but they do require clamping pressure for several hours (read the label) to achieve a proper bond. Like the white glues, these dry almost clear and usually leave no noticeable glue line.

"Instant" or "one-drop" adhesives. Best suited for use on nonporous materials, including glass, metal, ceramics, and some plastics, these are technically known as cyanoacrylates (Krazy Glue is probably the most widely known brand, but there are literally dozens of others). They form a very strong, permanent bond and come in very small tubes (from 1 to 3 ounces) because only one or two drops is required in most cases. In fact, they will not adhere properly if applied in too thick a film.

They set very rapidly—less than a minute in most cases—and require no clamping pressure. Temporary pressure with the fingers to bring surfaces in firm contact is usually enough. However, because they set up very fast, there is little or no room for shifting things around once the two surfaces make contact. The adhesive bonds almost instantly, so you have to line everything up correctly the first time.

Most cyanoacrylates form a bond that is almost as strong as an epoxy (probably the strongest of all adhesives available to the consumer), but they are not quite as resistant to moisture. Also, they must be used with caution—they will stick to skin as well as to most other materials, and there have been cases where careless handling has resulted in eyelids being glued shut or fingers getting glued together. Acetone will dissolve it, but this should not be used around or near the eye (go to a doctor or hospital if this happens).

OTHER ADHESIVES YOU MAY WANT TO KNOW ABOUT

There may be times when you will run across a problem that cannot be solved by these three "multipurpose" adhesives, so it is a good idea to know what other types of glue or adhesive are available. Following is a brief description of some of the most widely sold varieties you will find at local dealers.

Plastic household adhesive. Usually packaged in metal squeeze tubes, these are the comparatively inexpensive clear adhesives that have been around for years and usually have the word *cement* on the label or as part of the brand name. They are solvent-base adhesives that dry clear and very quickly without need for clamping. Extremely versatile in that they can be used on both porous and nonporous materials, they form a quick bond adequate for light-duty use when only moderate strength is required. They dry in a matter of minutes in most cases, though full strength doesn't develop for about 24 hours. Most are moderately resistant to moisture.

Epoxy adhesive. This is also a two-part adhesive that must be mixed together before use. Once mixed, it leaves you only a limited amount of working time—from a couple of minutes up to several hours. Epoxies are more expensive than most other adhesives, but they are also probably the strongest of all. They cure by chemical action, so they don't have to be exposed to air, and they are excellent for filling gaps and voids in poorly fitted joints. All are sensitive to heat and cold when curing—the chemical action is slowed up by cold—and they work best at room temperature.

Epoxies will bond wood, metal, masonry, ceramics, glass, and most plastics, and they can be used indoors or outdoors—the cured adhesive is completely weatherproof. Some epoxies are packaged in tubes, while others come in cans, jars, and various containers designed to simplify measuring and mixing when only part of the package is used. Epoxies vary from a thick liquid to a putty-like paste, and generally require no clamping pressure while drying—you simply keep the parts in contact and in proper alignment while the adhesive cures.

Contact cement. Made with a synthetic rubber or neoprene base, and available in both solvent-thinned and water-thinned varieties, contact cements do just what their name implies—bond almost instantly on contact, with no need for clamping or applying pressure. They are most widely used for bonding plastic laminates to tabletops, countertops, furniture, and cabinets, but they can also bond metal, rubber, plastic, or leather to wood, or any of these materials to each other. The bond formed is of moderate strength, fine if very little stress will be encountered.

Contact cement differs from most other adhesives in that you apply a coat to both surfaces, then allow each coat to dry before bringing the pieces in contact with each other. A surface coated with contact cement will stick only to another surface coated with the same cement—but then once the two parts are brought together they bond instantly, so there's no room for error. Surfaces must be properly aligned the first time.

In actual practice, a "slip sheet" of brown wrapping paper is often put between the two coated surfaces while you line them up, one on top of the other. Then, while holding the pieces in place, you slide the sheet of paper out from between the two. As the cement-coated surfaces come in contact with each other, an instant bond is formed.

Silicone rubber adhesive. Both an adhesive and a sealant, silicone rubber is probably best known as a caulking material. It is used around bathtubs and sinks, as well as for many hard-to-seal joints around the outside of the house. As an adhesive it remains rubbery almost indefinitely and under a tremendous range of temperature extremes—from 60 degrees below zero to 450 degrees above. Excellent for bonding glass, china, and ceramic materials, silicone adhesives cure slowly, taking anywhere from 8 to 24 hours to dry. Though flexible, the joint is usually not as strong as those formed by the epoxies and some of the other new multipurpose adhesives.

Plastic resin glue. Designed specifically for jobs that require extra-strong woodworking joints, plastic resin glue comes in powdered form and generally has a urea formaldehyde base. It is very water-resistant, though not always completely waterproof if the joint is to be immersed frequently in water or continuously ex-

posed to dampness. When properly used, however, plastic resin glue will form a joint that is stronger than the wood itself.

Plastic resin glues work well only on snug-fitting joints that leave practically no gaps to fill. They should not be used when temperatures are lower than about 68 degrees, and overnight clamping is required for a strong bond. A word of warning: Be sure you clean off promptly any excess that oozes out. Once the glue dries it turns quite dark and becomes very hard to remove.

Resorcinol glue. This is a two-part adhesive consisting of a powder and a liquid that you mix together just before use. Designed specifically for use with wood it forms an exceptionally strong bond that is also completely waterproof and thus is suitable for outdoors and even when the joint will be constantly immersed in water. It can fill moderate-size gaps and requires clamping for at least 8 to 10 hours to ensure a strong joint.

WHAT YOU SHOULD KNOW ABOUT LUMBER

As a rule, condominium owners and apartment dwellers do not get involved in a major remodeling project, but there are occasions when you may want to tackle some smaller improvement projects that involve the use of lumber—for example, if you want to put up some wood shelves or you decide to tackle some of the other storage projects described in chapter 9.

For most of these projects, and for various other repair and maintenance projects that will come up from time to time, you are likely to find that you will have to buy some boards, moldings, or other type of

lumber. That's why it is a good idea to save yourself time, money, and frustration by learning something about how wood and lumber products are graded and sold.

The first thing you must remember is that the so-called nominal sizes of most lumber is not the actual size. A "standard" 2×4 does not actually measure 2 inches by 4 inches; it's usually more like $1\frac{1}{2}$ inches by $3\frac{1}{2}$ inches (give or take about $\frac{1}{8}$ inch). In the same way a nominally sized 8-inch-wide board that is supposed to be 1 inch thick (called a 1×8 and often used for shelving) is not actually 8 inches wide—it is more like 7½ inches wide, and it is only ¾-inch thick (all finished lumber that is referred to as being 1-inch thick is actually ¾ inch in thickness).

LUMBER GRADES

Lumber is graded according to several criteria: appearance, strength (ability to withstand stress), and the number of knots, sap streaks, splits, and other blemishes that are visible. The better the grade, the better the appearance of that lumber (important when the wood is being used around the inside and a clear or "natural" finish will be applied) and the stronger that lumber will be (less likely to crack, warp, or split).

Most of the lumber you will buy for around the home will fall into one of two broad categories: Select and Common.

Select is the top-of-the-line quality you'll want when appearance is important and a fine finish will be applied. In the Select category three grades are sold: Clear, also called B and Better; C Select; and D Select.

B and Better grade provides the ultimate in appearance, with few if any knots, and a clear straight grain that is ideal for natural finishes. The C Select grade has some very minor defects, such as a few small knots, but it is often very close to B and Better in appearance. In the D Select grade the imperfections will be slightly larger (knots, and so on), but they will always be minor enough to be easily covered by paint—and often barely noticeable even when a clear finish is applied.

Common grades of lumber cost much less than the Select grades, and very often you'll have to settle for one of these—not only because of the difference in price, but

also because some lumberyards do not carry Select grades in many sizes (of those that do carry Select, very few will carry them in B and Better).

There are five grades of Common lumber, numbered 1 through 5, 1 being the highest and 5 the lowest grade. The number 1 grade contains very tight knots and few if any blemishes, but you'll seldom see this stocked locally because boards this close to a Select grade usually wind up in the D select category.

Number 2 Common has slightly larger knots and blemishes and is usually adequate for most projects, including wood paneling if you do a bit of careful selection when choosing the boards.

Number 3 Common may have some loose knots and actual knotholes, as well as other noticeable flaws. It is the grade most often used for shelving, fencing, and similar structural purposes where appearance is not an important consideration.

Number 4 Common is a utility grade of fairly low quality and is quite a bit cheaper than the other grades. It is most popular for general construction such as sheathing, subflooring, and building concrete forms.

The Number 5 grade is not really suitable for many jobs around the home, and not all lumberyards stock it. It is primarily for industrial and commercial use, where strength and appearance are minor considerations.

WORKING WITH PLYWOOD

Plywood is a dimensionally stable form of wood paneling made up of several thin layers of wood veneer (plies) glued together under pressure. The ply grains are alternated in each layer, so they run at right angles to each other. This makes plywood much stronger and less susceptible to warping than conventional wood of equivalent thickness.

Most common forms of plywood have an odd number of layers so that the grain in the two outside layers of veneers runs in the same direction—for uniformity of appearance, as well as for increased stability. Plywood is usually made from fir, pine, or similar softwood, but there are also hardwood-faced plywoods that have softwood on the inner plies. These are most practical for wall paneling, as well as for building furniture and cabinets.

Most local lumberyards stock plywood in 4×8-foot sheets, although longer sheets are sometimes available on special order. Local yards will often cut sheets when you need only part of one, though there may be an extra cutting charge. The most commonly available thicknesses are ¼ inch, ⅜ inch, ½ inch, ⅝ inch, and ¾ inch.

CHOOSING PLYWOOD

Plywood is usually available in two types—interior and exterior. The primary difference between the two is that exterior plywoods are supposedly made with a more waterproof glue, and the quality of the inner plies is higher—fewer knots and other defects—thus creating a stronger panel.

Interior and exterior grades of plywood are classified according to the quality of the outside plies or layers of veneer on each side of the panel—qualities that affect appearance more than anything else. They are graded from A through D, with A the best quality and D the worst.

Grade A plywood has only minor blemishes that have been neatly repaired and a smooth surface that takes paint better than any of the other grades. Grade B may have a few tight knots up to 1 inch in diam-

eter and may also have repair plugs in places, although the overall surface is solid and fairly smooth.

Grade C allows for tight knots up to 1½ inches in diameter, as well as a few splits of limited size. Grade D permits knotholes up to 2½ inches across, plus other defects that may be slightly larger than those allowed in grade C.

When you buy a full sheet of plywood you should find the grade stamped on each sheet. Two large capital letters will indicate the grade for the two sides. A sheet stamped A-A has a smooth attractive grade A outside ply on both sides. If the appearance on one side is not as important as that on the other, then you will probably select a sheet stamped A-B or A-C. Few, if any, lumberyards stock all combinations.

There is also a type of plywood known as MDO (stands for medium-density overlaid) that has an exceptionally smooth resin-impregnated finish ideal for painting. It needs no sanding and almost eliminates the later problems of checking and splitting that often plague conventional plywood.

MDO plywood comes in exterior type only and costs more than interior types—but it is well worth the extra cost for indoor projects when you want a really smooth painted finish that won't show cracks or checks after a few years.

POINTERS ON CUTTING PLYWOOD

Cut plywood with a fine-tooth saw to minimize splintering and to give the cleanest possible edge. Make sure the panel is firmly supported on both sides of the cut. If you are cutting with a handsaw, place the panels with the face—the good side—up.

A handsaw cuts on the downstroke, so any splintering will occur on the bottom side.

On the other hand, if you're using a portable power saw, then cut with the face down. Power saws (circular saws as well as saber saws) cut on the upstroke, so any splintering will occur on the top side. When cutting panels on a table saw or radial-arm saw, however, you'll want to cut with the face up, because these saws cut down through the wood.

There will be occasions when it is important to avoid splintering either face—for example, when both sides will be visible and smoothly finished. You can do this best with a portable circular or table saw equipped with a special hollow-ground blade made for cutting plywood. The best of these give a smooth, splinter-free cut that looks and feels sanded. Special fine-tooth blades for cutting plywood are also available for most saber saws, but these cut much slower and are less likely to give you a really straight cut unless you clamp a straightedge to the plywood for a guide.

When you're cutting with a handsaw, there are a few tricks to help minimize splintering:

1. Make sure the saw has sharp, fine teeth.

2. Score the plywood along the cutting line on both faces with a sharp knife and a metal straightedge.

3. Lay a strip of masking tape along the line on the back side and saw right through it.

These steps will minimize splintering, though they may not prevent it completely in every case.

Splintering can also be a problem when drilling holes through plywood, so always try to drill from the good side so that any

splinters will be on the back side. And when the back side is accessible, you can avoid splintering entirely. Clamp a scrap piece of lumber to the back side of the plywood before you start, then drill through both pieces at once; if any splintering does occur, it will be on the back of the scrap piece of wood, not on the plywood.

• •

Finishing Plywood Edges

If the plywood is to be painted, the simplest way to smooth off exposed raw edges is to fill in their end grain with a wood putty or ready-mixed latex (acrylic or vinyl) spackling compound. Smooth this on with a flexible putty knife or with your finger, rubbing it well into the grain, then sand smooth after it has dried hard.

Another method for concealing exposed plywood edges is to cover them with a piece of solid wood molding. If the plywood will be stained and varnished, the molding should be of the same species as the plywood so that the color will match. It can be half-round, flat, or grooved and fluted, but it should ideally be the same width as the plywood's thickness. After sanding the plywood edges reasonably smooth, fasten the molding with glue and small brads.

You can also cover plywood edges with thin strips of wood tape (actually wood veneer) that you can buy in rolls. It comes in widths of ¾ inch and wider and in various species of wood (pine, mahogany, and so on), and is sold in many lumberyards and hardware stores. It is fastened to the edges with contact cement. It forms a clean edge that makes the plywood look like solid lumber and can be matched to most plywoods on which a clear finish is being applied.

• •

Another way to prevent splintering, especially when boring large-diameter holes, is to stop drilling when the tip or point of the drill bit just barely breaks through on the back side. Pull the bit out and finish drilling the hole from the other side.

PLYWOOD JOINTS

When joining plywood with nails or screws, remember that these fasteners do not hold very well when driven into the edges of the plywood. Make sure the fasteners are longer than normal, and use glue along with the nails and screws.

Better yet, try to arrange joints so that nails or screws will go into one of the faces instead, and be kept as far away from the edges as possible. When nailing, drive nails in at oblique angles to each other, rather than straight in. Always reinforce joints with glue and screws or dowels. If appearance on the inside of the joint is no problem, triangular or square blocks of wood can be glued into the inside corner.

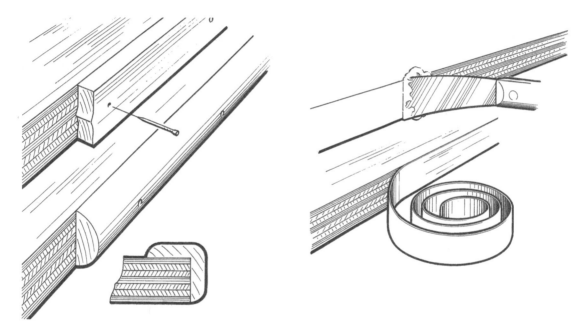

Several ways to cover exposed plywood edges in order to create a smooth surface for painting or finishing.

Repairing Doors and Windows

Doors that stick, bind, or otherwise fail to open and close smoothly can be a real nuisance, yet in most cases the problem is relatively simple to correct. Muttering curses under your breath or slamming, banging, and kicking the door rarely helps. The only sensible solution is to make the necessary repairs as soon as possible, but in order to do this you have to first diagnose the problem so you will know what has to be done to correct it.

Generally speaking, the doors in most apartments and condominium dwellings will fall into one of two categories: doors that are hinged so that they swing open or closed, and doors that slide on overhead tracks or rails so that they move from one side to another instead of swinging on hinges (some sliding doors are hinged together so that they fold up as they slide to one side or the other). The problems that may occur with each type, and thus the repair techniques required to correct these problems, will differ.

HINGED DOORS

Although there are some instances when a hinged door that sticks, binds, or won't open or close easily can be cured only by planing or sanding the edges of that door, more often than not sanding or planing is not really necessary—or even desirable. (Usually it is required only when the door has swollen or warped and sometimes when the door frame has settled or buckled.) In most cases there are simpler and less drastic solutions that will solve the problem more effectively.

LOOSE HINGE SCREWS

When a door that has been working smoothly starts to stick, bind, and become hard to open or close, one of the first things you should suspect is a loosening of the screws that hold the hinges in place against the door or against the door jamb. If these screws are loose, they will allow the hinge (and the door) to sag away from the frame—resulting in rubbing or sticking along the opposite edge.

To check on this, swing the door wide open to expose the hinges and screws. Check each of the hinge screws with a large screwdriver. Don't use a small or narrow screwdriver; it must have a blade wide enough to almost fill the slot in the screw head. If you find, as so often happens, that the screw head's slot is filled with paint, scrape all this paint out before you try to tighten the screw so that you can get a firm grip when the blade is inserted.

Sometimes you will find that no amount of turning tightens the screws because the wood is so chewed up that the screw no longer holds. The solution to this problem is to remove the screw and then fill the hole with slivers of wood (wooden toothpicks work fine). Keep packing wood in until no more pieces will fit, then break each one off flush with the surface.

If the hole seems to go all the way through so that the slivers fall through on the inside, use wood plugs or small pieces of dowel instead. Provide a snug fit inside the hole (whittle a piece to fit if necessary), then dip the plug or dowel in glue and tap it in. Allow the glue to harden before you trim off the plug flush with a sharp chisel.

If hinge screw can't be tightened because hole is enlarged, fill hole with wood toothpicks before reinserting screw.

After the hole has been packed with wood slivers or a small plug as described above, reinsert the screw and tighten securely. (Make sure first that the old screw head is not badly chewed up; if it is, don't try to reuse it—throw the screw away and replace it with a new one of the same size.)

IMPROPERLY MOUNTED HINGES

If loose hinge screws are not the cause of the door's sticking or rubbing, then the next most frequent possibility is the way the hinges are mounted. The first step in checking for this is to find out exactly where the rubbing or sticking occurs.

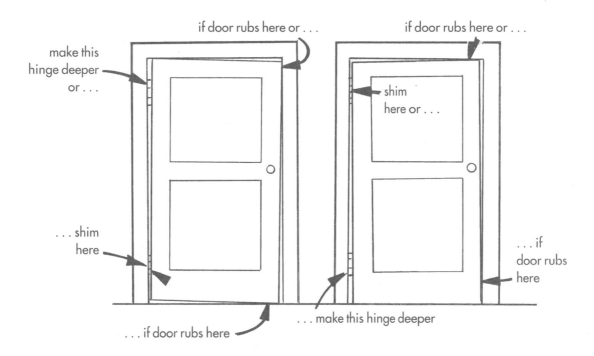

if door rubs here or . . .   if door rubs here or . . .

make this
hinge deeper
or . . .

shim
here or . . .

. . . shim
here

. . . if
door rubs
here

. . . if door rubs here   . . . make this hinge deeper

Inserting shim behind hinge leaf, or setting hinges deeper, will often correct door rubbing problems that are due to improperly mounted hinges.

Look for signs of abrasion along the edges or close the door over a sheet of paper, then slide the paper along and note where it sticks or won't pull out easily.

When this happens along the closing edge near the top or bottom of the door, or along the top and bottom edges near the outside corners, chances are that the problem is being caused by one of the hinges—it is set either too deep in the wood or not deep enough.

As you can see from the illustrations, if the top hinge has not been mortised (recessed) deep enough into the edge of the door or into the door jamb, the top of the door will tend to sag away from the jamb, causing it to rub along the lock edge near the top of the door or at the bottom near the lock edge.

On the other hand, if the bottom hinge is the one that is not mortised deep enough into the wood (as shown in the second illustration), the door will rub along the lock edge near the bottom or at the top of the door near the lock edge.

In all of these cases you'll notice that you have a choice, an alternative method for solving the problem. You can either set one hinge deeper (the one that is not deep enough) or you can shim out the other hinge, the one that is set too deep. You do the latter by placing pieces of cardboard behind the hinge leaf, thus bringing it out slightly to straighten the door's vertical alignment. Shimming out one hinge will have much the same effect as recessing the other hinge slightly—the end result is that the door hangs straight without rubbing along the top or the bottom. To determine which method you should use, swing the door wide open and examine the two hinges. You should be able to tell if one hinge leaf is not set deep enough: It will not be quite flush with the surface. In a majority of cases this will not be the problem—the problem will be that one of the hinge leaves has been set too deep. To correct for this, prop the door open by wedging a magazine under the outside corner, then remove the hinge screws that hold that hinge leaf against the door frame or door jamb. Cut a piece of cardboard the

Shim consists of piece of heavy cardboard cut to fit behind hinge leaf.

same size as the hinge leaf and slip it behind the hinge, then replace the screws and tighten securely. Now try the door again. You may find that a single thickness of cardboard is not quite enough—the door closes better but still sticks or binds slightly. If so, add a second or even a third piece if necessary to build up the required thickness.

Shimming can be impractical when there is not enough clearance between the lock edge of the door and the door frame to allow for the added thickness of a cardboard shim behind the hinge. You will be better off in that case if you set the other hinge slightly deeper. This is only feasible, however, if the hinge is not already recessed below the surface of the wood—that is, if it actually sits above the surface of the wood.

To recess a hinge more deeply on the edge of a door, you will have to remove the door from its hinges so that you can prop it up on its other edge while you work on the hinge mortises. Removing the door is not very difficult. With the door closed and latched, use a large screwdriver and a hammer to drive each of the hinge pins upward. Remove the bottom hinge pin first, then the top one (if there are three hinges, leave the middle one for last).

With all the hinge pins out you can grasp the door by the knob, unlatch it, and swing it open while lifting slightly. The hinges will come apart quite easily, allowing you to lift the door and lay it over on its edge. To support the door in this working position, you can either clamp it against the side of another door or wedge it into a corner of the room where two walls meet.

Of course, you do not have to remove the door if the leaf you want to work on is the one that is fastened to the door frame—just prop the door wide open by wedging something under the free edge, then unscrew the hinge leaf on the frame and swing it out of the way so that you can use a chisel to deepen the mortise (recess) in which it fits.

DEEPENING A MORTISE

Cutting the existing mortise slightly deeper calls for careful work with a very sharp chisel. Since the hinge outline is already cut out, all you have to do is cut within it. Start by tapping the chisel around the perimeter while holding the blade at right angles to the surface, then make a series of light cuts across the recessed surface by tapping the chisel.

To actually remove the excess wood you push the chisel in with your hand, along the grain, shaving off only a little at a time until the mortise is deep enough. Push with a sideways shaving or slicing action, using the thumb of one hand and the forefinger of your other to guide the cutting edge. Use a hammer or mallet if

you must, but if possible avoid it. You'll be running the risk of taking off too much wood or splitting the edge of the door.

DOORS THAT BIND OR SPRING OPEN

Up till now we have been talking about doors that swing closed easily until the edge of the door comes in contact with the door frame and starts to rub or stick. There is another problem that occurs almost as often: a door resists closing and seems to spring open when you swing it shut.

Nine times out of ten this is also a hinge problem—at least one of the hinges has been recessed too deeply, either into the edge of the door or into the door frame.

You can check this out by watching the hinges carefully while someone else swings the door closed. Probably you will notice that as the edge of the door starts to make contact with the door frame the hinges are still not fully closed. Then, in the effort to close the door the rest of the

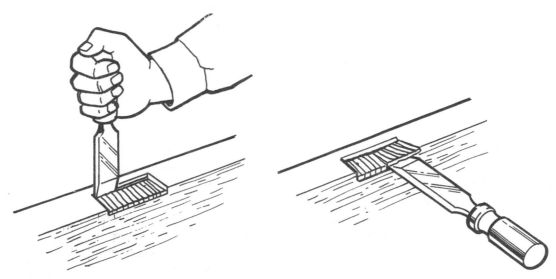

To deepen hinge mortise, first use chisel to cut around edges (left), then make a series of cuts across the mortise. Remove the excess by pushing chisel in from face of door as shown (right).

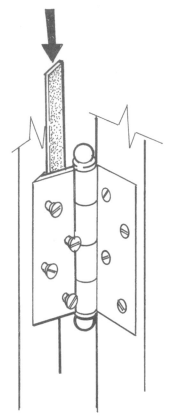

Half-width shim, inserted next to hinge pin, will cause hinge and door to swing more into its opening.

way, the hinges seem to spring or bend slightly (the hinge leaves cannot meet). This condition is usually caused by the hinges having been improperly set. Either they were recessed too deeply, or they were not recessed uniformly (the pin edge of the hinge leaf was set deeper than the inside edge of the same hinge leaf).

In the first case—when the whole hinge has been set too deep—it's simply a question of the door meeting the frame before the hinge closes fully. In the second case—when only the pin side of the hinge is deeper than the rest of the hinge leaf—the metal leaves of the hinge come together

before the door is fully closed. In both cases the door will tend to spring open before it latches.

Either problem is solved by installing cardboard shims behind the hinges. If the full hinge has been recessed too deep, you install one or more cardboard shims as described on pages 51–52. If only the pin edge of the hinge leaf has been set too deep, you still install shims behind the hinge leaf, but in this case you use narrow pieces of cardboard that are only about one-third the width of the hinge leaf. These go behind the pin edge of the hinge as illustrated, so that they cause the hinge to swing around slightly (more into the door opening). This should eliminate the springy, last-minute resistance to closing that can cause binding when the hinge edge is set too deep near the pin.

To install full-size shims you'll have to remove all the hinge screws so you can swing the leaf out of the way. However, for narrow shims that only have to fit behind the pin edge of the hinge, you need only loosen the screws, then slide the strip of cardboard into place as shown.

WHEN ALL ELSE FAILS—GET OUT THE PLANE

There are, of course, cases where shimming alone simply will not solve the problem—for example, if the door sticks along its entire length or if it is rubbing or sticking in several different places along the top and bottom. Chances then are that some planing or sanding will be required to trim off extra wood along those edges where the rubbing occurs.

If only a slight amount of trimming is required you may be able to do it without actually taking the door down, particularly if the rubbing occurs along the lock edge (as long as it is not right near the lock itself) or along the top edge. Prop the door open by wedging a book or magazine under the bottom, then use a small block plane or wood rasp to trim the edge where the rubbing occurs. Take off only a little at a time and keep testing by swinging the door shut to make sure that you're not taking off more than is necessary. When finished, sand the edge smooth, then touch up with paint, shellac, or varnish to seal out moisture.

Working on the door within its frame is impractical when wood must be trimmed away along the full length of the door, and it won't work when wood must be removed next to the lock itself. Obviously

To support door while planing its edge, shove one end into a corner of the room while straddling it.

you cannot plane past the lock without removing the lock and then resetting it—a tricky job even for an experienced carpenter.

Under these circumstances it is best to take the door down and trim the needed amount off the *hinge* edge, rather than along the lock edge. The hinge leaves are easy to remove, and after the necessary planing has been completed they can easily be reset by chiseling out the mortise slightly deeper (as described on page 53), until the hinge leaves are once again flush with the edge of the door. Since you will be working on the edge opposite the lock (where the rubbing actually occurs), you'll have to approximate the amount that has to be trimmed off, then hang the door back on its hinges temporarily to see if you have removed enough.

The easiest way to support the door in a position for planing the hinge edge is to lay the door on the lock edge and push one end into a corner of the room as shown here. You can then straddle the door while planing from one end to the other.

If trimming is required on the top or bottom edge of the door, make sure you plane from the corners in toward the center, never out toward the corners. Running the plane past the edge on a corner is almost certain to cause splintering. With the door lying on one of its long edges, this will mean planing downward for about half the width of the door, then turning the door over so that it rests on the opposite long edge and planing the other half of the door's width, again in a downward motion.

After you have removed the required amount of wood, replace the hinge leaves in the mortise to see how much deeper the mortises will have to be in order for the face of the hinge leaf to once again sit flush with the edge of the door, then shave the mortise to the required depth as previously described.

WHEN THE LOCK WON'T LATCH

This is another annoying door problem—the door closes easily without sticking or binding, but it won't stay closed or snap shut because the latch bolt on the door lock is not quite in line with the opening in the strike plate on the door frame.

You can almost always correct a condition of this kind by moving the strike plate slightly in order to line up its opening with the latch bolt when the door is finally closed. The trick is in finding which way to move it.

You start by closing the door slowly while your eye is level with the strike plate. Have someone else stand on the other side of the door, shining a bright light on the latch bolt so you can watch the action of the bolt as it slides across the curved part of the strike plate and tries to slip into the opening. In this way you should be able to tell whether the opening in the plate is too high or too low to line up with the latch bolt.

Depending on exactly how much out of line it is, you have two options: you can remove the strike plate and reinstall it slightly higher or lower to compensate for the misalignment; or, having removed the plate, you can use a metal file to elongate the opening slightly at the top or bottom (depending on whether the strike plate was sitting too low or too high) and reinstall it in the same position.

Generally, if the distance the plate must be moved is ⅛ inch or less, it is easier to file the opening to compensate for the misalignment. If the plate is more than ⅛ inch

If latch bolt doesn't engage the opening in strike plate when door is closed, move the plate up or down slightly to correct the problem.

out of line, however, it is better to remount the plate in a higher or lower position.

You remove the plate by taking out the two screws that hold it in place. Then fill the old screw holes by jamming in as many wood slivers (pieces of wood toothpick work fine) as you can. Break off each piece flush at the surface. Hold the plate in its new position, then drill pilot holes for the screws and mount the plate in its new location. You may have to chisel away a little extra wood to permit recessing the strike plate flush with the wood, and you may have to enlarge the opening in the wood slightly so the latch bolt can slide all the way in.

Sometimes the problem is horizontal rather than vertical alignment. The strike plate may be too close to the stop molding (against which the door closes) so that the door hits the stop molding before the latch bolt can slip into the strike plate's opening.

To cure a condition of this kind you again have two choices: you can remount the strike plate slightly farther away from the stop molding; or you can pull the stop molding off and move it slightly farther away from the strike plate (so the door can swing a little more into its opening when fully closed).

Sometimes a door will close easily enough, and then will rattle to show that it isn't really snug, even when closed all the way. In this case the stop molding is too far away from the door when the door is fully closed—or, to put it another way, the strike plate is too far away from the stop molding. Again, two options: you can remount the strike plate slightly closer to the molding; or you can pry off the stop molding with a stiff putty knife or small pry bar. If you can't force the blade in behind the molding by hand, tap gently on the handle of the putty knife or pry bar with a hammer or mallet. You can then renail the molding against the frame so that it is slightly closer to the face of the door (with the door closed and the latch bolt engaged in the strike plate, the edge of the molding should just make contact with the face of the door).

There is also another simple solution that will work when only a slight amount of "play" needs to be taken up: place a strip of foam-type self-adhesive weather-stripping on the inside of the stop molding to take up the slack. This will not only eliminate the rattle, it will also cut down on sound transmission.

SOLVING DOOR LOCK PROBLEMS

An interior keyless door lock is normally referred to as a knob set or knob-and-latch set. The most popular type is the cylindrical or tubular set, which is installed by boring two holes in the door—a large one through the door and a smaller one into the edge of the door. The small one intersects the larger hole so that the latch bolt assembly (which fits into this hole) can engage the main lock mechanism.

In older homes there may be mortised lock sets or knob sets that have the whole mechanism recessed into the edge of the door. This is done by drilling a series of vertically aligned holes in the door edge and then using a chisel to hollow out a rectangular-shaped mortise or recess in which to fit the lock.

From the description above you can see that there are several different types of locks used on residential doors, so this would be a good time to explain the principal types and how they differ.

Broadly speaking, all door locks fall into one of four categories: tubular, cylindrical, mortise, and rim (often called night latches or auxiliary locks).

Tubular and cylindrical locks are similar in appearance, and both are easy to install—all you have to do is bore two holes through the door as described above (one in the edge of the door and one through the door). Cylindrical locks, which cost more, are more rugged and are designed for use on exterior doors where security is essential. They usually require a key to unlock them from the outside (a push button or turn button on the inner knob serves to lock or unlock them from the inside). Tubular locks are used only on interior doors and do not come with a key, although they may have a push button on one side that enables them to be locked from that side (you can usually unlock these from the other side in an emergency by pushing a thin nail or heavy piece of wire into a hole in the center of the knob).

All door locks have moving parts, so occasional lubrication is required to keep them operating smoothly. Often this is the only thing wrong with a balky lock or a knob set that isn't working smoothly. Powdered graphite is the best lubricant to correct such a condition. It comes in plastic squeeze tubes with a narrow nozzle that enables you to puff the powdered lubricant into a lock, through the latch bolt opening. Never use ordinary oil, which can cake up and gum the mechanism (there are some lubricating liquids that contain graphite and, used like oil, also work well on locks).

Squirt the graphite in around the latch bolt while turning the knob back and forth, then remove the knob and squirt some more alongside the knob stem while turning the knob on the other side back and forth. It may also help to rub a little paste wax on the face of the strike plate, or spray a small amount of silicone lubricant onto the plate and the sloping face of the latch bolt, which should then slide in more easily when the door is slammed shut.

Lubrication is especially important on outside door locks—not only because they are exposed to the weather, possibly causing oxidation or corrosion of the metal parts, but also because lubrication is your best protection against the lock freezing up when wind-driven rain or snow gets inside.

(When a lock does freeze up, the easiest way to thaw it out is to heat the key with a match or cigarette lighter, then work the heated key gradually into the cylinder until the ice on the inside melts. You may find at first that the key goes only partway in; keep heating the key and reinserting it until it goes all the way in and the lock

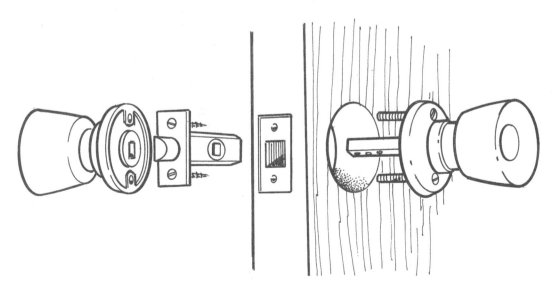

Tubular and cylindrical lock sets are installed merely by boring two holes in the door—one through the face of the door and one into the edge of the door.

turns smoothly. Never force the key in, and never use a pair of pliers or similar tool to turn the key when you can't turn it with your fingers.)

As a rule, when a tubular or cylindrical lock set (sometimes referred to as a bored lock set because it is installed just by boring two holes) starts to act up, the simplest solution is to replace it with a new one. Replacement locks are widely available in all hardware stores and home centers, and they come complete with installation instructions and templates for boring the necessary holes (for installation in a new door).

Most of these locks are designed to fit holes of the same size spaced the same distance from the edge, but some do vary. So to play safe when buying a new lock, either bring your old one with you or measure the size of the holes and the distance in from the edge for the larger hole. That way you will be sure the new lock will fit the original holes in the door.

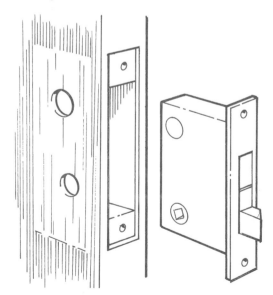

Mortise locks fit into a deep recess chiseled into the edge of the door.

To take off the old lock, you first have to remove the knobs. In cylindrical locks, and some of the better tubular ones, these knobs are usually threaded onto the shaft and will have a setscrew to lock them on. After this screw is loosened, the whole knob can be unscrewed. In tubular locks the knob is usually attached to the decorative escutcheon plate—or rose, as it is sometimes called—so that loosening the two screws or bolts that go through it will enable you to pull the whole thing out of the door, the knob with the spindle attached.

In a cylindrical lock, the rose is a separate plate fastened to the door with two screws; once the knob is removed, the plate can be slid off. You then take out the two screws that hold the latch bolt mechanism in place against the edge of the door and pull out the latch bolt and faceplate. This frees up the lock mechanism so that you can pull out the whole assembly.

In the case of a tubular-type lock, you cannot pull out the latch bolt mechanism until you have pulled out the knob with stem attached, since the stem goes through a square hole inside the latch bolt assembly, as shown in the accompanying illustrations.

Mortise locks are long, rectangular-shaped units that have to be mortised or recessed into the edge of the door. Mortise locks are not widely used on interior doors nowadays, but they are excellent for entrance doors for which maximum security is desired, since they are especially hard to force.

Many older houses still have mortise locks on interior doors, and when one of these acts up your best bet is to replace the lock entirely with one of the new tubular or cylindrical types. To cover up the holes left by the old knobs on the mortise lock, you can buy special modernization kits that include oversize escutcheon plates. These will not only cover the old holes in the door, they also allow for holes to be bored that accept the knob handles and latch bolt mechanisms of the new lock set.

HANGING A NEW DOOR

There are times when you will want to replace an old interior door with a new one—either because the old one is badly warped or cracked or because you want a "newer look" in that room. Fortunately, installing a new door is a relatively simple task that any home handyman can tackle safely. Lumberyards and home centers sell new doors in an almost unlimited variety of sizes and styles to meet every need, or they can order them for you. You can also buy doors that are predrilled to accept any standard-size lock or knob set, and there are even some that come with all hardware (locks and hinges) already mounted.

The first step after getting the door home is to trim it to proper height. There should be about ⅛-inch clearance at the top and ¼-inch clearance at the bottom. If the door will swing into a carpeted room after it is hung, make sure you allow for the additional thickness of the carpet so it will clear easily and won't rub when the door is open.

If you have to remove ¼ inch or more from the top or bottom of the door, use a carpenter's saw to trim off the excess. If you have to remove less than ¼ inch, it is usually best to use a bench plane rather than a saw to trim off the excess. Just make sure that if you use a plane for this job, you run the plane from each edge in *toward the center*, not from the center out toward the edges. *Never* allow the plane to

run off past the edge of the door—this will almost certainly result in splitting or splintering of the end grain on the outside edge of the door.

After trimming the door to the correct height, the next step is trimming to width (if necessary). The width of the door should be about ¼ inch less than the width of the opening in which it will fit—in other words, there should be about ⅛-inch clearance on each side of the door when it is centered inside the door jamb. Use a bench plane to trim the vertical edges if necessary to provide this clearance, but work carefully with long straight strokes to avoid creating a wavy or irregular edge on the door.

To install the hinges, prop the door in place in its opening, using ¼-inch wedges (scrap pieces of plywood or hardboard work well) along the bottom to raise the door to the height at which it will actually hang. Wedge additional pieces along each side to center the door in its opening, then use a sharp knife or chisel to mark the location of the hinges on both the door and its frame. If the door is being hung in an opening where originally there was a door of the same size, then the hinge mortises will have already been cut in the door frame; use these as a guide to mark the top and bottom of each mortise to be cut in the edge of the door. If, on the other hand, you are hanging a new door where there was none before, locate the hinges so the upper one is about 7 inches down from the top and the lower one about 10 inches up from the bottom.

After marking the location for each hinge, take down the door and prop it on its lock edge so you can chisel out the mortises. Use the hinge leaf as a pattern to mark the outline of the new mortise, then score around this outline by tapping lightly with a sharp chisel. To chisel out the mortise, start by making a series of shallow cuts across the surface, along the grain, then remove the excess wood by tapping the chisel in from the side while holding the blade horizontal. Remove a little bit of wood at a time to avoid digging too deep; cut the mortise just deep enough so the face of the hinge leaf will be flush with the surrounding wood. Now hang the door by interlocking the hinge leaves and tap the hinge pins into place.

The final step is to install the door lock or knob set. Use one of the tubular or cylindrical models described on pages 57–59. These locks come with special templates that help you locate the holes that must be bored through the door, along with other detailed instructions. Your dealer may also have a jig for rent which can make the job even easier. These are metal guides that clamp to the edge of the door and have openings to guide you in drilling holes exactly where needed.

SLIDING DOORS

Most full-length sliding doors—opening into closets or rooms—are suspended from an overhead track by means of small rollers that are attached to either the top edge of the doors or the inside face of the door near the top. The rollers ride inside the track as the door slides back and forth, and floor guides attached to the floor keep the doors from swinging in or out as they move. The floor guides also keep the edge of one door from banging into or rubbing against the edge of the other door as it passes behind or in front of it.

Interior sliding doors come in three basic types or styles: bypassing doors, pocket doors, and bifold doors (doors that fold and slide).

Bypassing doors consist of two doors that slide past each other, with each riding in its own track or groove, one behind the other. With bypassing doors you can expose only one half of the opening at a time. The two doors can be slid over to allow access to either side of the opening, or they can be used to completely close off the opening by sliding one to the right and the other to the left (actually they will overlap slightly in the center when fully closed).

Pocket doors are those that slide into a "pocket" or cavity inside the wall. With a single pocket door there is only a single channel or track at the top, and the door slides into the hollow wall at one side. In the case of a double door, there is a two-channel or double track at the top; one door slides into the wall to the right, and the other slides into the wall to the left.

Bifold doors (also called folding-sliding doors) consist of narrow hinged doors or panels that can fold together and then slide over to one side. They may all slide together in one direction (to either side), or they may fold from the center out to each side. Each door or panel has rollers or guides attached to the top corner, and these rollers ride in an overhead track the way conventional sliding doors do. Pivot mounts under the inside corner of the

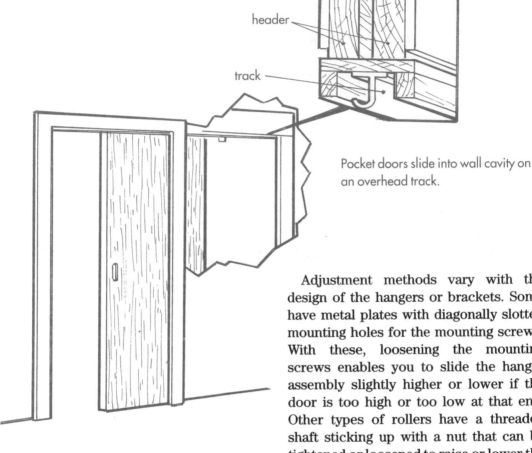

header

track

Pocket doors slide into wall cavity on an overhead track.

door (see illustration) are fastened to the floor or the bottom of the jamb against which the doors fold.

On all bifold sliding doors the mounting brackets that secure the rollers to the top corner of the door are almost always adjustable—that is, they allow you to slightly raise or lower that edge of the door in order to compensate for a minor misalignment. Raising or lowering may be necessary due to poor installation when the doors were hung or when the door frame was built, or it may be necessary later on because of warping or settling of structural members that caused the door frame to twist or sag.

Adjustment methods vary with the design of the hangers or brackets. Some have metal plates with diagonally slotted mounting holes for the mounting screws. With these, loosening the mounting screws enables you to slide the hanger assembly slightly higher or lower if the door is too high or too low at that end. Other types of rollers have a threaded shaft sticking up with a nut that can be tightened or loosened to raise or lower the height of the roller above the door. Directions furnished with the hardware, or close study of the actual brackets, should enable you to figure out how adjustments can be made in each case.

When a regular bypass sliding door binds or becomes hard to move, or if it constantly jumps off its overhead track, the first thing you should check is the hangers or brackets at the top of the door. Make sure the track is not clogged with dust or dirt, and inspect the brackets or roller to see if they are bent or otherwise damaged. If they are damaged, replace them. In most cases, however, it will sim-

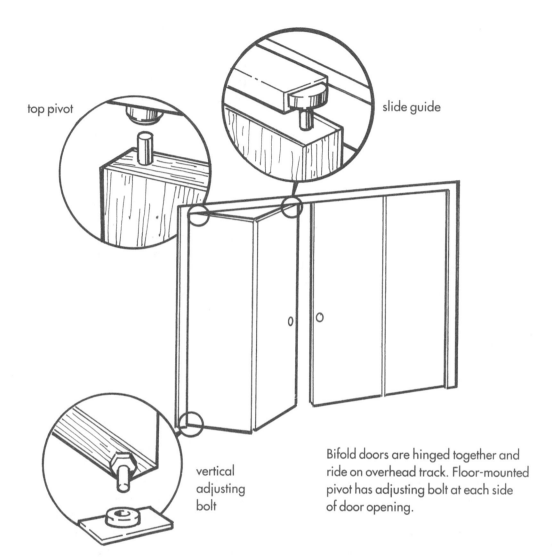

top pivot

slide guide

vertical
adjusting
bolt

Bifold doors are hinged together and
ride on overhead track. Floor-mounted
pivot has adjusting bolt at each side
of door opening.

ply be a matter of adjustment—that is,
slightly raising or lowering one to keep the
door from dragging at the bottom. In most
cases these adjustments can be made
without having to take down the door or
remove it from its track.

If the door does have to be taken off its
track, here is how you do it:

First remove the bottom guides (usually
fastened to the floor with one or two
screws) to allow the bottom to swing free,
then pull the bottom of the door toward

you while pushing upward simultaneously. This will lift the rollers out of the
track at the top, after which the door can
be taken down and set aside.

With the door off inspect the overhead
track to see if it is bent or dented at any
point, and see if the screws holding it in
place have begun to come loose.
Straighten dents with a block of wood and
a hammer or by bending back with a large
pair of pliers. Tighten all loose fasteners
that hold the track in place, and clean out

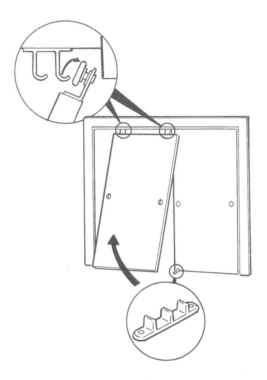

Bypassing sliding doors can be taken down by first removing the floor guide, then pulling the bottom of the door toward you and lifting the top out of its track.

the inside of the track. Then spray lightly with a silicone lubricant before replacing the door. Don't use oil or grease on the track or on the rollers. These will attract and hold dirt and will tend to gum things up. If rollers, bracket wheels, or guides are badly worn, replace them.

Sliding glass patio doors that lead to the outside usually differ from inside sliding doors in that these have tracks under the door rather than at the top. There is an overhead channel in which the door travels as it slides from side to side, but this serves only as a guide for the top of the door, not as a sliding track. The doors have small sheaves or rollers set into the bottom that ride on the track under the door.

When one of these doors stick or become hard to move, it usually means that the rollers or sheaves have jumped off the track at the bottom. In most cases you can set it back on track simply by lifting up on the door and then moving the bottom end in or out slightly until it fits back onto the track and rolls easily once more.

If the sticking or binding is not due to the wheels having jumped off the track (you can bend down close to the floor and shine a light under the edge of the door to check this), then the trouble can usually be traced to one of three things: the track along the bottom has become partially clogged with dirt or debris; the track has been bent or otherwise damaged; or the rollers at the bottom of the door are damaged.

If dirt inside the track is the culprit, clean it out with a stiff brush and a vacuum. If the track is bent or dented, use a block of wood and a hammer to straighten the damaged sections. Cut two pieces of wood the exact width of the tracks and tap one of these into each channel at an undamaged section. Then force them along the inside of the tracks in order gradually to straighten the damaged sections. In some cases simultaneously tapping against the outside of the track with another hammer may be required.

If the sheaves or rollers under the door are damaged—usually indicated by a stubborn, hard-to-slide door and often accompanied by a grinding noise with metal particles showing inside the track—the only cure is to take down the door and replace the rollers with matching new ones.

Slide the door about halfway over, then lift up on the bottom until the lower edge clears the floor track. Pull the bottom of the door toward you (inward), then let the door drop. Now you can lay the door on its

Sliding cabinet doors are removed by first lifting up until bottom clears track, then pulling down and out.

side to get at the rollers set into the bottom. Replacement rollers or sheaves are available from dealers who sell and install sliding patio doors—but make sure you get the size and style that matches the original ones.

SMALLER CABINET SLIDING DOORS

Small sliding doors that are found on many cabinets usually ride in tracks or channels set into the bottom and the top of the cabinet frame. In some cases the tracks may consists of nothing more than grooves cut into the wood above and below the sliding doors, while in other cases there may be separately installed metal or plastic channels inside which the door slides.

The track at the top is always deeper than the one at the bottom, and the door is never high enough to completely reach up into the top of the upper track. This provides enough clearance at the top so that the door can be easily removed and replaced. To remove the door you simply lift it straight up until the bottom edge clears the track at the bottom. Then pull the bottom of the door toward you until it swings clear of the track and comes free from the upper track.

When these sliding doors stick or become hard to move, chances are one of the doors has jumped out of its track—either because the track is bent or warped or because the tracks are a little too far apart for the height of that door (this can happen if the top or bottom of the cabinet warps or sags, allowing the tracks to spread farther apart than they were originally). The top of the sliding door can then slip out of the upper track, causing it to bind or jam when you try to move it back and forth. To correct this, remove one of the tracks and insert a thin strip of wood or a strip of heavy cardboard under or over the track before replacing it. This will bring the tracks closer together and keep the top of the door from slipping out of its upper track.

Another reason a sliding cabinet door will sometimes stick or bind is the accumulation of dirt or other debris inside the tracks. To clean this out, use a small, stiff brush—or an old toothbrush—and a vacuum. When clean, spray the tracks with a silicone lubricant (don't use oil or grease). If the track is damaged or bent, you can try to straighten it by tapping with a small block of wood and a hammer, but if this doesn't work, you will probably have to replace the track completely.

WINDOWS

Residential windows may be made of metal, wood, vinyl, or a combination of two or more of these materials. Wood windows are by far the most common, but in recent years the trend in new construction, as well as in remodeling, has been to favor metal (usually aluminum) and plastic (vinyl) windows. Most metal windows and all plastic windows have a permanent finish that does not need painting, and neither of these will swell or warp, so these types of windows are almost maintenance free.

The windows found in most homes and apartments can usually be classified in one of four categories: double-hung windows that have two movable sashes that slide up or down, one at the top and one at the bottom; casement windows that are hinged at the side and swing open like a door; horizontal sliding windows that move from side to side; and awning windows that have sashes that are hinged at

Double-hung window.

Casement window.

Horizontal sliding window.

Awning window.

the top and swing out from the bottom when open (they look like an awning when open—hence the name).

REPAIRING DOUBLE-HUNG WINDOWS

In a double-hung window each movable sash slides in its own vertical window channel—the upper sash in the outer channel and the lower sash in the inner channel. Since you can lower the top sash and raise the bottom one at the same time, these windows provide maximum flexibility for ventilation. (Some of the newer models have only a single movable sash at the bottom—the top one cannot be lowered—so there will be only one channel.)

Probably the most frequently encountered problem with a double-hung window is that it gets stuck and can't be opened because dried paint has accumulated around the edges of the sash, or because the wood has swelled. If the window can be reached from the outside, the quickest way to unstick the lower sash is to force the blade of a small pry bar or wide chisel under the bottom edge of the sash from the outside, tapping carefully with a hammer if necessary. Work from side to side, prying upward each time the blade is forced under the sash, until the window

breaks free and can be pushed open.

If this technique doesn't work, or if you cannot get at the window from the outside, you will have to work from the inside, prying along the sides rather than along the bottom. Try forcing a stiff putty knife in between the inside face of the sash and the edge of the stop molding as shown in the illustration on page 68 (don't use a chisel; it will leave dents in the molding). Use a hammer if you can't push the blade in by hand, and each time the blade is forced in wiggle it slightly while twisting back and forth to break the "seal" between the molding and the sash. Work your way up one side and down the other side, twist-

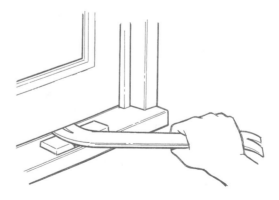

Small pry bar and block of wood are used to pry open stuck window from the outside.

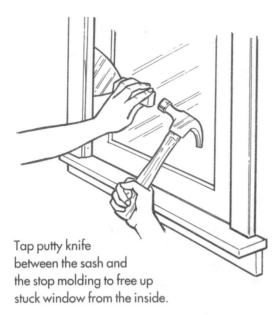

Tap putty knife between the sash and the stop molding to free up stuck window from the inside.

ing and wiggling the blade repeatedly before moving on to the next spot.

If this doesn't free up the sash, there is another technique that often works. Trim a small block of wood so that it is just about the width of the window channel in which the sash rides. Push this into the channel just above the stuck lower sash (if it's the upper sash that is stuck, place the

If window can't be pried open, remove stop moldings, then lift out sash.

block of wood inside the channel *below* that sash). Now with a hammer rap this block of wood sharply against the inside of the channel two or three times, then do the same inside the channel on the opposite side of the window. This should jar the window frame and spread it momentarily—enough to break the "seal" between the sash and its frame and thus enough to free up the stuck sash.

If you cannot unstick the window this way, your best bet is to pry off the stop moldings on each side, using a wide chisel or stiff putty knife as shown in the illustration. Starting near the bottom, tap the putty knife in between the molding and the frame and wiggle it back and forth to pry the molding loose at that point. Then move the blade up a few inches and repeat. When the molding is loose along its entire length, take it off and lift the sash out of the window frame (you can leave the sash cords or chains still attached).

Now you can get at the window channels on each side to clean them out, using a small scraper or putty knife and a stiff brush to remove caked-on paint, dirt, and other foreign matter. While you are at it, also scrape off the edge of each stop molding where it comes up against the inside face of the sash in order to minimize rubbing when the moldings are replaced, then lubricate the window channels and the edges of the sash by spraying with a silicone lubricant or rubbing with wax or paraffin. Replace the sash inside the window frame and nail the stop moldings back into place.

If these measures have not solved the problem, it is likely that the wood has swelled and the edges of the sash have to be trimmed down by planing or sanding. Remove the stop moldings as previously described, then lift the lower sash out of the window and disconnect the cords or chains that are attached to each side. Attach a large safety pin or paper clip to the end of each cord or chain before releasing it so that it won't fall through the pulley openings at the top of the channel (remember, the other end is attached to a weight inside the window and this weight will drop to the bottom when the cord or chain is disconnected). Once the sash is free you can lay it on its side and then use your plane or sanding block to trim off the edges a little. Be careful to avoid trimming too much—to play it safe, trim off only a little at a time and then try it before continuing to trim off more.

If your window does not have sash weights but instead has spiral-type spring balances, you'll find that you won't have cords or chains to contend with, but you will have to unscrew the tubular balance from the window frame in order to get the sash out. You will then have to detach it from the sash at the bottom, so that you can get at the edge of the sash with a plane or rasp.

Although taking off the stop moldings on the inside will make it easy for you to remove the lower sash, it still will not enable you to remove the upper sash. This sash rides in a separate, outer channel which is separated from the inner channel by a strip of wood molding known as a parting strip (see illustration on page 70). To get the upper sash frame out you will have to remove this parting strip, having first removed the lower sash and the stop moldings as described above.

Start by lowering the upper sash as far as it will go. Then grasp the square parting strip near the top with a pair of heavy pliers. Pull straight out with a firm grip until the upper end comes free. Chances are that it won't come out easily, having over

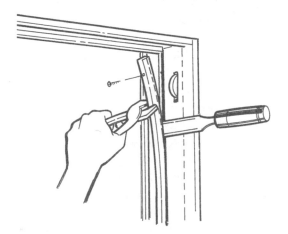

To remove upper sash, parting strip must be pried out first. Remove nail or screw at the top, then grasp strip with pliers and pull firmly.

the years become virtually glued into place with layers of paint. But if you work carefully, prying along the edges with a sharp chisel or knife and pulling steadily with the pliers, you should be able to get it out in one piece (don't worry if you don't—a new parting strip can be bought readily at any lumberyard). As soon as the top of the parting strip starts to come loose, move your pliers down a few inches and start pulling again till you gradually get more of it loose.

There are two precautions to remember when you are trying to remove this parting strip: (1) Sometimes there are small nails or screws that hold it in place, so look carefully for any of these and pry around them rather than between them. (2) In many instances you will find that the bottom rail of the lowered upper sash will overlap the parting strip; in that case you cannot pull it straight out along its full length but will have to bend the top end out past the side of the window frame, then pull up and out while gripping hard in order to get the whole length out.

REPAIRING BROKEN OR JAMMED SASH CORDS

Older windows have sash cords and weights, and these frequently present problems. When the upper sash keeps falling down, or when the lower one won't stay up after you raise it, chances are that the ropes connected to the sash weights are broken. These sash weights are on the inside of the window frame, riding up and down in concealed pockets on each side as shown in the illustration .

Sometimes a window sash will jam or stick because the rope that goes over the pulley is jammed—the rope has "jumped the track" and come out of the pulley groove. When this happens the rope often gets caught between the edge of the pulley and the wood frame in which it is mounted, and the harder you pull, the tighter the rope gets jammed in. To correct this, raise the sash enough to give you some slack, then use a blunt screwdriver or the side of a dull putty knife to work the rope free by pushing it upward. If necessary, tap the tool with a hammer. When the rope is clear of the pulley's side, guide it over the top of the pulley and back into the groove where it belongs.

In most cases, however, the problem is not that simple. You will probably find that the rope going up and over the pulley is slack—or it will be missing entirely, because it has broken and the weighted

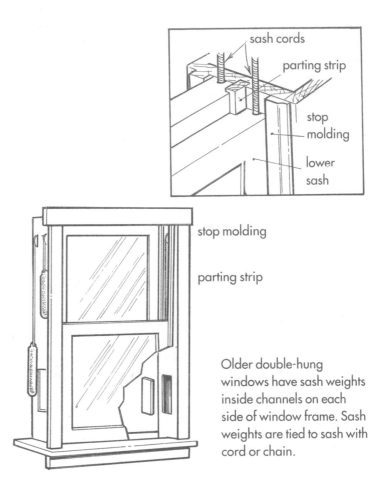

Older double-hung windows have sash weights inside channels on each side of window frame. Sash weights are tied to sash with cord or chain.

end has fallen back down inside the window frame's pocket. To repair this properly, you will have to replace the broken rope with sash chain (sold in all hardware stores and lumberyards).

Start by removing the stop moldings on each side, as described on page 68, then lift the sash frame completely out of the window and disconnect the cords from both edges of the sash. After the bottom sash has been removed, examine the window frame inside the channel on both sides. Along each, you should be able to discern the barest outline of a cut-out panel.

Called the pocket cover, this panel may be hard to see at first if the outline has been covered over by many layers of paint. If you cannot find it, try tapping hard against the lower part of the channel with a hammer; this may cause the paint to crack around the panel and allow you to see its outline more easily.

In some cases the panel is held in place with two small screws, one at the top and one at the bottom of the panel, but in others it will just be a force fit. In still others the pocket cover may never have been completely cut out around the edge, so you may have to use a keyhole saw to complete the rest of the cut. If the panel is partially covered by the parting strip, then you will have to take this strip out first (see illustration on page 69). After you have located the cut-out or panel, either unscrew it or work a chisel carefully around the edges to pry it out. This will reveal an opening through which you can reach inside the pocket and find the sash weight.

If your window has no pocket cover or removable panel inside the channel—or if you just cannot find it on your window— then the only way to get at the sash weights inside the frame is to pry off the window trim around the inside. This will expose the hollow space where the sash weights are suspended.

After the pocket cover (or the trim around the inside of the window) has been removed, reach in and lift the sash weight—it will be sitting on the bottom if the cord is broken. Untie the old cord, then cut a new piece of sash chain the same length as the old cord. If you are not sure of the correct length, start with an extra-long piece of chain so that you can trim it off afterward.

Feed the new chain over the top of the pulley, starting at the outside. Let it fall down inside the pocket until you can reach through and grab the end as it comes down. Attach this end to the sash weight, using the small hooks or clips sold for this purpose, then set the sash weight back inside the pocket; make sure the free end of the chain (the end that will be attached to the sash) can't pull through by pushing a nail or large paper clip through one of the chain links on the other side of the pulley. Now install the chain on the other side of the window frame in the same way.

Set the sash frame back into the window so that it rests on the sill, then pull down the free end of one chain until you have raised the weight up high enough (inside the pocket) so that it almost touches the pulley. Slide a small nail through one of the links in the chain to keep the weight from dropping (the nail will get caught in the pulley opening), then fasten the other end of the chain to the side of the sash frame in the same place where the old rope was fastened; use one or two small nails or the clips provided on some windows.

Repeat this on the other side of the sash frame, then test by raising the sash as high as it will go—the weight should clear the bottom by at least a couple of inches.

Replacing the cords for the upper sash frame is done in much the same manner, except that you have to take the lower sash out first (even if only one cord is broken it's a good idea to renew all four cords while you are at it and have the window apart). You can then remove the parting strip on each side in order to get the upper sash out. Since this is harder than just replacing the cords on the lower sash, there is a temptation to do only the lower ones when the upper cords are not broken—but this is only delaying the day when you will have to do the whole job over again.

REPAIRING WINDOWS WITH TUBE-TYPE SPRING BALANCES

Many windows installed over the past two or three decades have tubular-type spring balances, instead of the older sash weights and cords. Some of these spring balances permit some adjustment to increase tension as they wear, but others cannot be

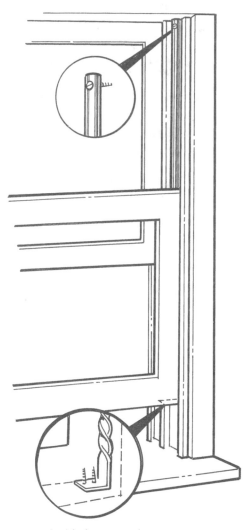

Newer double-hung windows use spring balances that fit inside the window channels, instead of sash weights.

adjusted at all and must be replaced when they start to lose tension.

If your windows are equipped with the adjustable type, here is how you can increase tension:

Hold the tube firmly with one hand and remove the screw holding it in place at the top. When the screw is out (keep holding the tube firmly because it will try to spin away from you!), you can adjust the tension by turning the tube clockwise two or three turns.

If the spring is too tight (the window creeps up), then you want to decrease tension, and you do this by letting the spring unwind slowly after the screw at the top has been removed.

If the balance doesn't work at all, or is not the adjusting type, or if adjusting the tension doesn't solve the problem, you will have to replace the balance entirely. To do this you first raise the sash as high as it will go, then unscrew the brackets on the bottom of the sash frame that attach the spring balance to the sash. Now remove the stop moldings and lift the sash out of the window frame.

The new spring balances are installed simply by reversing the order—screw the upper end of the tube in place against the window channel, then replace the sash and attach the brackets that fasten the end of the spiral rod to the bottom of the sash. When you are buying a replacement unit, bring along the old one to make sure the new one will fit.

REPAIRING CASEMENT WINDOWS

Unlike sliding double-hung windows, casement windows are attached by hinges so that they can swing open and be closed much like an ordinary door. Made of wood

Installing New Window Channels

One way to rejuvenate an old double-hung window with broken sash cords, or with poor weatherstripping and hard-to-move sash, is to install replacement channels that eliminate the need for weights and cords—or balances of any kind.

Sold in home centers and lumberyards, these replacement channels come with permanent weatherstripping, as well as a friction-type channel that holds the sash in position regardless of where you leave it. They are available in various lengths to fit most standard-height windows.

You install them by first removing the stop moldings on either side, then taking out the lower sash and the upper sash, disconnecting the cords or chains attached to the sides of each. Taking out the upper sash will usually require removing the parting strip first (see page 69). With both sashes out, the cord pulleys at the top of each channel are removed next, either by prying them out or simply by driving them into the hollow space behind the frame with a hammer. Don't worry about the holes that remain—these will be covered by the new channels.

Now use sandpaper to clean the edges of each sash and scrape off any ridges of paint that remain. Then, as illustrated, stand the two sashes up behind each other and place one channel on each side. Press everything firmly together and lift up the whole assembly and set it in place inside the window. Set the bottom ends of the channels in place first, then tip the upper ends into position. The channels are then fastened in place against the sides of the window frame with screws—first at the top, then at the bottom. The job is finished when you replace the stop moldings on each side (they are no longer needed to hold the sash in place, just to give the frame a finished look).

Old double-hung windows can be rejuvenated by installing new window channels. These eliminate the need for weights, cords, or balances.

or metal, they usually operate with a lever-type mechanism that is activated by a crank on the inside. Some older models do not have cranks, but rather a rod or lever that you push to open or pull to close. The rod slides through a pivot bearing that in turn slides in a track on the sill.

When a casement window starts to stick and bind, the trouble almost always has one of four causes: (1) The hinges that support the window need lubrication. (2) The window frame's edges are caked with paint and/or dirt. (3) The opening and closing mechanism—crank, rod, or tracks in which the guides slide—needs lubrication. (4) The rod or pivot lever that actually pushes the window open and pulls it closed has been bent.

Start by lubricating the hinges or pivoting supports on which the window swings, using a few drops of lightweight oil and working it in by opening and closing the window a few times. Next, lubricate the crank mechanism that activates the rod or lever that opens and closes the window. To do this you will have to take off the handle assembly (it is held in place by two screws), then clean out the gears and the inside of the case and repack with fresh grease.

If the window still doesn't work right, swing it all the way open and inspect the track along the bottom edge of the sash (on some wood casement windows this track will be on the inside face of the sash, not under the bottom). Use a wire brush to clean out dirt, paint, or encrusted grease, then rub a little fresh white grease (Vaseline works fine) along the track.

When a casement window swings open easily until the last inch or so, but then "gets stubborn," look for an accumulation of dirt and hardened paint along the edges of the sash frame or inside the window frame itself where the sash contacts the casing. Use steel wool and a wire brush to clean off any such accumulation on metal frames, and a scraper and sandpaper for wooden frames.

If none of these steps makes the window work easily, the trouble is most likely either the crank mechanism or in the actuating rod slide (where the end of the rod slides along the track on the bottom of the sash frame). If the rod or lever is bent, or if the part that slides along the track is sticking, you can try, in the first case, to straighten the rod or, in the second, to unstick the sliding track and guide by cleaning and lubricating.

One sure way to make certain whether or not the problem lies with the crank

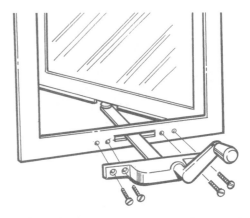

Crank mechanism on casement windows can be removed by taking out bolts that hold it in place.

mechanism, rather than with the slide or the rod, is to disconnect the rod from the sash frame. You can usually do this by swinging the window open as far as it will go, then slipping the sliding guide out of one end of the track (depending on its style, and on which way the window swings, the guide will come out of either the left or right end of the track).

After the rod or arm is disconnected, turn the crank handle to see if it works easily. If it does, you know the problem lies with the track or guide. If it doesn't, then you know the crank mechanism is the trouble. Take the whole thing off (it is held in place by two screws), then examine the gears on the inside (wiping off any excess grease to help you see). Note whether any of the gears or other moving parts are bent, or if the teeth are chipped and broken.

If everything looks okay, flush out the mechanism with kerosene or paint thinner, then squirt some fresh oil inside and try again. If the handle still does not work easily, your best bet is to replace the entire mechanism with a new unit. You can buy it at many large building supply outlets and home centers, or your local dealer should

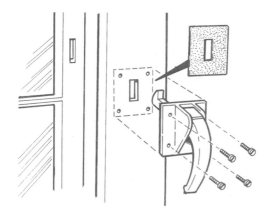

If handle doesn't pull window tightly closed, add cardboard shim behind mounting plate.

be able to tell you where you can order one. Bring along the old one to be certain you get a new one that will match.

Casement windows are often plagued with one other type of problem—drafts caused by the fact that the window doesn't shut tight enough. This is particularly true of metal casements, which have a lever-action handle with a hook-shaped lock on the outside that swings up through a slot to engage the sash frame. The mechanism is supposed to pull the sash up against the window frame and create a tight seal, but in some cases it does not pull in tight enough. To correct this condition, remove the handle from the inside, then slide a shim or spacer made of cardboard or plastic behind it, as shown in the illustration above. The effect will be to move the handle slightly farther inward and thereby apply greater closing pressure as the hook part swings to close.

REPAIRING SLIDING WINDOWS

The most common cause of trouble with a horizontal sliding window—wood or metal—is dirt or paint inside the track or on the edge of the sash frame. This is especially true in older houses with wood windows on which multiple layers of paint have built up over the years.

Sometimes you can correct the problem simply by cleaning out the track with a wire brush or by scraping the edges of the movable sash frames with a narrow putty knife. In most cases, however, you will have to take out the window sash, then use a scraper and some sandpaper to remove the hardened paint from both the window frame and the sash frame. (Horizontal sliding windows can be removed by lifting up and swinging the bottom end out of the track, then pulling the top out.) Spray the track and the edges of the sash with silicone lubricant, then replace the sash.

Lubrication is also the answer on metal sliding windows—after tracks and sash edges have been thoroughly cleaned with fine steel wool and a wire brush. Use a silicone spray or rub with paraffin, but don't use oil in this case—it will only attract and hold dirt that will then cake up and cause more trouble.

If lubrication doesn't solve the problem, the track is probably damaged or bent. Examine the inside of the track carefully to find the damaged section. If it is just bent in one place, you should be able to straighten it with a hammer and a small block of wood or by using a pair of heavy pliers. If it is bent in many places, or is cracked and broken, you should replace the entire window frame.

REPAIRING AWNING WINDOWS

These windows are practically the same as casement windows, except that they are hinged along the top and thus swing out from the bottom instead of from one side or the other. Most of the cleaning and lubricating techniques described for casement windows will also apply to awning windows.

While most awning windows have crank mechanisms similar to the ones used on casement windows, some have a scissors-type lever-arm action that helps support the opened window sash. Like the operating levers or rods that are used on a casement window, the pivot points on the operating mechanism should be lubricated regularly with a lightweight penetrating oil. Don't forget the pivoting arm at the side that rides up and down in a track as the window frame swings up and down. Very often when a window is hard to work, cleaning and lubricating the track in which the end of this arm rides is all you need to do.

REPLACING BROKEN PANES OF GLASS

The hardest part of replacing a windowpane is, more often than not, getting out the broken pieces of the old glass and then removing the old hardened putty. For safety's sake, you should wear heavy work gloves to protect your hands, and when you are pulling the broken pieces of glass out of the frame, play it safe and grab with an extra piece of cloth (in addition to the gloves) or with a pair of pliers before you start twisting or pulling.

After the broken pieces of glass have been removed, scrape out all the old, hardened putty or glazing compound, using a narrow chisel or a stiff putty knife. If you find the putty to be exceptionally hard and stubborn, you can make things easier by first applying heat to soften it using either an electric heat lamp or a hair dryer set on high. An electric heat lamp will take

longer, but it is safer and less likely to scorch the wood or the surrounding paint. Either way, it is a good idea to keep a bucket of water or a small fire extinguisher handy—just in case.

After the glazing compound has been removed, clean out the rabbet thoroughly (the rabbet is the groove or recess into which the glass fits), either scraping or rubbing with steel wool. Then coat the exposed wood inside the rabbet with boiled linseed oil or with a thin coat of exterior primer. This seals the wood and helps to ensure a better bond (otherwise the wood will absorb the oil in the glazing compound, which then, in time, dries out excessively). If the window is metal, make sure you clean off all rust and corrosion and apply a coat of metal primer before glazing.

When measuring for the new pane of glass, make sure you allow for a slight amount of clearance on all sides—usually about ⅛ inch less around all four sides. Bring these measurements to your local dealer (be sure you tell him you have already made the needed allowance for extra clearance), and have him cut a new piece to size.

A word of caution here about the kind of glass to buy: If the window or door is in a location where it can be easily broken (by children throwing balls, for example, or by accidental encounters with large packages or big dogs), you should buy safety glass or tempered glass or instead of glass get a clear plastic such as one of the break-resistant acrylics. In many communities there are laws or building codes that require such materials for hazardous locations.

Before installing a new pane of glass, you should first apply a layer of glazing compound behind it to ensure a waterproof seal. Roll a wad of glazing compound

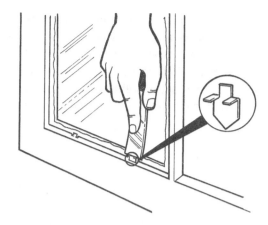

Glazier's points that secure glass in frame are pushed into place with putty knife or screwdriver.

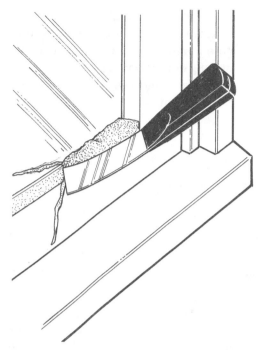

To bevel putty smoothly, hold putty knife at an angle while pressing down firmly to trim off excess.

into a long thin strip (about ¼ inch in diameter), place it along the rabbet where the glass will go, then press the pane of glass into place, shoving it in hard enough to squeeze the compound flat, with the excess oozing out around the edges.

Glazier's points—triangular-shaped bits of metal—are what actually hold the glass in place, not the glazing compound. Use two such points on each vertical side in smaller windowpanes, more on larger ones. You install glazier points by pushing them in with the blade of a screwdriver or stiff putty knife, or you can buy the kind that has a slight flange at one side and, very carefully, tap them in with a tack hammer.

The last and final step of window replacement is applying the glazing compound around all four sides to seal the edges of the glass with an airtight and watertight fit. The easiest way to do this is to roll the glazing compound into a long strip—a "bead" slightly thicker than a pencil—then press it firmly into place with your fingers. Knead it down so that it makes firm contact with both glass and frame. You are then ready to form a neat

bevel with your putty knife, smoothing off any excess in the process.

Hold the blade at such an angle to the surface that only a corner of the blade contacts the glass (see illustration), and press down firmly while dragging the blade smoothly along the surface. This will shave off excess compound so that it can be peeled away with your other hand. The idea is to form a neat beveled surface that will be both flush with the wood on the outside and tight against the glass on the inner side. If you have trouble getting the compound smooth because the knife tends to "drag" or crumple the surface, try heating the knife slightly—the warm blade will make the glazing compound easier to finish smoothly.

The glazing compound should come up

just high enough on the glass to cover the wood that is visible through the glass, but not high enough so that you see the edge of the glazing compound from the inside.

Metal-frame windows are glazed in much the same manner as wood windows except that you don't use glazier's points to hold the glass in place. Instead there are special clips that snap into the channel in the window where the glass fits. Some windows have plastic splines that hold the glass in place instead of glazing compound.

Cutting Glass

Although all hardware stores and lumberyards will cut glass to size, there are times when you may want to cut your own—for example, when trimming down a large piece for a small pane or when using scrap pieces for a picture frame. Fortunately, you'll need only two tools: a glass cutter and a straightedge. A pair of square-jaw pliers may also come in handy if you have to break off small strips, though this is not always necessary.

Lay the piece of glass on a flat surface that you have covered with several layers of newspaper (to serve as padding). Then place the straightedge along the line of cut and hold it down firmly with one hand. Now grip the glass cutter with your thumb and index finger, as shown, and dip the cutting wheel into a little kerosene or very light machine oil.

You make the cut by scoring the glass *only once* with a single stroke, bearing down with firm, steady pressure during the entire length of the stroke. *Do not bear down hard*—just press with moderate pressure and move the cutter along steadily. The idea is to score the surface of the glass with a single smooth stroke so that the cutter makes a crisp, crackling sound and leaves a uniform score mark without skipping and with no tiny chips flying off the surface. Going over the stroke almost always results in breaking or chipping the glass at some point.

Now place a pencil, dowel, or strip of wood under the glass so it is positioned directly under the score mark you've just made. Then press down on both sides of the glass, more smartly on the smaller piece. It should snap off neatly along the line of cut. If any narrow slivers remain, grasp these with a pair of pliers and snap off by twisting up or down.

When cutting glass, hold cutter almost vertical and score glass with single stroke of cutter.

REPAIRING WINDOW SHADES

Window shades consist of a length of fabric or plastic material that is rolled around a central roller that may be made of wood, metal, or plastic. This roller is hollow and has a long spring on the inside that is wound up as the shade is pulled down. The tension built up in this spring provides the power needed to raise the shade—that is, when you are ready to roll it back up.

The roller has two ends—one end has a fixed, round pin, and the other end has a flat, rotating pin. If you rotate the flat pin while holding firmly on to the outside of the roller so it cannot turn, you wind up the spring on the inside. Conversely, if you hold the flat pin in one position (say, with a pair of pliers) so it can't turn while you rotate the entire roller, you also wind up the spring on the inside. And in fact that is exactly what happens when you pull a shade down.

Here's how it works: When the shade is in position with the pins at each end placed inside their respective brackets that hold it across the window, the flat pin at one end fits into a slotted bracket that keeps it from rotating, even when the roller is turning (while the shade goes up or down). The fixed round pin at the other end of the roller fits into a bracket with a round hole, also mounted on the window frame. This allows it to rotate freely when the roller is rotating (again, each time the shade goes up or down). When you pull the shade down you are actually winding up the spring on the inside (because the flat pin at the other end is kept from turn-

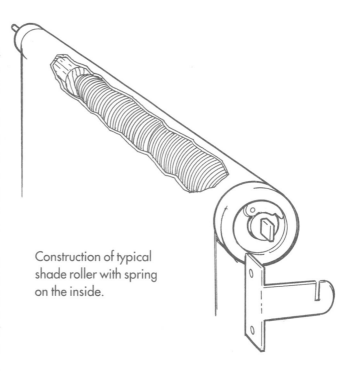

Construction of typical shade roller with spring on the inside.

ing by its bracket). This winds up the spring on the inside and builds up the tension that will be needed to raise the shade back up later on.

To keep the shade from rolling back up as soon as you release it, there is a gravity-operated pawl-and-ratchet mechanism around this flat pin. The pawl engages a notch around the outside of the flat pin as the shade is pulled down, keeping the spring from unwinding and rolling the shade back up as soon as you let it go.

When you are ready to raise the shade, you give it a short downward pull to disengage the ratchet mechanism so that the pawl falls out of its notch. This allows the spring on the inside to unwind, pulling the shade back up. When you have raised the shade as high as you want it to go, you give the shade another short downward pull to make the pawl fall back into place inside its notch, thus keeping the spring from unwinding any farther. If the pawl were to stick or fail to function properly (more about this below), the shade would go flying up as soon as you released it.

When a window shade is too loose— that is, when the spring is not wound tight enough—the shade won't raise or roll up the way it should, or it may simply keep unrolling (dropping) after it is released. On the other hand, when a shade is wound too tight so that there is too much tension in the spring, it will be hard to pull down and will have a marked tendency to go fly-ing up out of control when you let go of it.

To fix a shade that keeps falling because there is not enough tension in the spring, all you have to do is wind the spring tighter. Here is the simplest way to do this:

Pull the shade down as far as it will go, then reach up and lift the roller out of the brackets that support it at the top of the window. Holding the roller in both hands, roll the shade up as shown in the accompanying drawing. When you have rolled it up completely, replace the shade in its brackets and try again. This time the ten-

If shade is too tight . . .

If shade is too loose . . .

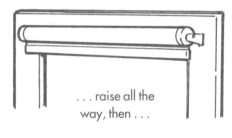

. . . raise all the way, then . . .

. . . pull down, then . . .

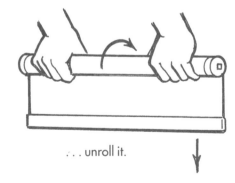

. . . unroll it.

. . . roll it up.

How to partially unwind a shade that is too tight (left) or tighten a shade that is too loose (right).

sion should be much stronger, probably adequate for making the shade work properly. If not, repeat the process, only this time roll the shade up by hand just about halfway—rolling it all the way up once again would probably built up too much tension and cause it to fly up out of control when released.

If winding the spring in this manner has no effect at all on increasing tension, then the spring is broken and you need a new shade roller. Replacement rollers are available from stores that sell window shades, as well as from many hardware stores.

To correct a shade that is wound so tight that it has too much tension and flies up out of control when released, you do just the opposite. Raise the shade carefully as high as it will go on the window, then reach up and lift it out of its brackets while it is still fully rolled up. Holding the roller in your hands, unroll about half to three-quarters of the length of the shade by hand, then, holding the shade in the same position, replace it in its brackets. Now check the tension again. If it is still too tight, repeat the process, but this time unroll it only about half as much as you did the first time.

Sometimes a shade roller will have the right amount of tension in its spring yet still won't stay in position when you release it. This usually means that the ratchet mechanism at the end of the roller is not working properly—or, to be more exact, that the metal pawl is not swinging into place when it should to engage the notch next to the flat pin. The most common cause of this malfunction is dust or lint in the mechanism, so take a small brush and clean out any foreign matter. In some cases it also helps to lubricate with a little silicone spray or graphite powder,

Replacing a Window Shade Roller

To replace the wooden roller, you will have to buy a new one that is as long as the old one or, if the frame opening is not standard width, a longer one that will then have to be cut to the exact length that is needed. To do this you have to pull out the round pin at one end, then pry off the metal cap that covers that end. Use a fine-tooth saw to cut the wood roller to the length you need (some stores will do this for you). Remember when measuring the length of the roller to allow for the added length of the metal cap and pin when they are replaced.

With the roller cut to length, replace the metal cap and the pin that goes into the center (you just tap them into place with a hammer), then unroll the old shade on the floor and pry out the staples that hold the fabric to the roller. Restaple the top of the fabric to the new roller, being sure to line up the top edge of the fabric with the line drawn on the roller—if you don't get this aligned, the shade will roll up at an angle and will bind. Also make certain the shade cloth is centered on the roller so that the same amount of roller projects at each side (as measured from the tip of each pin).

but don't use oil—it will eventually cake up and clog the works.

If cleaning and lubricating don't solve the problem, and if a visual examination of the ratchet-and-pawl mechanism seems to indicate that these parts are working properly (the pawl swings back and forth easily when you turn the shade roller in your hands), the next thing you should suspect is the mounting brackets on the window frame. The slotted bracket is supposed to hold the flat pin vertical when the shade is in position on the window; the pawl then falls into place when the shade stops. If the bracket is bent or worn, however, the flat pin can turn sideways and the ratchet will not engage when it should. The cure for this is to replace the bent or distorted bracket with a new one.

There are also times when the trouble is due to the fact that the shade was never mounted properly in the first place. If, for example, the shade keeps falling out of its brackets, you know that the brackets are too far apart for the length of the shade roller. Moving one of them slightly closer to the other will solve the problem. If the brackets are mounted inside the window frame, so that moving them closer together is not practical, the solution lies in lengthening the roller. Usually only a small fraction of an inch is involved, so all you have to do is pull out the round pin slightly (it is like a nail that has been driven into the end of the roller). If this is still not enough, you will simply have to buy a longer roller and remount the shade.

The opposite condition—brackets that are too close together—cause the shade to stick so it won't roll easily up or down. If the brackets are mounted outside the window frame, the condition can usually be cured simply by bending the brackets slightly away from each other. If they are mounted inside the window frame, hammering them to flatten them a little will often do the trick.

If this slight amount of additional clearance is not enough, it may pay to shorten the shade roller slightly. Pull out the round metal pin, then pry off the metal cap that covers that end of the wood roller. Now use a fine-tooth saw to trim off a small amount on the end, then replace the metal cap and tap the round pin back into its original hole. This will leave the shade

cloth slightly off center on the roller, but if only a slight amount of wood has been removed, the difference should scarcely be noticeable.

REPAIRING WINDOW SCREENS

Nowadays very few window screens are made of wood; most have aluminum frames. However, if you live in an older building that still has wood screens, make sure the wood frames are painted regularly, otherwise the wood will soon start to rot and deteriorate. Another problem with wood screens is that as they age they eventually become loose and wobbly in the corners. The quickest and easiest way to reinforce these corners is to screw on flat metal corner braces or mending plates. Be sure you paint these brackets—not only to make them less noticeable, but also to protect them against rusting (most are zinc-plated and are marked "rust resistant," but they will still rust when exposed to the weather).

The mesh used on these screens may be either metal (usually aluminum) or plastic (usually fiberglass). Today even most aluminum frames use some type of plastic mesh, as do most replacement screens. One of the main reasons is that plastic mesh is a lot easier than aluminum wire to work with and simpler to install. It is more flexible than metal mesh and can be stretched smoother without crimping or wrinkling. However, metal doesn't burn or scorch as easily as plastic, so with aluminum mesh there is less chance of damage from a careless cigarette smoker or from flying barbecue sparks.

To replace torn or badly worn mesh on a wooden screen, lay the screen flat, then pry off the moldings that are covering the edges. If you work carefully, you should be able to save these moldings for reuse, but if the moldings do crack or break, don't worry—similar moldings are sold in all lumberyards. After the moldings are removed, strip off the old wire mesh and pull out all staples or tacks, then use a narrow scraper to clean out the rabbet or recess in which the moldings originally fit.

Your new piece of mesh should be at least 12 inches longer than the screen frame and at least 4 to 6 inches wider. Position it on top of the frame and fold a small hem at one end (about ½ inch wide) before stapling this across the screen frame. To avoid wrinkles, start at the midpoint or center of the hemmed end and staple out toward each corner.

With one end stapled, move to the opposite end of the frame and pull the mesh tight with your hands (that is why you wanted the extra foot of material—it gives you something to grab). Now staple this

end down, again working from the center out to each of the corners. Then do the two long sides, starting in the midpoint of each side and working both ways out to the corners. In this way, any slight wrinkling or bunching of excess will take place in the corners where it can more easily be hidden or trimmed off. Replace all moldings with rustproof brads, including those on the center crossbar. Use a sharp utility knife or a single-edge razor blade to trim off excess mesh that sticks out from under the moldings.

Replacing the wire mesh on a metal-screen frame is usually easier, because the mesh is held in place by a plastic or metal spline that eliminates the need for stapling or tacking. The spline fits into a groove on the face of the screen and serves to wedge the edges of the screening in place, avoiding the need for separate moldings to pry off or renail.

To remove the old screen wire you sim-

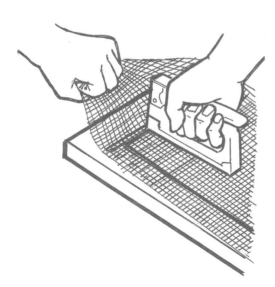

Staple gun is best for fastening screen mesh to wood frame.

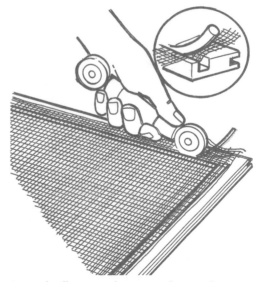

Special roller is used to press plastic spline into channel on metal screens. Spline holds mesh firmly in place.

ply pry out one end of the plastic or metal spline on each side, then pull the whole length of spline out of its groove and peel off the screen wire.

Cut the new mesh slightly oversize to allow for some excess material to grab when you try to stretch the screening, then lay the mesh over the screen frame and align it evenly around all four sides. Trim off each corner of the mesh at a 45-degree angle so that the material just cuts across the corner of the screen groove. This prevents bunching up or jamming in the corners when the spline is replaced.

Start replacing the splines on one of the longer sides—either by tapping with a hammer and a block of wood or by using one of the special rollers that are sold for this purpose. (This inexpensive tool makes the job faster and easier to complete.) Begin at one end and force the spline snugly down into its groove, then do the other side in the same manner. Be sure you pull the mesh tight across the surface of the screen frame as you proceed (one hand pulling outside of the spline, the other rolling or tapping the spline down on top of the mesh). When all four sides are secure, use a sharp knife or razor blade to trim off any excess material sticking out beyond the spline.

CHAPTER THREE

Wall and Ceiling Repairs

· · · ·

Chances are that if you live in a building that was built after about 1950, the walls and ceilings are surfaced with gypsum wallboard (commonly referred to as drywall), and the joints or seams between the panels are filled in with joint cement and perforated paper tape. Gypsum wallboard provides a strong, even surface that is much less subject to cracking than plaster, and it is relatively easy to work with and install—especially when making additions or alterations. It is also easier than plaster to patch or replace. (For information about repairing plaster walls and ceilings in older buildings, see pages 91–95).

Gypsum board panels are usually either ½ inch or ⅝ inch in thickness, and they are

nailed to the wood studs inside the wall (the 2×4s or 2×6s) with special drywall nails—that is, nails that are ringed or "threaded" to resist "popping" (pulling out). In newer buildings that have walls framed out with metal studs, the wallboard is attached to the studs with drywall screws instead of nails.

In all cases the nail heads (or screw heads) are recessed slightly below the surface by an extra blow of the hammer—just enough to "dimple" the paper facing on the wallboard without actually tearing or breaking it. The cavity or recess that remains is filled with joint cement at the same time as the joints; seams are filled later on.

WORKING WITH GYPSUM WALLBOARD

Gypsum board is most often sold in 4×8-foot panels (although 4×10s and 4×12s are also available), and it is easily cut with an ordinary utility knife, using a metal straightedge as a guide. Lay the straightedge along the line of cut, then use the knife to cut through the paper facing on one side and to score partway through the gypsum core. Turn over the panel and fold toward you along the score mark to break the gypsum core, then use the knife to cut through the paper facing on the other side. Snap back in the opposite direction to break the sheet off neatly along the score mark.

When you have to make curved cuts, the scoring system described above won't work. The easiest way to cut a curve is to use an ordinary keyhole saw or utility saw with a narrow blade (even a coarse hack-saw blade can be used). A keyhole saw can also be used to make "pocket cuts" in the middle of a panel (for example, when you have to cut out a damaged section to replace it with a new piece of wallboard, or when you want to cut an opening in the middle of a panel for an electrical outlet). To provide an opening for starting the tip of the saw blade, drill a hole with a large-diameter bit or cut through in one corner of the cut-out with the point of your utility knife.

TAPING WALLBOARD SEAMS

To achieve a smooth, unbroken wall surface, drywall seams and joints are filled in and smoothed over with joint cement and then covered with specially treated paper tape that has very fine perforations in it (to allow trapped air and moisture to escape). The joint cement (also called joint compound) is most often sold as a ready-mixed paste in one-gallon and five-gallon cans. About the consistently of soft butter or cream cheese, it is ready for use as it comes from the can and can be smoothed out to form a slick surface that will need little or no sanding.

To apply the compound you will need a putty knife or taping knife at least 6 to 8 inches wide. Start by spreading a layer of joint cement over the seam, filling the recess formed where the boards meet (where there is no recess, as on the end seams, just spread the com-

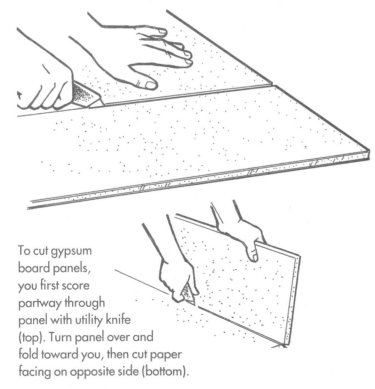

To cut gypsum board panels, you first score partway through panel with utility knife (top). Turn panel over and fold toward you, then cut paper facing on opposite side (bottom).

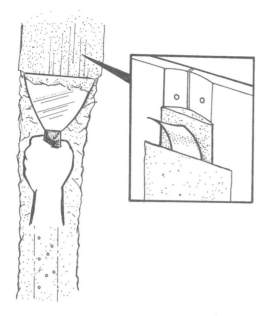

Wallboard seams are covered by first filling joint with layer of compound, then pressing paper tape into place over this. When dry, cover with another, wider layer of the same compound.

pound over the seam in a wide band). The paper tape is then pressed down on top of this, using the blade of the knife to smooth it down and partially embed it in the compound. If you do the job right, the tape should be almost—but not completely—covered. Excess cement or compound is smoothed off with the blade of the knife as you work it down along the seam.

Allow this first coat to dry hard (usually overnight), then apply a second coat of the compound alone, again using the wide knife. This time you want to cover the tape completely and fill the seam to bring it up level with the surrounding surface. To accomplish this you will have to "feather out" the compound on each side, forming a still wider seam anywhere from 8 to 10 inches across. This second coat is not a thick layer—it is just heavy enough to

cover the tape and fill in all the low spots in the first coat.

If the joint to be filled does not have the usual recess formed when two sheets are installed alongside each other, you still use the same technique, except that a bit more effort is required to feather out the compound, even more to avoid a bulge or ridge along the seam.

Although it is not always required, walls that are to be painted will usually look better if a third coat of the joint cement is troweled on over the seams (again without tape) for a final smoothing. This coat can be applied with the same wide joint knife previously used, but you will get better results if you use one of the special extra-wide drywall tools made for this purpose (some have a flexible edge that makes it much easier to feather out to a smooth finish). If this is done right, the surface of the seam should be smooth enough so that little or no sanding will be required to get it ready for painting.

Nail heads are covered with two or three applications of the same joint cement—only without any paper tape. You can do this with the wide joint knife or with an ordinary 4-inch spackling knife. Again, try to apply the last coat so smoothly that no sanding will be required. If you do have to sand, use a fine grade of paper, and avoid sanding the paper facing surrounding the plastered area—sanding will make the paper fuzzy.

Inside corner joints are taped and filled in much the same manner, except that here you have to fold or crease the tape lengthwise down the center. You spread compound over one side of the joint at a time and give the first side a chance to stiffen before you start spreading compound on the other side. If you don't follow this procedure, you may find the edge of the putty knife marking up the wet compound on the adjoining wall.

Outside corners are another matter. They really need reinforcing to keep them from getting banged up and dented, so there is a special type of rigid metal bead to be used on corners. It has a flange attached to each side of the rigid metal corner, and you cover these flanges with layers of joint cement on each side after nailing the strip in place against the outside of the corner joint. Allow the first coat of joint cement to dry hard, then apply a second coat to bury the flanges completely, along with the heads of the nails that hold the bead in place. Some of the rigid metal along the corner may still be slightly exposed, but you won't see this at all after the wall is painted or papered.

REPAIRING POPPED NAILS IN DRYWALL

Popping or working loose of nails can be due to warping or shrinking of the wall studs or to the fact that the wrong type of nail was used. In either case, the problem is cured by removing the loose nail or, if you can't remove it easily, driving it deep enough so that the head is well below the surface of the wallboard, then driving in another nail an inch or two away from the original one—only this time using a ringed or threaded nail with a regular head (not a finishing nail).

Before you drive this new nail all the way in, push hard against the wallboard to press it against the studs, and hold it in until you are finished driving the nail. Drive the nail head just slightly below the surface of the wallboard—deep enough to create the slight dimple required, but not so deep as to tear the paper facing of the panel.

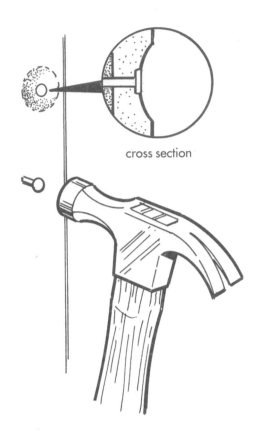

cross section

Recess nail heads slightly below surface by "dimpling" paper facing with hammer head, but do not tear paper.

After the new nails are in, use a ready-mixed vinyl or acrylic spackling compound, or regular joint cement, to fill in and smooth over the depression and to cover up the nail heads and holes. Apply one coat to fill in and bring the surface almost smooth, let it dry, then apply a second coat for final smoothing. Crisscross your strokes to avoid score marks and give an extra-smooth finish that should need no sanding. If you must sand, use fine paper and a sanding block, and avoid sanding the paper facing around the patch.

PATCHING CRACKS IN DRYWALL

Cracking along seams or joints are not as common as popped nails, but they do sometimes show up. If it is only a hairline crack with no sign of the tape actually pulling loose, and is no more than a few inches long, you can repair it with ordinary spackling compound, similar to the way you would repair a crack in plaster (see pages 91–92). But if the crack is larger and there are definite signs that the tape is pulling loose, you will have to do a more thorough job of patching. Start by pulling off any cracked or loose tape and any cracked or flaking cement. Then use joint cement and fresh tape to redo the joint from scratch.

REPAIRING HOLES IN DRYWALL

To patch a small hole—for example, one left by a crashing doorknob or by the removal of an electrical fixture or outlet—you can use several methods. One that works particularly well on openings that are no more than a few inches across is the technique illustrated here.

1. Start by cutting out the damaged section of wallboard with a keyhole saw, using a straightedge to guide you in making the cuts. Shape the cut-out so it forms a neat square or rectangle.

2. Cut a patch out of a scrap piece of gypsum board, about 2 inches larger on all sides than the cut-out (for a total of 4 inches wider and 4 inches longer).

3. Place this piece face down on a flat surface and with a sharp utility knife cut away the excess 2 inches of gypsum core and the paper backing on all four sides as shown in the drawing. *Do not* cut away the paper on the face side of the wallboard.

You will be left with a 2-inch-wide paper flap around all four sides and with the solid core (including backing paper) sized to make a neat fit inside the rectangular hole cut in the wall.

4. Smear a layer of joint cement over the back of the paper flaps, as well as around the edges of the hole in the wall, then push the cut-out patch into place so that it fits into the opening with the flaps on all four sides overlapping the face of the wall. Use a wide putty knife to smooth flaps onto the surface and to squeeze out excess compound from around the edges.

5. Allow the patch to dry hard, then apply a second coat of compound on top of and around the flaps to feather out the patch neatly so that it will blend in smoothly with the surrounding surface. A third coat of cement may or may not be required for the final smoothing, depending on how careful you have been with the first two.

For extra-large holes and extensively damaged sections for which this technique is not practical, there is another patching method you can use. Cut out the section of damaged wallboard, extending the cut-out to expose half the thickness of the studs on each side (leaving the old wallboard backed by the other half) to allow for wood against which the new patch can be nailed. Then all you have to do is cut a new piece of the same size and shape and nail it to the studs to fill the opening.

Cut out the damaged section with a keyhole-type saw or by making repeated cuts with a sharp utility knife. The cut-out should be at least 10 inches high so that the new patch, itself 10 inches high, will be strong enough to resist bending. Since you cannot use a saw for the side cuts (which will be directly over the center of each

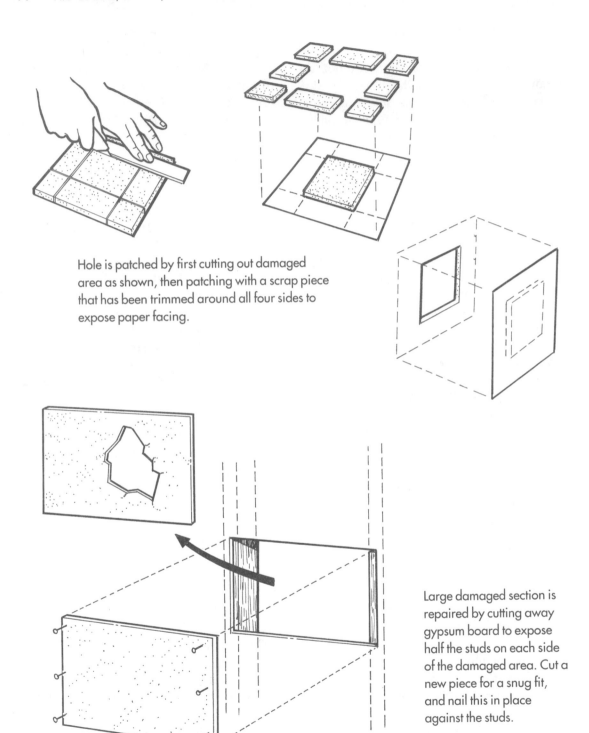

Hole is patched by first cutting out damaged area as shown, then patching with a scrap piece that has been trimmed around all four sides to expose paper facing.

Large damaged section is repaired by cutting away gypsum board to expose half the studs on each side of the damaged area. Cut a new piece for a snug fit, and nail this in place against the studs.

stud), you will have to employ a hammer and chisel or score repeatedly with a sharp utility knife until the piece comes off neatly.

The new piece of gypsum board should make a reasonably snug fit inside the opening and should be nailed against the studs on each side with ringed or threaded nails. Space the nails no more than 4 to 6 inches apart, and angle them slightly to make sure they go into solid wood.

Complete the job by applying joint tape and cement around all four sides of the patch, feathering the compound out neatly on all sides. The technique for applying the joint cement and tape is exactly the same as when finishing new wallboard seams.

PATCHING PLASTER WALLS AND CEILINGS

Small holes and cracks in plaster walls and ceilings are normally patched and filled with spackling compound—a material you can buy ready-mixed in paste form or as a powder that must be mixed with water. The paste type costs slightly more, but it is much easier to work with and forms a stronger bond because it contains a vinyl or acrylic latex base. And since you use only what you need, there is less waste. If you mix too much of the powdered material, the excess hardens up in a comparatively short while and cannot be saved.

The best tool for patching cracks and holes in plaster is a flexible putty knife with a blade made of springy, polished steel. It should be at least 3 inches wide—narrower blades won't bridge the crack or hole as well, making it harder to "feather" the patch out neatly.

The first step is to widen and undercut the crack, using a chisel or a V-shaped tool such as a "church key" can opener. The idea is to make the crack wider on the inside or bottom than along the surface (see illustration) in order to ensure a good bond with the old plaster. Brush out dust and loose particles, then wet the crack thoroughly with water before starting to apply the spackling compound.

Scoop up a wad of the compound with a

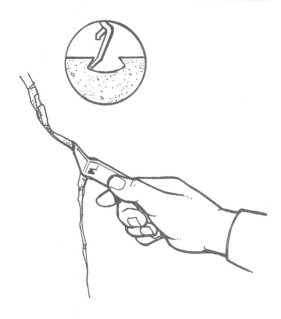

Before filling crack in a plaster wall or ceiling, undercut the crack with a pointed tool to ensure better grip for patching material.

corner of the spackling knife, then spread it into the crack by wiping it across with the full width of the blade, pressing hard enough to flex it slightly, while at the same time forcing the patching material down to the bottom of the crack or hole. Draw the knife back and forth until the whole length of the crack is filled, then remove the excess and smooth off the surface by wiping with

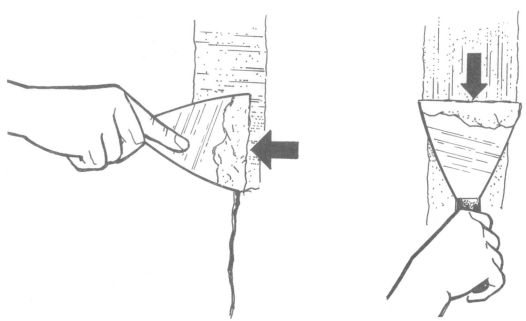

When filling crack in plaster, start by first packing compound in across the length of the crack. Finish by smoothing parallel to crack.

strokes almost parallel to the length of the crack, as illustrated. Do this with reasonable care, and you should be left with a surface that is smooth enough to need little or no sanding when the patch is dry.

Small holes are filled in much the same manner, except that undercutting is seldom required.

FILLING HOLES AND LARGER CRACKS IN PLASTER

Holes and larger cracks (more than about ⅛ inch wide) are generally filled with patching plaster, although spackling compound is often used for the final smoothing. Patching plaster does not set up as fast as regular plaster (which the amateur can find hard to work with), but it does set up faster than spackling compound and will not sag or shrink as much as spackling compound (which is why spackling compound is not used on large patches).

Begin by removing loose, crumbling, or flaking material, either scraping or chipping it out. Be ruthless—any part of the plaster that seems soft or crumbly should be scraped out or chipped away until only solid material is left or unless you are down to the lath.

Next, wet the surface of the exposed lath and the edges of the old plaster with a sponge or brush. Mix a batch of patching plaster, using only enough water to form a plastic, workable mass, then trowel onto the area to be patched. Press firmly into all crevices to make sure of solid contact with the exposed metal or wood lath, as well as with the edges of the surrounding plaster. You can use a wide putty knife for this, but if the area to be covered is more than just a few inches across, you are better off using a metal plasterer's trowel.

The first coat of plaster should fill the depression about halfway to the surface,

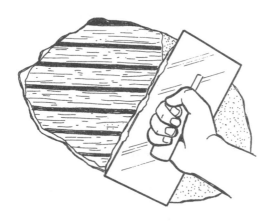

Large patches in plaster wall should be filled in two layers. First layer should be forced into spaces between the exposed lath and should fill depression only about halfway to the surface.

and it should be left relatively rough at the surface to help ensure a good mechanical bond when the second coat is applied. If necessary, use a piece of wire lath or mesh, or even the corner of the trowel, to scratch or score the surface of the first coat while it is still soft.

Allow this first coat to dry hard, then wet the surface again and spread on a second coat of plaster—this time bringing it up just about flush with the surrounding surface. This part of the job definitely requires a metal plasterer's trowel, rather than a putty knife; you will be able to bridge the area more easily with less chance of score marks. In addition, you can bear down harder with a trowel—and this pressure is essential for a smooth finish and elimination of air pockets.

There is another method for filling in a large patch, whereby you eliminate the need for troweling on multiple coats of

*R*epairing Plaster When a Hole Has No Backing

Sometimes you have to patch a hole that goes clear through the plaster—for example, when a light fixture or electrical outlet is removed. You will then have to create some sort of backing for the first coat of plaster. One way to do this is to stuff enough wads of newspaper or folded cardboard into the hole to fill it in to the back side, with the wads tight enough to stay in place. This paper or cardboard can then be dampened and covered with a base coat of patching plaster, which is packed in around the edges and spread lightly over the surface of the paper. As this coat hardens it forms enough of a backing so that additional coats of plaster can be troweled on until the hole is filled flush with the surface.

A better way to create a backing that will also be more stable and less likely to shrink or crack is to use a piece of wire lath or coarse wire mesh of some kind. Cut this patch a little larger than the hole, then tie a string to the middle of the mesh. Push the mesh through the hole in the wall and use the string to pull it tight against the back of the plaster (see illustration, page 95).

Apply the first coat of patching plaster by pressing it in around the edges of the hole and over the face of the wire mesh. You don't want to cover or fill the hole completely—just get a layer over the mesh to form a complete bond with the edges of the old plaster. Allow this to harden, then cut the string, wet the surface, and apply a second coat of patching plaster, this time filling in about two-thirds the way to the surface. Allow the surface to remain rough.

Let this second coat dry hard, then apply your third and final coat to finish the job, using the smoothing techniques described on pages 94–95. As mentioned previously, you can use a wide flexible putty knife if the patch is small; for sizable patches a steel plasterer's trowel is much easier to use and will do a better job.

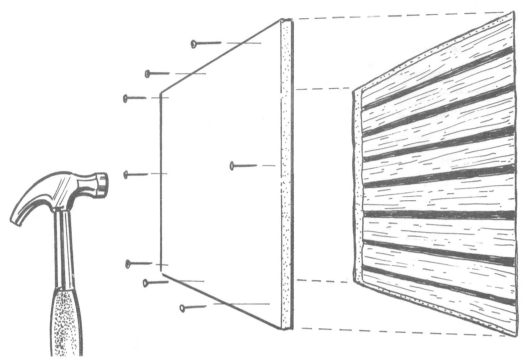

Alternate method for repairing large areas of damaged plaster: scrape away all old plaster to expose lath, then nail a piece of gypsum board to the lath.

plaster, which in turn makes it much easier to get a smooth finish on your patch. You fill in the depression with a patch cut out of a piece of plasterboard or gypsum board. This is nailed into place inside the cavity as illustrated, after which patching plaster is troweled in around the edges to fill in the spaces that remain between the board and the edges of the old plaster. The plaster should be applied in two layers, the first filling in the joints about halfway to the surface, and the second filling them in flush with the surface. Spackling compound can then be used for the final smoothing, if necessary.

Regardless of whether you are using a steel plasterer's trowel or a putty knife, there is one professional trick that will help ensure a smooth finish on the final

For extra-smooth finish on final coat, wet down patch with water as you drag trowel over the wet surface.

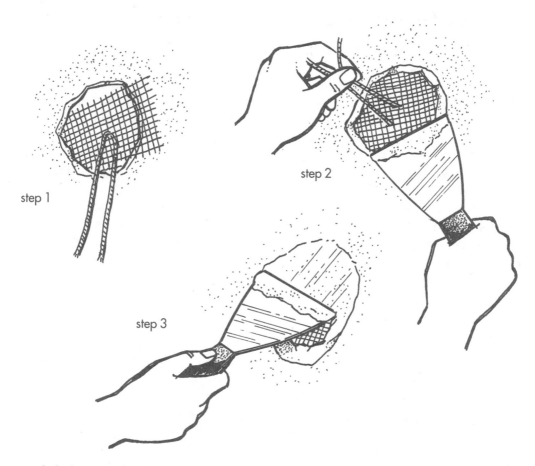

step 1

step 2

step 3

To repair hole that goes clear through the plaster, insert an oversize piece of wire mesh, then use string to hold this mesh in place against the back of the plaster while you trowel on a first coat of patching plaster.

coat of plaster or spackling compound. Wait till this coat starts to stiffen slightly (about 3 minutes), then use a clean paintbrush to spread a film of water over the patch. Immediately drag the trowel over the surface of the patch while bearing down hard with the front edge slightly raised. Keep wetting the plaster in front of the trowel or putty knife with your brush,

or keep dipping the tool in water to keep the surface wet as you work. You'll wind up with a supersmooth, glazed finish that would be impossible to match otherwise.

After this final coat has hardened, spackling compound can be used as necessary to fill in any visible defects or low spots. No sanding should be required, but if it is, use a fine-grit paper.

• • • • • •

REPAIRING CERAMIC TILE WALLS

Although ceramic tile walls will last almost a lifetime, there are occasions when a damaged tile will have to be replaced or when the grout in the joints between the tiles will crack, crumble, or start to fall out. Defective or missing grout not only looks messy and attracts dirt, it also may allow water to soak in behind the tile, and eventually this water will cause considerable damage to the backing behind the tile or to other structural components inside that wall.

Most tile grouts consist of a cementlike mortar that dries to a hard, waterproof compound something like the mortar that is used to bond bricks. However, the grout that goes between the tiles to fill in the joints has nothing to do with bonding or holding the tiles in place—the grout's only function is to seal and fill in the joints between the tiles. Some grouts are sold in powder form and must be mixed with water before use; others come ready-mixed in cans and are ready to use as soon as the can is opened. Ready-mixed grout costs a little more, but for the do-it-yourselfer who has only a few repairs to make, the ready-mixed type is usually less messy and easier to work with.

In addition to the cement-based grouts, there are also silicone rubber grouts that are used by those manufacturers who sell tile in pregrouted sheets rather than as individual tiles. However, when installing sheets of tile of this kind, the same type of silicone grout must also be used between the sheets after they are put up on the wall. Silicone rubber is also the best material for the apartment dweller to use for filling in the joint between the top of the bathtub and the wall tiles when regrouting of this joint is required.

The reason silicone rubber is better is because it remains flexible for years; ordinary grout is very brittle and tends to crack out with the slightest movement—for example, when a bathtub settles slightly after it is filled with water or if any structural supporting members warp or move the least bit. Under these conditions a brittle cement grout may crack out, but a flexible silicone rubber caulking compound won't. Just make sure you buy a brand that is formulated to be mildew-resistant.

Before using this to fill in such joints, however, you must scrape out most of the old grout, using the edge of a stiff putty knife or the point of a beverage can opener. Brush out loose dust and particles and make sure the joint is dry and clean before you start. If there are signs of mildew, wash with a solution of one part liquid laundry bleach to four parts water, then rinse with clear water and wipe dry.

Cut off the end of the plastic nozzle on the tube or cartridge at approximately a 45-degree angle, and hold this nozzle against the inside of the joint so that it projects up at about the same angle from the joint. Start squeezing the cartridge while moving it

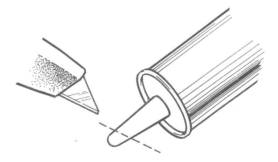

When starting a new cartridge, cut off plastic tip at approximately a 45-degree angle.

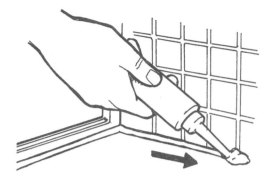

For best results, move cartridge or tube forward while squeezing it, instead of pulling it toward you.

along at a slow but steady pace—but move the nozzle of the tube away from you, rather than pulling it toward you (see illustration above). The reason for this is that pushing away from you helps to pack the compound more firmly into the joint as you move. Pulling the nozzle toward you—as seems more "natural" to most people—would cause the bead of rubbery compound to stretch out and become stringy, especially if you move a little too fast.

REPLACING A LOOSE OR DAMAGED TILE

When you are faced with the task of replacing a badly cracked or damaged ceramic tile, the first step is to make sure a replacement tile is available that will match (often impossible if you live in an old building). What do you do if you can't find one? Try to find a decorative tile that will blend in, or see if

you can have one hand-painted to match or blend in. In some cases you may find it desirable to remove several tiles so that you can arrange a grouping of decorative or contrasting colored tiles that will form an interesting pattern on that wall.

To actually remove the damaged tile, start by scraping out most of the grout around that tile, using the corner of an old chisel, a screwdriver, or a similar tool. Work carefully to avoid damaging adjoining tiles. Then use a hammer and small cold chisel to break up the damaged tile so it can be pried out in pieces without disturbing the other tiles. Start hammering in the center of that tile, striking with moderate to light blows with the chisel to crack the tile without loosening those next to it and without smashing or cracking up the cement behind that tile.

After cracking up the old tile, or at least breaking it in the center, start chipping away the pieces and prying them out where possible. Also remove all of the grout

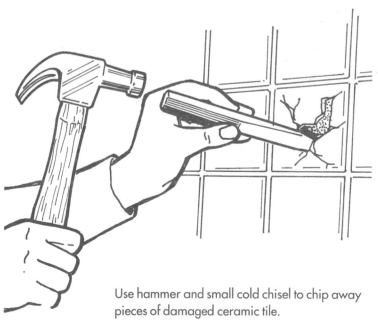

Use hammer and small cold chisel to chip away pieces of damaged ceramic tile.

around it. If there is mortar behind the tile and it is still solid, you can cement the new tile in place on top of it. If the tile was put up with a mastic adhesive of some kind, remove as much of this as you can, then cement the new tile back on top of the solid material that is left. If the surface behind the tile seems to be covered with partially exposed wood or metal lath, scrape off any of the cement that is loose or powdery before trying to install the new tile.

Most hardware stores and home centers sell ready-mixed mastic adhesives that are made for installing ceramic tile. However, if large amounts of cement are missing so that the wood or metal lath is exposed, it would be best to cover the lath with a layer of regular mortar first. Wait till this hardens, then use the adhesive to cement the new tile in place on top (make sure you don't apply too much mortar cement over the lath or the new tile will be higher than the surrounding tiles).

If you find there is a whole section or group of tiles loose, make sure you remove all of them—then inspect the wall or supporting surface behind the tiles. Chances are you will find that this surface is badly deteriorated (usually from moisture). New tiles cannot be successfully put up over plaster that has crumbled or rotted, over drywall that has started to delaminate and fall apart, or over lath that has rotted or rusted away. If any of these conditions are present, the old surface should be removed entirely and then the wall covered with a gypsum board or drywall (make sure it is the special moisture-resistant type that is sold for use in damp locations). Only then are you ready to glue in your tiles.

Special mastic adhesives for putting up ceramic tile or replacing loose tiles are

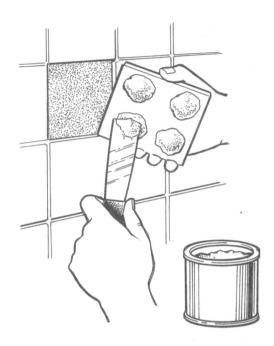

Tile is cemented in place with several large dabs of mastic cement.

sold in most hardware stores and home centers. If you have only one or two tiles to replace, or if the old mortar cement is still in place so that you don't have much of a recess for the new cement, you will probably be better off using a silicone rubber adhesive. This will bond firmly even in comparatively thin layers, and it is completely waterproof.

Apply the cement or mastic to the back of the tile, keeping it at least ½ inch away from the edges, then push the tile firmly into place. Use toothpicks or small slivers of wood as spacers around the edges if necessary to make certain it is uniformly spaced around all four sides, and tap carefully with a rubber mallet or wood block to seat the tile firmly.

After the tile is in place, use a small stick or similar tool to scrape out any of the adhesive that has oozed up into the joints.

You want the joints left open so they can be filled with grout—though not until the adhesive is fully cured.

• •

Cutting Ceramic Tile

The simplest way to cut a tile to fit is with an ordinary glass cutter. Score the glazed face with a single smooth stroke along the line to be cut, then place the tile face up directly over a pencil centered under the score mark. Press down hard on both sides of the cut to snap the tile neatly in two. Use a piece of medium-grade abrasive paper to smooth off any rough edges.

If you have to make a curved cut—for example, to fit around a pipe or faucet—score the curved line with the glass cutter, then make a series of radial cuts from this curve out to the edge. Now use a pair of end-cutting pliers or nippers to "nibble" away at the waste areas, splitting off one small piece after another until you have the shape you need.

• •

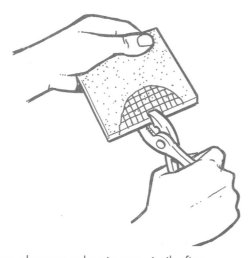

To make a curved cut in ceramic tile, first use a glass cutter to score marks across the waste section. Then break away the waste in pieces by using a pair of heavy pliers or nippers.

REPAIRING OR REPLACING A BROKEN CERAMIC TILE FIXTURE

When a ceramic soap dish, toothbrush holder, or similar tile fixture falls out or starts to work loose, replacing it is in most respects similar to replacing a broken or damaged tile. Start by first scraping out all of the old grout from around the edges of the fixture, as described in "Replacing a Loose or Damaged Tile," then follow the steps outlined in that section for installing a new tile. However, because these fixtures usually weigh considerably more than a single tile, you probably would be better off using a two-part epoxy adhesive (rather than an ordinary tile adhesive) to cement the new fixture in place.

If the old fixture has broken off cleanly and the base is still stuck solidly in place on the wall with no pieces missing, chances are that your best bet is to glue the broken section back into place rather than trying to replace the entire fixture. You can use a clear two-part epoxy adhesive to glue the broken section back, but remember that you will have to rig up

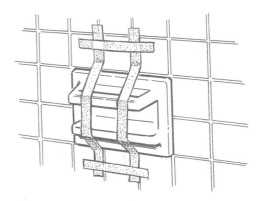

Long strips of masking tape or duct tape will hold broken pieces of soap dish in place until mastic adhesive dries.

some way to hold the pieces firmly in place until the adhesive cures (there are fast-drying epoxy adhesives you can use that will set up in about five minutes, but you still have to support the weight for at least that length of time). The simplest way to arrange this is to use strips of duct tape or cloth adhesive tape as shown in the illustration on page 99 to support the broken-off section while the epoxy is curing.

SOLVING CEILING PROBLEMS

Ceilings made of plaster or gypsum board (drywall) are repaired exactly the same as walls made of the same material—except, of course, that you are usually working overhead while standing on a ladder.

The most common problems encountered with ceilings in older buildings are extended peeling or flaking and large sections that are very lumpy and uneven, caused by repeated, poorly executed patching and repainting. If the problem is peeling or flaking paint, complete removal of all paint with a chemical paint and varnish remover is probably the only answer.

Sometimes, if the condition is not too bad, you can get by with scraping off most of the loose or flaking material, then lining the ceiling with canvas—a special fabric-like wallcovering that is sold by all wallpaper stores for covering walls or ceilings that are plagued with cracks or are otherwise in very poor condition. The lining canvas is put up with a regular vinyl adhesive (the kind sold for putting up vinyl wallcoverings) and when properly done creates a smooth new surface that can be either painted or papered. However, doing the job properly does require some skill and experience, so this is one job where it is generally best to call in a professional paperhanger.

In many cases plaster ceilings in old buildings will be so badly cracked, flaky, and bumpy that patching is almost hope-less and lining with canvas is impractical. Under these conditions the only way to end up with a smooth ceiling is to re-cover it completely—either by nailing up new drywall (gypsum board) or by putting up some type of ceiling tile.

Sold by most lumberyards and home centers, ceiling tiles are most often 12-inches square and are available in a wide range of patterns and styles. Some have a fibrous, textured finish, while others have a plasticized finish that is moisture-resistant and washable (ideal for kitchens and baths). Most have some acoustical qualities (some more than others), and some are fire-retardant. All can be put up in one of three ways: by cementing them directly to the surface of the old ceiling, by stapling them to wood furring strips that are nailed up beforehand, or by snapping them into metal channels or rails that are nailed to the ceiling in place of wood furring strips.

Cementing the tiles directly to the old ceiling is, of course, the simplest procedure, but this is seldom practical, because by the time an apartment owner decides to re-cover the ceiling, it is usually much too rough and bumpy. Even when the old ceiling is still reasonably flat and solid, it may be necessary to strip all the old paint off first for the cement to adhere properly. That is why it is almost always advisable to nail up wood or metal furring strips to

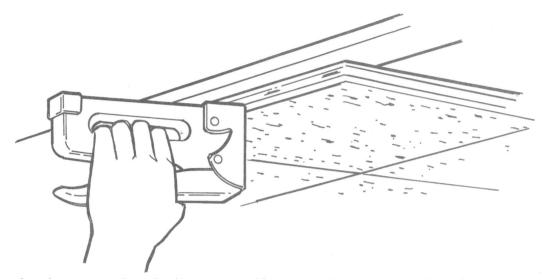

Ceiling tile is put up with staples driven into wood furring strips that have been nailed up first.

create a solid, uniform surface for the tiles and then staple the tiles to these strips.

The furring strips may be 1×2-inch wooden pieces that are nailed up to the ceiling beams, or they may be special perforated metal channels or tracks that are nailed up in the same way. The ceiling tiles are attached to the wooden strips with long staples or the metal tracks with special metal clips. Using metal tracks and clips makes it much easier to take down or replace individual tiles when necessary. Also, wood furring strips must be carefully spaced the right distance apart so they will fall exactly under the edge of each row of tiles, while the metal tracks do not require the same precise spacing.

The furring strips should be nailed up at right angles to the direction of the overhead beams—in other words, running across the beams. If you are resurfacing a finished ceiling and are not sure which way the beams run, you can usually assume that they run across the shortest dimension of the room. This can be checked by drilling small holes in the ceiling where you think the beams are (the holes will eventually be covered by the new ceiling), then probing the holes with a short length of bent wire, working it from side to side until you strike solid wood.

Before nailing up the strips, you will have to plan the layout for the whole ceiling so that you wind up along each side of the room with border tiles of a reasonable width, rather than with very narrow strips of tile. Each border piece should be at least 6 inches wide (half a tile). Your best method is to draw a small-scale plan on graph paper, penciling in the furring strips to see how the layout works out, then erasing and moving as necessary until you get borders of uniform width on each side of the ceiling.

PUTTING UP A SUSPENDED CEILING

Wherever you have enough headroom so you can afford to lose a few inches of height in the room, one of the best ways to

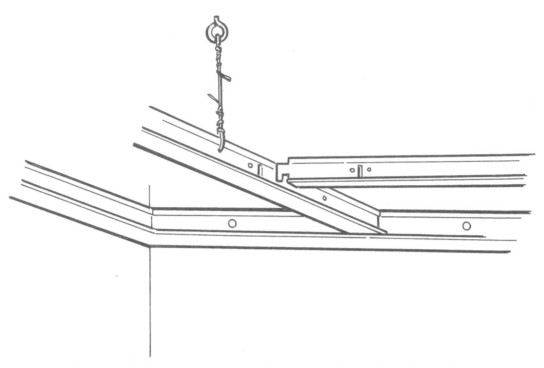

Suspended ceiling consists of aluminum runners and crosspieces that are hung from ceiling with pieces of stiff wire.

cover up a problem ceiling—or put up a new one—is with a suspended ceiling.

The framework for such a ceiling consists of an aluminum grid suspended by wires fastened to screw eyes driven into the existing ceiling or, where there is no existing ceiling, into the overhead beams. This system eliminates the need for nailing up furring strips or installing individual small tiles. It is also an easy way to hide unsightly pipes, wires, and other overhead eyesores.

The aluminum strips that form the supporting grid for this type of ceiling are designed to snap together with special clips, making it easy to assemble the suspended frame in place. There are holes or slots at regular intervals for tying the wires that suspend the framework, and the strips are usually designed to form a grid that accepts 24×48-inch acoustical ceiling panels.

The panels rest on the flanges of the T-shaped moldings and are easily dropped into place when the suspended framework is finished. They can be just as easily lifted out when it becomes necessary to gain access to the space above the ceiling. For some systems you need at least 6 inches of clearance between the original ceiling and the suspended framework in order to tip the panels into place, but for some of the newer ones, which have semiflexible panels that can be bent slightly for installation, this space can be as little as 2 or 3 inches.

The first step in installing a suspended ceiling is to measure the area. Then take these measurements to your local lumber-

Ceiling panels are dropped into opening so that they rest on top of the aluminum runner's flanges.

yard or home center to compute the materials you will need: main runners (the long pieces that serve as the main support for the ceiling), crosspieces (which clip to the main runners), angle-shaped border moldings (which are fastened to the wall around the perimeter), and the actual ceiling panels.

The companies that make these ceiling systems supply detailed instructions on how to assemble the main runners and crosspieces and how to join them to the angle pieces around the walls of the room. You start by nailing the angle-shaped pieces to the walls, using a tightly stretched string and a line level to mark the height at which each strip will be fastened. *Don't* depend on measuring down from the ceiling or up from the floor to achieve a level line—few ceilings or floors are themselves that level.

The T-shaped main runners are installed next by suspending each one with a length of wire from screw eyes or hooks driven into the overhead beams. Space these according to the directions recommended by the manufacturer, and take time to make sure that each runner is hanging straight with its ends resting on the angles previously fastened in place against the walls. A stretched length of string is the best way to align each row of hooks. The individual lengths of the wire are adjusted by bending them to keep the runners level and thus ensure a level ceiling.

The final step is installing the actual panels. Push each one up through its opening, then tilt it forward and allow it to drop into place on the flanges of the T-shaped runners. Being acoustical, the panels will also help absorb or muffle noise in that room.

Some are also plastic-coated to resist soiling, a feature useful in kitchens, laundry rooms, and similar locations.

One big advantage of this type of ceiling is that with it you can install modular fluorescent lighting fixtures, fitted into the same framework as one of the ceiling panels. In other words, the lighting fixture will rest on, and become part of, the ceiling, providing recessed lighting where needed. Translucent panels fit under and conceal each lighting fixture—all you see is the light-producing panel. This panel is usually hinged to let you reach into the fixture to change bulbs or for routine cleaning and service without the need to take down the whole fixture.

F loors and Stairs

Squeaking floors or a creaky set of stairs may provide great atmosphere for a mystery movie or a television show, but in a home or apartment these are almost always considered a nuisance—especially at night when everyone is asleep. Fortunately, repairs required to silence such noisy floors are usually minor and can be taken care of by the do-it-yourselfer willing to take the time to track down the source of the trouble.

CURING A SQUEAKY WOOD FLOOR

Although the problem is not always easy to isolate, one thing you can almost always be sure of is that the squeaking or creaking noise is being caused by one or more loose boards. These boards tend to "give" or move up and down when stepped on so that the edge of one board rubs against the edge of an adjoining board—and it is this rubbing that often causes the squeaking or creaking noises that you hear. In other cases the movement of these loose boards may cause them to rub against the nails that are supposed to be holding them firmly in place—again causing a noise.

What causes floorboards to loosen? In some cases the boards may have buckled or warped after they were put down. In others the joists or beams under the flooring may have warped, shrunk, or twisted after the flooring was installed. And in some other cases it may even be that the flooring was never nailed down properly

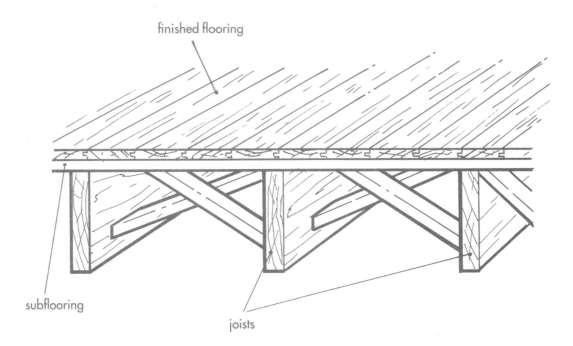

Construction of a typical wood floor.

in the first place (not enough nails were used, the wrong kinds of nails were used, or nails were placed improperly).

In most homes the wood flooring will consist of two layers—one layer of subflooring and one of finished flooring. The subflooring may consist of 6-inch or 8-inch wide tongue-and-groove boards laid across or diagonal to the supporting joists, or the subflooring will consist of large panels of plywood or particle board that have been nailed across the joists. It may be either the subflooring or the finished flooring that has loosened—or both may be loose (although in most cases it is the finished flooring).

(*Note:* High-rise buildings that have concrete slab floors may have no wood subflooring. The finished wood flooring may have been put down directly on top of the concrete in a single layer, using a spe-cial mastic adhesive. This finished flooring may consist of wood "tiles" that form a parquet pattern, or it may consist of strip wood flooring that is glued down.)

The first step in silencing a noisy floor is to locate the loose boards that are causing the problem so that you can take steps to fasten them down properly with nails or screws. This will keep them from moving or "giving" when stepped on. Have someone walk over the floor slowly while you listen carefully. When you hear a squeak, mark the location with a piece of tape or with chalk so that you can come back to work on that area later on. Sometimes even if you hear no squeak you will see the floorboards or parquet squares actually move slightly when stepped on, but in other cases—especially when the problem is in the subflooring—you may not actu-ally see anything.

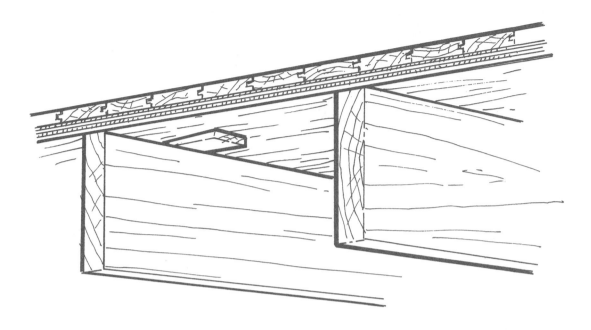

Glue-coated thin wood wedge driven under flooring will stop movement that causes squeaking.

Most squeaks can be silenced temporarily by lubricating the edges of the boards that are rubbing against each other—that is, by squirting some powdered lubricant into the cracks between those boards. This type of lubricant is usually sold in hardware stores and home centers for use on sticking drawers, or you can use powdered graphite (sold for use in locks). In a pinch, you can even use talcum powder, although this won't last as long as a powdered lubricant.

In town houses or other condominium units where there is a basement or garage with an unfinished ceiling under the noisy floor, it is generally simpler, neater, and more effective to work from below. Working from below is also easier when the squeaking floor is covered with wall-to-wall carpeting, tile, or sheet vinyl. Have someone walk slowly around the room in a predetermined pattern while you watch and listen from below. Listen for sounds of movement in the flooring and watch for subflooring that moves up or down even slightly when the person above steps on that area (it helps to shine a bright light up between the joists as your upstairs "helper" steps on each section).

When you see any movement in the flooring, there are several things you can do to correct this from below. One is to drive thin, glue-coated wood wedges in between the top of the joist and the underside of the flooring in that spot—pieces of wood shingle make excellent wedges for this purpose. Another option is to screw a short length of 2×4 against the side of the joist with its top edge pressed firmly up against the underside of the flooring as shown in the illustration on page 108 (coat the top edge of this block with glue before screwing it into place).

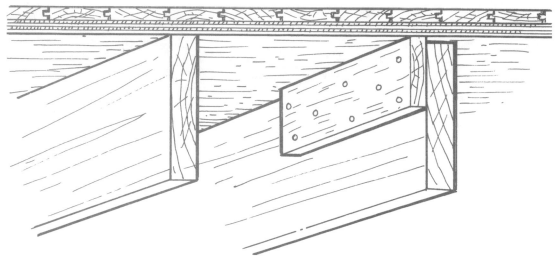

Another way to keep floor from moving is to fasten wood block against side of joist.

If you locate a squeaky area but do not see any sign of the subfloor moving when you shine your light at it, it is likely that the finished flooring on top is the cause of the problem. Either it is loose or has buckled upward slightly. To correct this from below, you can drive several wood screws up through the subflooring and into the finished flooring. These screws should be just long enough to go completely through the subflooring and then penetrate about three-quarters of the way up into the finished flooring (but you don't want the point to come through on top!).

If each layer of flooring is ¾ inch in thickness, then the screws would have to be 1¼ inches in length. Drill a clearance hole through the subflooring and a pilot

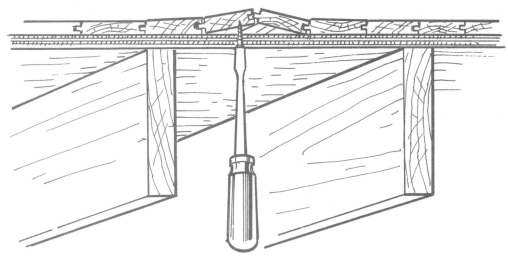

Screw driven up from below will pull down and secure loose floorboard.

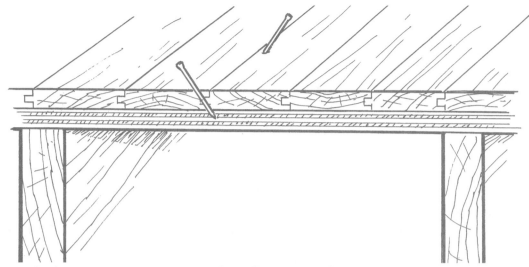

Two nails, driven into joint at opposing angles, will secure loose floorboards.

hole into the finished flooring for each screw, then draw them up as tight as possible while someone stands on top of the flooring to press it down. This will draw the boards together and prevent the top flooring from bulging or buckling up away from the subflooring.

Unfortunately, the floors in most apartments and in a majority of condominium units are not exposed from below, so you will have to try to correct the problem while working from above. If there is carpet or vinyl on top, you will usually have to take this off or peel it back to expose the wood floor underneath before making the necessary repairs.

In most cases the quickest and simplest way to fasten down loose boards is to drive two nails down through the boards at opposing angles as shown in the illustration above. Ideally these nails should go through both layers of flooring and into one of the floor joists as shown. To do this you have to use finishing nails that are at least 2½ to 3 inches long. They should penetrate the joist by at least 1 inch (1½ would

be better). The nails should be driven in next to (or into) the joint between the two suspected boards so that one nail angles down through the tongue edge of the adjoining board while the other nail goes through the grooved edge of that board.

Even when the floor is over an unfinished basement, you may find in some cases that the place where the nails or screws are needed is inaccessible from below because of pipes or other structural members. The solution in that case is to drive screws in from above. But then you will want to cover up or hide the screw head after the job is done. The neatest way to do this is to counterbore the screw hole slightly so that its head will be recessed below the surface of the wood. You can then fill the remaining hole with a colored wood plastic or with a wood plug that can then be stained and finished to match. If you can't buy a suitable wood plug, cut off a short length of dowel, coat it with glue, and drive it into the hole. After the glue dries, use a sharp chisel to trim the top off flush with the surrounding wood.

Replacing a Damaged Board

When a floorboard is badly warped and/or split, simply fastening it back down is probably not enough. The only way to do a proper repair is to replace the damaged section of board entirely. But most flooring is joined together with tongue-and-groove edges that interlock, and removing the damaged section of flooring without ripping up an entire section of floor (from that board to the nearest wall) requires careful carpentry. It can be done, and here's how:

1. Draw a line across the board at each end of the damaged section, then drill a series of holes across the board as shown in the illustration, keeping the holes just inside (on the waste side) of the line. Use a bit about ¾ inch in diameter, and overlap each hole slightly. Drill through the finished flooring only, not into the subflooring.

2. Use a hammer and sharp chisel to split the damaged piece lengthwise, from one end to the other—that is, from one line of holes to the other—then pry up the split pieces of board and lift them out.

3. Use the chisel and hammer to trim off the remaining ends and "inside" bits of the board still on the floor; each cut-off end should be straight and square across, necessary if you want to fit in a new piece neatly.

4. Cut a new strip of matching flooring so that it is an exact fit between the trimmed-off ends—it should be snug enough to require pressing into place, but not so tight that you have to hammer it in. Because of the tongue-and-groove edges, you won't be able to just drop it in. Turn the board over and trim off the lower part of the grooved edge, as shown. Now, with the trimmed-off edge on the bottom, you will be able to tip the board slightly as shown to engage the tongue edge of the insert piece with the grooved edge of the board on the floor. Tap down the other edge for a snug fit, with its remaining lip overlapping the tongue edge of the board on the other side.

5. Finish securing the board by driving two nails in at each end, using cement-coated or ringed nails for maximum holding power. Countersink each nail head slightly, then fill the holes with a colored wood plastic or filler.

After removing damaged section of flooring, new piece can be inserted by first trimming off lower lip of grooved edge.

Although in most cases the problem is solved if the screws go only into the sub-flooring, you can be surer of the job if you locate the screws where they will also go into the joists and then secure both layers of flooring. In this case you will want to use screws at least 1½ inches longer than the combined thickness of the two layers of flooring.

Any time screws are to be driven into or through an oak floor, regardless of screw length and regardless of whether you are driving from above or below, make sure you drill pilot holes first. Otherwise you may wind up with split floorboards, or you may break the screws, or both. (Even when driving nails into oak, very small pilot holes are a good idea.)

SANDING AND REFINISHING WOOD FLOORS

Sanding a wood floor down to the raw wood and then applying a new finish is the only way to really rejuvenate an old floor that has been so badly neglected as to show severe wear and ugly discolorations. The job is best done with a heavy-duty floor-sanding machine, which can be rented from many hardware stores, as well as from tool rental agencies and lumberyards or home centers.

Your first step is to remove all the furnishings from that room—not only the furniture, but also any pictures hanging on the wall, as well as curtains or draperies. This is necessary because the fine dust created by the sander will coat everything, so the more you remove, the less tedious the cleanup job will be.

It is also a good idea to pry off all the floor moldings before you start, although this is not absolutely necessary. As you sand near the walls you will tend to scratch these moldings if they are left in place, so they will have to be repainted anyway. And if you do take them off, sanding around the edges will be that much easier because you won't have to worry about getting so close to the baseboard (with the moldings off, you can count on the last ½ inch of flooring being covered by

the moldings when they are eventually replaced).

Next, examine the floor to see if there are any nails sticking up that might damage the sanding machine, and replace any damaged sections of flooring that are badly split or warped. Also, nail down any boards that are loose or show signs of squeaking (see pages 105–109).

You will actually have to rent two different machines from your dealer: a large drum-type sander to be used on most of the floor and a smaller disk-type sander (called an edger) for sanding around the edges and in places where the large machine will not fit. The edger is also useful on stairs or steps.

If the floorboards are at all cupped or warped in places, three sandings will usually be required—the first with coarse paper while moving the machine at about a 45-degree angle to the length of the boards in order to level the surfaces off; the second straight and parallel to the grain with a medium-grade paper to remove the scratches left by the coarse paper; and the third with a fine paper that smooths off the scratches left by the medium-grit paper. You can buy the abrasive papers you need from the same dealer who rents you the machine.

On most floor sanding jobs first cut is made at 45-degree angle to the boards.

Sometimes when a floor is really not that bad you can get by with only two sandings, both parallel to the grain. In this case the first sanding is done with a medium-grit paper and serves to remove all of the finish. The second sanding is done with a fine-grit paper that will remove the scratches left by the first sanding and give the wood its final smoothing. Parquet flooring usually requires three sandings—the first at a 45-degree angle to the length of the room, the second at a 45-degree angle in the opposite direction, and the final one along the long dimension of the room.

Before starting, close all doors leading into the room (to confine the dust), and open all the windows. Begin sanding at one end of the room and work your way down to the other end. When you press the switch to start the motor, always have the machine tipped back so the drum is *not* in

contact with the floor. After it starts, lower the drum gradually till it touches the floor while beginning to move forward even before contact. The idea is never to start the machine while it is in contact with the floor—instead, start it and bring the drum down as you slowly move ahead—and to be moving as soon as and whenever the machine is sanding.

You don't have to really push the machine forward, because when the drum comes in contact with the floor it will "grab" and try to pull you forward. So be prepared—you just have to maintain a firm grip on the handles to keep the machine from "running away." And always keep moving while sanding to prevent gouging or digging in. As you approach the end of the room, raise the drum so that it loses contact with the floor just before you come to a complete stop, and never allow the rotating drum to remain in contact with the floor while the machine is standing still.

After you have completed one pass by walking forward, make the next pass by moving the machine over a couple of inches, then walking backward and pulling the machine after you. For the third pass you move over a couple of inches again, then start walking forward again. And so on. Work your way back and forth across the room in this manner, overlapping each pass by a couple of inches to make certain none of the boards are missed. Sand to within a couple of inches from the baseboard on all sides.

After you have sanded the entire floor with the coarse paper, switch to the smaller disk sander to do all the edges next to the walls. You won't be able to reach into all the corners even with this machine; just leave those spots until all the machine sanding is done. For these

Disk-type edge sander is used for sanding next to baseboards.

spots you will have to get down on your hands and knees with a small hook-type wood scraper, followed by some hand sanding.

Reload your sanding machine with the next finer grit of paper, then repeat the process. Remember to remove the dust bag on the machine and empty it (*outside*) as soon as it is half full (and won't be so heavy to handle).

Hook-type hand scraper is used in corners where edge sander won't fit.

SELECTING AND APPLYING THE NEW FINISH

Although you may find it confusing trying to differentiate among the many different brands of finishing materials available for wood floors, all of them can be classified roughly into two broad categories: penetrating sealers and surface coatings.

Penetrating sealers soak into the pores of the wood and bond with the fibers to seal and protect the wood without leaving any appreciable surface coating and therefore little or no gloss on the surface. Since there is no surface film to scratch, they do not show scratch marks (although you can scratch the wood itself). All such sealers require at least two coats on freshly sanded floors, and any of them will give you a beautiful finish that is easy to maintain or touch up when necessary (worn or damaged areas can be touched up by rubbing a little of the same sealer into the wood with a pad of fine steel wool, then buffing with a cloth). They can be applied with a brush, roller, or lamb's-wool pad; of the three methods, mopping it on with a long-handled lamb's-wool applicator is by far the easiest and most foolproof. Directions furnished with the various brands of sealer vary to some extent, but as a rule you simply wipe on the sealer and allow it to soak in, then wipe off the excess with a dry cloth. Once it is thoroughly dry, the floor should be given a light coat of wax and buffed to bring up the luster. Penetrating sealers come in clear as well as in various wood-tone colors (walnut, dark oak, and so on). If you cannot find the shade you want, colors can be intermixed, or you can mix your own by adding regular tinting colors (the kind sold for tinting paints) to the clear or to

The easiest way to apply a floor sealer or stain is with a long-handled lamb's-wool applicator.

any of the ready-mixed shades. Be sure to test the color first before you start applying it to the entire floor, and avoid adding too much color, since this can interfere with proper drying. If you want a dark shade, start with a ready-mixed tone that is close to what you want, then add your own colors to darken it. If it is too dark, you can lighten it by thinning or by buffing with steel wool after the stain is dry.

Surface coatings differ from penetrating sealers in that they build up a decided surface coating on the wood. The best finishes in this category are both hard and tough, and they build up to a beautiful shine, but they will also show scratches more readily than a penetrating sealer. Also, surface coatings can be much more difficult to touch up (when only one part of the floor shows signs of wear). Most of the surface

coatings sold for use on floors fall into one of three broad classifications: shellac, varnish, and lacquer or synthetic-type finishes.

Shellac is probably the oldest of clear floor finishes, and it is still used frequently. It dries very clear, so it does not darken the wood, and it dries very quickly—45 to 60 minutes in most cases. Thus, two or three coats can usually be applied on the same day, and the room can be used that same night. However, shellac does stain easily if water or other liquids are not mopped up promptly (it turns white in most cases). On the other hand, it is easier than varnish and most other surface coatings to touch up, because each new coat of shellac tends to dissolve the old coat, so patches blend together more easily.

Varnish comes in dozens of variations sold under many brand names, but you will want one that is made specifically for use on floors. It will dry to a hard, abrasion-resistant finish that is also highly resistant to staining and discoloration when liquids are spilled on it. Most varnishes tend to darken with age, and almost all take at least 6 to 8 hours to dry hard, so you can seldom put more on than one coat in a single day. In most cases this means you can't use that room for a couple of days.

Probably the toughest and longest-lasting floor varnish you can use is a polyurethane varnish. A clear synthetic finish that is radically different from most conventional varnishes, it still falls into the varnish category. Available with either a high-gloss or semigloss finish (also called satin gloss), polyurethanes dry to a much harder finish than most of the other surface coatings—hence their exceptional resistance to scratching.

Although some polyurethane manufacturers claim that waxing is unnecessary, these tough finishes will start to show scratch marks in time, and waxing will help prevent or at least minimize this. On the other hand, waxing may also make the floor more slippery, so if this is a serious consideration for the room, you may prefer to skip the waxing and accept the fact that the finish will wear a bit more rapidly than it would with a coating of wax.

Lacquers and similar fast-drying synthetic finishes are not as popular as they once were. They dry so fast that they are often difficult to apply, and they are not as durable or long-lasting as the polyurethane varnishes. However, they don't darken a floor as much as varnish does, and their quick-drying characteristics make them useful for floors that cannot be kept out of use for days at a time, so many people still prefer them.

All surface coatings can be applied with a brush or roller or with a flat painting pad. The coating should be applied liberally but uniformly, and without leaving pools or puddles on the surface. You must allow adequate drying time between coats, and if you plan to use a wood stain on the floor, make sure the stain you choose is compatible with the type of finish you intend to apply over it. Read the specifications on the label, and if still in doubt, ask your dealer. Wait at least three days after the last coat has dried hard before applying the first coat of wax.

Caring for Wood Floors

A few important rules should be observed in maintaining any type of finished wood floor:

1. Keep the surface as clean as possible—cleaning every day in heavily trafficked areas and at least once a week in other areas, using a vacuum to pick up dust, and wiping up spills as soon as possible after they occur. If dirt gets ground in, it shortens the life of the finish and also darkens and discolors the wood.

2. Never scrub the floor with water, and do not use water-based cleaners or waxes to clean it. Water is the natural enemy of a wood floor and of most of the finishes used on wood floors.

3. Keep the surface waxed, and renew this wax coating as soon as it shows signs of wearing off, usually when the surface starts to look dull.

4. When simple sweeping or vacuuming won't get the floor clean, use a solvent-based cleaner-wax to get up the dirt. The solvents will dissolve the old wax on the surface so that it comes off on the applicator as the new coat is applied, with the dirt embedded in the old wax as it comes up. The applicator cloth should be changed frequently as you work—otherwise you will be merely spreading the same dirt around.

5. Waxes, liquid or paste, should be applied sparingly, for a thin film dries harder and thus is less likely to absorb and hold dirt. A light film of wax is also less slippery than a heavy one. Most waxes stand up better if each new coat is buffed vigorously after application, not only to bring up the luster, but also to make the wax harder and remove any excess.

As a rule, waxing should not be required more than once or twice a year, even in frequently used rooms. An exception might be an entrance hall or similar area where people walk in from the outside. Here waxing may be needed more often, if only for the cleaning action rewaxing provides.

REPAIRING STAIRS

A squeaking or creaking set of stairs may be only a slight nuisance if you don't mind the noise, but it can also be an indication of loose treads or risers that need fastening down if they are not to deteriorate into a potentially hazardous condition.

Most stair noises are caused by loose or warped treads (the tread is the part you step on), but the problem can also be caused by a loose or warped riser (the vertical piece on which the tread rests). Either one may be rubbing against the stringer along the side of the staircase, or it can be rubbing against one of the other treads or risers when stepped upon.

As can be seen from the illustration below, treads usually have grooves on the bottom that fit over the top of the riser. If such a groove is not down tight, its edges will rub on the top of the tread when you step on it, and this creates a squeaking or rubbing noise. To check for this, shine a light under the bottom edge of the tread where it projects out over the top of the riser to see if there is a slight gap. (In some cases there will be a small molding under the nose of the tread, so you will have to pry this off first in order to see if the top of the riser goes inside a groove on the bottom of the tread.) Another way to check this joint is to have someone step on and off the suspected tread to see if you notice any slight up-and-down movement. If the back of the staircase is open so that you can get at the steps and risers from underneath (for example, on steps that go down to the basement), it is neater and easier to make repairs from underneath. A loose tread notched to fit over the riser can be secured from below by driving thin wood wedges up into the groove. Pieces of wood shingle are ideal for this, but any piece of wood that is planed to a taper will work just as well. Trim for a snug fit, then coat with glue and drive the piece upward.

If driving wedges is impractical because

Showing how treads and risers fit together in typical stairs.

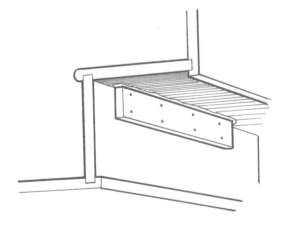

If underside of stairway is accessible, squeaks can be cured by screwing glue-coated wood block up against bottom of tread.

the space left is too small or because the tread is not grooved on the underside, you can secure the tread by bracing wood blocks against tread and riser as shown. Use screws and glue to secure them snug up against the bottom of the tread and the back of the riser. If the problem seems to be a matter of the bottom edge of the riser pulling away from the back edge of the tread it helps to support, the solution lies in driving long screws in from the back. These should be at least 2 inches long, and pilot holes should be drilled first to avoid splitting the wood.

Sometimes rubbing occurs where the side of a tread or riser meets the stringer at the side; if this joint is loose, the tread will move slightly each time it is stepped on, and there may be enough play to permit it to warp slightly. If you are able to get at the joint from underneath, you can fix it in the same way as you would a loose tread—either by driving glue-coated wedges into the gap or by installing wood blocks against the back of the tread or riser.

When the back of a staircase is finished or closed off, and therefore is inaccessible, you will have to work from the top. Loose treads can usually be fastened down by driving in nails or screws at an angle as pictured above. Be sure you drill small pilot holes for the nails or screws first, especially if the treads are oak—nails will bend otherwise—and have someone stand on the tread to hold it down while you are driving or nailing the screws down. Screws will do a better job of pulling the tread down, but their heads will be more noticeable unless you countersink them (predrilling the top of the pilot hole with a countersink bit, then screwing the head below the surface of the wood) and fill the depression with wood putty or a wood plug. If you use finishing

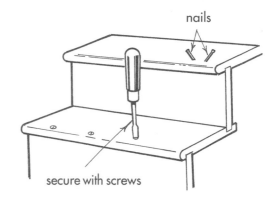

nails

secure with screws

When back of stairs is not accessible, loose treads can be secured by driving screws or nails down into top of riser.

nails, the heads can be neatly countersunk, and the small holes that remain can then be easily concealed by filling with a putty stick (sold for use on paneling) or with a wood plastic of the right color.

One problem that should be attended to promptly is a cracked or split front edge or "bullnose" on a tread. This makes the tread unsafe, as well as unsightly. A neat-looking permanent repair can be made in most cases by working some glue into the split with a thin spatula or blade of some kind, then driving a few small brads in to hold the split together (drill small pilot holes for the brads first to avoid splitting the wood). If the front of the tread has split off completely, you may be able to shape a new piece of hardwood to fit, using a rasp and some sandpaper, then glue this onto the front of the tread with epoxy glue. Make the filler piece slightly oversize, then trim it to a neat fit after the adhesive hardens, using a plane or rasp, and finish with sandpaper.

If a tread is so badly split or warped that repairs are impractical, it should be replaced entirely. Getting off the old tread can be a tricky job if it fits into mortises (grooves) in the stringers at each side of the stairway. You will have to pry up the tread carefully by working from the center along the front edge, then reach underneath with a hacksaw blade or pair of metal cutters to cut off any screws or nails that hold it in place. In some cases you may also have to cut an opening in the riser to enable you to reach in with a keyhole saw and cut off the riser (you will then have to replace both the riser and the tread).

If, on the other hand, the tread merely butts against the stringer and is attached to it by nails or screws, the job is a lot easier—you should be able to pry the tread up and out without having also to ruin the riser on which it rests.

Because there are many variations in how stairs are assembled, and unless you are really sure of yourself, you will probably be better off calling in a professional carpenter when altogether new treads or risers are required on a finished staircase.

REPAIRING DAMAGED RESILIENT TILE FLOORS

Small scratches, dents, and other minor imperfections in vinyl, vinyl-asbestos, or asphalt floor tiles can sometimes be repaired without replacing the entire tile, if you have a few scrap pieces of the same or a closely matching tile on hand. You can use these scrap pieces to make your own matching color patching compound with which to fill in and hide defects, the same way you use a wood filler for dents and scratches in wood. Use a coarse piece of sandpaper or a rasp to shave off or shred

some of the scrap material, then save the powder that you scrape off (you can also pulverize or powder the tile by working its edge against a rotary rasp chucked in an electric drill). The powder or shavings can then be mixed with a little clear varnish or shellac to form a pastelike putty, which you then apply with a small trowel or putty knife. Fill the scratch or dent flush with the surface and allow the compound to dry hard. Buff with steel wool to smooth it off, then rub wax on to restore the luster.

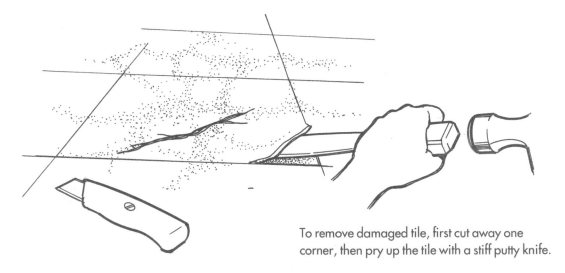

To remove damaged tile, first cut away one corner, then pry up the tile with a stiff putty knife.

REPLACING A DAMAGED TILE

Of course, the best cure for a damaged tile is to replace it with a new one. To simplify removal of the old tile, it often helps to apply mild heat to the tile, which softens it and makes it more pliable. The heat also helps to soften the old cement or adhesive that holds it down, making it easier to lift the tile off the floor. Heat can be applied with a hot clothes iron. A heat lamp would be faster than the iron, but be careful not to scorch nearby tiles, and always keep a pail of water or fire extinguisher handy—just in case.

After heating, lift out the damaged tile by inserting a sharp knife or thin putty knife near one of the corners and prying up carefully. Sometimes the tile will come up easily, but other times it won't come up without damaging the tiles next to it—something you definitely want to avoid. The safest procedure is to cut away one corner of the damaged tile first, using a knife or small chisel. Pry out this corner piece, working from the center of the tile, and you should then be able to slide a putty knife or chisel under the rest of the tile to get it up.

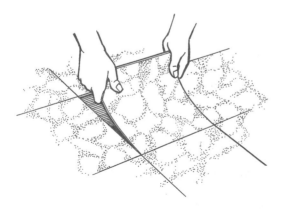

Set new tile in place by lining up one edge first, then press down without sliding.

After the entire tile is up, any cement left on the floor should be scraped away. Make sure no lumps remain, and clean out all dirt and debris. Test-fit your new tile to see how it matches (sometimes it helps to turn it 90 degrees in one direction), then set it aside and spread a thin layer of adhesive over the area. Use the type of adhesive recommended for the kind of tile involved, and put it down sparingly. Most adhesives are applied with a finely notched spreader, but some can also be applied with a brush. Either way, keep the adhesive about ¼ inch away from the edges to avoid excess oozing up through the seams after the tile is pressed down.

If the new tile feels stiff and brittle, warm it first in order to make it more pliable. Set it into place by bringing one edge down first, snug against the adjoining tile, then flex it slightly and lower the rest of it onto the adhesive-coated area. Pat down hard with both hands, then place a few heavy books or other weights on top. Leave the weights in place for a couple of hours to keep the tile from curling or raising.

PATCHING SHEET FLOORING

Patching a damaged section of a sheet vinyl floor covering is usually done by cutting out the damaged section and replacing it with a matching piece of the same material—but this can be done only if you have, or can get, a piece of the same material (or one that matches very closely). And in order to do the job right, you will have to cut a patch that perfectly matches in size and shape the piece you cut out. The best way to do this is to cut out both pieces at once.

Place the new piece on top of the damaged section and move it around till the pattern exactly matches that on the original floor, then tape it down with a few strips of tape. Using a straight-edge and a sharp utility knife, cut through the new material and the old flooring underneath simultaneously, making the patch either diamond-shaped or rectangular in outline.

Lift off the cut-out new patch and lay it aside, then lift out the damaged section under it. The cut-out in the old floor will be exactly the same size and shape as the patch that was just laid aside. Next, scrape off as much of the old adhesive from the floor as you can, then clean the area thoroughly to remove all dust and specks of dirt or old adhesive (a vacuum cleaner is best for this job).

You can now spread new adhesive (sparingly) over the exposed floor inside the cut-out, then fit the newly cut-out patch into place by bringing one edge or one corner in contact with the edge or corner of the old material, then gradually lowering the patch into place. Try to avoid

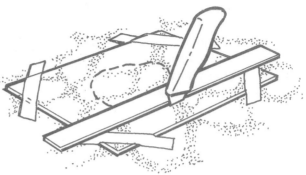

Place matching piece of flooring over damaged area, then cut through both at once with sharp knife to create matching patch.

sliding it by positioning the first edge properly the first time (just as if you were installing a tile), and if the flooring material seems a bit stiff or brittle, warm it first by placing it in a warm oven for a few minutes or by heating it carefully with a heat lamp. Place weights on top of the patch to hold it down around all edges.

CARPET REPAIRS

A burn or scorch mark caused by a hot ash or match dropped on the carpet is often only on the surface—that is, only the tips of the individual fibers have been scorched. A simple way to get rid of such

Scorched carpet fibers can be trimmed off with sharp scissors. If necessary, new fibers can then be glued in to replace them.

damage is to snip off the burned tips with a sharp pair of scissors, holding the blades almost flat against the carpet as shown. If slight scorch marks still are noticeable, rub the spot lightly with a pad of fine steel wool, then vacuum up the residue before it can soak in and cause more staining.

When cosmetic surgery of this kind won't do the job, you can operate more drastically by trimming off the burned fibers completely. This will leave a slight "hole" in the carpet, but one can fill in neatly in the following manner.

Snip some extra fibers or tufts from a scrap piece of the same carpeting—if you have an extra piece. If you don't then snip the tufts from under a large piece of furniture where a similar "hole" will never be noticeable. Bundle these in your fingers, then cover the bottom end of the tuft with some white glue (the kind that dries clear). Push the glue-coated end down into the place where you clipped off the burned fibers and wait till the glue dries. Then snip off the tops of the newly inserted tuft to make the new fibers the same height as the rest of the fibers around it.

To replace a damaged piece of carpet, place a matching piece over the damage and then cut through both layers with a sharp knife.

When there is a burn or bad stain too large to be repaired by the technique above, you can often make a neat patch by cutting out the damaged section and then inserting another piece of the same material. If you do not have a spare piece of the same carpet, and cannot buy any, there is yet another possibility, similar to the method of repairing a "hole," that can save the day:

Cut a patch out of the existing carpet in a place where it will not show—for example, under a couch, breakfront, or similar large piece of furniture that is seldom if ever moved. After you have cut out the damaged piece you can install this piece in the hole where you cut out the patch, thus "moving" the damage from a conspicuous spot to a place where it will probably never be seen.

Use a metal square and a sharp utility knife to guide you in cutting out the patch you will need (again, make it rectangular or diamond-shaped), then lift out this piece and lay it in place over the damaged section of carpet, making certain you have positioned it to cover all of the damaged section. Hold this piece firmly in place

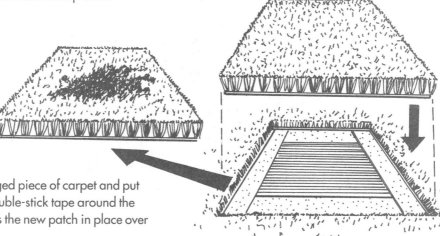

Lift out the damaged piece of carpet and put down strips of double-stick tape around the edges. Then press the new patch in place over the tape.

with one hand and cut around it with the other, bearing down hard enough to cut through the carpet completely. The idea is to cut out a section of the carpet on the floor that will exactly match the outline of the patch you are holding on top. The two pieces will be exactly the same size and shape, so the patch will match perfectly when the cut-out piece is lifted out and the patch is inserted in its place.

If the carpet is a type that tends to unravel around the edges, brush a light coat of clear-drying white glue around the edges of the cut-out after the damaged section has been removed, then brush more glue around the edges of the piece that will be inserted as a patch. Don't get any glue up near the tips of the fibers, only down near the base (gluing the tips will make them stiff).

Your best bet to hold the new patch in place is a double-faced carpet tape (sticky on both sides). Apply strips of tape to the floor around the perimeter of the cut-out, then press the piece of fresh carpet down on top to secure it. The damaged piece that you remove can then be put back into the place from which you cut out the patch.

*P*ainting and Wallpapering

. . . .

Of all home repair or maintenance projects, one chore that even the least enthusiastic do-it-yourselfer is likely to tackle is some type of painting. It may be a sizable project such as painting the entire apartment, or it may be simply repainting a small set of shelves, but chances are that even the person who claims he or she is "all thumbs" will still pick up a paintbrush at one time or another. It's not hard to understand why.

Painting is a fairly simple job that is relatively safe for anyone, and it can seldom do permanent damage—you can always go over it. Painting is also a labor-intensive job, so doing the work yourself offers a substantial saving—usually anywhere from 60 to 80 percent of the total cost of a professionally completed job. And the results are almost always instantly gratifying—you see a bright new finish as soon as you are done.

Fortunately, today's paints and finishes are easier than ever to apply, and they are generally more versatile than ever before. But remember that despite what some advertisements may claim, there is still no one paint that is ideal for every surface or good for use under all conditions. Before you buy, read the label on the can carefully to make certain that the product you select meets your particular needs and to make certain you are familiar with what preparation, if any, is required before actually applying the paint (priming, sanding, cleaning of the old surface, and so forth). A knowledgeable dealer or salesman can be a big help there, but unfortunately not all sales clerks are as well informed as they should be—particularly in large "discount"-type stores where you are expected to help yourself from bulk displays.

CHOOSING THE RIGHT PAINT

Latex paints that thin with water, rather than with a solvent such as turpentine or mineral spirits, are by far the most popular type of paint used, especially on the inside (even on the outside latex paints are largely displacing solvent-based paints). There are several easy-to-understand reasons for this:

• Latex paints thin with water, so they permit you to clean tools, hands, and clothing with water. No harsh or smelly solvents are required—as long as you scrub away the smears and stains before they dry completely.

• Since there is no need for keeping open cans of solvent or thinner on hand, painting with a latex paint poses less of a fire hazard than painting with a solvent-thinned formulation—and there are no solvent-soaked rags to dispose of.

• Although some latex paints do have a slight ammonialike odor, these paints don't have the pervading "painty" odor that most people find objectionable, and they pose much less of a problem for those with allergic tendencies.

• Latex paints generally dry faster than solvent-based paints, so you can often apply two coats in the same day, and you can put rooms back into service quicker.

• Flat latex paints—the ones most often used on walls and ceilings—tend to cover better in one coat because they build up to a thicker film with one coat.

Despite these obvious advantages, some still prefer solvent-based alkyd paints for certain jobs, and in some cases they may be right. For example, some "old-timers" feel that alkyd or solvent-thinned paints are more durable and will withstand more scrubbing than latex paints—but this is mainly true of the glossy enamels, not the flat finishes. When it comes to high-gloss enamels, a good-quality alkyd or polyurethane enamel is generally tougher than an equivalent-quality latex enamel—it will withstand more scrubbing and hard wear—and where constant exposure to water is a consideration (such as inside a tub or shower enclosure, for example), a solvent-thinned alkyd enamel will shed water better than a latex.

Another plus is that in most cases latex colors are not as vivid as those that can be obtained with solvent-thinned paints; they tend to be more muddy. So where a very dark or very bright color is desired—for example, a dark red or bright blue—an alkyd enamel is more likely to give you the color and the effect you desire.

CHOOSING THE BEST FINISH

Interior paints are available in a choice of finishes—flat, semigloss, or high gloss. Unfortunately there is really no set of standards to define these terms—not all high glosses have the same amount of shine, and not all flat finishes are as dull or flat looking as others. Perhaps the greatest variation is in the so-called semigloss finishes (also referred to as satin finishes or, when slightly duller, eggshell finishes). The only way to be sure how much sheen the paint will have when dry is to see a dried sample of the actual paint on a surface similar to the one you will be applying it on—and that sample should be at least one day old (the luster often changes as the paint cures).

Generally speaking, most people prefer a flat finish on walls and ceilings, except perhaps in kitchens, bathrooms, and laundry rooms, where dampness is apt to be more of a problem and where occasional scrubbing may be required. In these rooms, as well as in children's rooms and utility rooms, many will find a satin finish or semigloss enamel more serviceable. In fact, where young children are constantly present, a low-luster "eggshell"- or "pearl"-finish paint is often preferred (rather than a flat) for use on walls, since flat paints really do not wash or clean very well.

In most rooms an enamel (high gloss or semigloss) will be most suitable for use on doors, windows, cabinets, and other woodwork—again because these surfaces are likely to be washed or scrubbed more frequently and because they get a great deal more wear than walls or ceilings. Just remember that the higher the gloss, the more washable the finish will be, but also keep in mind that the higher the gloss, the more noticeable the imperfections in the surface (a flat finish tends to hide bumps and irregularities better than a gloss).

CHOOSING AND CARING FOR PAINTBRUSHES

Although rollers have largely displaced brushes for painting large flat areas, there are still many places and many types of surfaces around the home that can be properly coated only with a good-quality paintbrush—for example, windows, paneled doors, trim and woodwork, furniture, and cabinets. In addition, even the finest roller covers will leave a slight stipple or texture on the surface, so when a really smooth, glassy-looking finish is desired—for example, when applying shellac or a high-gloss enamel or varnish—no roller will give you as smooth a finish as a good-quality brush.

The most important point to remember is that as with most other tools, using a poor-quality brush is almost always a foolish economy. A cheap or poorly made brush will make it almost impossible to smooth the paint on evenly and smoothly—no matter what quality paint or varnish you use—and it is certain to create more spatters and runs than a good brush. Inexpensive "throwaway" brushes may be convenient for quick touch-ups when you want to avoid washing the brush after you are done, but they will almost always leave brush marks, streaks, and runs in the finish. In addition, a cheap or poorly made brush will be likely to shed bristles and drip excessively while you are working—especially when working overhead or on vertical surfaces—and it will make it almost impossible to "cut in" neatly to a sharp edge when you want to avoid smearing paint onto other surfaces.

A good-quality brush, on the other hand, not only holds more paint and spreads it on more smoothly, it will actually enable you to get the job done faster and with less effort.

Years ago the only good-quality paintbrushes were those made of 100 percent Chinese natural hog bristle—and to a great extent this bristle is still used in top-quality brushes. Good-quality hog bristle is tapered and has naturally "split ends," which are "flagged" at the tip as shown in the illustration on page 127. These flagged or split ends not only help the brush pick up and hold more paint, they also spread the paint on more smoothly and more uniformly without as much dripping, running, or spattering.

However, natural bristles have one serious drawback for many paint jobs around the home: when used with water-based (latex) paints, they tend to absorb water and swell, losing their shape and flexibility and making the brush floppy to work with. As a result, natural bristle brushes are definitely not suitable for use with latex paints—inside or outside. In addition, natural Chinese bristle is not as abrasion-resistant as synthetic bristles, so they will wear down faster in prolonged use, especially when painting over rough or textured surfaces.

Fortunately, synthetic bristles are now made with tapered shapes and with flagged or split ends that closely rival those found in the best of natural bristles. As a result, many top-quality synthetic bristle brushes are just as good as—or in some cases better than—the natural bristles. This is particularly true when working with latex paints (which accounts for the vast majority of the paints used by do-it-yourselfers).

Two types of synthetic bristles are used in paintbrushes—nylon and polyester. Brushes may be made of all nylon, all polyester, or a mixture of both (some mixtures or "blends" also include a percentage of natural bristle, although this is much less common). This blending or mixing of different types of synthetic bristle in one brush is done to take advantage of the best features of each type in order to maximize wear and working qualities, while keeping costs down. Needless to say, not all agree as to what is "best," but before you can make a wise selection you must know something about the principal characteristics—and thus the advantages and disadvantages—of each type of synthetic bristle.

Nylon, which is the oldest type of synthetic bristle, will wear longer than either polyester or natural bristle, especially when used on rough or heavily textured surfaces such as cement or stucco. Good-quality nylon bristles have a nice springy feel and tend to spread the paint on smoothly, but when used in water-thinned latex paints nylon tends to get soft and floppy. Nylon also gets soft and floppy when used in very warm, humid weather—and this can be a problem when working around the outside during the summer, even if you are using an oil paint. Another problem encountered with nylon is that it tends to lose its springiness and shape when used in shellac or any finish that thins with alcohol, acetone, or lacquer thinner (this includes some of the highly volatile solvents that are found in many two-part epoxy paints and some polyurethane coatings).

Polyester, on the other hand, is not affected by immersion in water-thinned paints or any of the other solvents that affect nylon. These synthetic bristles will retain their stiffness and shape better than nylon when used in shellac or alcohol-thinned finishes or with the strong solvents found in lacquer and in many of the quick-drying "synthetic" finishes (for example, most two-part epoxy and polyurethane paints). However, the flagged tips on polyester generally are not quite as efficient as those found on a comparable nylon bristle. This is one of the reasons most companies make their best synthetic bristle brushes with a mixture of nylon and polyester—polyester around the outside for its stiffness and ability to retain the original shape of the brush, as well as its resistance to heat and humidity and most solvents, and nylon for its superior working qualities and its ability to pick up and hold more paint without dripping and streaking.

Recently DuPont has introduced a new type of modified nylon bristle—one that is claimed to be superior to the older forms of nylon. Called Chinex, this new synthetic offers two big improvements over conventional nylon: the flagged tips and split ends are more effective than those on traditional nylon bristles, and most important of all, as the bristles wear the tips continue to split and form new "flags." A third advantage of Chinex is that it does not get as floppy or soft as regular nylon when used in warm, humid conditions.

In spite of all the improvements made in the design and manufacture of synthetic bristle brushes, most experts still agree that the best paintbrush you can buy for fine varnishing and for achieving a mirror-like finish with a top-grade enamel is a brush made of pure Chinese hog bristle. Top-quality natural bristle still gives you the smoothest finish and still does the best job of picking up, holding, and spreading the paint or varnish. As a rule, a top-quality natural bristle brush will cost a little more than its equivalent in a synthetic bristle brush, but in most cases the difference, if any, is relatively small. If you can't find them in your local hardware store or home center, look in a regular paint store—the kind that caters to professional painters.

Paintbrushes also differ as to the shape or style of the handle. Generally speaking, most pros prefer a wooden handle over a plastic one, and the most popular style is the so-called beaver tail shape. However, the shape and the length of the handle usually has nothing to do with the working or handling qualities of the brush—although a longer handle is usually preferred on a so-called sash brush (one designed for cutting in windows and painting narrow trim). As a rule, the size and shape of the handle is strictly a matter of personal preference—the one that feels most comfortable to your hand is the one that is best for you.

When shopping for a paintbrush, you should look for certain manufacturing features that are common to all good-quality brushes (manufacturing and assembling methods are just as important as the quality of the bristles used).

Hold the brush by the handle so that the bristles are pointing upward, then examine the ends of the bristles carefully. A high percentage of them should be "flagged"; in other words they should have split ends, as shown in the illustration. In addition, each of the individual bristles should be slightly tapered so that they are actually thicker at the base (near the ferrule) than they are at the end.

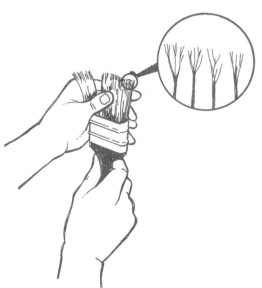

Good-quality brush should have a high percentage of tapered bristles with split ends and "flagged" tips.

• Now turn the brush sideways so that you are looking at it from the edge and examine the shape of the tip on the brush. The bristles should not have been cut off square (with all bristles trimmed to the same length). A good-quality brush contains a mixture of different-length bristles, with the longest ones in the center and the shortest ones around the outside. When viewed from the side, the bristle tips should form a tapered edge with a profile that looks something like a blunt chisel.

• Select a small clump of bristles from one side of the brush and bend them out till they are almost 90 degrees from the ferrule or base of the brush, then release them. The bristles should snap right back to conform to the original shape of the brush without remaining bent or flared out away from the rest of the bristles.

heel plug

Wood or plastic plug in center of brush creates a pocket for holding paint.

• Spread the bristles apart by grabbing a clump in each hand and separate them as shown to expose the inside. Look down into the base of the brush. You should see a wood or plastic block whose purpose is to create a "pocket" in the center of the bristles for holding paint. However, on a cheap brush this block, or plug, will be a lot wider than it should be in order to make the brush look thicker and thus to make it look as if it has a lot more bristle than it really has. The block should actually be no more than about ⅛ inch to ¼ inch in thickness, and it should be made of wood rather than plastic or paper (found in some of the cheaper brushes). Comparing a few brushes of similar size in different price ranges will soon point out the difference.

• Hold the brush by the handle as though you were going to paint with it, then press the bristle tips down lightly against the back of your hand. The bristles should feel springy and have a natural tendency to fan out smoothly, forming the sharp, chisel-like edge that will make it a lot easier to do a neat job of trimming or "cutting in," as well as applying the paint smoothly.

• Try to select a brush that is wide enough to minimize the amount of back-and-forth brushing that will be required— excessive brushing not only means a lot more work when putting the paint on, it also adds to the likelihood of leaving brush marks. As a rule, a 2-inch or 2½-inch brush will be about right for narrow trim and most moldings, while a 3-inch or 4-inch brush will be about right for doors. An angled 2-inch sash brush (which has a longer handle than a regular brush) is usually preferred for painting window sash, while a 2½-inch or 3-inch brush will work best on wide baseboards and some furniture.

CLEANING BRUSHES

The job that people seem to dread most when painting is cleaning the paintbrush afterward—yet this does not have to be a particularly messy or time-consuming job if you tackle it immediately after you finish working for the day. And, contrary to popular opinion, thorough cleaning does not require gallons of solvent or thinner (even when working with oil-base paints).

First rub as much excess paint out of the bristles as possible by wiping the brush across the rim of the can, then by rubbing back and forth on a stack of old newspapers. Discard the top sheet as soon as it becomes loaded with paint. To clean the brush of water-thinned paint, simply wash it in running water, or in several changes of water, preferably with a little detergent added. Be particularly careful to wash up near the heel of the brush, and work the bristles between your fingers to make certain that you get out all the paint. Then smooth out the bristles and separate tangles with an old comb or a special metal brush comb that many stores sell. Lay the brush flat to dry, after which you should wrap the bristles with paper as illustrated.

Brushes used in solvent-thinned paints are most often washed in solvent or thinner—turpentine or mineral spirits for oil-base and alkyd-base paints, lacquer thinner for lacquer, and alcohol for shellac. First wipe out as much of the paint as you can, then pour about an inch of the thinner into a can wide enough to take the bristles easily. Press the bristles down and work them vigorously against the bottom of the container.

Pour out the dirty liquid into another container (don't throw it away yet), then pour another inch of solvent into the origi-nal container and repeat the process of working the bristles against the bottom until the solvent is saturated. Pour this dirty liquid into the second container, then rub the brush out hard on newspaper or scrap pieces of cardboard. Repeat this two or three more times, then finish by washing in a little warm water and detergent. Shake out the excess water, comb the bristles smooth, let them dry, then wrap as shown.

Most of the dirty solvent can be saved. Allow it to settle for a few hours, then pour off the top and discard the sediment-filled portion at the bottom—usually less than about one-fourth of the solvent used to clean the brush.

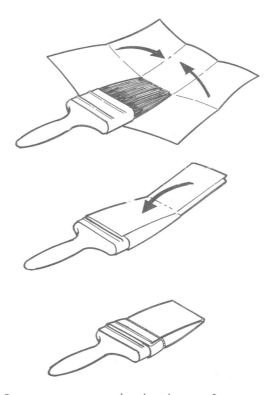

Proper way to wrap a brush with paper for storing it. Brush should be washed thoroughly first.

CHOOSING AND USING PAINT ROLLERS

Paint rollers have almost completely replaced brushes for painting walls, ceilings, floors, and other large flat surfaces in the home or apartment. They are certainly much faster than brushes and usually a lot neater, and they can be used to apply almost any type of paint—regardless of the coating (water-thinned or solvent-thinned) and regardless of the amount of gloss involved.

Most rollers are either 7 or 9 inches in width, but there are also narrower rollers that can be used on flat trim and moldings, as well as on cabinets, furniture, and shelving. All paint rollers have removable covers or sleeves that slide on over a wire "cage" or slotted metal "drum." This metal or plastic frame rotates when pushed over the surface. Most roller handles have a threaded hole in the bottom end that will

"Cage"-type paint roller has replaceable cover that slides on.

accept a standard extension pole for painting ceilings. In most cases a standard threaded mop handle or floor brush handle can be used as the extension pole, but there are also telescoping extension poles available that will reach up to 20 feet or more for those jobs where extra height is required.

Fortunately, all 7-inch and 9-inch roller frames have the same outside diameter, and all covers have the same inside diameter, so covers are usually interchangeable as long as they are of the same width.

Roller covers vary as to the length of nap or fiber used. Generally speaking, the shorter the nap or fiber length, the smoother the finish that it will apply (and the less paint it will pick up). On smooth walls a cover with a ⅜-inch or ½-inch nap will usually work best (stick to a ½-inch nap if the surface has a slight stipple), while roller covers with a ¾-inch or longer nap will work better on heavily stippled or textured surfaces (such as brick or the so-called sand finish and popcorn-textured ceilings).

At the other end of the scale there are also roller covers with a relatively smooth mohair-type fiber (something like a plush carpet material) and even some that are made of a special foam for applying enamel and other high-gloss finishes. These are designed for use on flat surfaces when you want an extra-smooth finish, especially when applying a high-gloss or semigloss coating. They leave practically no stipple or texture on the surface (most "lamb's-wool"-type covers do leave a slight stipple).

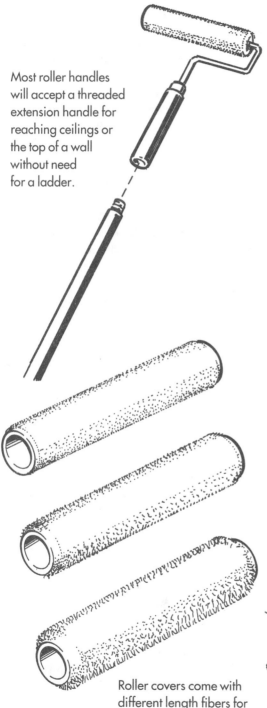

Most roller handles will accept a threaded extension handle for reaching ceilings or the top of a wall without need for a ladder.

Roller covers come with different length fibers for painting over different types of surfaces.

POINTERS ON USING A ROLLER

To avoid spattering when painting with a roller, be careful not to spin the roller too fast as you push it over the surface. Each time you go back to pick up more paint, make sure you roll off a little of the excess on the highest part of the tray. Then roll the paint onto the wall with a slow, steady rhythm and with only a moderate amount of pressure on the handle.

To ensure the application of a liberal coat and uniform coverage, get in the habit of picking up more paint as soon as the roller starts to feel as though it is running dry. Don't just press harder on the handle. Even if pressing harder makes it look as though you are still applying enough paint to cover adequately, there is a good chance that when the paint dries the coating may look translucent in that area and a second coat may be required—particularly with a radical change of color or when there are stains or patches to be covered over.

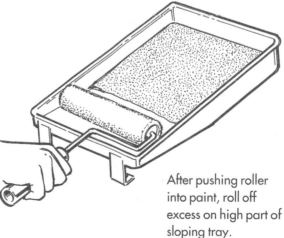

After pushing roller into paint, roll off excess on high part of sloping tray.

CLEANING PAINT ROLLERS

The most important thing to remember about cleaning a roller is that the job should be done immediately after you stop working. Start by rolling it back and forth on a stack of old newspapers to work out as much paint as possible. Discard the top sheet as soon as it is saturated.

Next, slide the cover off the roller handle for a thorough washing. Leaving it on when you clean it will cause paint to wash inside, where, after it dries, it will glue the cover on so that it will be impossible to get off later. Wash it in the appropriate solvent or thinner—water if the paint was a latex and paint thinner if it was an oil paint. For washing in water, you can use a bucket or container, but if you have a sink in the basement or can take the cover outside, rinsing under running water is probably the easiest.

To wash out oil paints, pour some thinner into the paint tray (after wiping most of the paint out), then roll the cover around and work the solvent into the fibers with your fingers. You will have to change thinner several times, but you don't need a lot each time—an inch or so in the bottom of the pan will do the job. Finish by washing in a warm detergent solution and rinsing with plain water. Squeeze out the excess by wringing the cover almost dry with your fingers. Stand the cover on end until it dries to avoid creating a flat spot in the nap. After the cover is clean, dip a cloth in thinner or solvent and wipe paint off the cage on the roller handle.

FLAT PAINTING PADS

Usually made of resilient plastic foam and faced with a replaceable, synthetic fiber material similar to the mohair-type fabric used on paint rollers, flat painting pads were originally introduced primarily for outdoor painting (siding and shingles). However, smaller versions are now also widely sold for use in painting all kinds of flat surfaces on the inside of the home or apartment.

These painting pads are mounted on a rigid plastic holder with a handle attached, and they come in a wide range of sizes—from little ones that may be less than 1 inch in width and are used for "cutting in" around windowpanes or painting narrow moldings, to larger ones that measure up to 9 inches in width and are used for painting walls, ceilings, and other large flat surfaces.

Painting pads can be used on most of the same surfaces that rollers can, but they require more care to avoid drips and runs and to prevent lap marks and streaks.

For interior painting the smaller painting pads are the most popular. They are useful for painting in corners instead of using a brush—for example, next to windows, doors, and other trim before using a roller or in the corners where walls meet or where a wall meets the ceiling. Some models have a plastic lip or rim along one side so they can be used to paint right up to an adjoining surface without smearing paint onto that surface, while others have little wheels along one side for precise "cutting in" (the wheels keep the edge of the pad from coming in contact with the adjoining surface).

PAINTING WALLS AND CEILINGS

Before painting any room, always remove as many obstacles as possible—pictures, curtains or other hangings, area rugs, and furniture. Large pieces that cannot be easily removed should be pushed together in the center of the room, then covered with suitable drop cloths such as old bedsheets or inexpensive lightweight plastic covers. For covering floors you are better off with canvas or cloth covers, unless you can get heavier-weight plastic tarps; very light weight plastic covers tend to lift and slide too easily.

If you do cover the floors with plastic— light or heavy—it is still a good idea to spread some old sheets, pieces of canvas, or even old newspapers on top; plastic doesn't absorb paint, so drips and spills will just get smeared around by your shoes if you happen to step on them. Papers or rags will help prevent this.

Use a vacuum to remove dust from walls and ceilings, and use detergent to wash sections that are really dirty or greasy. If you paint over dirt or grease, chances are that the paint will peel or wrinkle quite soon. So a thorough cleaning is especially important in kitchens and utility rooms.

In addition to cleaning the walls and ceilings, you should also patch all cracks and holes (see chapter 3) and smooth over rough spots by sanding. If you are using a latex paint, spot-prime any patched areas before you go ahead with the entire wall or ceiling. If you are using an alkyd paint, then a primer-sealer or an undercoat may be required for touching up.

Paint the ceiling first, then the walls. Woodwork and trim are normally done last. A roller is generally best on ceilings (painting pads are harder to control overhead). You can eliminate the need for a stepladder on most of the ceiling if you attach an extension handle to your roller—these handles simply screw into a threaded hole or socket in the base of most roller handles.

A standard roller will not reach all the way into the corner joints where the ceiling meets the wall, so you will need a brush to cut in this area. If the walls are the same color as the ceiling, you don't have to cut in, but you will still need to reach into the corner. A brush, a narrow doughnut-shaped roller, or a small flat painting pad designed for cutting into corners will do the job.

As a rule, it is best to paint in the corners and around the edges first, with the brush or other applicator. Then go ahead on the main part of the ceiling with your roller. If you are fortunate enough to have a helper, then one person can paint around all the edges while the other follows with the roller on the larger areas.

After the edges have been done, start with the roller in one corner and work across the shortest dimension of the ceiling in a wide band. When you reach the opposite wall, come back and start painting another wide band across the room. The idea is to always keep a wet edge for the next lap. That is why you should never stop in the middle of a ceiling or wall. Wait until the whole ceiling is done before you stop for a rest—or at least until you come to a break in the surface, such as where a room divider or other large built-in meets the ceiling.

Roll the paint on slowly in a series of diagonal back-and-forth strokes, applying

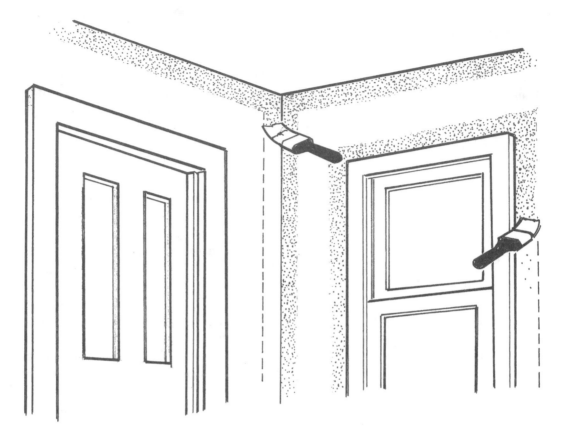

Use brush first to paint in corners and in wall-to-ceiling joints where roller cannot reach.

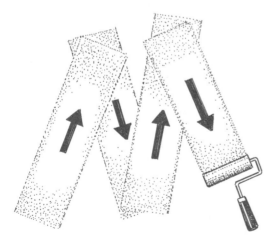

First stroke with roller should be in an upward direction, then alternate strokes with overlapping up and down passes.

only a moderate amount of pressure to the handle to avoid dripping or spattering. After you have covered several square feet, start smoothing out the paint by going back and forth over the same area with parallel strokes at approximately right angles to the direction in which the paint was originally applied.

When painting close to the wall with the roller, try to overlap as much of the brush-painted area as you can—the roller will cover any noticeable difference in texture between the brushed and the rolled areas.

Painting walls is not much different from painting ceilings, except that you don't have to worry about reaching overhead or working in an awkward position. Also, on a wall there is much less dripping, running, and spattering than when painting overhead.

If you are applying paint with a roller, make your first stroke in an upward direction to minimize drips or runs, then come down at an angle to the first stroke before rolling upward again. Each stroke should overlap the previous one and go off at a slight angle so that you actually wind up painting a sort of inverted W on the wall.

As soon as you have completed these first three or four up-and-down strokes, cross-stroke lightly, alternating between strokes that are parallel to the floor and those that are more vertical. The idea is to smooth off the paint just applied and even up any noticeable irregularities. Pick up more paint as soon as you start to feel the roller running dry—don't just press harder to get more coverage out of the same amount of paint.

PAINTING WINDOWS, DOORS, AND TRIM

Most experienced painters will agree that a good paintbrush is definitely the preferred tool for painting most woodwork and trim inside the house. However, on flush doors, bookcases, and similar flat surfaces, some may find that it is faster to use a small paint roller or flat painting pad instead—although a brush may still be needed for tight places and inside corners. Flat painting pads and small rollers can also be used on shelving, as well as on some types of furniture and cabinets, but in most cases you can still get a smoother and more professional-looking job with a good-quality paintbrush, especially when applying a varnish or an enamel (remember, the emphasis here is on using a *good-quality* brush).

For baseboards, door frames, window frames, and similar trim, a brush about 2 or 2½ inches wide will be about right. For painting window sash, a 1½- or 2-inch angled sash brush will work better (sash brushes have a longer handle than a conventional trim brush and are designed especially for "cutting in" around windows, with bristle ends shaped or trimmed off at an angle to make trimming close to

the glass easier). On doors, a brush about 2½ or 3 inches wide will make the job go faster and is less likely to leave brush strokes (the idea is to use as wide a brush as possible in order to minimize the amount of brushing and cross-stroking required to cover the surface smoothly).

When you are painting both sides of a door, it is best to paint the edges first, then paint the two sides before the edges dry (that way you can brush over and smooth down any runs or drips that took place on each side). On flush doors, work from the top down to the bottom, first applying the paint across the short dimension and then smoothing it out by cross-stroking lightly with vertical strokes, using the tips of the bristles without picking up additional paint.

On paneled doors, paint all the panels first, then the rails between the panels. Start by painting the edges or moldings around each panel, then coat the panel itself—again cross-stroking lightly as you finish each panel. After all panels are done, paint the horizontal rails on the door between the panels and those across the top and bottom of the door, then do all the vertical rails (called stiles) last.

Sequence to follow when painting a typical paneled door: 1. molded edges, 2. panels, 3. horizontal stiles, 4. edges, 5. vertical stiles.

Painting conventional double-hung windows should also follow a definite sequence if you want to avoid smearing paint onto your hands because you have to move a freshly painted sash—and if you want to be sure you don't accidentally skip some parts of the window. Start by lower-

ing the top sash until it is almost down to the windowsill at the bottom, then raise the lower sash within an inch or two of the top of the window frame, as shown.

With the two sash units reversed in this manner, you will now be able to paint most of the lowered top sash. When this is done, push the top sash back up to within an inch of the top, then lower the bottom sash to its normal position, but leave it open an inch or so. Now finish painting the top of the upper sash where you couldn't reach before, then paint the entire lower sash. In each case, paint the mullions (the narrow strips of wood or metal between the glass panes) first, then paint the frame of that sash. After both sash units are painted, finish by painting the entire window frame, starting across the top and then working your way to the sill at the bottom.

For many people, the hardest thing about painting windows is keeping the paint off the glass. Some use masking tape to avoid the need for careful "cutting in," but this is almost more trouble than it is worth—you have to be very careful when applying the tape, and you have to be sure to remove it promptly when the paint starts to get tacky. If you leave the tape in place for days, you may find it difficult to remove, and it can pull some of the paint off with it.

A better way to keep paint off the glass is with a metal or plastic shield that you hold against the molding and move along with the brush as you paint. This works well if you remember to keep wiping the edge of the shield with a rag—otherwise it will start to smear as it becomes heavily coated with paint.

Cutting in freehand—that is, without any help from a shield or masking tape—is

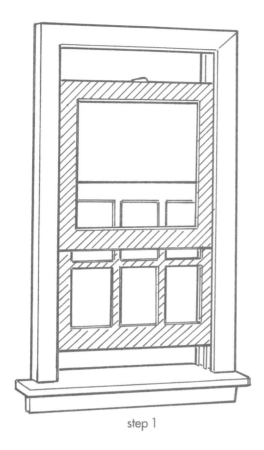

step 1

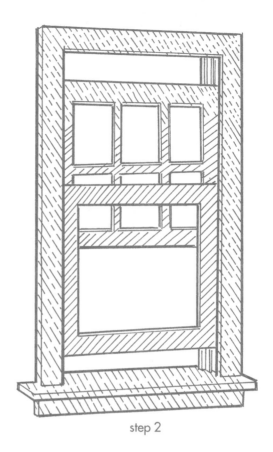

step 2

Sequence to follow when painting a double-hung window.

not as hard as it seems, but you need a good-quality sash brush that fans out to a nice sharp edge. Touch the loaded bristles to the wood at a short distance from the glass, then move the brush along the length of the molding, pressing down enough so that the bristles fan out to a clean edge. Move the brush in a slight arc that will bring the bristle tips gradually in contact with the glass, then keep moving in a straight line along this joint. Remember: The paint should overlap onto the glass by a tiny fraction of an inch. This is essential for a truly tight seal.

When painting windows touch bristles to wood away from glass, then press down to fan them out as you stroke closer to glass.

SPRAY PAINTING

Using a sprayer is probably the fastest way to apply paint or varnish on most surfaces—but particularly on those that are textured or heavily carved and irregular. This is especially true of objects that would be hard to coat with a brush or roller—for example, louvered doors and shutters, wrought-iron railings, children's toys, wicker and rattan furniture, and small cabinets or chests that have molded edges. As a rule, a good spray job will almost always come out smoother and with a higher gloss than a job done with a brush or roller—but this is true only if the spraying is done by a reasonably skilled applicator who has the right kind of equipment for the job at hand and knows how to use it.

There are three different types of spray equipment that the amateur is likely to use for spray painting: a conventional spray gun that is used with a separate air compressor; an "airless" spray gun that needs no separate compressor because it requires no flow of compressed air; and an aerosol-type disposable spray can that requires no separate equipment—you just push the spray nozzle and spray out the paint contained in that can.

Conventional compressed-air spray guns mix a stream of air with the stream of paint brought up from the cup to atomize it so that a fine mist comes out of the nozzle when the trigger is pressed. The air comes in through a hose that is attached to a separate compressor (on larger units there may be a separate storage tank that stores the compressed air and feeds it to the gun as needed).

Generally, two different types of spray guns are used with these sprayers—pressure-feed guns and siphon-feed models. In a pressure-feed gun the air coming in from the hose goes into the cup and builds up pressure on the inside to force paint up into the nozzle. In a siphon-feed gun the air does not go into the cup at all; instead it

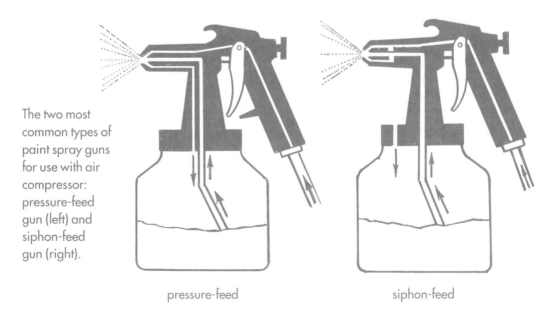

The two most common types of paint spray guns for use with air compressor: pressure-feed gun (left) and siphon-feed gun (right).

pressure-feed   siphon-feed

is forced at high speed past the top of a suction tube (leading from the cup) so that it literally "sucks" or siphons the paint up through the tube. The flow of air mixes with the paint as it goes out through the nozzle.

Pressure-feed guns usually work best with heavier-bodied finishes such as outdoor paint and most flat wall paints. Siphon-feed guns give a smoother finish when spraying lighter-bodied or thinner finishes such as varnish or enamel. Some spray guns come with convertible heads that permit you to use them either way.

Spray guns also differ in the types of nozzles they have. Some are external mix and some are internal mix. External mix means the paint and the stream of air come out of the gun through separate orifices; the two separate streams do not mix or come in contact with each other until after they are outside the nozzle. Internal mix means the air and the paint are mixed together inside the nozzle. As a rule, external mix is better for quick-drying, light-bodied finishes such as lacquer and fast-drying enamels; internal mix is better for slower-drying or heavier-bodied finishes.

Airless spray guns differ from compressed-air sprayers in that they do not need a compressor and do not mix air in with the paint at all. Instead, a tiny high-pressure pump built into the head of the gun forces the paint out through a tiny orifice in the nozzle when the trigger is pressed. The paint comes out with enough pressure to atomize it and produce the fine mist needed for spraying without being mixed with air at all.

Airless sprayers dispense paint much faster than a compressed-air sprayer because the spray that comes out is solid paint—there is no air mixed in with it.

Generally speaking, these guns will not give as fine a finish, or produce as smooth or glossy a finish, as a compressed-air sprayer. However, they are faster and more convenient to use when painting large surfaces such as walls, fences, or similar surfaces. They also are more suitable for use with latex paints because they are less likely to clog or cake up inside the gun—always a problem when using these paints in a conventional sprayer (especially when you stop for a short break).

Aerosol spray cans provide a quick and convenient way to spray small objects that would be difficult to paint with a brush or roller. As each spray can is emptied, you simply throw it away, so there is no messy and time-consuming job of cleaning spray guns or other equipment. However, for anything other than a very small job, they are expensive—remember that only about 20 percent of the contents is actually paint; the rest is all propellant gas. In addition, with most aerosol cans you are limited to the "standard" colors that are available; you can't mix or match colors when needed.

To get around this, however, you can buy aerosol-type spray units that come with an empty glass jar that screws onto the bottom of a can of propellant (no paint is mixed in with this propellant). You then fill the empty jar with any color or type paint you want (suitably thinned, of course). There is a spray nozzle on top of the propellant can that you press when you want to start spraying. Paint will be drawn out of the jar by suction action—otherwise spraying is the same as with any other type of aerosol-type spray can. Additional cans of replacement propellant are sold separately, and you can refill the jar with more paint as often as necessary.

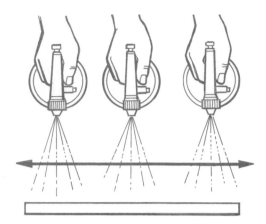

Move gun so spray is always parallel to surface. Press trigger after gun is in motion and release it before stopping motion.

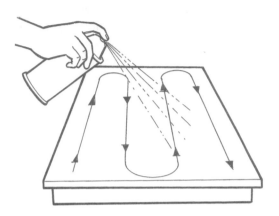

When spraying horizontal surface, start on part closest to you, then work away from yourself.

SPRAYING TECHNIQUES

With any type of spray equipment there are certain rules to follow if you want to ensure the best possible results. There are also some working techniques that will make the job come out better.

1. Before filling any spray gun, make certain the paint has been carefully strained by pouring it through a piece of nylon stocking or a regular fine-mesh paint strainer, and be sure you thin it to the proper consistency. If the manufacturer's instructions do not tell you how much thinner to add, experiment with a small amount of paint first. Add about 10 percent thinner the first time, then gradually increase this amount until the paint sprays out in a fine mist yet does not run or sag. Practice on some scrap surfaces similar to what you will be spraying.

2. If you are using an aerosol can, be sure you shake the can vigorously until the little ball on the inside rattles around loudly, and keep this up for at least 30 seconds before you start to spray.

3. Remember that two thin spray coats are always better than one heavy coat—a single heavy coat is more likely to sag or run after a couple of minutes.

4. Hold the spray gun or can so that the nozzle is about 8 or 9 inches away from the surface, and if possible aim it so that the spray strikes at a right angle to the surface.

5. First press the trigger, *then* sweep across in a continuous stroke, releasing the trigger only after you are past the surface. The idea is always to have the gun in motion while paint is coming out. Starting and stopping a stroke with the trigger depressed will cause an uneven finish.

6. Do not arc your strokes by swinging your arm while holding your wrist straight. Instead, move the gun so that its stroke is parallel to the surface, with the nozzle always remaining at the same distance from the surface. This calls for arcing the wrist as you swing your arm from one side to the other.

7. When spraying a horizontal surface such as a tabletop, start spraying the part closest to you first, then work away from yourself till you get to the opposite side. This technique is less likely to result in some of the spray mist settling on parts that are already coated—a problem that often occurs when you start at the far side and work back toward yourself. (Since you are spraying downward at an angle, the spray tends to spread away from you. If the farthest points are already coated, the spray will settle on top of those surfaces). Also, paint the hard-to-reach areas first; leave the tops, fronts, and other prominent parts for last.

8. Avoid shooting straight into an in-side corner; spray one side first, then the other. Spraying straight into the corner usually results in runs and drips.

9. When possible, take the work outside to spray it. If this is impractical, make sure everything nearby is covered to protect against overspray and drifting mist. If the object is small, you can set it up inside a large carton or build a small "spray booth" out of large sheets of cardboard, or hang sheets of plastic around the spray area.

10. When working indoors, make sure there is plenty of ventilation and no open flames or lit cigarettes, pipes, or cigars nearby.

HANGING WALLPAPER AND OTHER WALLCOVERINGS

Although most people refer to every decorative material that is pasted up on a wall as wallpaper, in reality many are not made of paper at all—some "wallpapers" are made of (or faced with) vinyl or other plastic material, or they may be made of canvas, burlap, or other fabric. That is why the industry long ago adopted the term wall*coverings* when talking about a decorative material that is pasted up on walls or ceilings—regardless of whether or not it is actually a wall*paper*.

Practically all wallcoverings are sold and priced by the roll or "single roll," although they almost always come packed in two- or three-roll units called double or triple rolls. A single roll is supposed to contain 36 square feet of material, but when normal waste is figured in, you will probably get between 30 and 32 square feet of usable material out of each single roll (it's best to figure 30 square feet out of each roll in order to play it safe).

To figure the amount of wallcovering needed for a particular area or room, you first have to add up the square feet of wall and/or ceiling areas to be covered. Multiply the height of each wall (in feet) by its length (in feet) to give the area of that wall in square feet. Then add all wall areas together to get the total number of square feet to be covered. Divide this by 30 to get the number of rolls required. If there are normal-size windows and doors on these walls, don't allow for these at this time—measure the walls as though there were no openings. After you have totaled everything, deduct one roll for every two windows or doors.

PREPARING WALLS AND CEILINGS

Before hanging any wallcovering, you must see to it that all cracks and holes are filled in and smoothed over, rough patches sanded smooth, and loose, peeling, or flaking paint scraped off. (For more information on repairing walls and ceilings, see chapter 3). In addition, the wall or ceiling to be covered must be reasonably clean and free of dust, grease, wax, or oil to ensure a good bond when the wallcovering is pasted up. Slight irregularities in the surface will be scarcely noticeable with many patterns, but if you are hanging a solid color, or a material that has little or no pattern, even the slightest bump or rough spot will be quite noticeable after the wallcovering is hung.

Hanging new material over old is always a bit risky and usually not a good idea. However, if only one layer of paper is up on the wall, chances are that you can safely hang another layer of wallpaper directly over this—but only if you are hanging *paper* over *paper*, and only if the old paper is still bonding firmly. If there are any loose seams, bubbles, or blistered areas where the old paper is not sticking, then remove these areas or—better yet—strip off all the old paper before starting to hang new material over it.

Never hang a canvas, fabric, or vinyl wallcovering over paper. Strip off the paper first. In fact, in most cases you should not hang vinyls or fabric-type materials over *any* type of existing wallcovering, but if you are in doubt, check the manufacturer's instructions. If the instructions are not clear, or if there is any doubt at all, then removing all the old material first is always the safest choice.

Removing most fabric-type materials, or those that have a fabric-type backing, is usually easier than removing paper. That's because in most cases all you have to do is scrape one corner loose, then peel off the rest of the material in large sheets. This also holds true if you are removing a wall-covering that was put up with a strippable paste or adhesive or if you used one of the so-called strippable wallcoverings—these should allow you literally to peel off the material when you are ready to remove it.

Stripping off ordinary wallpaper is usually a bit more difficult—normally you have to soak the paper or use a wallpaper steamer to soften it, then scrape off the paper by hand with a wide scraper. If the paper was hung over a plaster wall, scraping poses no serious problems—other than the amount of work involved. However, if the paper is over drywall (gypsum board), then the ease of removal will depend on whether or not the drywall panels were painted or coated with some type of sealer before the wallcovering was put up. If the walls were painted or sealed, scraping off the paper poses no serious problems.

However, if the drywall was not painted or primed before the wallcovering was put up, removal will be quite difficult—in some cases almost impossible. The reason is that as you soak the paper to soften it, you will also be soaking and softening the paper facing on the wallboard under the wallcovering. Then as you start to scrape the wallpaper, you almost always wind up digging into and damaging the paper facing on the wallboard. Sometimes you can get the paper off with a minimum amount of damage to the wallboard by using a long-handled wallpaper scraper that uses disposable, razorlike blades. Sold in many paint and wallpaper stores, these are designed to hold the blade at a very shallow angle that minimizes the likelihood of digging into the wallboard. If even this doesn't work, then your only other option (short of putting up new wallboard) is to paint over the old paper, using an alkyd-base primer. You can then paint over this with a regular flat wall paint or hang a new wallpaper on top.

The quickest and easiest way to remove any wallpaper is by using a wallpaper steamer. These time- and work-saving machines are rented by most paint stores, home centers, and tool rental agencies. They are actually small boilers that generate steam, which then flows through a hose to a flat pan with a perforated plate on one side. Some use a kerosene-fired burner to generate the steam, and some use electricity. When you hold the perforated plate or pan against the wallpaper, the steam comes out through the holes and saturates the paper. Scraping off the wet and soggy paper then becomes comparatively simple.

To remove wallpaper without a steamer, you first soak it with water (preferably hot). The water will soften the paper and penetrate it more effectively if you add a wallpaper-removing liquid to the water (sold in all paint and wallpaper stores). For applying the water, you can use either a large sponge, a sponge mop, or—best of all—a garden-type sprayer. Wet each wall from the bottom up, then wait a few minutes for the water to soak in. It's usually a good idea to wait about five minutes and then wet the wallpaper a second time before starting the actual scraping.

Garden-type sprayer can also be used to soak wallpaper prior to scraping it off.

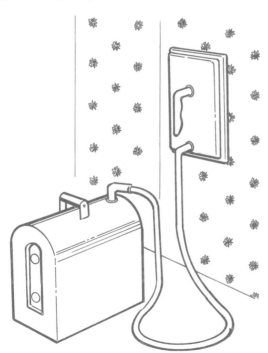

Steam from wallpaper remover flows through hose to flat pan that has perforations on side facing wall.

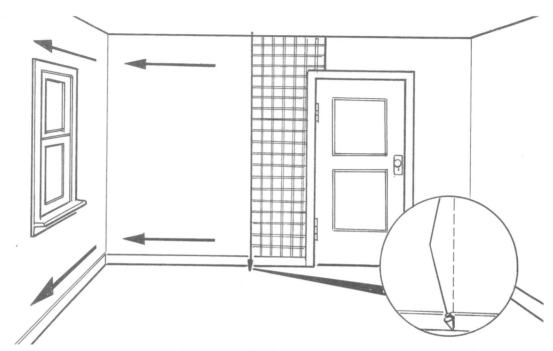

A good place to start hanging the first strip is behind the door leading into that room or in the corner next to that door.

Some wallpapers shed water and thus will not soften when you wet them—for example, most foil papers and many papers that have a plastic coating on the surface. This is also an even greater problem when trying to remove any wallpaper that has been previously painted over. In all these cases the water (or steam) will not penetrate and thus will not soften the backing or the paste—making scraping *very* difficult.

The way to handle this problem is to buy a few sheets of the coarsest open-coat sandpaper you can find (very coarse floor sanding paper is ideal for this purpose), then use this abrasive paper to thoroughly scratch up the face of the wallpaper before you use your steamer or before you try to wet it. The scratches will allow the water or steam to penetrate and soften the backing, and scraping the paper off will then be much easier.

Regardless of what kind of wallcovering you have removed, and regardless of the method you used to remove it, chances are that some of the old paste or adhesive will remain on the wall in some places. It is essential that this residue be completely removed, or new wallcovering may not adhere properly or paint that is applied over it will peel. Scrub this old paste off thoroughly, using hot water and detergent or using the steamer to go over the walls a second time.

CUTTING AND PASTING

Measure the height of the wall, then unroll enough wallcovering to allow for a strip about 6 inches longer than the height of the wall. This allows a margin for trimming along the baseboard at the bottom and along the ceiling-to-wall joint at the top after the wallcovering is in place. Before actually cutting the strip, however, hold up the design to see how it looks along the top—you may want to cut at a point slightly farther along even if it means wasting a few more inches of material. For example, if the pattern has people in it, you might not want to cut strips in such a way that the top of the wall will have rows of headless people showing.

Now decide where to hang the first strip. The usual procedure is to work your way around the room in sequence after the first strip has been hung, so that the last strip will end up next to the first strip. Chances are the pattern on this last seam will not match; you will most likely have to cut one strip to less than its full width. So you want to select the starting point with care.

One of the best places to start is next to the door frame through which the room is entered—a mismatch will be scarcely noticeable there, being visible only above the door. Another good starting point is in a corner behind an entrance arch or door or next to a large window or built-in wall-to-ceiling bookcase.

Next, snap a vertical chalkline on the wall, using a chalked string with a plumb bob or weight of some kind on the end. This line should be at a distance from the starting corner equal to the width of the wallcovering, less about ½ inch. When you hang the first strip, line up its edge with this line and allow the extra ½ inch to fold around the corner onto the adjacent wall. If you are starting next to a door or window frame, this extra ½ inch will be trimmed off with a razor blade after the strip is up.

Don't make the common mistake of merely lining up the edge of the strip with the wall corner or with the edge of the door or window frame. These are seldom if ever really plumb (vertical), and if the first strip is not plumb, all subsequent strips will not be plumb. The error will be magnified as you work your way along the wall.

After the first strip is hung plumb (along the line), subsequent strips on that wall will not have to be plumbed, because you will be butting adjacent strips together until you get to the next corner. Then the first strip on the next wall will have to be plumbed again before continuing on that wall.

Many of today's wallcoverings are prepasted—with these all you have to do is dip the rolled-up strip in water after cutting it to length. With those that are not prepasted, applying paste to the back of the material is the next step after cutting.

For this you will need a large flat surface. You can rent a special pasting table, or you can use a Ping-Pong table or a large kitchen or dinette table. Or place a large sheet of plywood across two sawhorses. The table or work surface should be about 6 feet long and at least half again as wide as the wallcovering.

Lay the first strip face down on the table so that the top end is even with one end of the table as shown in the drawing. The edge closest to you should be lined up with the edge of the table and the excess material left hanging over the other end of the table. To keep from smearing paste onto the table where it is exposed past the far edge, slide sheets of newspaper or other scrap material under the wallcovering to cover the exposed part of the table. After each strip is pasted, slide the paper

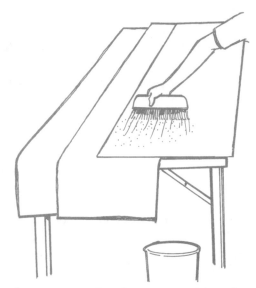

Wallpaper strip is placed on pasting table so that its end and one edge are aligned with the end and edge of the table.

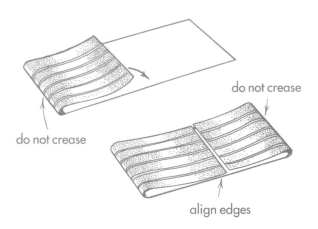

To simplify carrying the pasted strip, fold it for carrying as shown here.

out a little to expose a clean surface on which the next strip can rest.

The paste can be applied with a large brush or a roller. Make sure you use the adhesive recommended for that material by the manufacturer, and be sure there are no skips or misses. This is especially important along the edges, where even a small skip will leave a dry spot that can cause the seams to open or lift after the wall is finished. But don't apply the paste too liberally—just enough to cover the entire surface evenly.

As you finish coating the part on the table, lift up the pasted end and fold it over loosely, with the pasted sides on the inside, the pattern showing on the outside. The folded portion should now contain a little more than half the strip's length. Slide the strip along the table until all of the unpasted part (that was hanging over the end) is now up on the table. Paste this

Unfold top half and allow the end to lap up onto the ceiling, then smooth down and unfold the bottom half.

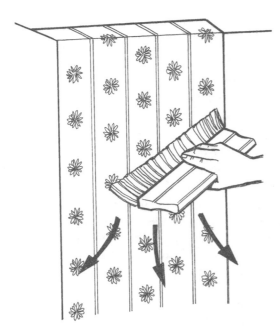

Stroke smoothing brush downward firmly, working from the center of strip out to edges on each side.

Razor knife is used to trim off excess that laps onto baseboard at bottom and onto ceiling at top.

part, then fold it over in the same way so that the bottom end now meets the top in about the middle, as shown. This makes it much easier to carry the strip over to the wall and simplifies handling when you start hanging it.

When you're ready to hang the wallcovering, unfold the top half and smooth it onto the wall with a couple of inches overlapping onto the ceiling and with the edge lined up with a plumb line tied to a nail driven into the wall up near the ceiling. For regular wallpaper and most lightweight vinyl or fabric wallcoverings, a paperhanger's smoothing brush is the best tool, but a large flat sponge can also smooth the paper onto the wall. For heavier-weight materials, a wide metal trowel or a special type of roller may be required.

After the top half of the strip has been smoothed into place, the bottom half is unfolded and peeled down carefully. Smooth this part down in the same manner, then go over the entire strip with the smoothing brush once more to remove air bubbles and wrinkles. Work from the top down and from the center out to each of the edges. If excess paste is squeezed out along the seams, wipe it off immediately with a cloth or clean wet sponge.

The next step is trimming off the excess material at the top and bottom. Crease the material into the corner joint with your smoothing tool, then trim along this crease with a single-edge razor blade. The razor blade will dull fast, so buy plenty of them and throw each blade away after you have used it on two or three strips (buy the commercial kind from a paint or hardware store—they are much cheaper than the ones in a drugstore). Wheeled cutters, called trimmers, are also sometimes used, but these require frequent sharpening and

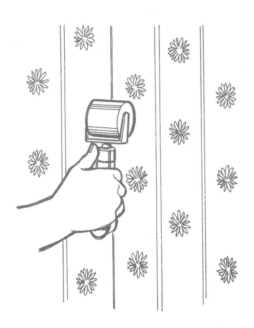

Seam roller is used to smooth down edges.

several passes—so razor blades are faster and cleaner. And the blades are cheap enough to throw away when dull.

After trimming off the excess along the ceiling and baseboard, go over the seams and top and bottom edges with a seam roller (made of plastic or wood) to smooth them down. Be careful to wipe off excess paste that gets squeezed out or else you'll smear it around.

Before you cut the second strip of paper, unroll it against the wall and hold it next to the first one to see how the pattern matches. In some cases the match is straight across, but in others there is a "drop match"—that is, to get a match at the top you will have to raise the material by half a pattern.

Since this means wasting half a pattern length on each strip as you keep cutting from the same roll, cut the first strip off one roll and the second strip off another

roll. Then back to the first roll to cut the third strip and back to the second roll for the fourth strip. By alternating rolls in this way, you will have waste only on the second strip—after that you will be able to measure from the beginning of the roll each time without having to waste any at the top.

As each strip is pasted and hung, butt its edge against the edge of the previous strip by first applying it to the wall a fraction of an inch away, then sliding it over by pressing with your hands until it just meets the other edge. Then follow the same procedure of smoothing, trimming, and rolling the edges of that strip, before wiping excess paste off the face. Don't forget to keep rinsing the sponge frequently in clean water; otherwise you will just wind up smearing the paste over the covering.

When you get to an inside corner, do not simply fold the paper around the corner and continue on the adjoining wall with the same strip—this would almost certainly result in the material wrinkling and pulling out from the corner as it dries. Instead, stop and measure the space left between the edge of the last strip and the corner, then slice the next strip to the same length as the space left on the wall, plus about ½ inch. To ensure a straight cut, use a straightedge and a razor blade rather than the scissors you normally use to cut across a strip. Do this while the strip is still folded and on the table—that way you won't get paste on the straightedge.

When you hang this narrow strip, fold the extra ½ inch around the corner onto the next wall, then smooth it down and trim top and bottom in the usual manner. Be sure you press it tightly into the corner from top to bottom on both sides of the fold.

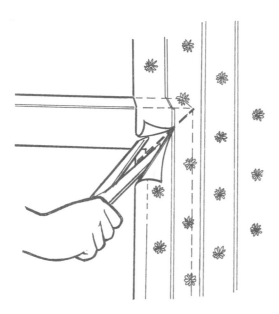

Use sharp scissors or a razor blade to cut diagonally into the corner when fitting around window and door frames.

Take the rest of that same strip and hang it on the adjacent wall next to the folded edge. The match should be practically perfect, because both came from the same strip. If the corner is not straight, however, you may find it necessary to overlap the cut edge slightly here and there in order to avoid gaps between the two edges. On outside corners this is generally not necessary; you can safely fold a full-width strip around an outside corner if the corner is reasonably straight and plumb. If it isn't,

then you should cut the strip as described above and apply it in two parts.

When trimming around windows, doors, and similar openings, it is generally best to apply the full-width strip on the wall so that it overlaps the opening. Line up the one edge with the last strip hung, then carefully crease the wallcovering material into the joint formed between the wall and the trim around the door frame or window frame. To do this without tearing the paper, you will have to make several "relief" cuts so the material will lie flat against the wall.

Cut inward at a diagonal where the frame forms a corner joint, as shown, then gradually trim away the largest areas of excess. Make enough cuts to permit the material to lie flat against the wall, then, with the single-edge razor blade, trim off the rest. On these strips it is generally better to trim around the window or door before you go ahead with trimming along the ceiling and baseboard.

If the wall has light switches or electrical outlets, be sure you remove the cover plates first. Hang the wallcovering as though there were no opening. Before trimming and smoothing, slit the wallcovering over the opening with your razor blade so that you can cut it out with scissors. Make sure you shut off power to that switch or outlet before doing this, and don't replace the cover plate until the paste has dried.

*M*aking Electrical Repairs

The idea of working with electricity or making your own electrical repairs does scare many people, yet it really shouldn't in most cases. It is definitely true that working with electricity does call for a certain amount of caution and a reasonable degree of common sense, but this doesn't change the fact that there are still many simple electrical repairs that any do-it-yourselfer can tackle safely. However, before starting anything, you should be familiar with some elementary facts about electricity and should have at least a basic knowledge of home wiring techniques and wiring systems.

Needless to say, an inexperienced amateur should never tackle a sizable project like rewiring an entire room or adding new circuits to the existing wiring—in fact, many communities forbid anyone but a licensed electrician from doing such work—but you can safely handle such jobs as repairing a faulty lamp, replacing a lighting fixture or wall switch, or repairing a doorbell system that no longer works properly (or doesn't work at all). All you have to do is take the time to read and follow the directions on the pages that follow, as well as make certain you always observe some well-established safety guidelines.

WHAT YOU SHOULD KNOW ABOUT ELECTRICAL WIRING

All properly wired electrical circuits in your home or apartment are protected by either a fuse or a circuit breaker. Its purpose is to keep the amount of current flowing through the wires in that circuit from exceeding safe limits. If the flow of current were to exceed the current-carrying capacity of those wires—as happens when a short develops—the wires would dangerously overheat, scorching and possibly melting the wires and the insulation and eventually starting a fire.

The fuse or circuit breaker prevents this from happening because each fuse or circuit breaker is precisely rated—it will "open" and stop the flow of current before the wires become overloaded (and overheated). That is also why you should *never* replace a blown fuse with another one of larger capacity (this cannot happen with circuit breakers because you don't replace

these when they blow; you simply flip the switch off fully and then back on to reset).

Most household circuits carry voltages that will range anywhere from 110 to 120 volts, depending on your local utility company (to simplify we will refer to all of these as 120-volt circuits). However, some large electrical appliances such as electric stoves and clothes dryers require 220 (or 240) volts to run properly—which is why most modern buildings are wired for that voltage. In all such home installations the voltage coming into the main service entrance panel will be 240 volts, but inside the panel this voltage is separated or broken down into various 120-volt circuits that are then used for lighting and for receptacles throughout the house—except for those large appliances that do need the full 240 volts.

The way that this current is divided or

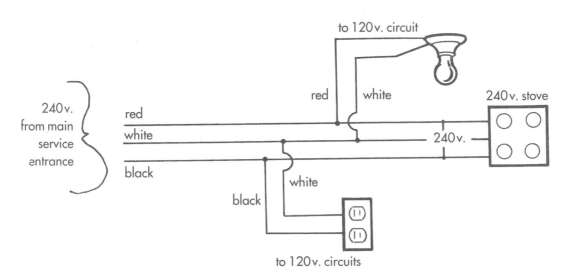

Typical three-wire, 240-volt power supply is normally split up to supply 120 volts to most circuits and 240 volts to stove and other large appliances.

broken up is fairly simple: The incoming 240 volts comes in on three wires—a common wire (which is colored white) and two "hot" wires that each carry 120 volts (one may be black and the other red, or both may be black). To get the full 240 volts, power is taken from the two "hot" wires, thus giving you 120 volts from each or a total of 240 volts. For those circuits or appliances that need only 120 volts, power is drawn from only one side (called one phase) of the incoming circuits. In other words, the 120-volt circuit draws power from only one of the "hot" wires (red or black) and the common (white). You can consider the common as the "return," since all circuits must form a full unbroken loop if power is to flow. When this loop is broken—for example, when a fuse blows or a switch is opened (turned to the off position)—then no current flows. Switches and fuses are always located along the "hot" wire (the black or red wire), because breaking the common (white) wire only could still allow current to flow through a ground connection, inasmuch as the white wire is itself "grounded"—that is, connected at the fuse box to a common ground connection.

To simplify this—think of voltage as being similar to the pressure applied to a flow of water in order to keep it flowing through the pipes. In other words, the higher the voltage, the higher the "pressure" that is actually "pushing" the current through those wires. The other quantity or term used in measuring current is the number of amperes involved (usually abbreviated as amps). To continue the comparison with plumbing, the number of amps might be compared to the "gallons per minute" flowing through a pipe—in other words, this is a measure of the actual "quantity" of current flowing through that wire.

But to know the total amount of electrical power consumed by any appliance or fixture, we must take *both* voltage and amperage into consideration (more water will flow through the pipe in a given length of time if the pressure is higher). The term used to measure this total flow of power is watts, determined by multiplying volts by amperes. For example, if an appliance draws 10 amps at 120 volts, it will be drawing a total of 1,200 watts (10×120).

WHEN A FUSE OR CIRCUIT BREAKER BLOWS

Although most home wiring circuits now use circuit breakers, many older buildings still have fuses. The most commonly encountered type of fuse is the plug-type fuse—the kind that looks like a small electric plug and screws in much like a light bulb. These have a transparent plastic "window" on top, underneath which is visible a strip of fusible metal or wire that

"good" fuse

When fuse "blows," fusible metal link melts to break circuit.

blown fuse

melts at a relatively low temperature. All current in that circuit flows through this fusible link, so that as soon as the current exceeds a safe limit and the wires start to heat up (from a short or an overload caused by plugging in too many appliances), this metal strip or wire will melt—thus causing the fuse to "blow." This immediately cuts off the flow of current in the same way that opening a switch would stop the current. When a fuse does blow, the transparent window usually turns dark or clouds up, making it easy to spot which fuse is blown.

In addition to plug-type fuses, many older fuse boxes also have several cartridge-type fuses, especially in the larger-capacity circuits such as those that carry 240 volts or those located in the main service entrance. Unlike a plug-type fuse, a cartridge fuse gives no visible indication when it has blown. The only sure way to check is to take it out and replace it with a new one that you *know* is good.

Cartridge-type fuses are held in place by spring metal clips (usually copper) that are mounted inside the box and serve as the connections or contacts for that fuse. When you pull out the fuse, the connection is broken. Because these are in the "hot" side of the circuit, care must be taken not to touch the metal clips that hold the fuses. Wear gloves when removing or replacing a fuse, and use a pair of pliers to grasp the cartridge in the center when you want to remove one. Yank firmly by pulling it straight out. Some cartridge fuses are mounted on a special removable block with a handle in the center of this block. When you pull out this block you are actually pulling the fuses out with it, instantly shutting off all power to that circuit. You can then remove and replace the

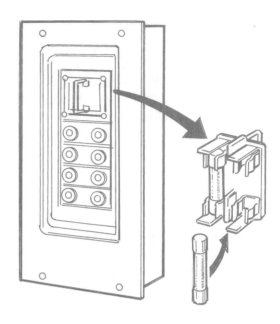

Cartridge-type "main" fuses are often mounted on back side of removable block. Pulling block out shuts off all power.

cartridge fuses mounted on that block in complete safety, without worrying about getting a shock.

Circuit breakers perform the same function as fuses, but they do not have to be replaced when they "blow." They are like switches that flip to the off position when overloaded. They can be readily reset simply by pushing the toggle switch back to the on position after the overload is corrected (on some brands the toggle takes a middle position when the breaker opens; these have to be flicked to the off position before they can then be flipped back to the on position).

When a fuse or circuit breaker blows, simply replacing the fuse or flicking the circuit breaker back on will not solve the problem. The overload that caused the fuse or breaker to blow must be corrected

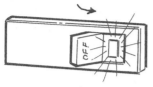

red shows when blown

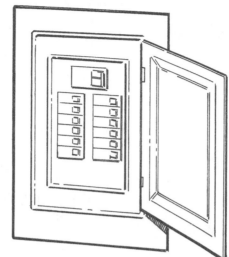

When circuit breaker "blows," red square is visible in window. Throwing switch handle back and forth resets breaker.

first; otherwise the same thing will immediately happen again.

How do you know what caused the problem? If the fuse blew just after you plugged in an appliance or power tool, chances are that the trouble is a short or other defect in that appliance. If it did not occur immediately, however, then the likelihood is that the circuit was overloaded by your plugging in that particular appliance in addition to all the other appliances or lights on that circuit.

If the fuse blows without any new load having been added, then the problem could be an overload caused by something that kicked on automatically (a refrigerator, for example), or it could be a defect that has developed in the wiring or in one of the appliances plugged into that circuit.

To locate the source of the trouble before turning the power back on, start by unplugging all the lamps and other appliances on that circuit. Then turn the power back on. If the fuse or circuit breaker

blows with nothing plugged in, the trouble is in the wiring or in one of the receptacles or permanently connected lighting fixtures. Unless you are pretty familiar with electrical wiring, you will probably have to call in an electrician at this point to track down the problem.

Assuming the fuse (or circuit breaker) does not blow with everything unplugged, you then start plugging lamps and appliances back in one at a time to see which one caused the problem. If there is a short or similar defect in one of the appliances, the fuse or breaker will pop immediately after the device is plugged in. If the fuse doesn't blow until a few seconds later, then the addition of that appliance has probably overloaded that circuit and you will have to move one or more appliances or lamps to a different circuit. You can, of course, check for this simply by plugging the suspect appliance into a different circuit (one that has very little or nothing else plugged in) to see if it works okay.

THAT ESSENTIAL THIRD WIRE—THE GROUND

In addition to the "hot" (black or red) wire and the common or "neutral" white wire that is found in every 120-volt electric circuit in the home, every building that was wired (or rewired) after the early 1960s is also required to include a third, non-current-carrying conductor or ground

If appliance was not grounded, short inside appliance could cause metal housing to be "hot" so that current would flow through any person touching it.

wire in each circuit. This ground wire is usually colored green, but in some older houses the ground wire may be a bare, uninsulated wire inside the same cable. It is this third wire, the ground wire, that connects to the third (round) hole in all three-prong receptacles and to the third (round) prong on all three-pronged plugs.

The ground wire forms a continuous, unbroken loop that connects all switches, receptacles, boxes, and appliance housings to the main ground conductor or bus bar inside the central fuse box for that electric system. Its function is to do just what the name implies—to ground that circuit if a short should develop in one of the current-carrying wires. This could happen if the insulation was defective on one of the wires inside an appliance or if a wire loosened and somehow came in contact with the metal housing or an appliance or fixture. A person touching that appliance or fixture could then receive a serious, possibly lethal, shock because the

current, which is always trying to find its way to earth (ground), would then flow through that person's body on its way to the ground—particularly if that person was standing on a damp surface.

However, in a properly wired circuit the ground wire would prevent this. As soon as the short occurred, there would be a heavy flow of current through that ground wire directly to the earth ground (a metal water pipe or a separate metal bar that is buried in the ground). This would cause the fuse or circuit breaker to blow, thus shutting off the flow of current to the defective appliance.

If the house was wired in the days before three-prong receptacles were required, there will be a problem when you try to plug in motor-driven tools or appliances that come with three-prong plugs. This is usually solved by using an adapter between plug and receptacle; the adapter has a separate pigtail wire that you connect to the screw in the center of the receptacle plate to continue the ground connection. All too often people do not do this—or they don't first scrape paint off it to ensure a good connection. Even then

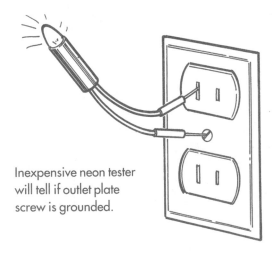

Inexpensive neon tester will tell if outlet plate screw is grounded.

there is no guarantee that the screw holding the plate on is itself grounded properly—in a nonmetallic cable system a careless electrician may never have attached the separate ground wire to the metal box.

To make sure the screw in the center of the cover plate will work as a ground, use a small inexpensive neon test light as shown in the illustration. Push one prong of the test lamp into one of the slotted openings in the receptacle. (If the test prod on the trouble light won't fit into the narrow slot, use heavy gloves to insert a paper clip or short piece of stiff wire into the outlet, then touch the test prod to this piece of metal; do not touch any of the bare metal with your bare fingers!) Hold the other prod of the test light against the screw as shown, pressing or rubbing slightly to ensure good contact. If the test light glows, the screw will make a good ground; if it doesn't, try the same test with one prong of the test in the other slot of the outlet. If you cannot see the light glow in either case, then the screw is not properly grounded.

It is because of all these uncertainties that many communities now have codes that no longer allow the use of adapters. Old-style two-prong receptacles can be replaced by approved three-prong receptacles that have the third hole connected to a proper ground (the metal housing of the cable or the third wire inside the box). It is a job best done by a licensed electrician or someone qualified to do work of this kind, though you can do it yourself if you are reasonably careful about following directions and if there are no local regulations against doing your own wiring (check this with your local building department).

Start by first shutting off all power to that circuit, then remove the cover plate and take out the two screws that hold the receptacle in place against the front of the box. Now pull the receptacle out of the box and disconnect the two wires connected to it—one white and one black. If there is more than one white and one black connected to it, disconnect all of them, but make a note of where each wire was connected. If other wires inside the box are connected together, leave them alone.

Now connect the new three-prong receptacle to the same wires, making certain that all the same color wires go to the same connections on the receptacle. This means that all white wires go to the silver or lighter-colored screw on one side, and all the black (or red) wires go to the darker, brass-colored screws on the other side. It is essential not to mix this up. *Never* allow a white and a black (or red) wire to be connected together or to be connected to the same terminal strip or screw.

When attaching the wires to the terminal screws, always twist the strands together tightly, then wrap the wire around the screw in a clockwise direction—in other words, in the same direction as the screw will be turned when you tighten it. As you tighten the screw head down on the wire, it will then tend to wrap the wire even more tightly around the terminal. If you wrap the wire in the opposite direction, you will find as you tighten the screw that the wire tends to loosen rather than tighten.

In addition to the terminal screws on each side, the new receptacle has a separate green-colored terminal screw at one end. This is for the ground wire inside the box. In some cases this wire will itself be green, but in most it will be bare metal and probably be connected to a screw on the side of the metal box. Connect this wire to the green screw on the receptacle. If the house is wired with BX metal-sheathed cable, there may be no separate ground wire evident inside the box. In that case connect the green screw to the metal box with a separate piece of wire, running it from the receptacle screw to one of the screws that clamp the cable in place at the back or side of the box.

Once all wires have been connected, push the receptacle back into the box and fold the wires neatly out of the way so none get crimped or pinched against the sides. Then tighten the screws that hold the receptacle against the front of the box and mount the cover plate on front to complete the job.

GROUND FAULT CIRCUIT INTERRUPTERS

Even if all circuits and receptacles in your house are properly grounded, it is still possible for you to get a serious, even lethal, shock if you are standing on wet ground or holding a metal pipe while you happen to touch an appliance whose metal housing is "hot" or charged with current because of an internal short. It is true that the fuse or circuit breaker will blow, but in the fraction of a second it takes for this to happen enough current could flow through your body (on its way to the ground) to give you a fatal shock. The primary function of a fuse or circuit breaker is to protect the wiring and equipment, rather than people. In addition, a fuse or circuit breaker may not suffice when only a "partial" short develops—that is, when there is not enough current leaking to ground to actually blow the fuse or circuit breaker, but still more than enough to give someone a serious shock.

That is where the ground fault interrupter (GFI) comes in. Something like a circuit breaker in function and appearance, these protective devices are required by the National Electrical Code for installation in all circuits that lead to an outdoor receptacle, as well as in all circuits that supply power to receptacles in garages, bathrooms, and laundry rooms and near kitchen sinks or anywhere else dampness may normally be encountered and electrical tools or appliances are often used.

A GFI continuously monitors, measures, and compares the amount of current flowing through the black (hot) and white (neutral) wire of the circuit. If everything is normal, the amount of current in each wire will be exactly the same, and the GFI does nothing. However, if there is even the slightest amount of variation, indicating that there is some current leaking to ground from one of the current-carrying wires, the GFI will sense this and instantly shut off the flow of current. It will do this even if the variation is only a few thousandths of an ampere, and it will do this in a tiny fraction of a second—much quicker than a fuse or circuit breaker can and long before there is enough current flowing through the ground wire (or grounded housing) to cause any bodily harm to anyone.

GFIs come in three different types or styles. One type is designed to be installed inside the fuse box or service panel in place of a regular circuit breaker. This is a combination unit that serves as both a circuit breaker and a GFI, and it will provide GFI protection for all outlets and receptacles in that circuit. However, in some homes this can be a nuisance because GFIs tend to "blow" easily with even the slightest amount of leakage—something

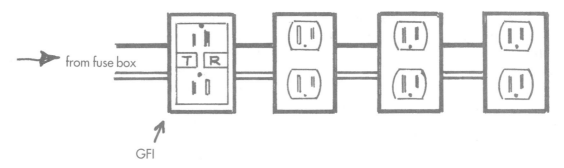

from fuse box

GFI

GFI receptacle provides protection for all receptacles that are "downstream" from that one.

that is almost "normal" in some older buildings.

The second type of GFI is the receptacle style, which is installed in a regular outlet box in place of a standard duplex outlet or receptacle. One GFI will serve to protect all other receptacles in that same circuit as long as the other outlets are all "downstream" of that one (not between it and the fuse box). In other words, if you had a receptacle in one bathroom with a GFI installed and that same circuit continued on to a receptacle in another bathroom, the one unit would protect the receptacles in both bathrooms.

The third type of GFI is the portable one that simply plugs into an existing wall outlet and then has its own duplex receptacle on the front so that anything you plug into it has GFI protection. In some cases the portable GFI is also part of an extension cord. One end of the cord plugs into a standard outlet; the other end has a GFI receptacle into which you can plug tools or appliances when working outside or in a damp location.

All GFIs come with a reset button on the front panel. This will pop out when there is a problem of any kind, even a small overload. Pressing it back puts the circuit into service once again. However, if the button pops out immediately after you reset it, then the circuit should be checked to see if there is a short or an overload. In addition to the reset button, all GFIs have a test button. This should be pressed about once a month to make certain the unit is still functioning properly.

Portable GFI plugs into regular receptacle, after which tools or appliances can be plugged into it to provide protection when working in damp locations.

REPLACING A WALL SWITCH

Whether you have to replace an old switch because it is no longer working properly, or because you just want to update the system with an energy-saving dimmer switch that will permit you to lower the amount of wattage consumed when full brightness is not required, changing a wall switch is a fairly simple electrical repair that normally takes only a few minutes and requires no special tools or skills.

As with most jobs that involve house wiring, the first step is to shut off the power by pulling the fuse or throwing the appropriate breaker. Next, remove the screw in the center of the cover plate and take off the plate. The switch has two screws to hold it in place against the front of the metal box, one at the top and one at the bottom, so loosen these screws until they come out of the threaded holes in the metal box. Now pull the whole switch straight out of its box so the terminal screws on each side are exposed.

Some switches have push-type terminals instead of terminal screws. Bared wire ends are simply pushed into openings in back until they lock in place.

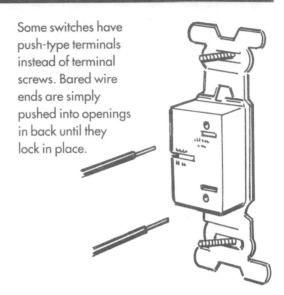

Loosen these screws and disconnect the wires at each one. In many cases both wires will be black, because switches are always installed in the "hot" line, never in the white or "common" line. However, if the switch is at the end of the circuit and controls a light or outlet without power going on from there to other parts of the circuit (as evidenced by the fact that only one two-wire conductor or cable will be coming into that box), there may be one white wire and one black wire connected to it. The reason for this exception is that electricians have no choice: there are no household two-conductor cables with both wires black. An electrician who installs a switch in this manner is supposed to paint the end of the white wire black to show that it is actually serving as a black wire, but unfortunately this is not always done. So if you find both a black and a white wire going to the old switch, it probably makes no difference, but play it safe and hook them up on the new switch the same way they were on the old one.

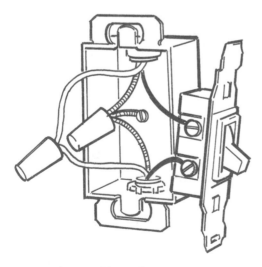

When replacing old switch, connect new one to the same wires.

If there are other wires inside the box that do not connect to the switch, leave them alone. Don't disturb any of the connections—just push them back into the box. Then connect the wires that originally went to the old switch onto the same terminals on the new switch. If the new switch has screw terminals like the old one, simply wrap the bent wire ends clockwise around the screws, then tighten firmly. If the new switch has push-type terminals instead of screw terminals, clip off the bent wire ends and then use the strip gauge on the back of the new switch to strip off the amount of insulation specified on each wire. Push each bare wire end firmly into the terminal holes until they are locked solidly into place.

Most single-pole switches will have only two wires connected to them, but in some cases there will also be a third ground wire (either a bare metal wire or a green covered wire). Connect this ground wire to the green ground terminal screw on the new switch (if there was a ground wire connected to the old switch, make sure your new switch also has a ground terminal).

If you are installing a dimmer switch in place of a conventional switch, make sure this switch is one that does *not* control wall outlets where you might occasionally plug in an appliance. If you were to plug in an appliance and turn it on while the dimmer was turned down to low, that appliance could be seriously damaged. Some dimmer switches have wire leads coming out instead of terminals, for connecting to the wires in the box. To splice these wires to the wires coming out of the box, use standard twist-on solderless connectors. Strip off the proper amount of insulation on each wire, then push each pair of wires into the solderless connector

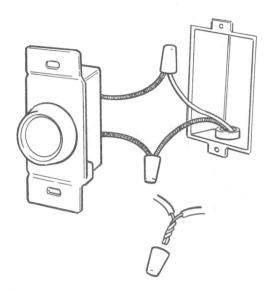

Dimmer switches often come with wires that must be attached to wires inside the box, using solderless, twist-on connectors.

and twist clockwise until it won't tighten anymore. Another point to keep in mind when installing a dimmer switch is to make certain you purchase one that is rated to handle the total wattage of all the lights it must control.

If you are replacing a three-way switch —one that enables you to turn lights on and off from more than one location— make sure the new one is also three-way, and be very careful about tagging or labeling all the wires before you disconnect them from the old switch. You want to be certain that you are connecting them to the proper terminals on the new switch.

For some installations there is also another type of wall switch you might want to install—one that has a built-in timing device that turns off the switch automatically after a preset length of time (usually up to 60 minutes). This can be useful for controlling exhaust fans or built-in heat lamps in a bathroom, for controlling attic fans, or for similar uses where you want the power to go off automatically after a predetermined length of time. Like dimmer switches, timer switches are available to fit into standard wall outlet boxes, and they usually come with their own cover plates marked with numbers to indicate time spans. You turn a knob to set the lengths of "on" time, then a clock mechanism turns it slowly to off.

REPLACING A RECEPTACLE

Although it doesn't happen often, there are times when a receptacle will go bad—either the fuse blows every time that receptacle is used, or the outlet remains dead even if the wiring to all other outlets on that circuit is okay. Another sign that you may need a new receptacle is finding that a light or appliance flickers or runs intermittently every time you plug something into its outlet (this could also be the fault of the plug or the cord on the appliance, so test with more than one plug and cord before deciding that the outlet is faulty).

Changing a receptacle is similar to changing a switch. Start by shutting off the power, then removing the cover plate and loosening the screws that hold the receptacle in place so you can pull it out to expose the terminal screws on each side (or on the back of some models). However, you have to be more careful about seeing how the old wires are connected before you disconnect them. With a receptacle it *does* make a big difference where the white and the black wires are connected.

To avoid mistakes, make a sketch to show where each white and black wire goes before you disconnect it, or label each wire with a piece of marked masking tape before you disconnect it. You will notice that all the white wires go to one side and all black wires to the other side.

Also, the screws to which the white wires connect will be lighter in color, while the black wire terminals will have darker-colored screws. Be sure you hook up the new receptacle in the same way. Some of the new receptacles are back-wired—that is, they do not have screw terminals; instead, they have holes in the back, and you simply push the bared wire ends into these to make the connection without using the screw terminals.

All receptacles now have three-prong outlets with a green grounding screw on one side. If your old outlet does not have this, there will be an extra wire that will have to be connected—a ground wire running to a screw inside the metal box.

ADDING AN EXTRA RECEPTACLE

Adding an additional receptacle to an existing circuit does not increase the total capacity of that circuit—it merely serves to locate receptacles more conveniently, or it permits plugging in more lights or appliances at one time (so you won't, for example, have to pull the lamp plug every time the vacuum cleaner is to be used). Just remember that a typical lighting circuit fused at 15 amps can only carry a total load of 15 amps (about 1,650 to 1,750 watts), no matter how many receptacles it has.

In most cases the simplest way to get power to one or more additional receptacles is to connect the wires for this new one to one of the nearest existing receptacles or switches in that room. However, before selecting a switch or receptacle that you will tap into, make sure it is not controlled by a wall switch—unless, of course, you don't mind having the new outlet also controlled by that same switch.

If you decide to tap into a box that contains a wall switch rather than a wall outlet, make sure you pick one that contains at least one "hot" wire that will be "live" at all times, regardless of whether the switch is in the off or the on position. The way to check for this is to shut off power to that circuit, then take off the switch plate and loosen the screws that hold the switch in place against the front of the wall box. Pull the switch out of its box to expose the terminals and the wiring, then turn the power back on. Now use a small neon test lamp to test the "hot" wire. Try it first with the switch on, then with the switch off to make sure it carries current even when the switch is in the off position. You can then connect the black

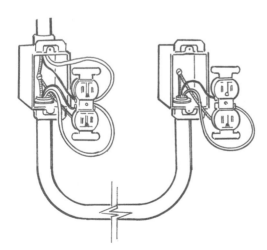

The usual way to add permanent outlets is to wire the new receptacle to one of the existing outlets.

wire for the new outlet to this "hot" wire, while connecting the white wire from the new outlet to the white wire that goes to the existing switch.

In some cases you will find that the wall box you select (for either a wall switch or a wall outlet) may contain more than just one pair of wires. It may contain wires that are not connected to the switch or receptacle at all; they are simply joined together with solderless connectors. This is because that particular wall box is being used as a junction box for those wires, so it's best not to disturb them.

Just remember this important rule: You must *always* connect white wires to white wires and black wires to black (or red) wires. Also, the white wires in that circuit must always be continuous and should never be broken or interrupted by a switch; switches are always wired into the black (or red) wires—the "hot" side of each circuit. Wires can be attached or connected together by using solderless, twist-on connectors similar to those shown on page 161, or they can be attached to unused terminal screws that are often available on existing receptacles and switches (terminal screws for white wires are normally silvery or light in color; those for black wires are usually brass in color).

After deciding on the location for your new outlet, it's best not to cut the actual opening in the wall until after you have located the nearest wall studs (by using a stud finder or by drilling some test holes first). If possible, mount your new electrical box against the side of a stud. However, if this is impossible, then you can buy special wall boxes that come with attached "ears" that enable the box to be safely mounted on plaster or wallboard without need for fastening to a stud.

Check with your electric supply dealer or home center; they stock electrical wall boxes in many different configurations— some for fastening at the top, some for bottom mounting, and some for side or back mounting.

In most cases, the most difficult part of the job when adding additional electrical outlets is the problems encountered when you try to run the new electric cables from the existing outlet to the location of the new one. One simple method that is often used is to pull off the wood baseboard along the bottom of the wall, then run the cables along in the space behind this trim (you may have to dig a groove in the plaster or wallboard in order to recess the cable before the baseboard is replaced). After you replace the baseboard, it conceals all the wiring. There will be other times when you will have to bore holes through the wall or through a floor, then fish the cables through, using a flexible electrician's "snake" or stiff piece of wire to help pull the wires through.

ADDING OUTLETS WITH SURFACE WIRING

Another way often used to add receptacles to an existing circuit is to use a surface wiring system. These are simpler and easier for do-it-yourselfers to install, and they eliminate the need for removing baseboards or other trim in order to conceal wiring as well as for boring holes in walls or floors. Surface wiring systems are widely available in electrical supply houses as well as in most home centers.

These generally consist of long metal or plastic channels, usually called raceways, that are mounted directly to the surface of a wall or baseboard. All wiring for the new outlets is installed inside this hollow channel. The most popular style comes in two parts: the channel that is U-shaped in cross section and is screwed directly to the wall or baseboard, and a matching cover that snaps on over this channel to cover all the wiring on the inside.

The snap-on channel cover usually has recessed receptacles (electric outlets) installed along the face at regular intervals, so that after the cover is in place the strip already has multiple outlets that can be used for plugging in lamps, appliances, portable electric tools, and so on. Some surface wiring systems do not have outlets installed in the cover. Instead these systems use separate low-profile outlet boxes that are mounted on the surface of the wall.

Most surface wiring systems are designed to be permanently connected directly into the house wiring through an existing receptacle. A few are more portable and come with a short electric cord and plug attached to one end so that no permanent wiring is required—you simply mount the raceway channel on the wall, then plug the attached cord into the nearest existing outlet.

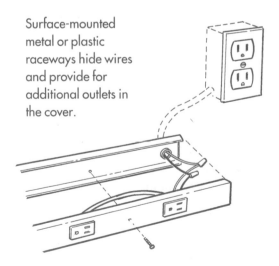

Surface-mounted metal or plastic raceways hide wires and provide for additional outlets in the cover.

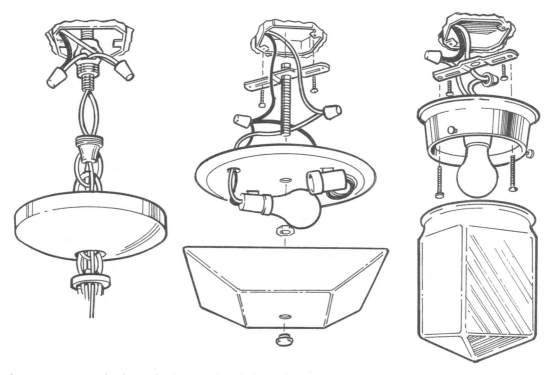

Three common methods used to hang ceiling lighting fixtures.

Ideal for kitchens, workshops, family rooms, and similar locations where the raceways or channels would not look objectionable, all surface-mounted systems offer matching end pieces, T-connectors, and corner pieces for making right-angle bends and for going around corners. The channels and fittings usually come finished in a beige or off-white color, but most can be easily painted to match the walls or woodwork if desired.

REPLACING A CEILING FIXTURE

Changing or replacing a ceiling lighting fixture is about the same electrically as changing a wall switch or replacing a defective wall receptacle—after disconnecting the wires from the old fixture you recon-

nect them to the corresponding terminal screws on the new ones. However, unlike wall outlets, ceiling fixtures do require different methods for mounting or hanging. All are hung from a metal outlet box that is recessed into the ceiling, but this box must be solidly mounted in order to support the weight of the hanging fixture. In some cases this ceiling box will be fastened against the side of one of the beams in the ceiling, but in most cases the box is mounted on a metal brace or strap that goes across the top of two of these beams.

The illustrations above show some of the most commonly encountered methods used to hang a ceiling fixture from its box. Some ceiling boxes have a threaded metal stud that sticks down in the center of the box, and in many cases the ceiling fixture is hung from this threaded stud—either by means of a metal strap that fits over the threaded stud and is held in place with a large nut or by means of two bolts that go up into threaded holes on each end of the metal strap. With very small fixtures there may be two bolts that go up through the canopy and into threaded holes in the metal "ears" located on opposite sides of the ceiling box.

Chandeliers that hang from a chain are often suspended from a threaded stud at the top of the chain. This stud fits through a hole in the center of the fixture's ceiling canopy, then goes up through another hole in the center of the metal mounting strap, to be secured by a nut on top of the strap. In many cases there will be another nut under the canopy to hold it in place against the ceiling.

Most chandeliers and other ceiling fixtures are designed so that either the heads of the bolts that hold them in place are covered up by the canopy or globe that fits over the bulbs, or the canopy is held in place by a decorative escutcheon plate or collar that screws on over the bottom end of the threaded stud or pipe. When the fixture is the type that hangs from a chain, this decorative nut will often serve also as the securing point for the chain from which the fixture is suspended.

Whatever the type of fixture, the first step is to shut off the power, then remove the decorative globe or canopy. Glass globes are usually held in place by screws around the perimeter. After the globe is off, the canopy and the socket can be dropped by removing the two screws that go up into the metal supporting strap or into the metal box itself. Taking these out will enable you to lower the canopy and expose the wiring. Remove the wire nuts or solderless connectors that join the incoming wires to the fixture, making sure you support its weight with one hand—or have a helper hold the fixture for you if it is an especially heavy one—then finish removing any bolts, nuts, or other hardware holding it in place.

During all this, note carefully how the parts go together so you will have no trouble mounting the new one. It's possible that the new one will mount differently, but if you note how the old one was hung, you will know what adapters or other fittings will be needed for the new one. Hardware stores and electrical supply houses that sell fixtures have the metal straps, threaded studs, cap nuts, and so on, used for hanging ceiling fixtures, so you should have no trouble getting any additional parts you may need if they were not included.

To mount the new fixture in place of the old one, simply reverse the steps. If the fixture is very heavy, have someone help you hold it while you insert the bolts through the canopy, or thread it onto the center stud through which the wires may also go—this all depends on the style and construction of the fixture.

Don't tighten anything yet; just secure the bolts or nuts sufficiently to support the weight of the fixture. Now connect the wires to the new fixture, using the old fixture's plastic twist-on, solderless connectors. If the old ones are cracked, or if you lost them, new ones can be purchased in any hardware store. Twist the bared wire ends together, then push them into the connector and twist firmly until the connector won't turn anymore. If any bare wire shows outside the connector, too much insulation has been stripped off. Take off the connector and cut off a little of the bare wire to shorten it.

After all connections have been made, with no bare wire showing, turn off the power and test. If all seems well, tighten all nuts and bolts and finish mounting the fixture by installing the decorative globes or canopies that cover the bottom end.

REPAIRING LAMPS AND REPLACING PLUGS

When a lamp starts to flicker, or won't light at all, chances are that the trouble is caused by either a bad socket or a defective plug at the end of the cord—assuming you have checked the bulb by trying it in another lamp that you know works, and assuming there is power in the outlet into which the lamp is plugged (you test this by plugging something else in, something you know works).

Occasionally the problem is merely some dirt or corrosion on the metal at the bottom of the socket preventing good electrical contact with the base of the bulb. To eliminate this possibility, unplug the lamp and remove the bulb from its socket, then use a table knife or similar tool to scrape clean the metal strip at the bottom of the socket. If the strip is not bent upward enough to press against the base of the bulb, pry it up a little, using the tip of the knife blade or a very small screwdriver. Wipe the base of the bulb clean with a small piece of fine abrasive paper, then replace the bulb and try the lamp again.

If it still does not light, you can be pretty sure the problem is either a bad plug, a bad socket, or a loose connection in one or the other. You can't tell which without actually checking the connections in or replacing each part, but you may be able to pinpoint the source of the trouble by wiggling the wires near the plug to see if this causes the light to flicker or produces sparking at the plug. If you see sparks, pull the plug out immediately. If you notice flickering, the plug is bad or one of the connections is loose, so you will have to take off the plug and possibly replace it.

When you still can't decide which is the source of trouble—the plug or the lamp socket—the simplest thing to do is change one and then the other. Since replacing a plug is cheaper and quicker, you're usually better off starting with this, especially if the plug is an old one that shows signs of cracking or that has bent or badly oxidized prongs.

REPLACING PLUGS

Electric plugs come in many different styles, some made for use with flat lamp cords (also called "rip cords" because they consist of two conductors that you can "rip" apart) and some made for heavier-duty use with round cords and

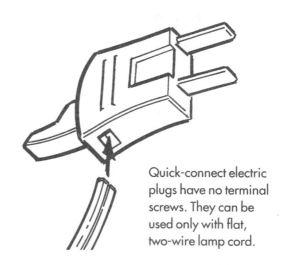

Quick-connect electric plugs have no terminal screws. They can be used only with flat, two-wire lamp cord.

heavier-gauge wires (the type often used on power tools and appliances, as well as on many extension cords).

For lamps and similar light loads you can use one of the light-duty, flat plugs that do not have terminal screws—many do not even require stripping the insulation off the ends. As shown in the illustration on page 167, you simply cut off the old plug, then separate the two halves of the wire for a short distance and push the wire ends into the hole provided at the side of the plug. Pressing down a cam or lever forces metal prongs into each conductor and establishes electrical contact.

Another version of this type of plug that also eliminates the need for stripping allows you to slip the housing off the plug, then slide it back on over the wire. This causes pronged levers to close over the wires and pierce the insulation to make contact. Sliding the housing back on clamps the whole thing together.

Round plugs designed for use with heavier-duty wires, and flat plugs with terminal screws, do require that the ends of the wire be stripped bare of insulation. Use a knife or stripping tool to shave off about ½ inch of insulation at each end, taking care not to nick the wire.

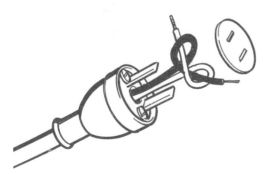

When connecting heavy round electric cords to a three-prong plug that has terminal screws, an underwriter's knot should be tied in two wires first.

The bared ends should be just long enough to permit wrapping around the terminal screws next to each prong. It is important that you wrap the wire *clockwise* around each screw so that the wire will tend to tighten as the screw is tightened. In this type of plug the wire comes in through the back, then the two conductors are separated and an underwriter's knot is tied to take strain off the cord before attaching it to the terminal screws. Make certain there are no loose strands protruding from under the screw head, which could cause a serious short.

REPLACING THE LAMP SOCKET

Most lamps have sockets with built-in switches, but some have separate switches on the base, so you should always make certain the switch is not the source of the trouble before you go ahead and change the socket. The easiest way to do this is to disconnect the wires leading to the switch, then simply join them together temporarily in order to "jump" or bypass the switch. If the wires happen to be soldered to the switch and you don't want to cut them, leave them connected and just run a short piece of wire from one side of the switch to the other for the test. If the lamp lights with the switch not in the circuit (when the wires are connected directly to each other), then you know the switch is defective and needs to be replaced. Replacement switches are widely available in most hardware and electrical supply stores.

If your lamp has no separate switch (other than the one in the socket), or if shorting out or "jumping" the switch does not solve your problem, replacing the lamp socket is your next step. Not only is this an

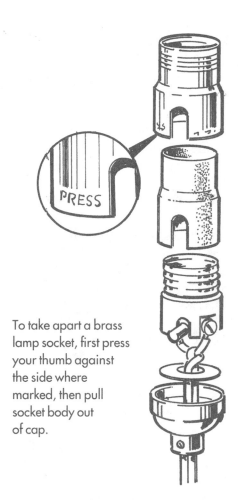

To take apart a brass lamp socket, first press your thumb against the side where marked, then pull socket body out of cap.

word "PRESS" is embossed in the metal. Simultaneously, use your other hand to push the top half sideways and upward. The socket will snap apart, enabling you to lift off the top half of the metal shell as shown in the illustration.

Inside the metal shell there is a fiber liner (resembling cardboard) that serves as an insulator. If this does not come off with the metal shell, slide it off separately to expose the terminal screws. Loosen each screw and pull off the wires, then remove the rest of the socket body.

The bottom half of the socket, called the cap, is threaded onto the top of the small metal pipe or hollow stud that comes up through the base of the lamp and contains the wires. To remove the cap, simply unscrew it by turning counterclockwise while holding the lamp base firmly. (In most cases there will be a small setscrew that locks this cap onto the threaded stud to keep it from turning, so make sure you loosen this before you start unscrewing the cap.)

To install the new socket you first take it apart so that you can remove the cap from the bottom end. Thread the lamp wires through this cap, then screw it onto the end of the threaded stud or pipe through which the wires project (and tighten any setscrew that secures the assembly). Then take the body of the new socket and connect the wires to the terminal screws on each side as shown. Make sure you wrap the wires clockwise around each screw before tightening securely.

Next, slide the fiber insulating liner down over the socket body, then slide the upper half of the metal shell over this and snap the two parts of the socket together by pressing down into the previously mounted cap.

easy job, it even offers you the chance to upgrade the lamp by replacing its conventional socket with a socket that takes three-way bulbs or, for maximum control of light, a socket with a built-in dimmer with which you can adjust the light from full brightness to all the way off just by turning a built-in rotary switch. These dimmer sockets fit all standard lamp bases and require no rewiring of any kind.

After pulling the plug out of the wall, remove the lamp shade and the harp that supports it, then take out the bulb. Pull the socket apart by pressing with your thumb just above the cap on the side where the

REWIRING THE LAMP WITH NEW CORD

While you are replacing the lamp's socket, it is also a good idea to check the lamp cord itself to see if it is cracked or dried out or if the insulation has been damaged or cut in any way. If any such conditions exist, this is a good time—while you have the lamp apart for replacing its socket—to replace the whole cord.

The lamp cord should run in one continuous length from socket to wall plug, so rather than trying to splice in a short section you should play it safe and replace the whole length of wire—even if only one section looks worn. You start by removing the lamp socket as just described. Then remove the felt or other material covering the base so that you can see up inside the lamp base. Very often there will be a knot tied in the cord inside the base, and this will have to be untied before you can pull out the cord.

After disconnecting the wires from the lamp socket, tie a length of short string to the upper end of the lamp cord, then pull the lamp cord out from the bottom (through the base). The string will be pulled along with it. As soon as the end of the wire emerges, untie it from the string, but leave the string in place inside the lamp. Now you can tie the new lamp cord to the bottom end of the string so that by pulling the string back up you will draw the new cord up through the lamp and socket cap. You finish the job by adding a new wall plug to the other end of the new wire.

REPAIRING FLUORESCENT LIGHTS

A fluorescent lamp gives off much more light than an incandescent bulb of the same wattage, and it will last anywhere from four to five times as long. Although it is true that a fluorescent lamp costs more initially, in the long run it will almost always cost less—both to replace and to operate.

Once limited almost entirely to kitchens, bathrooms, utility rooms, and similar areas, fluorescent lighting is now much more widely used in homes and apartments—primarily since the introduction of fluorescent lamps that come in a variety of pleasant shades (warm white, daylight white, living white, and so on)

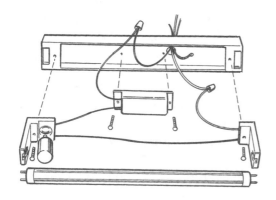

Wiring for fluorescent lamp with starter.

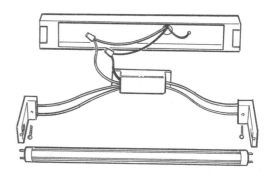

Wiring for rapid-start fluorescent lamp that has no starter.

instead of only in the original "cool white" that many feel is too cold and commercial looking for use in the home. These new lamps give off a "warmer" light that blends in better with incandescent lighting and is also more comfortable to live with.

Although the life of a fluorescent lamp is determined to some extent by how many hours it is in use, its life is determined primarily by how frequently it is turned on and off. Fluorescents use the most current when they are first turned on—a small filament on the inside heats up and then serves to vaporize the gas on the inside. This gas becomes an excellent conductor of electricity so that a short surge of high-voltage current flows through the tube—causing the phosphorescent coating on the inside to glow. At this stage light is being given off, but comparatively little power is actually being consumed. That, plus the fact that tube life is shortened by frequent turning on and off, is why most experts believe that it is best not to turn off fluorescent lights when leaving a room for a short period.

Fluorescent lights that are used in homes and apartments will generally fall into one of two categories: those that have a separate starter and the rapid-start type that has no separate starter. As its name implies, a rapid-start fluorescent is one that comes on almost instantly when the switch is activated. The separate-starter types do not come on immediately; when the switch is turned on, these lights often blink once or twice and then there is a slight delay before the light stays on steadily. The lamps used in either type of fluorescent fixture all have two pin connectors at each end of the tube. When the lamp is installed these pins snap into special sockets at each end of the fixture.

Both types of fluorescent fixture also have a built-in ballast on the inside—a special type of transformer that is located inside the base of the fixture.

The rapid-start type of fixture is by far the most popular these days, although many of the older starter types are still in use. As a rule, both types of fluorescent are relatively trouble free and usually fairly simple to repair if and when a problem does develop. The illustrations on page 170 show how typical fluorescent fixtures of each type are wired and assembled.

Here are the most common problems liable to crop up with fluorescent lighting fixtures in the home, along with the steps you can take to correct them:

Light flickers and blinks continuously. This is fairly common with brand-new tubes, but it should not occur after the tube has been on for an hour or two. It can also be a frequent problem with cold tubes—tubes that are in an unheated or colder-than-average room (below about 50 degrees). Special tubes are available for low-temperature installations.

The most frequent cause of flickering is a poor connection at the sockets. Take out the tube by giving it a quarter turn and pulling straight down, then wipe the pins clean at each end and replace the tube, making sure it is firmly seated this time—line up the pins with the slot in the sockets, then push in firmly and give it a quarter turn to seat it solidly. If the tube still flickers, try twisting back and forth slightly. If that doesn't work, replace with a new tube (or one from another fixture that is not flickering).

If none of these measures solves the problem, your next alternative is to replace the starter, a small can-shaped device that fits into a special socket under one end of the tube or lamp. You remove it by pressing it in and giving it a quarter turn counterclockwise. Then install the new one by pressing it in and turning clockwise a quarter turn. Starters come in sizes to match the tubes used, so make sure your replacement is of matching size (a 40-watt starter for a 40-watt tube, and so on).

Tube won't light at all. Check the obvious things that might affect power to the fixture—the fuse on that circuit and the switch that controls the fixture or circuit. If the ends of the tube are blackened, then the tube is probably worn out and needs replacing. Otherwise, take out the tube and check the pins to see if any are broken or if the socket seems damaged.

If all seems well here, then likely the starter needs replacing. Take it out and try a new one (or one that you know is good from another fixture of the same size).

If the fixture is the rapid-start type that does not have a starter, wipe the tube clean with a dry cloth—dirt on the outside of the tube can interfere with proper starting. If that doesn't do it, chances are that the ballast inside the fixture has gone bad and needs to be replaced.

To get at the ballast you have to take out the tubes, then take the cover off the housing. Ballasts are secured with two small screws or bolts and are connected up with solderless wire nuts or similar connectors. When you are shopping for a new ballast it is a good idea to take the old one with you to make certain you get the right model for replacement.

Ends of tubes are discolored. A brown discoloration is fairly normal as the tube ages, but if it starts to turn very dark or black, you will know that the tube is nearing the end of its life and is no longer working efficiently. If only one end of the tube turns black, take it out and turn it over (reverse its ends) before replacing it. If the darkening develops while the tube is still relatively new, then the starter is defective and should be replaced.

Fixture hums. This is almost always a problem with the ballast. Either it is the wrong type, or it is not properly secured and tends to vibrate slightly when current flows through it. In some cases the hum may be due to a defective ballast that is starting to go. First, try tightening the mounting screws and checking all electrical connections to make sure they are tight, and if this doesn't help you will have to replace the ballast. Be sure to ask for one of the special low-noise types.

Tube glows at the ends only. First, try a new tube. If this doesn't work, the trouble is probably your starter. If the fixture is the rapid-start type, it could be the ballast.

All of the above problems apply equally to circular fluorescents and those with straight tubes. Like the straight-line fixtures, circular fluorescents are available in both rapid-start (no separate starter) and regular types (with replaceable starter). Service them just as you would a straight fixture; the only difference is that circular fixtures have a single socket with a four-prong plug on the tube instead of two sockets with two pins at each end.

FIXING DOORBELLS AND CHIMES

Because doorbells and chimes operate on low voltage—anywhere from 10 to 24 volts in most cases—this is one type of electrical repair that any do-it-yourselfer can tackle safely without fear of getting a shock.

The low voltage used to operate these signaling devices comes from a transformer connected to the house current, a device that reduces or "steps down" the voltage to the lower amounts required. This transformer is usually mounted on one of the electrical outlet boxes in the basement or utility room, or it may be on the outside of the fuse box in the basement. It has two wires that are connected to the 120-volt house current inside the metal junction box on which it is mounted, so you really can't get at them without opening that box.

The other exposed side of the transformer has two terminals that deliver the lower voltage needed to operate the bell or chime. You can easily connect wires to these more accessible terminals—the light-gauge wires that are normally used in circuits of this kind. Some transformers are made with multiple taps to take off different voltages—for example, 10 volts if that is all your bell requires, 20 volts if you have a chime that needs greater power.

To intelligently troubleshoot a doorbell or chime that does not ring, you should know something about how the system is wired. The accompanying illustrations show the most common installations, from a simple one-button system such as would be typical of an apartment, to the more common two-door installations with a second button at the back or side door. Two buttons usually mean that the chime gives a different signal for the back door than for

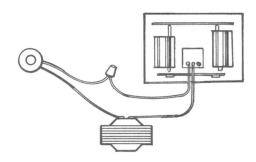

Single-button doorbell wiring system with one chime.

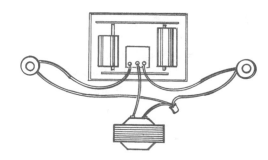

Two-button doorbell wiring system (front door and rear door) with one- or two-tone chime.

the front door or indicates a bell-buzzer combination that sounds a bell for the front door and a buzzer for the back or side door.

TEST THE BUTTON FIRST

Generally, when a doorbell or chime fails to ring each time the button on the outside is pushed, or if it operates only spasmodically, the most likely source of the trouble is the push button itself. Being constantly exposed to the weather, it tends to corrode and fail quicker than any other part of the system.

To test for this, unscrew the push button from its position on the door frame or, if it is set into a hole in the frame, pry it out of its recess. Check the terminals on the back or side to see if the wires leading to it are loose or broken. If so, disconnect the wires, clean off the wire ends and terminal screws by scraping with a pocket knife, then reconnect the wires to the terminal screws and try again.

If this doesn't help, or if the wires seem sound, your next step is to "short out" the switch to see if the bell rings—in other words, connect the wires as though there were no switch. The simplest way to do this is to press a screwdriver blade or similar metal object across the two terminals. If this is awkward to manage, just disconnect the two wires and rub them against each other for a moment. This should make the bell or chime ring. If it does, then you know that the push button is defective. Buy a new button and install it in place of the old one.

CHECK THE POWER SUPPLY NEXT

If shorting out the button or touching the wires together doesn't give you a ring (or a chime signal), you know that something else is wrong, most likely the power supply. First, check the fuse or circuit breaker controlling the transformer's circuit to see if it has blown.

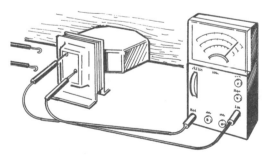

Using small voltmeter to test doorbell transformer.

If it is okay, indicating that power is getting to the transformer, then the next thing to check is whether power is coming *out* of the transformer—in other words, that the transformer is still working (they normally last for years, but they can fail).

The simplest way to check the transformer is with a small voltmeter or continuity tester capable of reading low voltages. If you don't have one of these, there is another simple method you can use. Bare each end of a short piece of copper wire, then press one end of the wire firmly against one of the exposed terminal screws on the transformer while you rub the other bare end across the terminal screw. This should be done in dim light while watching closely. You should see some small sparks where the wire rubs across the screw—if the transformer is working. This may not be quite as sure a method as testing with a voltmeter, or with a small 12-volt test lamp wired to a small socket, but it does show if the transformer is delivering power.

If the transformer is not working, it will have to be replaced with a new one. To do this, first shut off all power to that circuit, then open the junction box on which the transformer is mounted so that you can reach the wires on the inside. If it is mounted directly onto the fuse box, you will have to remove the front panel on the box—first making sure to shut off all power by pulling the main fuse.

The transformer is normally mounted with two bolts that can be reached from inside the box after the cover has been removed. The black and white wires coming from the transformer will be connected to matching black and white wires by means of solderless connectors or wire nuts. Untwist these and disconnect the transformer, then loosen the screws that hold it in place and remove the unit. Make sure the new one is the proper size for your particular system (some chimes require larger transformers than others, so if in doubt check the label on your unit), mount it in place, and connect up in the same way.

SOMETIMES IT'S THE BELL OR CHIME

When the trouble is not the transformer or the push button on the outside, the next thing to check is the actual doorbell or chime. Take off the cover to expose the terminal board or connecting screws and see if all connections are still tight. If so, inspect the exposed mechanism to see if the clapper or any other moving parts are clogged with dust or lint. Use a soft brush to clean them, or blow out the dust. Chimes have small plastic rods that slide up and down (or in and out) to strike the metal bars that make the sound, so check also to see whether these rods are moving freely. Remove dust and lint with a small brush or by blowing it out, but do not use oil or other lubricant.

If you find nothing wrong here and can't decide whether the trouble is in the bell or chime itself or in part of the wiring that connects it to the transformer or push button, you should test the bell or chime by running a pair of wires directly to it from the transformer terminals. Take off the unit, carry it down to the transformer, and run wires directly between the two, one from a transformer terminal screw to the bell terminal marked "TRANS" or "Transformer" and the other from the other transformer terminal directly to the terminal on the bell (or chime) where one of the push-button wires normally goes—

marked "Front" or "Rear." This completes the circuit just as though one of the buttons were being pushed. If the bell or chime still fails to ring, and you have already tested the transformer, you know the unit is defective and has to be replaced.

If all these tests indicate that the bell or chime, the transformer, and the push button are all okay, then the problem is obviously in the hidden wiring. Either there is a break somewhere or one of the connections where wires were spliced together has come loose.

Finding this spot may be tricky, even impossible, if the wires are mostly buried in walls and floors. Usually it is simpler and quicker just to run all new wiring from the transformer to the chimes and perhaps also to the push buttons. Use the type sold for low-voltage doorbell circuits.

ADDING AN EXTRA BELL OR CHIME

In homes that have a centrally located unit, it is sometimes difficult to hear the doorbell from more remote parts of the house such as a garage or basement—particularly if noise-making tools or appliances are in use. Adding an extra bell or chime to the circuit that rings along with the central unit often solves this problem.

This is not an especially difficult wiring job, since you are working with low-voltage wires. Wires can be routed with safety anywhere that is convenient. In many cases you don't even have to snake them through walls or floors—you may be able to go through closets or even fasten them along the base of the wall.

There is one electrical problem you may encounter, though: the original transformer may not be large enough to carry

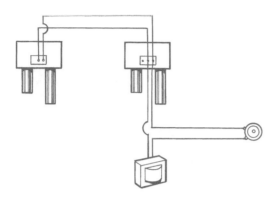

Wiring extra chime or bell to existing system involves running wires from new chime to old one.

point to the existing bell or chime unit so that the two bells (or chime and bell) work in parallel. This means that when either of the door buttons is pressed, the new bell or chime will ring along with the old one.

In a typical installation that includes two door buttons (front and back, or front and side), there will be three wires going to your present chime—one from the front button, one from the back door button, and one from the transformer (see illustration). In that case you will need three wires going from your new unit to the old one (or a single length of three-conductor wire) in order to connect each of the terminals on the new bell or chime. With three-conductor wire or cable, each wire is of a different color, so you cannot mix up the three. If you have to use separate lengths of single-conductor wire, try to get them of different colors.

When the job is done, both bells or chime units should ring at the same time. If they sound weak or barely hum, then the transformer is overloaded and a larger one is needed to supply the additional power for activating both units simultaneously.

the additional load of a second bell, buzzer, or chime. If in doubt about this, ask your dealer—tell him the size of the present transformer and the size of the unit it is now operating. He should be able to tell you if the same transformer can carry the additional load. If the transformer is too small, you will have to replace it with a larger one.

After deciding where the new bell or chime will go, you run wires from that

WIRING FOR TELEPHONES AND EXTENSIONS

Ever since it became legal to install your own telephones and extension phones back in the early 1980s, adding wires for one or more additional extensions has become almost standard practice for most apartment dwellers and condominium owners because of the high price phone companies charge for such a service. Fortunately the job is relatively simple and completely safe for the do-it-yourselfer to tackle because only low voltages are involved; the possibilities of getting a

serious shock—or of creating any kind of safety hazard—are almost nil.

The telephone company always supplies and installs the wiring that connects the outside phone lines with the phone wires inside your home or apartment. The phone company wiring ends at a special terminal or junction box inside your dwelling, technically referred to as a network interface. Some older homes and apartments do not have a special network interface, so the first telephone jack or

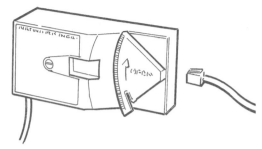

Network interface marks terminal point at which telephone company's wiring (and responsibility) ends. Your internal wiring plugs into the side as shown.

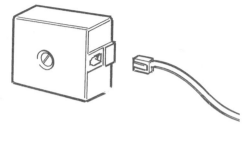

Modular telephone jack mounts on wall or baseboard.

junction box inside the home that is connected to the company's outside phone line becomes the equivalent of a network interface—otherwise referred to as the demarcation point between your wiring and that of the telephone company.

This network interface or demarcation point is not only the junction terminal where their wiring ends—it is also the point at which the telephone company's responsibility for maintenance and repair ends. Any problems that develop inside your apartment or condominium are your responsibility, not theirs. If a repair is required, you can request that the phone company come in and make the necessary repairs, but you will be billed for this work separately.

Inside your apartment or condominium, and past the network interface or demarcation point, you can add as much additional wiring or as many extension phones as you wish, but you must use equipment that meets the FCC's requirements, and all wiring must conform to local building regulations, as well as to the rules and regulations established by your state and local phone company. There is also a practical limit to the number of additional phones you can add to one line. Each additional phone cuts down on the volume and clarity of the signal; six or seven extension phones are usually considered the maximum. After that, service deteriorates sharply.

All telephone installations and all telephone equipment now being sold uses standard modular jacks and connectors. This means that you can plug any modular telephone cord into any modular wall jack, regardless of brand.

If your apartment or condominium still has the older-style four-prong wall jacks that were widely used years ago before modular jacks became standard, you can convert these in either one of two ways:

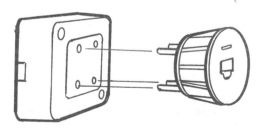

Special plug-in adapter can be used to convert old-style four-prong wall jacks to accept modular-style plugs.

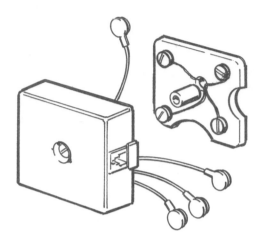

Easy-to-install modular converter changes old-style permanently wired terminal block to newer modular style.

you can buy a special plug-in adapter that will plug into the old wall jack and give you a modular receptacle to accept a standard modular phone cord; or you can install one of the modular jack conversion units that are sold for just this purpose in most hardware stores, home centers, and telephone stores. These come with simple illustrated instructions that anyone can follow and take only a few minutes to put in.

If, on the other hand, your phone is permanently wired to an old-style, square junction block or terminal block that is mounted on the baseboard or wall, then you need a different type of modular jack converter, as illustrated (these converters are available from most telephone companies and from local stores that sell telephones and supplies). Installation is simple. Take the cover off the old terminal block and discard it. Then connect the color-coded wires from the conversion unit to the matching color-coded screws

on the old terminal block (if the screws are not colored, they will be marked Y for yellow, B for black, G for green, and R for red). On some conversion units the connecting wires will end in colored caps that snap on over the old terminal screws, on others the wires will end in spade fittings that fit under the terminal screws of the terminal block.

If you find it desirable to plug more than one telephone into a single wall-mounted modular phone jack, or if you have to plug in an answering machine, fax machine, or other piece of equipment in addition to a telephone, all you have to do is buy a special duplex jack adapter similar to the one illustrated. This duplex plug has a male fitting at one end that snaps into the existing wall jack, while two female receptacles on the other side allow you to plug in two separate phone cords.

In most cases, however, when you want to add an extra telephone it will be in a different location or in another room, so you will want to extend the existing wiring and then install another modular jack at that point so that your phone (or phones) can be plugged in at either or both of these locations. To accomplish this you should first install a special wire junction box (sometimes called an entrance bridge) near the network interface. These wire

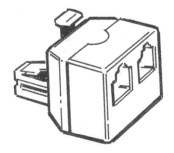

Duplex jack adapter enables you to plug two phone cords into a single wall outlet.

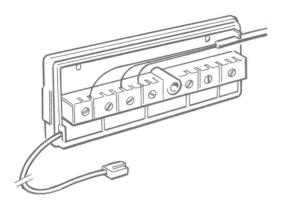

Junction box has four sets of terminals for running wires to four different locations.

junction boxes come with a short cable attached that is fitted with a modular plug at the far end. This enables you to plug into the network interface or into any jack, including the one that the phone company is using as a network interface.

This junction box usually has four sets of terminals on the inside, so that you can run up to four different cables from this box to four different telephone locations in various rooms. The terminals are color-coded to match the special four-conductor cable that is sold for telephone wiring (the colors on the four conductors or wires match those on the terminal screws). In most cases only two of the four color-coded wires in the cable are actually used to carry the signal and the bell-ringing current, but it's always best to connect up all four wires to their matching terminals in order to keep color coding constant throughout the system. (The other two wires are needed in case there is more than one line coming in, and they are sometimes used to replace the existing pair in an emergency when one of the original wires has been damaged or broken at

some inaccessible location). You will find that the job of stripping the thin wires of insulation will be a lot easier if you buy one of the special stripping tools that are sold for this purpose in most phone stores, hardware stores, and home centers.

If all that sounds too complicated, you can add an extension or additional modular jack to your existing wiring simply by plugging in a long phone cord with a modular jack at each end. You then extend that cord to where you want the new phone located. Long cords of this type are sold already made up in various lengths (with a modular plug at each end), or you can make up your own cord by buying the four-conductor cable separately and then adding plugs to each end yourself.

If you add a new extension jack in this manner, there will obviously be no provision for using a phone at the original location (the extension cable will be plugged into the jack). You can get around this in one of two ways:

1. You can buy a duplex plug as previously described, then plug it into the existing jack, and now you have jacks for both the extension cord and the phone cord.

2. You can strip the insulation off the extension cord and then connect the four color-corded conductors directly to the matching colored terminal screws inside the existing jack (thus leaving its opening free for plugging in your original phone). In order to use this second method, your system must already have a network interface or entrance bridge where the phone company's wiring terminates inside your dwelling.

As with any electrical wiring, when you run telephone wires from one location to another, do not run the wires under car-

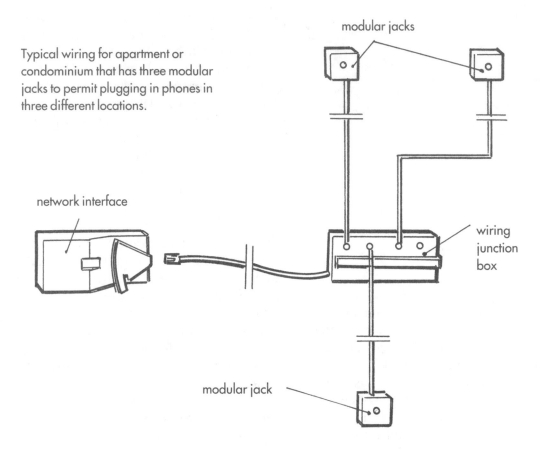

Typical wiring for apartment or condominium that has three modular jacks to permit plugging in phones in three different locations.

modular jacks

network interface

wiring junction box

modular jack

pets or where they can be stepped on. Also, avoid running the phone wires through areas that are exposed to dampness, and never fish telephone wires through a conduit or pipe that carries other electrical wiring. In fact, try to avoid running them even close to other electrical wiring (this could cause static or interference in the line). Wherever possible try to run the wires inside the walls or behind baseboards or other trim so they will be protected from damage, and try to run a single length of cable from one location to another to avoid splicing. If a cable must be spliced or joined, do this inside a junction box that will be accessible later on, so that the connections can be examined and tested if a problem does develop.

Plumbing Repairs and Maintenance

Like your electrical system, the plumbing system in your home must conform to certain regulations and code restrictions that have been established to protect the health and safety of all occupants in your dwelling, and to prevent contamination of the water supply in your community.

Your home plumbing system actually consists of two completely separate systems—the supply pipes that bring water from your municipal water lines to the faucets and water-using appliances inside the home, and the drain and waste pipes that carry away dirty water and sewage. (The drain-and-waste system also includes a vent system for noxious gases, which is more fully described in the pages that follow.)

The supply pipes that bring hot and cold water to the fixtures are relatively small in diameter—usually either ⅜ inch or ½ inch—because supply water is always under pressure, although the main supply line that brings water into the building is often larger, sometimes ¾ inch in diameter. The main line branches off into the smaller-diameter pipes that go to the individual fixtures and appliances. Although not always required by local codes, most well-planned installations will have a shut-off valve installed in the supply pipe under each sink or fixture—one valve for the hot water supply and one for the cold water. That way the water can be shut off quickly in an emergency or when repairs are needed without having to shut off the water going to other parts of the home.

Drain and waste pipes are always larger in diameter than supply pipes—usually anywhere from 1 inch to 3 inches in diame-

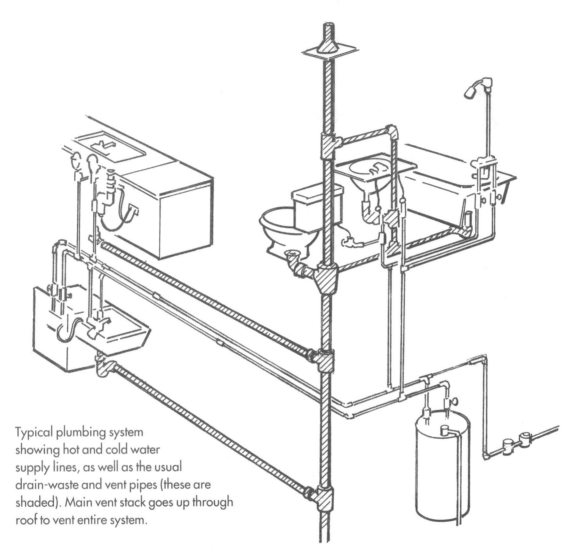

Typical plumbing system showing hot and cold water supply lines, as well as the usual drain-waste and vent pipes (these are shaded). Main vent stack goes up through roof to vent entire system.

ter—and the main vent stack that goes up through the roof is often 4 inches in diameter.

There are two reasons waste and drain pipes are larger: first, some drain lines will have to carry away solid as well as liquid wastes, and second, waste and drain pipes are never under pressure, so there is nothing to actually force the water through them. They depend entirely on gravity to keep the waste water flowing until it reaches the outside sewer or disposal site.

That is why all drain and waste lines *must slope downward.*

All plumbing codes require the installation of a trap in the drain line under each sink, tub, toilet, and so forth. This may be either an S trap or P trap, depending on whether the drainpipe goes through the floor or the wall. Each consists of a U-shaped section of waste pipe in the drainage line whose function is to always retain some water in the lowest part of the loop. The water creates an airtight seal that keeps sewer odors and gases from escaping up through the drain opening, as well as keeping out insects and small rodents.

Technically speaking, the entire drain-and-waste system is more accurately called the drain-waste-vent system (often referred to as the DWV system). That's because every drain-and-waste system also includes a vent system—a series of pipes that allows air to enter the system and also allows noxious sewer gases and odors to escape harmlessly to the outside. This venting is necessary to prevent a potentially harmful buildup of gases inside the pipes, as well as to help ensure smoother and more rapid drainage of the waste pipes.

All vent pipes eventually connect up with a large vertical vent pipe (called the main soil stack or main vent) that runs from the underground sewer line up through the roof of the house, as shown on page 182. Most vent pipes carry only air, but in a so-called wet vent system some vent pipes will also serve as drainage pipes. They must then be large enough in diameter to allow waste water to flow out in one direction, while allowing air to enter the system from the other direction.

In addition to venting sewer gases and odors to the outside, the DWV system also serves two other very important functions:

1. If there were no vent pipes or venting system (or if the vent pipes were clogged, as sometimes happens), the outflow of waste water could create a partial vacuum that could actually siphon water out of the traps under the various sinks, tubs, or other fixtures throughout the home, thus allowing sewer gases and noxious odors to enter through the drain openings.

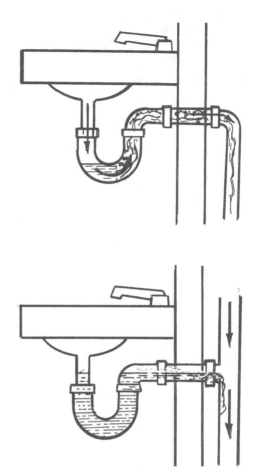

If drain had no vent pipe water running out into the drain, this could create a siphon action that might draw the water out of the trap under the sink (top). Vented pipe allows air to enter and break siphon so trap remains always full of water (bottom).

2. As mentioned previously, the vent system is designed to let air into the drainage system as the waste water flows out in order to help ensure a smooth and rapid flow at all times. If air could not enter the system as the waste water flowed out, the water would tend to make "gurgling" or "glug-glug" sounds like the kind often heard when liquid is being poured out of a narrow-neck bottle.

WHAT YOU SHOULD KNOW ABOUT PIPES AND FITTINGS

Depending on the age of your building, the water supply pipes in your condominium or apartment may be made of galvanized steel, brass, copper, or plastic. The pipes used in the DWV system may be copper, galvanized steel, cast iron, or plastic. It's not unusual to find several different types of pipe in use in either system—sometimes because of alterations or additions that were made after the original building was completed and sometimes because even in the newest buildings it is common practice to use more than one type of pipe in different parts of the plumbing system.

If you have to make any repairs, replacements, or additions to your plumbing—for example, if you are planning to install a new fixture or appliance, or if you have to replace some defective pipes—you should check with the plumbing inspector in your local building department to determine what type of pipe is acceptable for that particular application. When given a choice, the do-it-yourselfer is almost always better off using an approved type of plastic pipe—it is lighter and easier to work with and much simpler to assemble and install.

THREADED PIPE AND FITTINGS

Threaded pipe may be made of iron, galvanized steel, or brass. Galvanized pipe is by far the type most commonly encountered, especially in homes built prior to the 1950s when it was still widely used for water supply lines and waste lines. Brass pipe does not rust and lasts much longer than steel pipe, but it costs a great deal more than galvanized pipe and is seldom if ever used in

home plumbing systems anymore. Copper pipe and tubing and, more recently, plastic pipe and tubing have now largely replaced threaded pipe in most new homes built during the past couple of decades because they are lighter in weight, less bulky, and generally much quicker and easier to work with and install.

Threaded pipe is assembled with bulky threaded fittings. This means that the end of each piece of pipe must also be threaded, using expensive threading dies and other special tools. That, plus the fact that working with threaded pipe calls for careful measuring and fitting and a fair amount of experience, is why most do-it-yourselfers should avoid working with threaded pipe if possible. You can buy lengths of pipe that are already threaded from many plumbing outlets, as well as matching threaded fittings, and, if such pieces fit, assembling the pipe and fittings is relatively simple. All you have to do is thread the fittings onto the pipe and then tighten the joint firmly with a couple of pipe wrenches. Before you thread the fittings onto the pipe, make sure you apply a suitable pipe compound or Teflon tape over the threads to ensure against leaks.

Wherever possible, it is much easier, cheaper, and more foolproof to use copper or plastic pipe instead of threaded pipe when making repairs—assuming, that is, that your local codes permit it.

Fortunately there are all kinds of adapters and transition fittings available that enable you to connect threaded steel or brass pipe to copper or plastic pipe. In other words, if you have to replace a defective section of threaded pipe, you can cut out or remove the damaged section and then replace it with a length of plastic or copper pipe, instead of having to put in another length of threaded pipe. Likewise, if you are installing a new appliance and have to connect new pipes to existing threaded pipes, you can use transition fittings or adapters to accomplish the connection.

COPPER PIPE AND TUBING

Copper pipe and tubing, which has been widely used for water supply lines since the late 1950s, is assembled with fittings that require no threading, making it much simpler to cut, fit, and install. Since copper pipe is much smoother than steel pipe on the inside, it offers much less resistance to the flow of water, so that smaller sizes can be used without affecting the pressure or the quantity of water delivered by that pipe.

Two types of copper pipe are used in home water supply systems: rigid or hard copper pipe that cannot be bent and requires an elbow or other fitting wherever the pipe must turn a corner or go around an obstruction; and flexible pipe (often referred to as tubing) that can be

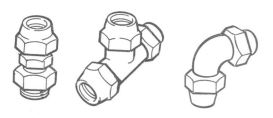

Compression fittings are available in a wide range of sizes, styles, and configurations.

bent around corners and obstructions so that fewer fittings are required. The decision whether to use rigid or flexible pipe on a particular job will usually depend on appearance and ease of installation. As a rule, flexible tubing is easier and quicker to install, but rigid pipe looks neater where appearance is important, and it is stronger, so that on long runs less supports will be needed for the pipe.

Copper pipe or tubing can be cut to length with an ordinary hacksaw, but the neatest, quickest, and most efficient way to cut this material is with a pipe cutter or tubing cutter similar to the one shown—especially when you have to cut a length of pipe that is already in place. Using a pipe cutter also ensures a square cut, important for a good joint when assembling fittings. This tool has one adjustable jaw that permits clamping it around the outside of the pipe, with a sharp steel cutting wheel that digs in and cuts the pipe or tubing as you revolve the cutter around the pipe. After completing each full revolution, you tighten the handle on the cutting tool about half a turn to make the cutting wheel dig in a little deeper on the next turn—until this wheel actually cuts all the way through and snaps the pipe in two. A small triangular file or pipe reamer (often attached to the cutter) is then used to

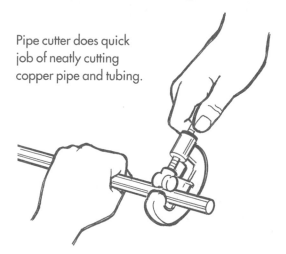

Pipe cutter does quick job of neatly cutting copper pipe and tubing.

remove any burrs or rims left on the inside of the pipe.

Three types of fittings are used with copper pipe and tubing: soldered fittings (usually referred to as "sweat" fittings because the soldering technique is known as sweat soldering), compression fittings, and flare fittings. The fittings are available in sizes to fit all common pipe sizes, as well as in a full range of styles or types—T's, elbows, couplings, valves, and so on.

In addition, there are adapters and transition fittings available that make it possible to connect one type of pipe with another, as well as reducers for linking different sizes of pipe or tubing. There are also transition fittings that allow you to go from one type of fitting to another—for example, from soldered fittings to compression fittings—as well as going from copper to plastic pipe or from hard copper pipe to soft copper tubing.

Soldered fittings are by far the most popular with professional plumbers, but most do-it-yourselfers will find that compression fittings are easier to use and install. These fittings require no soldering, so you don't need a torch, and they require no previous experience to assemble properly. They have threaded collars or nuts that slip on over the pipe or tubing first, with a tapered brass compression ring that fits inside this collar, as illustrated.

To assemble a joint with one of these fittings, you first slide the threaded collar or nut over the tubing with the open or threaded side facing the end of the pipe. Now slide the tapered brass compression ring on over the tubing, then push the end of the tubing firmly into the body of the fitting. Slide the threaded collar down over the compression ring, forcing it against the end of the fitting, and thread the collar

Tapered compression ring slides around outside of tubing and fits inside threaded collar that tightens down over it.

onto the outside of the fitting (as shown). Tighten securely with a wrench (actually two wrenches will be needed—one to tighten the collar and one to hold the nut on the outside of the fitting while the collar is being tightened).

Compression fittings do cost considerably more than "sweat" fittings—one of the reasons they are seldom used by professional contractors—but for the do-it-yourself apartment dweller or condominium owner who needs only two or three of these fittings for a typical repair job around the home, the extra cost is well worth it. This is especially true if you don't have a torch or if you are worried about using a torch next to a wood beam or other flammable material.

Another advantage of compression fittings is that they can be taken apart quickly and then reassembled when necessary—often handy when future repairs or replacements are needed. And for those jobs where the use of a torch (for soldering) would be dangerous or very impractical, compression fittings may actually be the only safe solution.

SOLDERING COPPER PIPE AND FITTINGS

Although good sweat soldering does take a little practice, it is really not a difficult technique to master. The only special tool required is a portable propane torch of the type that is widely available in all hardware stores and home centers.

Before doing any soldering on existing plumbing lines, make sure the water has been shut off and the pipes drained completely. If you will be soldering a valve in place, or if you will be using the torch near an existing valve, take the valve apart and remove the stem and the packing before you start; otherwise you may damage the valve mechanism with the heat from the torch. Take every precaution against fire: make sure the flame is directed away from wood beams or other flammable surfaces, and keep a fire extinguisher or bucket of water handy—just in case.

After cutting the pipe or tubing to length, remove any burrs left on the inside of the pipe, then clean off the outside of the pipe where it will slide into the fitting. Use fine steel wool or emery cloth and polish the pipe for the last inch or so until the metal is bright and shiny. After polishing do not touch the clean metal with your fingers because skin oils can contaminate the surface and could interfere with a proper solder bond.

Now clean the inside of the fitting in the same way. Then apply a light coating of paste flux (rosin-core soldering flux) to the inside of the fitting and to the cleaned section of the pipe. Slide the fitting onto the end of the pipe and turn it back and forth once to distribute the flux uniformly, then line it up in its final position for soldering. As a rule, when there are a number of fittings and various lengths of pipe to be soldered, the surest procedure is to cut and fit all pieces first—without applying flux—to be certain everything fits, then take the whole thing apart and apply flux to each joint in preparation for the actual soldering.

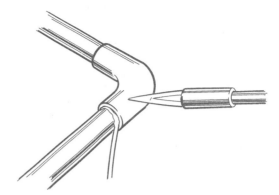

When soldering copper pipe fittings, direct flame of torch at thickest part of fitting, never directly at the solder.

Light the torch and direct its flame on the thickest part of the fitting, not on the pipe. In all sweat soldering you should direct the flame to the heaviest mass (the fitting), so that the other parts are heated by conduction. Have the solder ready in your other hand with a short bend in the end, but keep it out of the flame until the metal is hot enough to melt the solder instantly. Test for this after about 20 or 30 seconds by touching the end of the solder to the pipe just where it enters the fitting— but keep it out of the flame. The idea is to melt the solder by touching it to the heated metal, *not* holding it in the torch flame.

When the pipe is so hot that it melts the solder on contact, start feeding solder into the joint while moving it slowly and steadily around the perimeter of the pipe. Keep the flame aimed at the heavy part of the fitting, not at the pipe. The solder should melt and be sucked into the joint (even if it is vertical) by capillary action. As the joint fills, a slight bead will form around the outside. When this bead of solder is continuous all the way around, take away both flame and solder. Immediately wipe off excess solder with a heavy cloth while the metal is still hot and the solder is still liquid.

If you have more than one joint to solder on the same fitting—both sides of an elbow or the three legs on a T fitting—get all of them ready at the same time. In making multiple joints of this kind, you must direct the flame at the fitting, not at any of the pipes that connect to it. Remember— the general rule in all sweat soldering is to direct the flame at the heaviest mass.

Sometimes in the course of making repairs or additions, you will have to add to an existing fitting or valve that has a soldered joint on one side. To make sure the heat will not loosen up the old soldered joint, wrap the old joint with a thick layer of wet cloth and take extra pains to direct your flame away from this area. If the cloth starts to dry out or scorch, rewet it immediately. Use the highest flame so that the new joint is heated as quickly as possible.

WORKING WITH PLASTIC PIPE AND FITTINGS

When plastic pipe was first introduced for home use, it was used primarily for drain-waste-vent (DWV) installations, as well as for water lines that did not carry potable water—lawn sprinkler systems, fire sprinklers, and the like. However, most local and national codes now accept plastic pipe for use in hot and cold water supply lines, as well as for DWV installations. In fact, industry estimates indicate that the vast majority of new residential plumbing installations now use more plastic pipe than metal pipe. It's not hard to understand why. Plastic pipe

- costs less than copper or steel.
- is lighter in weight, making it much easier to handle and install.
- does not rust or corrode, so it will nor-

mally last longer than most metal pipe.

- takes less time to cut, fit, and install, so labor costs are lower (or do-it-yourselfers can get the job done faster).
- is work-intensive, requiring neither expensive tools nor specialized skills.
- is much smoother on the inside, so it does not build up scale and offers less friction to the flow of water (which means that a smaller size can often be used).
- offers better insulation against heat loss—an energy-saving benefit when used for hot water.
- is easily connected to copper or galvanized iron and to threaded pipe, as well as to soldered fittings or pipe, thanks to the wide variety of transition fittings and adapters available.

Although there are a number of different types of plastic pipe on the market, many of which are approved for use in home plumbing systems, some are suitable for use only as waste lines or for other parts of the DWV system inside the home, and some are for use only in large outside water supply lines or sewer lines.

For hot- and cold-water supply lines inside the home, two types are widely accepted by most plumbing codes: polybutylene (PB) and chlorinated polyvinyl chloride (CPVC). PB pipe is flexible, so it can be bent around corners and obstructions. CPVC pipe is rigid, so it requires the installation of a suitable fitting where the pipe must bend around a corner. As a rule, rigid pipe (CPVC) needs less support on long runs, and it looks neater where the pipe will be visible. Flexible PB pipe (often referred to as tubing) is easier to snake through walls and floors and is generally quicker to install because fewer fittings are required. Also, the fittings used with flexible tubing are simpler for most do-it-yourselfers to assemble since no cementing is required.

Rigid CPVC pipe can be cut to length with a regular hacksaw, crosscut saw, or tubing cutter equipped with a special cutting wheel that is made for use on plastic pipe. It is important that all cuts be perfectly square across the end and that burrs be removed from the inside as well as the outside of the pipe, using a sharp knife, file, or reamer.

The pipe is most often joined with fittings (elbows, T joints, and so on) that are secured with a cement formulated specifically for use with this type of plastic pipe. The fittings come in all standard configurations, styles, and sizes, but once a fitting has been cemented in place it is permanent; the only way to take that joint apart is to cut it apart.

Assembling CPVC pipe with these fittings is not really difficult, but it does require some care and attention to detail. Dry-fit every connection first without using any cement, and use a pencil or felt-tip pen to mark the outside of the fitting and the pipe to indicate proper alignment. Then take the joint apart and clean the outside of the pipe and the inside of each fitting carefully.

Use a clean cloth to wipe on the special primer that is sold for this purpose, coating the outside of the pipe and the inside of the fitting. Apply your cement immediately after this, smearing it liberally around the outside of the pipe and the inside of the fitting. Push the pipe into the fitting and give it about a quarter turn to spread the cement around and line up the fitting quickly. Then hold it in place for a few seconds while the cement sets. Don't try to shift or realign the parts after they

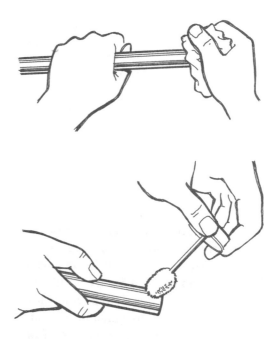

Before joining plastic pipe with cement, wipe on special primer (top), then spread cement on end of pipe with applicator (bottom).

are in place—this will ruin the joint, and it will no longer be watertight.

Flexible PB tubing can be cut to length with a sharp knife or with an inexpensive tubing cutter that is designed especially for use on plastic tubing. Just be sure that the cut is square and clean and that all burrs or ridges are removed from inside and outside the pipe.

The type of fitting most often used with PB tubing is a special type of threaded plastic compression fitting that is made by several different manufacturers and comes in all common tubing sizes. Similar to the metal compression fittings that are sold for use with copper pipe and tubing, these fittings also come in all standard configurations—elbows, T's, unions,

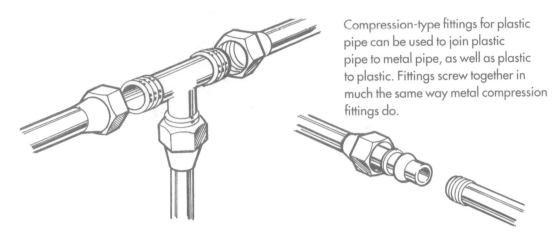

Compression-type fittings for plastic pipe can be used to join plastic pipe to metal pipe, as well as plastic to plastic. Fittings screw together in much the same way metal compression fittings do.

valves, and so on. In fact, many of these plastic compression fittings can also be used on CPVC pipe, as well as on PB pipe. Some are also suitable for use with copper tubing as well as plastic pipe and tubing, so these can serve as versatile transition fittings to connect different types of plastic pipe and tubing, as well as to connect plastic to copper and vice versa. Like the compression fittings that are used with copper tubing, these plastic fittings have a large threaded collar or retaining nut that screws onto the body of the fitting.

PLASTIC DRAIN AND WASTE PIPE

There are currently two different types of rigid plastic pipe for home drain and waste systems; acrylonitrile butadiene styrene (ABS) and polyvinyl chloride (PVC). Both come in all standard sizes—from 1½ inches

to 6 inches in diameter—and both are commonly joined with solvent-welded fittings, similar to those for CPVC pipe. The fittings, however, are designed with a more distinct shoulder inside that, when assembled, covers the edge of the pipe so that it does not project into the path of the flow. (Even a slight ridge will trap solid material that can eventually result in a partial blockage.)

There is a full range of elbows, offset connectors, T's, traps, and other fittings available for plastic drain pipes, and the techniques for joining them are much the same as those for joining CPVC pipe and fittings, described previously. Special T's or Y fittings are also available with removable cleanout plugs that you can twist off when major blockages or clogs must be removed. This type of pipe is also used for vents and for the stack pipes that go up through the roof.

SILENCING NOISY WATER LINES

Hammering or banging noises that occur every time a faucet is turned on or off, or every time an automatic valve inside a washing machine or similar appliance snaps shut, may signal the development of

a condition that could eventually result in breaking open some soldered joints in copper plumbing and in loosening the system's mounting straps. This could further endanger the condition of the water lines and even result in the bursting of some pipes or fittings.

The banging noise is usually evidence of a condition known as water hammer. Water is not compressible, and when it is moving in a rapid stream and is suddenly brought to a halt by a swiftly closing valve, it tends to "bang" loudly against the walls of the pipes and fittings. If the pipe is also loose, it may actually move and bang against adjacent structural members or other pipes, making the noise louder.

To prevent such problems, plumbing systems often have "antihammer" devices (also called water-hammer arrestors) installed in various places—near washing machines and kitchen or bathroom sinks, for example. You can buy these devices ready-made, or you can assemble them yourself out of short lengths of pipe (see accompanying illustrations). All work on the same principle: a chamber with a cushion of air trapped inside is spliced into the water line with a T fitting (as shown). When the water in that line comes to a sudden halt, it forces itself partway up into the air chamber. Since air is easily compressed, this acts as a "cushion" that absorbs much of the water's kinetic energy and thus keeps it from banging around inside the pipe.

The illustrations below and on page 192 show two types of antihammer devices: one that you can make yourself out of a straight length of pipe at least 18 inches high and at least as large in diameter as the water line, and another that you can buy in local plumbing supply outlets.

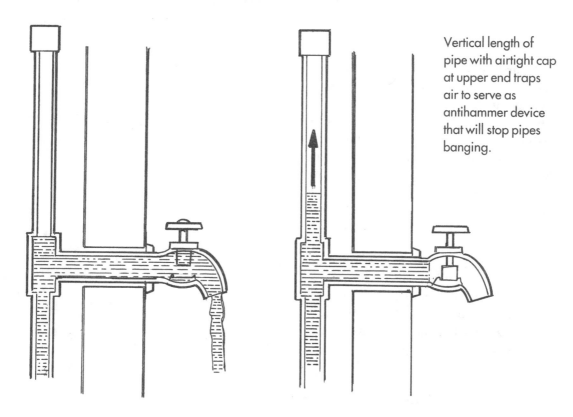

Vertical length of pipe with airtight cap at upper end traps air to serve as antihammer device that will stop pipes banging.

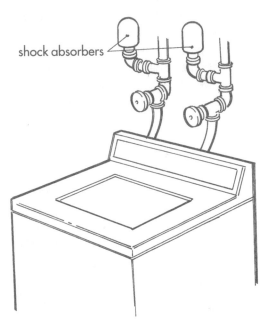

shock absorbers

Shock-absorbing antihammer devices can also be bought ready-made for quick installation behind washing machine and similar appliances.

The air chamber will once again be filled with air and should work as it originally did (if it doesn't, it is leaking air and should be replaced). In many homes these antihammer devices are required only near automatic washing machines; in other homes they may be required in several places—even near every faucet.

Another common reason pipes make banging, hammering, and squeaking noises is that the pipe does not have enough supporting straps or the pipe straps that are supposed to do the job are no longer tight. In places where the pipes are exposed and readily accessible—in a basement or crawl space, for example—you can usually spot the loose straps easily and then refasten them, or you can add more pipe straps where needed to keep the pipe (or pipes) from vibrating.

Regardless of which type you use, the device should be installed next to or behind the fixture or faucet that causes the hammering noise when opened or closed. Cut into the supply line and install a T fitting, then attach the antihammer device on top. If you assemble your own out of a length of brass or steel pipe, be sure you use compound on the threaded cap that closes off the top to ensure that it is airtight.

When the air chamber in an antihammer device becomes filled with water (even if it is absolutely airtight, some of the air in the chamber will be absorbed by the water over a period of time), it loses its effectiveness. To correct this condition, shut off the water supply to drain the pipes. Remove the air chamber and drain it, then replace it. Now turn the water back on.

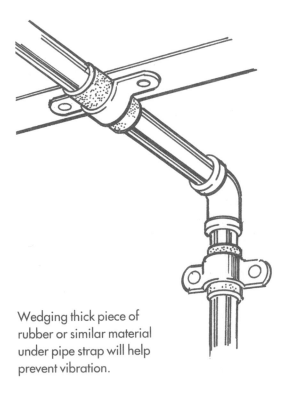

Wedging thick piece of rubber or similar material under pipe strap will help prevent vibration.

Pay particular attention to places where there are elbows or other fittings next to or almost touching a beam or other structural member. It's possible that each time the water goes slamming around the bend of this elbow it is causing the connected pipes to move just enough to bang against the beam. In most cases wedging a pad of thick rubber, cork, or similar material between the fitting and the wood beam will usually solve a problem of this kind. Adding another pipe strap on each side of the elbow is also a solution.

Loose pipes inside a wall are a bit more difficult to repair because this often involves ripping a hole in the wall so you can get at those loose pipes. If the situation is not too serious, most homeowners will elect to wait until the wall has to be torn open for other repairs or alterations, but if you don't want to wait that long, it may be worthwhile cutting a hole in the wall so that you can get at the pipes that are loose. When done you can patch the hole with a piece of drywall material and then repaint.

When banging or clicking noises occur in a hot-water line, it's possible that the pipe is expanding and contracting as the water is run through it (heating it) and then shut off (allowing it to cool). This can cause pipes to rub up against beams or other structural members, even against loose-fitting metal hanger straps. You can solve this problem by inserting a pad of rubber or plastic foam between the pipe and its mounting strap, or between the pipe and the nearby wood against which it is rubbing.

A whistling or squealing that occurs while the water is running—particularly when one of the faucets is only partway open or right after you open that faucet— is usually an indication of a loose washer, or one so badly worn that it no longer fits properly, or even one that is the wrong shape or size.

PROTECTING PIPES AGAINST FREEZING

Although water lines in a home plumbing system should be installed in such a way that they cannot freeze, all too often this does happen in very cold weather, particularly when the house is vacant for a while and the heat has been turned down. Or the freeze-up will occur at night when everyone is asleep and no one is using the water (moving water seldom freezes).

Unfortunately, water expands as it freezes, so a frozen pipe will usually split or burst if it is full of water. This makes quite a mess when the pipe finally thaws and the water starts running again.

To prevent this, pipes running through outside walls should have insulation installed between the pipe and the outer sheathing, not just between the pipe and the inside wall. And if pipes must run through an unheated crawl space, basement, or garage, they should themselves be insulated. You can use the self-adhesive foam type that comes in rolls with aluminum facing, or long foam sleeves that are slit down the middle so that you can slide them on over the pipe (the slit is then sealed with tape).

Bear in mind that insulation only conserves heat—if there is no heat inside the pipe, it can still freeze. So if you leave the house unheated for days at a time while on vacation, or if the heat is turned way down, even with insulation the pipes could freeze. The only sure way to prevent this from happening is to wrap the pipe with electrical heating cable (also called heating tape). The cable comes in various lengths, with automatic thermostat controls that will turn it on only when temperatures drop down close to freezing. You usually wrap the cable or tape around the pipes in a spiral, then wrap fiberglass insulation over it to keep in the heat and minimize energy consumption.

Obviously, heating cables can be installed only on accessible pipes, and they help only as long as there is electricity—a power failure will render them useless (though the insulation will help if the cold spell doesn't last too long).

Protecting pipes in enclosed outside walls is much more of a problem (even if you blow insulation into the wall later, you cannot be sure the insulation will get between the pipe and the outside sheathing). In extreme cases, where freezing is a frequent problem, your best bet is to cut an opening in the wall through which you can then cover the pipes with insulation.

Another trick that often works is to cut a small rectangular opening at the base of the wall and install a small louvered vent of the type used in hot-air systems. This will allow warm air from the room to get into the outer wall. The room will lose some heat, but you can keep the louver closed most of the time, opening it only in very cold weather when the water will not be running for many hours.

If the basement is heated, or is at least reasonably warm during cold weather, it may also be possible to cut openings from below that will allow some of the warm basement air to filter up into the hollow wall spaces where the pipes are located.

There are some occasions when none of these measures will help—when extra-cold weather will cause certain poorly located pipes to freeze every time: pipes in outside walls that have little or no insulation between the pipe and the outside, or pipes that come into a building from underground, but are not buried deeply enough (they should be below the frost line for that area). In all of these situations, relocating or rerouting the pipes, or burying them deeper if they are outside, is the only sure cure. However, until you get around to doing this, you can keep the pipes from freezing by allowing the water to run very slowly during very cold periods. A slow trickle or fast drip is all that is required in most cases, since moving water is much less likely to freeze.

DRAINING THE WATER SYSTEM TO PREVENT FREEZING

When a house is to be left vacant for a long period of time during the winter, especially if the heat will be turned off, it is necessary to drain the plumbing system in order to protect against freeze-ups. Even if the heat is left on, a danger still exists—there could be an extended power failure or some breakdown of the heating system. Pipes that freeze will often burst—and extensive flooding and other damage will result after the pipes thaw.

Some people feel safer if a plumber is called in to do this job, but if you are willing to take the time to do it carefully, there is no reason you cannot do the job yourself. Here are the steps to follow:

1. On the day you are leaving, turn off the water at the main valve out in the street (you may have to call your local water company to have this done). Turning off the main valve at the meter inside the house is not enough—if the pipe bursts *before* the valve (inside the house), your basement will still be flooded.

2. Open all the faucets and spigots inside and outside the house, and leave them open.

3. Turn off the power or fuel supply to your hot-water heater, then drain the appliance by opening the valve or spigot at the bottom.

4. Check the plumbing lines to see if the water-heater drain in the basement is the lowest point in the entire system (no pipes or valves should be lower). If it isn't, make sure there is some way to drain those lowest pipes in the system—either by opening a faucet or, if you must, by actually breaking open a connection. This is particularly important if you have a crawl space under the house with pipes running through it.

5. Disconnect and drain the hoses from your washing machine, then run the machine briefly in the drain cycle to remove the last of the water. Siphon out any remaining water. Do the same for your dishwasher.

6. Flush all the toilets, then sponge out any water that still remains in the tank (no more will come in because the water is off).

7. Pour about half a gallon of permanent-type auto antifreeze down each toilet bowl to fill the trap and to mix with any water left in the bowl, then pour at least a quart into each sink and fixture drain to protect the traps under each from freezing. Do the same in each shower drain, tub drain, laundry drain, and dishwasher and clothes-washer drain, in addition to kitchen and bathroom sinks.

8. If your house has a central humidi-fier, it's best to drain it as well, rather than merely fill it with antifreeze.

9. If you have a hot water or steam heating system, this too must be drained if you are planning to turn off the heat. There are many variations to these systems, however, and you should consult your local serviceman about the best way to close off your particular system. If you can get him to show you how to do your house once, then in subsequent years you can do it yourself.

• •

When Pipes Do Freeze

A frozen pipe must be thawed carefully or you can make matters worse. Heat must be slowly and gradually applied to keep the pipe from bursting, and you should always start at the faucet or valve end—making sure that this valve or faucet is all the way open. If the valve itself is frozen, thaw it first, then open it. Work your way along the length of frozen pipe so that the melting ice can run safely out through the valve or faucet. Otherwise trapped water might turn into steam—and this could literally explode the pipe open.

You can apply heat to the frozen pipe with an ordinary hair dryer (set on high) or with an infrared heat lamp. Regardless of the source of heat used, make certain you keep it moving constantly to avoid overheating and possibly building up steam inside the pipe, and avoid scorching wood or other flammable materials near that pipe.

An even safer way to do the job is to wrap the pipe with a thick layer of rags, then pour very hot water over the wrapping. Or you can wrap an electric heating cable around the pipe and plug it in for a while—the heat will melt the ice uniformly and safely (although more slowly than the other methods described).

• •

FIXING LEAKY FAUCETS

A leaking or dripping faucet is more than a mere nuisance that causes unsightly stains in the bottom of a sink, tub, or shower; it can be a sizable energy waster—especially when the faucet supplies hot water. Yet in the vast majority of cases, fixing a leaky faucet is a fairly simple project that will normally take less than half an hour and will cost only a few cents for parts.

Faucets come in a variety of styles, but practically all of them fall into one of three broad categories:

Compression-type faucets have regular washers made of neoprene or rubber that are secured to the bottom end of the stem with a brass screw. The handle is attached to the top of the stem so that turning it causes the stem to move up or down on spiral threads inside the body of the faucet. Turning the handle one way raises the stem and its washer so that water can flow; turning the handle the other way lowers the stem and presses the washer against a seat to close off the opening.

Washerless faucets fall into two categories. One has a rubber diaphragm instead of a washer on the bottom end of the stem, and works similarly to the conventional washer-type faucet. The other is a noncompression type with metal or plastic disks to control the flow. The disk type usually has two disks—a movable one and a fixed one—with openings in both. Turning the movable disk in one direction will align the openings in both disks so water can flow through. Turning the disk in the opposite direction moves the openings out of alignment and thus cuts off the flow of water. Since this type of faucet has no washers to wear out and does not depend on a compression seal to shut off the water, it is generally much less prone to leaking than a regular compression faucet and can often go for years without repairs.

Single-handle or single-control faucets are mixing faucets that have only one handle controlling the flow of both hot and cold water, as well as the volume of water that flows out through the mixing spout. They have no washers or diaphragms; instead they have a special ball or cartridge assembly that serves as a valve when turned or rotated (depending on the design) by the handle. On some models there is a round, knoblike handle that you turn to adjust for hot or cold and that you pull out to adjust for volume. On others there is a lever-type handle that is moved from side to side to adjust for hot or cold and pushed forward or back to adjust for volume.

REPAIRING COMPRESSION FAUCETS

When a compression faucet leaks or drips from the spout, it usually means that the washer has to be changed. If it leaks around the stem or under the handle, the packing has to be replaced. And if the problem is a chattering or squealing noise when the faucet is turned on, it's likely that the washer needs tightening or replacing. In all of these situations you will have to take the faucet apart to get at the washer, so the first step is shutting off the water supply to that fixture. You can do this by closing the valve under the sink or by closing the main valve that supplies water to the whole house.

Turn the faucet handle as far as it will go to the fully open position, then take the handle off the end of the stem by prying out the little decorative button or cap marked "Hot" or "Cold" in the center of the handle (it may just have an "H" or a "C") and taking out the screw underneath. With the screw out, you should be able to lift the handle straight off, though it may take a little coaxing or prying.

If your faucet has no removable decorative button or cap in the center, and if there is no screw visible on top, then look for a small threaded collar on the underside of the handle. Unscrewing this and letting it slide down will enable you to get the handle off.

The next step is removing the decorative bonnet or cap nut under the handle. This is a hollow metal housing that often is held down by a thin flat nut. Loosen this and you will be able to slide it and the bonnet straight up and off the stem. Under it you will find a large cap nut that holds the packing down. Loosen this with a wrench and the entire stem can be unscrewed by turning it counterclockwise until it can be lifted out of the faucet body.

On some faucets there will be no decorative bonnet or housing, just a chrome-plated threaded cap nut that can be unscrewed after the handle has been taken off, enabling you to then unscrew the entire stem and handle assembly by turning it counterclockwise until it comes all the way out. (When loosening this with your wrench—or when using a wrench or pliers on any chrome-plated fittings—protect the hardware with a few wraps of tape.)

With the stem out you can remove the small brass screw that holds the washer in place on the bottom, then replace the

Washer-type compression faucet.

washer with a new one of the proper size and shape. The size (diameter) should be a neat fit inside the rim or hollow on the end of the stem, and the shape should match that of the original. Bear in mind that some washers are flat and some are beveled, so make sure you use the right kind.

If the old washer is so deformed that you cannot tell what it originally looked like, your best bet is to take apart one of the other faucets—of the same type and brand—so you can see what the right washer looks like. If the brass screw that holds the washer in place is chewed up and corroded, replace it at the same time with a new one.

Screw the stem back into the body of the faucet, then slide the packing nut down on top and tighten it. Before you replace this packing nut, however, check the condition of the packing to see if it looks worn or stringy. If it does, or if the faucet was leaking under the packing nut,

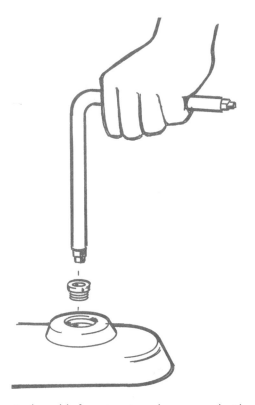

Replaceable faucet seat can be removed with special hex wrench or sometimes with a large screwdriver.

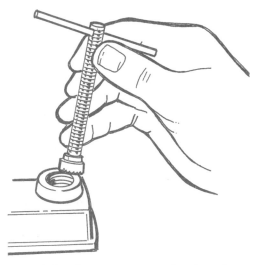

Instead of replacing seat, smooth it down by polishing with a valve seat dressing tool.

you should replace the packing with new material. It comes in string form that you wrap around the stem before you screw the packing nut down on top. Some faucets have a thick rubber washer instead of packing under the bonnet. If this is worn, it should be replaced with a new one of the same size and shape.

One caution: When you screw in the stem, turn the handle (or rotate the stem) so that the faucet is left partly open and the new washer is not forced tight against its seat. This is important; forcing the washer down on top of its valve seat could crack the metal.

In general, don't tighten the cap nut more than is necessary to ensure a snug fit against the packing. Overtightening can cause the faucet to bind or can even strip the threads on the nut. If it's too loose, at worst there will be a slight leak around the cap stem when the faucet is turned on; all you have to do is tighten the cap nut a bit more. If this still doesn't stop the leak around the stem, you will have to remove the cap nut and replace the packing under it.

Sometimes you will find that even after the washer is replaced, the faucet continues to drip from the spout. This usually means that the valve seat—the metal seat against which the washer presses—has been damaged. In some faucets you can remove the valve seat by unscrewing it with either a large screwdriver or a special oversize Allen wrench (some dealers rent or lend these out) and then replacing the old seat with a new one. You can usually tell if your valve seat is replaceable by shining a bright light down the stem hole and using a small mirror to inspect the seat. If it has an octagonal-shaped opening in the center, there is a good chance that it is removable.

Instead of replacing the valve seat, you may be able to repair it with an inexpensive valve seat dressing tool. Sold in most hardware stores and plumbing supply outlets, these tools grind down the valve seat to remove burrs and scratches that may be preventing a proper seal. First remove the faucet stem as described previously, then screw the seat dressing tool down into the faucet body. A few turns on the handle while pushing down with moderate pressure will dress the seat to make it smooth.

REPAIRING TWO-HANDLE MIXING FAUCETS

Most kitchen and bathroom faucets have two handles and a single mixing spout for hot and cold water to adjust the water temperature. In bathroom faucets this single spout is fixed, but in kitchen faucets the spout can usually swing from side to side.

When both handles are fully closed and the faucet drips, either the hot or cold side, or both, could be leaking. The easiest way to tell is to turn off one of the supply valves *under* the sink to see if this stops the drip. If turning off one eliminates the drip, then you know that is the one that is at fault. If that doesn't eliminate the drip, turn the first valve on again and turn off the other. If the spout still drips water after a few minutes, it could be that both faucets need new washers.

Either way, these faucets are repaired in exactly the same way as previously described—depending on whether the faucet is a compression type or one of the washerless types.

If a kitchen faucet leaks around the neck of the spout when you turn it on, you can usually stop it by tightening the knurled collar around the base of the spout. If tightening doesn't do the trick, then unscrew the spout completely and pull it up and out of the faucet body. Under the collar you will see a rubber O-ring or washer. Remove this and replace it with a new one of the same size, then replace the collar on the spout and tighten it back down again.

REPAIRING TWO-HANDLE WASHERLESS FAUCETS

Faucets that have rubber diaphragms instead of washers are taken apart in almost the same manner as faucets with washers—and in many ways repair techniques are just about the same. The rubber diaphragm snaps on over the end of the stem (there is no screw to hold it in place). Like a washer, this diaphragm presses down against an internal seat when the faucet is closed, but it does not wear as fast as a regular washer because the diaphragm rotates when the handle is turned.

Many of these faucets do not have packing under the cap nut or bonnet to prevent leakage. Instead they have O-rings that fit into grooves around the shank of the stem, and these keep water from seeping up around the stem and then leaking out over the cap nut or bonnet.

To repair a diaphragm-type faucet that has no regular washers, follow the steps for repairing a conventional compression-type faucet with washers. After shutting off the water supply, take the faucet apart as described on page 197, then pry the old diaphragm off the end of the stem and replace it with a new one of the same size and style (simply press it on over the "button" or tip).

If the faucet is the disk or cartridge type, you will probably have to replace the entire valve assembly when the disks are worn or damaged, although most disk models are designed so that only the rotating disks need be replaced (take the whole thing to your dealer if in doubt). If the O-ring around the stem looks damaged or worn, replace it with a new one at the same time.

When finished, reassemble the entire faucet by replacing the parts in reverse order, then turn the water back on.

One word of caution: Unlike washer-type faucets, which have parts that are more or less interchangeable brand to brand, washerless faucets usually do *not* have interchangeable parts, so check the brand before buying replacement parts. You won't run into this problem when you need only an O-ring, or possibly a diaphragm, but you might when you need replacement disks, stem assemblies, or other parts. So play safe and take the old

Two-handle washerless faucet has replaceable cartridge or diaphragm.

parts with you when you go shopping for new parts—that way you will be sure of getting parts that fit.

REPAIRING SINGLE-HANDLE FAUCETS

Often referred to as "one-arm" faucets, these are mixing faucets that have only a single handle to control both temperature and volume. The handle may move in and out to control volume and from side to side to control temperature. These faucets do not have washers or diaphragms to wear out and will usually last for years without repairs.

Of course, like any faucet, single-handle faucets will eventually start to leak—especially if you live in a hard-water area where sediment tends to build up and clog the small orifices inside the faucet.

Although designs vary, most single-handle faucets are of the following three types: tipping-valve faucets, rotating-ball faucets, and cartridge-type faucets.

Tipping-valve faucets have a spring-loaded valve and a cam-shaped lever that is rocked or tipped when the handle is moved from side to side. The water enters from each side in proportion to how much this valve is tipped in either direction. The cam action also regulates the size of the openings to control the water volume.

Two problems are most likely to occur with this type of mechanism. The first is a partial clogging of the small internal screen that surrounds the tipping valve; the second is wearing of the small gasket that fits between the valve and its seat. Your best bet is to buy a repair kit that contains all of these replaceable parts, then follow the directions supplied with the kit. Most parts are not interchangeable among

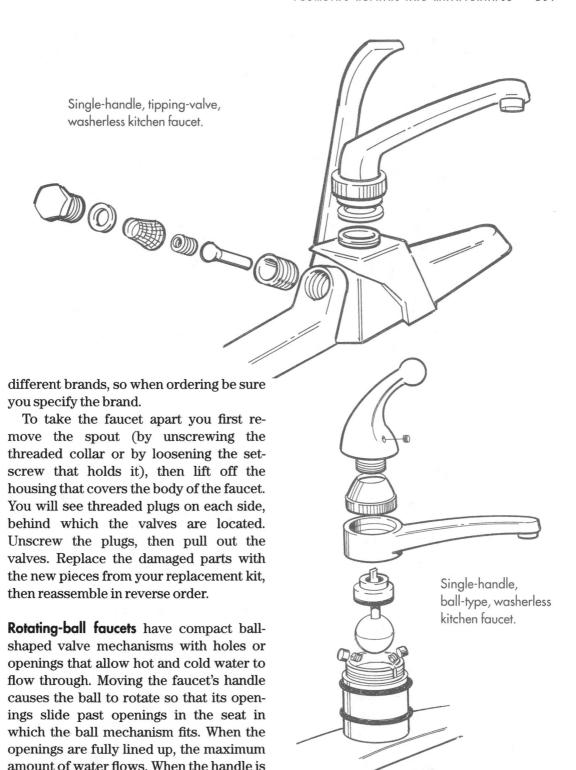

Single-handle, tipping-valve, washerless kitchen faucet.

Single-handle, ball-type, washerless kitchen faucet.

different brands, so when ordering be sure you specify the brand.

To take the faucet apart you first remove the spout (by unscrewing the threaded collar or by loosening the setscrew that holds it), then lift off the housing that covers the body of the faucet. You will see threaded plugs on each side, behind which the valves are located. Unscrew the plugs, then pull out the valves. Replace the damaged parts with the new pieces from your replacement kit, then reassemble in reverse order.

Rotating-ball faucets have compact ball-shaped valve mechanisms with holes or openings that allow hot and cold water to flow through. Moving the faucet's handle causes the ball to rotate so that its openings slide past openings in the seat in which the ball mechanism fits. When the openings are fully lined up, the maximum amount of water flows. When the handle is moved to bring the openings out of alignment, the flow of water (hot or cold) is diminished in proportion to the degree of the ball's rotation.

The most likely source of trouble with this mechanism is wear—either in one of the springs that maintain tension between the ball and the round housing inside which it fits or on one of the gaskets or seals. The procedure for taking apart the faucet to replace the gaskets and springs will vary to some extent from one brand to another, but generally you first have to loosen a setscrew under the handle, then lift off the handle to expose the ball mechanism (in faucets with a swing spout the spout will come off with the handle).

Each manufacturer makes his own ball mechanism replacement kit, as well as a repair kit containing just the gaskets, springs, seats, and O-rings. Locate a plumbing dealer who carries your particular brand of faucet and get your parts from him. The instruction sheet that comes with the replacement unit or repair kit will tell you how to install the new parts.

Cartridge faucets, also called cartridge-sleeve faucets, have a rotating-valve mechanism with several O-rings around the outside to act as seals. As the cartridge is rotated or moved in and out by the handle, openings in the cartridge line up with matching openings in the housing to control the flow of water from the hot or cold lines.

When this type of faucet starts to leak, simply remove the entire cartridge and replace it with a new one. Replacement cartridges are generally available from plumbing supply houses, but again, brands are not standardized and not all are interchangeable, so make sure you buy one that will fit your particular model.

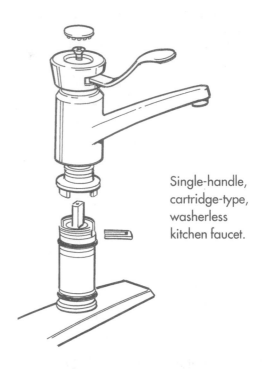

Single-handle, cartridge-type, washerless kitchen faucet.

To take these faucets apart, first remove the handle, normally held on by a screw that goes through the top (it sits in a recess under the decorative button or cap on top of the handle). Pry off the cap or button, then remove the screw and lift off the handle (in swivel-spout faucets, the spout will come off with the handle). With the handle removed you will have to take out a small clip or retainer, often called a keeper, that holds the cartridge in place in the faucet body.

In some faucets you won't be able to see this retainer clip or keeper until you remove a ring or stop tube that slides down over the entire assembly. You can slide this off after the handle has been removed. Then pull out the retainer clip by grabbing its edge with a pair of needle-nose pliers or by prying it out gently with a small screwdriver blade. On some models the clip is under the handle; on others it fits in from the outside so you don't have to take off the handle first. Once the clip has been removed, the entire cartridge assembly can be slid out easily (the faucet stem is usually part of the cartridge).

Like the ball-type valve replacements, cartridges are not standardized. You have to buy the brand that matches your particular faucet. It will come with instructions for taking out the old one and putting in the new one. When installing the replacement cartridge, look for a flat spot or arrow on the stem; this will tell you which way to install it—usually with the arrow or flat spot pointing up.

REPAIRING WALL-MOUNTED TUB AND SHOWER FAUCETS

Recessed faucets mounted in the wall above your tub or in the shower compartment are essentially no different from the faucets in your sinks. The only real difference is that they are horizontal instead of vertical. They also come in the same varieties, including compression faucets that have washers and single-handle or double-handle washerless types.

Single-handle washerless shower and tub faucets are taken apart in the same way as the sink-mounted faucets described on the previous pages. Buy a repair or replacement kit for that particular brand and install the necessary parts simply by following the directions supplied with the kit.

When a compression-type wall-mounted tub and shower faucet needs repair, however, there may be more of a problem, because the body of the faucet is recessed below the surface of the wall. In such cases the packing nut or bonnet may also be below the surface, so you cannot get at it with an ordinary wrench. Instead you will have to use a deep-socket wrench—after you have removed the handle and the decorative bonnet or housing that fits over the stem and covers the opening in the wall. To remove this, take off the handle, then loosen the large, flat nut that goes around the stem and slide it off. The socket wrench is then slid on over the stem to remove the cap nut that holds the stem in place. Under this bonnet there may be a rubber seat washer below the packing, so slide this off carefully to avoid losing it. Now unscrew the stem and pull it out of the wall so that the washer can be removed and replaced with a new one. Before reassembling the faucet, replace the packing with new material.

REPLACING AN OLD FAUCET

Although most deck-mounted faucets in bathroom and kitchen sinks are fairly standard in size, they do vary in the spacing required between the holes in the top of the sink or counter. So when shopping for a new faucet, buy one with the same spacing as your sink. Many of the newer units, including most single-handle faucets, come with decorative housings or escutcheon plates that will cover widely spaced holes, as well as an assortment of fittings that will enable you to hook up to most existing connections.

Every hardware store also carries a wide range of other adapters to simplify connecting pipes of different diameters or connecting one type of pipe to another, such as threaded pipes to copper. There are also flexible supply tubes (often furnished with the new faucet) that make it easy to achieve proper alignment between the old pipes and the new fittings.

Usually the hardest part of the job will be getting off the old faucet—the new one

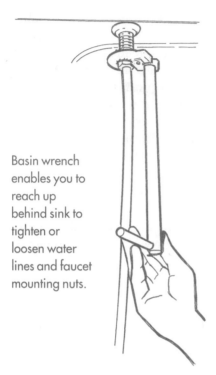

Basin wrench enables you to reach up behind sink to tighten or loosen water lines and faucet mounting nuts.

is seldom a problem to install if its connections are properly spaced to match the openings in your sink. Specific instructions may vary to some extent, but in most cases here is the sequence to follow when replacing an old faucet:

1. Shut off the water supply to that fixture by closing the valves under the sink, then with a basin wrench (see illustration) reach up under the sink and loosen the two supply pipes where they connect to the bottom of the faucet. There will usually be a threaded collar or nut that you loosen first, after which you can pull down the supply tube to disconnect it entirely.

2. Disconnect the supply tubes at the other end—where they go into the shut-off valve—to get them out of the way (sometimes you don't have to disconnect them entirely—you may be able just to swing them out of the way temporarily). Next, with the basin wrench, remove the large

locknuts holding the faucet in place from the underside. If these nuts are badly corroded and don't budge easily, squirt some penetrating oil on them and tap rapidly with a small hammer for a couple of minutes, then try again.

3. With the locknuts off (or dropped down along the supply pipe) you can lift the entire faucet off the sink top. Scrape off any old putty around the openings or the edge of the housing.

4. Take the locknuts and washers off your new faucet to ready it for insertion. Most new models come with plastic gaskets or bases that do not need sealing, but others will require bedding with plumber's putty before you set the faucet in place (the instructions should explain this). If you use putty, push down hard enough to bring the base of the faucet in contact with the surface so that none of the putty will show around the edges.

5. Reach up under the sink and screw on the locknuts and washers furnished with the new faucet. Tighten by hand, then finish tightening them with the basin

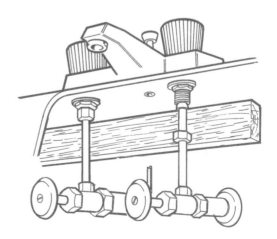

Installation of typical faucet, showing how water lines are connected.

wrench. You want these nuts snug, but be careful not to overtighten or you could crack the housing.

6. Connect the hot-water and cold-water supply tubes to the bottom of the new faucet with the fittings supplied. If none of these fit, you'll have to buy new ones. To play safe, bring along what you have so the dealer will be able to determine what you need. If you have trouble lining up the old supply pipes, or if the fittings are corroded or deformed, replace them with new flexible supply tubes. You can buy chrome-plated supply tubes that bend to shape easily or plastic ones with "universal" couplings for connecting up almost any kind of pipe or tubing.

7. Turn on the water and check all fittings for leaks. If you find one, tighten the fittings a little more—but go easy. Overtightening could strip the threads or crack the fitting.

FIXING CLOGGED DRAINS

Because the drain pipes in your house are not under pressure and depend entirely on gravity to carry away waste, it really doesn't take much to cause a blockage. Fortunately, in most cases freeing up a blockage is usually not very difficult (though it may be a bit messy at times), unless the blockage occurs down in one of the larger main drains.

If drains are slow in more than one sink or fixture, the trouble is probably in one of the large drains or the main vent stack. If fixtures make glugging and bubbling noises as they drain and drain slowly, there is a good chance that the vent pipe going up through the roof is clogged or at least partially blocked. When air cannot escape freely up the vertical stack, drainage will be slow.

In many cases the simplest way to unclog a blocked stack is to go up on the roof and shove a hose down into the vent from above. Turn the water on full force for a while, with somebody inside watching some of the drains—just in case the water starts to back up. If this doesn't free up the blockage, try running a power auger, which you can rent from a tool rental agency.

If these measures fail, you will have to remove a cleanout plug in the main drain line (usually in the basement) and run your drain auger in from there to the sewer to clean out the line. In most cases this cleanout plug will be at one end of a Y fitting at the bottom end of the main stack where it connects with the large waste line leading out to the sewer or septic tank system.

To remove the cleanout plug you will need a large wrench and plenty of muscle. Be prepared for a small flood of dirty water when you do get this plug out—there may be a lot of water backed up in the vertical line behind it. When you find it necessary to remove this plug because of a problem in one of the main lines, very often your best bet is to call in a professional plumber, who has the equipment needed for this kind of job.

CLEANING CLOGGED SINK DRAINS

A clogged sink drain is usually not hard to find, *if* you tackle it before things have gone too far. That's why it is best to take action as soon as you see a drain slowing up, rather than waiting until it is completely stopped.

In the case of a bathroom sink or tub, nine times out of ten the blockage is caused by an accumulation of soap and hair. If the trouble is in a kitchen or laundry sink, chances are that the blockage is caused by a mixture of soap, grease, and food particles congealed in the drain. In either case, the first thing you should do is check the drain opening inside the sink to see if it is clogged with hair or other solid material.

Kitchen sinks usually have a drain basket that you can remove and wash out. In bathroom sinks there is usually a pop-up metal stopper that closes the drain when a knob or handle behind the faucet is pushed down or pulled up. To clean out these drains properly this stopper will have to be removed first. Raise it as high as it will go, then turn it about half a revolution to disengage it from the linkage connecting it to the handle behind the faucet. Now lift straight up and remove it so you can clean off any accumulated hair or soap. If you can't lift out the stopper, take the linkage apart under the sink and pull the horizontal rod out of the drainpipe's tailpiece.

If the blockage is not in the drain opening, then the trouble is obviously under the sink in the trap or in one of the waste pipes leading from the sink or trap. In some cases—especially if the blockage is not yet complete—you may be able to clear it just by pouring a few potfuls of boiling water down the drain and then letting the hot water run for a few minutes

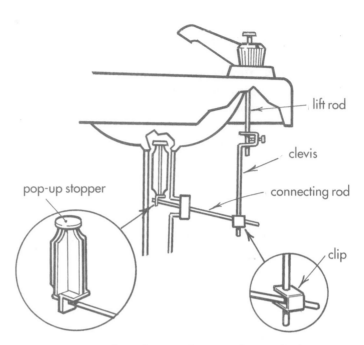

Linkage for typical pop-up drain in bathroom sink. Pop-up stopper opens (raises) when you press down on rod sticking up behind faucet.

before the drain can cool. The boiling water will soften up and liquefy the grease and soap, and the hot water will then flush it through.

When this doesn't solve the problem you have two recourses that do not require any dismantling: a chemical drain cleaner or a rubber force cup (also called a plunger or "plumber's friend"). Chemical drain cleaners are usually more effective on partial blockages, but if you are dealing with a completely stopped-up drain, then the positive action of a force cup will work better.

If you are in doubt, or if you think both will be needed, try the force cup first. If you use the chemical cleaner first, be careful. The caustic chemicals many of them contain will be mixed with the standing waste water, and you could be splashed when working with the force cup or when dipping out the waste water.

Although the rubber force cup is a simple tool, there are some "tricks of the trade" that will make it more effective. First, there should be enough water in the sink bottom to cover the rubber cup completely. Second, it's a good idea to smear a little petroleum jelly around the rim of the cup to ensure a tighter seal against the sink bottom. Third, make sure the overflow drain opening up near the rim of the sink is plugged (stuff a wet cloth into the opening). Fourth, if the sink is half of a double sink and shares a drain with the other half, make sure that that other sink's drain opening is plugged solidly—otherwise you will be merely forcing the water from one sink to the other.

After you press the rim of the force cup down over the drain opening, push up and down vigorously several times without lifting the cup off the bottom of the sink.

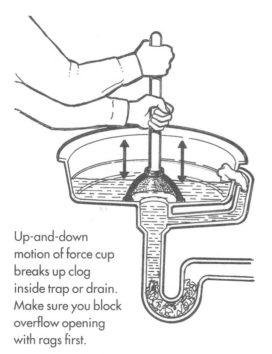

Up-and-down motion of force cup breaks up clog inside trap or drain. Make sure you block overflow opening with rags first.

The upward stroke creates a suction effect in the drain that is often even more effective than the downward compression stroke, so put more effort into the lifting or yanking action. After four or five such up-and-down strokes, yank the suction cup off the bottom with a quick motion to create maximum suction. The alternate suction and compression action is what breaks up the clog so that it can be flushed away by the backed-up water. If it doesn't break up on the first attempt, don't get discouraged. Try again. It often takes four or five attempts to break through.

If you decide to go ahead with a chemical drain cleaner, make sure you follow the manufacturer's directions exactly. Wear rubber gloves if the chemical is caustic (many are), and if the sink is full of water, dip most of it out before you start so that you can pour the chemical into the drain opening. Avoid contact with the porcelain if possible, and give the chemical plenty of time to work. The directions will specify how much time is needed; in some cases it may take several hours to really dissolve the blockage.

When you can't unclog the drain with a force cup or with a drain cleaner, you will have to try cleaning out the trap under the drain. This is a U-shaped or J-shaped bend of pipe under the sink that always has some liquid in it, so more often than not debris that gets flushed down the drain will get caught in this section.

Some sink traps have a cleanout plug on the bottom so that you don't have to remove the whole trap to clean it out. Place a bucket under this plug, then unscrew it carefully; these plugs have fine threads, so go easy. As the plug comes off, the water inside the trap will run out. You then take a stiff piece of wire to probe the

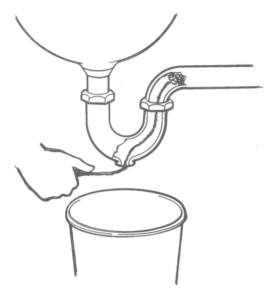

Stiff wire or plumber's snake pushed up through cleanout plug in bottom of trap will break up most clogs beyond trap.

inside of the trap and dislodge or break up whatever is caught there (see illustration).

If the trap does not have a cleanout plug on the bottom, or if pushing the snake up through the plug opening does not remove the blockage, take the trap off completely by loosening the two slip nuts that hold it in place at each end. Slide these nuts up along the pipe, then pull off the trap—making sure you do not lose the rubber gaskets under each nut. Turn the trap upside down to clean it out thoroughly.

If you find nothing inside the trap, then the clog is in one of the drainpipes. First, look down the tailpipe (the short length of vertical pipe between the bottom of the sink and the top of the trap) with a flashlight to see if anything's there. If not, use the plumber's snake to poke around inside the pipe beyond the trap, the one that runs into the wall or floor. Keep pushing and twisting with this flexible steel snake (it

will go around bends) until you feel it "bite into" the clog or obstruction. If possible, try to force the tip into the clog so you can pull it back out toward you. If this doesn't work, try alternately twisting and pushing or pulling the snake so you work the tip into the obstruction, to break it up so that flushing the water will wash it out into the main drainpipe.

When you replace the trap, make sure the rubber gaskets or washers are in place under each slip nut. Slide the end of the trap up onto the tailpipe sticking down from the sink, then tighten the nuts. These nuts also have very fine threads, so go easy to avoid stripping them. Screw each nut hand-tight first, then give them an extra quarter turn with a wrench to cinch them up. If the trap is bent or corroded, or if you strip the threads on the nuts, you'll have to replace the trap. Traps are not very expensive and are widely available in local hardware stores.

CLEARING CLOGGED TUB DRAINS

Most residential bathtub drains have a trip lever that sticks through an overflow plate located near the top of the tub, as shown in the illustration opposite. Some tub drains are the pop-up type that have a metal stopper that goes up or down to open or close the drain. Others are the so-called plunger type—they have no pop-up stopper, but there is a brass plunger inside the pipe that closes off the drainpipe when lowered by the trip lever. The most common complaints encountered with tub drains are water leaking out or water draining too slowly.

In both cases the first thing you will have to do is remove the trip lever and its linkage, as well as removing the pop-up stopper and its linkage (the plunger type has no pop-up stopper or linkage to remove). To do so, take out the two screws holding the plate in place, then pull out the linkage that is connected to it (you may have to do a little gentle tugging and twisting, but it should come out without too much difficulty). Now lift up and pull out the pop-up stopper and its connected linkage. In some cases you may have to give this a slight twist to free up the inside, but most will pull straight up and out.

If your tub drain is the plunger type and has no pop-up stopper—only a strainer over the drain opening—simply take out the screw that holds this strainer in place and remove the strainer.

If the problem is a poor seal when the stopper is down, you should replace the O-

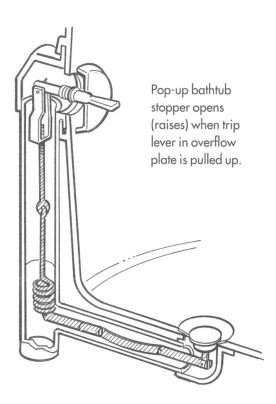

Pop-up bathtub stopper opens (raises) when trip lever in overflow plate is pulled up.

ring under the metal stopper. If replacing the O-ring doesn't do the trick, you probably need to adjust the length of the linkage that connects to the spring at the bottom (see illustration). This spring presses down on the end of the horizontal stopper linkage to open or close the stopper, so making it slightly longer or shorter will provide the proper closing pressure on the stopper. There is usually a nut or threaded rod at one end of the linkage that permits making such adjustments.

On plunger-type tub drains, adjusting the length of the linkage that connects the trip lever to the brass cylinder at the bottom end of this linkage may also be necessary if the plunger doesn't seal the drain properly. In either case, when adjusting this linkage, give the adjusting rod or screw only a couple of turns at a time—usually a slight adjustment is needed to make it work properly.

If the problem is a sluggish, slow drain where water flows out slowly even when the stopper is fully open, chances are there is a buildup of hair, sludge, and soap around the stopper or around the linkage connected to the stopper. Remove the stopper and its linkage as described previously, then clean everything off thoroughly. At the same time, clean out the inside of the drainpipe by probing with a piece of stiff wire or a bottle brush to remove any buildup that may have accumulated. Replace the stopper and its linkage by sliding it back down through the drain opening, making certain that the curved portion of the rocker arm is facing down when you do this.

After the stopper and its linkage is in place, the trip lever and its linkage must also be replaced by sliding it back down through the overflow opening. Then replace the screws that hold the overflow plate in place.

If the drain line is clogged farther down, past all the stopper linkage, then the drain line will have to be cleaned out the same way as described for a clogged sink drain (see pages 207–8). However, before you can do this you will first have to remove the stopper and its linkage, or the strainer (if there is no pop-up stopper). Before using a plunger, don't forget to block the overflow opening at the top with a wad of cloth.

CLEARING CLOGGED TOILETS

With toilets, even more than with sinks, it is much easier to free up a partial blockage than a complete stoppage, so take action as soon as you see the drain starting to act sluggish. Like a sink, a toilet has a trap, but unlike a sink the trap is actually built into the bottom of the toilet bowl—it is not a separate, removable one. There are several designs or styles, but the exact interior configuration really is not critical; the steps you must take to unclog a toilet are about the same for any design.

As a rule, chemical cleaners are not of much use in freeing up a clogged toilet— the volume of water involved and the size and type of clog all make a chemical much less likely to work. The two most effective tools are the rubber force cup and the auger or drain snake.

The kind of rubber force cup that works best on a toilet bowl is a bit different from the one for a sink—the toilet plunger has an extended cone on the bottom. This cone sticks down into the opening in the bottom of the bowl to form a tight seal when you press down on the handle. A sink plunger will work on some toilets, but in most toilets the shape of the opening at the bottom makes it difficult to get a tight

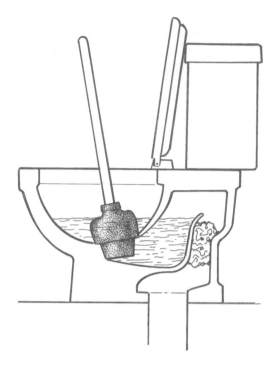

Toilet bowl plunger has extra rubber cone that folds out at the bottom to provide a snug fit inside opening at bottom of toilet.

seal with an ordinary force cup. Some rubber force cups have a folding cone designed for toilets, one that can then fold up inside the cup to leave a flat bottom that is just right for use on sink drains.

A rubber force cup is used on a toilet drain in the same way that it is used on a sink—you pump up and down vigorously and apply extra effort on the final upward yank.

If several tries with the force cup don't unclog the toilet bowl, you will need a drain auger or snake. An auger is more effective, especially if the clog is well inside the trap. You will have to do some pushing and twisting to force the tip of most snakes up and over the front rim of the trap. (It may help to slip a plastic bag over your arm, then reach down to the bottom of the toilet so you can guide the tip of the snake upward over the lip and into the trap.)

It's usually much easier to use one of the special augers designed specifically for toilets. Called a toilet auger or closet auger, this is a length of pipe with a sharp bend in the bottom end through which the first part of the spring-steel auger travels. This bent pipe serves to guide the tip of the auger up into the trap when you push it down into the opening at the bottom of the bowl. With the auger fully inserted, try to hook its tip into whatever is causing the blockage and then pull it back out. Augers come with a handle that enables you to twist the full length of the springy metal as you push into the drain, so keep turning and twisting on this handle as you feed the auger in. When you feel it dig into something, keep turning *in the same direction* while you slowly pull the snake back out, dragging the clog with it.

There are some rare cases when none of these measures will work—for example, when a solid object such as a hairbrush or plastic bottle, or something else that can't be hooked with the tip of the auger, has been accidentally dropped into the toilet and has worked its way up into the trap. The only solution is to take off the entire toilet bowl so you can turn it upside down and push the object out from below with a stiff piece of wire or a strong stream from a hose. Although some people may prefer to call in a plumber at this point, it is a job that can be handled by anyone willing to do a bit of heavy work. Here's how to go about it:

1. Shut off the supply of water to the flush tank, then empty it by dipping out the water.

2. Disconnect the toilet bowl from the tank behind it. If the bowl is connected to the tank by a large-diameter metal elbow, then the tank is hung on brackets that are fastened to the wall. Disconnect the elbow at both ends, then lift the tank off its brackets and set it aside. If the tank rests on the back of the bowl and is directly connected to it, there will be two bolts coming up through the bottom that you'll have to remove. In some cases you can reach the exposed heads from underneath the flange of the bowl; in others you can get at the heads by reaching down into the bottom of the tank.

3. A toilet bowl is fastened to the floor with bolts around its rim, and in most cases the bolt heads are covered with decorative porcelain caps. These have to come off first, and usually you can simply pry them off, though sometimes they are threaded on and must be unscrewed to expose the nuts. Such decorative caps are also often filled with putty, which you'll have to scrape away to expose the metal nuts. If you find the nuts badly corroded and hard to loosen, soak them with penetrating oil and tap lightly with a small hammer for a few minutes, then try again. Be careful when using the hammer to hit only the metal, not the porcelain.

4. After the nuts are off, remove the bowl by lifting it straight up. The best way to do this is to straddle the bowl and grip the rim on opposite sides with both hands. Rock it gently from side to side till it breaks loose, then lift straight up.

5. Take the bowl outside and turn it upside down so you can probe the inside with a stiff piece of wire, or backflush with a strong stream from a hose.

Before replacing the bowl, you should buy a new wax ring or seal to replace the original one that fit under the bottom rim

Wax ring under toilet seals joint between bottom of bowl and the floor fitting.

of the bowl (see illustration). Such rings are sold in all plumbing supply houses and fit over the horn that projects down from the bottom of the bowl. You will also need some fresh putty to put on the floor under

the rim before replacing the bowl against the floor (having first scraped all the old putty off both floor and rim). Set the bowl into place by sliding it down over the original bolts that project up from the floor, then press down hard to compress the wax ring and the putty around the rim.

Replace the nuts and work your way around with a wrench, tightening each nut slightly before going on to the next one. Repeat this until all nuts have been snugged down firmly, being carefully not to overtighten; you can crack the porcelain rim if you apply too much pressure on the nuts.

Finish by replacing the decorative porcelain caps over each nut, having scraped out the old putty inside each one and filled it with fresh putty. The purpose of the putty is to keep spilled water from washing down around the bolt holes and through the floor.

REPAIRING TOILET FLUSH TANKS

The inner workings of a typical toilet flush tank may seem like a complicated series of levers and valves, but once you understand the basic operating principle, there is nothing mysterious about it. And there is very little that you cannot fix yourself when a tank fails to flush properly.

The flush mechanism in a typical toilet tank consists of two separate valve assemblies: an inlet valve that fills the tank with water immediately after it is emptied in order to get it ready for the next flush, and a flush valve that lets the water go rushing out into the bowl when you press the lever on the outside of the tank.

The inlet valve mechanism is called the

ballcock. It refills the tank and adds some extra water to the bowl itself, so there will always be some standing in the bottom.

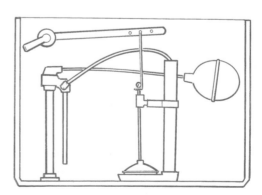

Working parts of old-style flush toilet tank.

The ballcock is activated by the dropping water level as the tank empties, and it shuts itself off when the water level inside the tank rises up to a preset level. This level is determined by a float ball carried upward by the rising water, thus raising the float arm with it. The arm is attached to the inlet valve mechanism and serves to shut it off completely when the float ball reaches the proper level.

Some models do not have a float ball. Instead, there may be a plastic float attached directly to the ballcock tube that rises with the water. In other models the float is replaced altogether by a pressure-sensitive valve at the bottom that senses the water level inside the tank and shuts off the inlet valve mechanism when the proper level is reached.

The flush valve is activated by the lever or handle on the outside of the tank. Pushing down on the lever raises the trip lever arm on the inside, and this in turn pulls up on the tank ball on the bottom of the tank. As this tank ball comes up off its seat on the bottom of the tank, the water inside the tank rushes out through the opening at the bottom and into the toilet bowl. Simultaneously, the tank ball floats up to the surface, then drops with the water level until it finally falls back into its original position over the seat opening at the bottom of the tank. Incoming water then builds up pressure on the ball, serving to hold it down and keep the seat opening closed while the tank refills.

Instead of lift rods and a tank ball, most of the newer flush tanks have a chain connected to a flapper-type valve that fits over the seat instead of a tank ball and is hinged so that when the trip lever is raised, the chain lifts the flapper off its seat and allows the water to rush out and down into the bowl. The flapper valve stays in the up (open) position because it floats, but when the tank is almost empty the flapper automatically drops back down over its seat to close the opening again. The weight of the rising water holds the valve down and seals the opening at the bottom until the next time the toilet is flushed.

Now that you understand how a flush tank mechanism works, repairs should not be difficult to make when something goes wrong. You first determine the source of trouble, then make the needed adjustments or replace any malfunctioning parts with new ones (inexpensive repair parts are available in every hardware store and plumbing supply outlet). Following is a list of the most common toilet tank problems and the steps that can be taken to repair each of them.

WATER KEEPS RUNNING, YET TANK DOESN'T FILL PROPERLY

This is often the case when you have to keep "jiggling" or flicking the handle up and down after each flush in order to stop the water from running out of the tank and into the bowl. It usually means that the tank ball (or the flapper valve) at the bottom is not seating properly, thus allowing water to continue running out through the bottom opening.

If the tank has a rubber ball that is pulled up by lift rods, the most likely cause of trouble is the lift-rod guide. The guide may have shifted slightly to one side or another, and as a result the ball does not fall squarely over the center of its seat. In other cases it may not fall at all and just gets hung up over the seat until you jiggle the handle a few times. This problem can usually be corrected by realigning the guide slightly so the ball drops onto the center of the seat without binding. To move the guide, loosen the setscrew that locks it onto the overflow tube, adjust it, then retighten the setscrew.

Sometimes the problem is due to lift rods that are slightly bent and thus stick as they try to slide up and down through the guide. You can straighten the wire rods easily, either with your hands or with a pair of pliers. Binding or sticking can also be caused by an accumulation of slime or mineral deposits on the rods, so clean them off with fine steel wool while you are at it.

If the ball is falling onto the center of its seat and water still keeps running out of the bowl, check for any dirt, rust, or sediment on the seat that could be preventing a watertight seal. If the seat seems clean, chances are that the rubber ball is dried out or cracked and has to be replaced with a new one. Just unscrew the old one from the bottom end of the lift rod, then screw on the new one.

A more permanent solution to this type of problem is to upgrade the entire mechanism by getting rid of the tank ball-and-lift-rod assembly (including the rod guide that is clamped onto the overflow tube) and replace it with a flapper-type tank ball. These flapper valves or flapper balls are shaped like a regular tank ball on the bottom, and they sit on the seat at the bottom of the tank just like the older-style tank ball. But instead of moving vertically upward when lifted off the seat, the flapper is hinged to the base of the overflow tube, so it simply flips up when the flush lever is pressed. It cannot move out of alignment, so when it drops it always falls back on the center of the seat.

Flapper-type tank balls are connected to the flush lever at the top of the tank by means of a light chain or flexible length of plastic, so there is no rod guide that can move the ball out of alignment when it drops back down onto its seat at the bottom of the tank. The flapper can be installed in minutes in place of an existing tank ball, after first removing the old lift rods, rod guide, and tank ball. They can also be purchased complete with a new replacement seat that will fit right over the existing seat—a good idea if the old seat is badly worn, chipped, or scratched. The new seat is quickly installed by cementing it in place right on top of the old seat.

WATER KEEPS RUNNING OUT THROUGH OVERFLOW TUBE INSIDE TANK

This can happen when the ballcock mechanism (the valve or mechanism that lets water into the tank to fill it after each flush) doesn't shut off as soon as the tank has been filled to the proper level. If water keeps pouring in, the level will keep rising until it starts running out through the top of the vertical overflow that sticks up in the center of the tank.

To see if this is the problem when you hear water running, take off the tank cover and look inside to see if water is up to the top of the tube and is overflowing into it. If it is, here is what you can do to stop the overflowing:

If your tank has the additional type of ballcock mechanism with a float arm and float ball (see opposite), it is likely that this needs adjusting. Try lifting up on the float arm and ball to see if this stops the flow of water. If it does, the problem can be corrected simply by bending the float arm slightly *downward*, as illustrated.

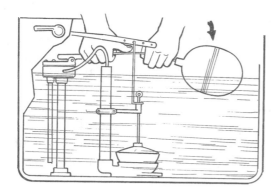

Bend float arm downward slightly to lower water level inside tank and prevent water running out the overflow tube.

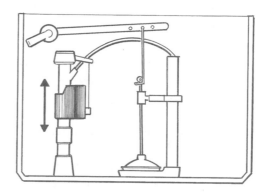

Newer-type ballcock eliminates need for float arm and float ball. Plastic cup rides up and down on ballcock instead.

That will cause the float arm to shut the water off sooner—before it gets high enough to reach the top of the overflow tube. Use two hands when bending this rod, and work carefully to avoid damaging the ballcock mechanism to which it is attached.

When simply bending the float arm doesn't solve the problem, it's possible that the float ball has developed a leak and is partially filled with water. This will keep it from floating as high as it should and therefore would keep the float arm from going high enough to shut off the water at the proper level. If you suspect this, unscrew the float ball and shake it. If you hear water on the inside, throw the old one away and buy a new one to replace it.

Some of the newer toilet tanks do not have a float arm and float ball attached to the ballcock. Instead, one type has a floating plastic cup that rides up and down on the outside of the vertical ballcock as the water level rises or falls. Another model has no float or floating cup; it consists of a low-profile mechanism that sits at the bottom of the tank and senses the increase in

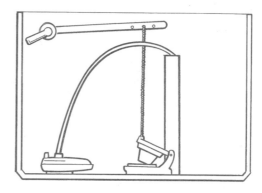

Low-profile ballcock sits on the bottom of the tank and senses depth of water by pressure. It has no separate float mechanism. In this tank flapper-type valve replaces older-type tank ball at the bottom.

pressure as the height of the water inside the tank rises.

With the first type, the water level inside the tank can be adjusted by turning a rod or screw that is attached to the floating plastic cup; with the second type there is a small adjusting screw on top of the unit that can be tightened or loosened to regulate the pressure at which it will shut off the flow of water—in other words, how high it will allow the water to rise before it closes the intake valve.

If you cannot adjust the height of the water to keep the tank from overflowing constantly by bending the float arm or by turning the proper adjustment screw (on the newer units), chances are you should replace the entire ballcock mechanism.

Widely available in local hardware stores, home centers, and plumbing supply outlets, the newer models are now made mostly of plastic and are generally quieter and more efficient than the older brands that were widely used years ago. All are relatively simple to install.

The first step is to shut off the water supply for that tank by turning off the valve in the supply line under it. Flush the tank to empty it, then use a large sponge to remove any water that remains on the bottom. Disconnect the water supply line from under the tank, then loosen and remove the large locknut that holds the ballcock in place from below. Lift out the old unit and install the new one in its place, then reconnect the water line.

If the old water supply line is corroded or hard to connect, replace it with a new flexible pipe or plastic or chrome-plated flexible copper. Most ballcocks come with adapters for connecting up to any size water supply lines, but other types of adapters are available if the ones that come with the unit don't fit.

BOWL DOESN'T EMPTY COMPLETELY OR FLUSHES POORLY

The most frequent cause of this problem is that the water level inside the tank is not high enough. A low water level when the tank is flushed means that the water pouring into the bowl is not coming in with enough pressure, thus it fails to flush the bowl properly. To check for this, take the cover off the tank and look at the water level in the tank when it is full. The water should come up to about an inch or less from the top of the overflow tube. In most tanks there will be a line marked on the back wall of the tank, or on the outside of the overflow tube, to indicate the proper level.

If the water level inside the tank is lower than this mark, bend the float arm slightly *upward* so it won't shut off the water as soon. If the tank does not have a float ball and float arm, turn the adjustment screw on the ballcock mechanism to increase the amount of water that will come into the tank after each flush.

If raising the water level inside the tank doesn't solve your flushing problem, the next most likely cause is a partially clogged drain and waste line. Use a plumber's force cup or plunger to try to break up the clog (as described on page 210).

When poor flushing is not caused by a low water level inside the flush tank or a partially clogged drain line, then the next thing is to make certain all the little holes under the rim of the bowl are clear—not clogged or partially blocked. This sometimes happens in older toilets, especially if the local water supply is naturally "hard"—loaded with minerals. When these small holes get clogged, water cannot come rushing in to flush the sides of the bowl the way it should and the toilet does not empty properly. To correct this, clean out these holes by poking under the rim with a stiff piece of wire or an ice pick.

There is one other possibility that can cause poor flushing—if you have already eliminated all the other possibilities previously mentioned. That is a blocked, or partially blocked, vent stack or soil stack. An obstruction in this line can restrict the amount of air that enters the system as waste water rushes down the pipe, and this can restrict the speed with which the pipe will drain. Since cleaning out a soil stack or vent line is not always an easy job, in most cases it would be best to call in an experienced plumbing contractor to do the job if necessary.

H ome Security

· · · ·

Although those who live in apartments or condominiums often think they are not as subject to burglaries or break-ins as those who live in single-family homes in the suburbs or in affluent areas, this has changed considerably in recent years. Of course, the incidence of crime does vary from one community or neighborhood to another, but most crime statistics seem to indicate that there are no truly "safe" or secure neighborhoods anymore—regardless of where you live.

In fact, there has been a steady increase in the number of burglaries and break-ins in medium- and low-income homes and apartments, as well as in the more expensive dwellings that most professional burglars used to favor. Drug addicts, professional "cat burglars," and even thrill-seeking teenagers have made crime

almost universal throughout the country, including in rural and suburban areas.

That's why it is not surprising to find that the public's interest in new and improved burglar alarms, locks, and other security devices has also been increasing steadily. Every hardware store, home center, and department store now prominently features security equipment of all kinds, and new and improved models that are easier than ever to install, even by the do-it-yourselfer, are being introduced constantly by national manufacturers.

Although installing better locks, or adding burglar alarms and other security devices to your home, will definitely help to discourage burglars, it must be remembered that regardless of how sophisticated an alarm system you install, and regardless of how many "burglarproof" locks you add to your doors and windows, none will keep out a really determined professional burglar who knows there are valuables in that home and who makes up his mind to break into your condominium or apartment.

This is not to say that good locks and alarm systems do not help prevent or deter such break-ins. Law enforcement officials have long said that most burglaries are not committed by determined or skilled professionals—most break-ins are committed on impulse by drug addicts, thrill-seeking teenagers, or other transients looking for an "easy mark." They will force their way in through one of the doors or windows, preferring dwellings that look unoccupied and as if they will be easy to break into.

Good locks and alarms will add to the time it takes to break in, and possibly to the amount of noise required to do the job—and noise is something all burglars try to avoid. In most cases they will avoid breaking glass or smashing through a door—they prefer to work quickly and quietly, especially if people are living close by. A lock that is very difficult to pick, or a door or window that cannot be forced open quickly, may be just enough of a deterrent to convince that would-be burglar to move on to an easier "mark." A burglar knows that the more time spent on the "job," the greater the likelihood that he will be detected and possibly caught. And the more noise he makes, the more likely he is to come to the attention of local residents who could call the police.

Therefore an alarm system does help, even if it only causes a local horn or siren to sound outside that building without actually ringing an alarm in a police station or private security company station. It's true that we have all heard false alarms from a security system that has gone off accidentally and that no one seems to be paying attention to, but the burglar doesn't know this, especially if the alarm goes off in the middle of the night while he is breaking in. That sudden loud noise may be enough to scare him off and convince him to move on to a different "job" where there is no alarm to worry about. This is particularly true if the burglars are thrill-seeking teenagers or drug addicts who have been "cruising" around the neighborhood to see what they can find, or if the burglar is relatively inexperienced and working on a sudden impulse because he sees what he thinks is a good opportunity for a quick break-in.

DOOR LOCKS

The locks on your entrance doors are your first line of defense against unwanted intrusion. Today most locks are of the pin-tumbler variety that are opened with a matching key that has the right number of accurately spaced notches, each cut to a precise depth so that a number of individual tumblers inside the lock cylinder will be raised by the correct amount when the key is inserted and turned. These tumblers must all be lined up by the key before the cylinder can be turned, and the more pins a lock has, the harder it is to pick. But even the best-quality pin-tumbler lock can be picked by a skilled burglar equipped with the right tools (though it will take him much longer to pick a good-quality five-tumbler lock than in inexpensive three-tumbler lock).

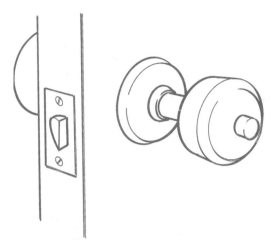

Spring-latch lock that snaps shut when door is closed is least secure type of lock and not recommended for entrance doors.

Spring-latch lock with extra deadbolt latch (arrow) offers a little better security.

There are also a number of more specialized types that are even harder to pick—some with multiple rows of pins instead of a single pin. Very often these more exotic mechanisms involve the use of special keys that cannot be duplicated locally, but only by the manufacturer of that lock (which can pose a problem if you ever lose your key).

On many homes, the lock originally put on by the builder is an inexpensive model that has an easy-to-pick mechanism. Rather than changing the whole lock, one can often upgrade it simply by changing the cylinder—the part that the key activates. However, this makes sense only if the lock itself is a good-quality unit with deadlocking capabilities (described on the pages that follow) and the strength to withstand easy forcing.

The type of lock that offers the least amount of security—and should never be used on an entrance door—is the spring-latch type. In this door lock the key fits into a keyhole in the knob (hence they are often called key-in-the-knob locks), and the spring-driven latch bolt (the piece that slides into the strike-plate opening in the door jamb) has a beveled face so that it can snap into place when the door is slammed shut. This type of lock is one of the easiest to force open—all you need is a stiff piece of plastic (such as a credit card) or a thin strip of flexible metal. If this is forced between the door and the jamb until it comes up against the sloping face of the latch bolt, the plastic or metal strip will push the bolt back into its recess in the edge of the door, releasing the lock and permitting the door to be opened.

Some additional protection is provided by those spring-latch locks that have a separate guardbolt or deadbolt located directly behind the main latch bolt. This extra bolt is also spring-driven—that is, a spring pushes it out—and it moves separately from the main latch bolt, so that even if the sloping latch bolt is forced back, the plastic or metal strip will encounter this second bolt, which cannot

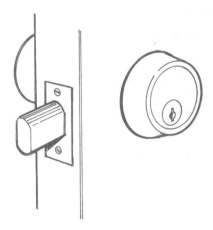

Maximum security is offered by separate deadbolt or dead latch, installed in addition to the conventional lock.

then be released by pushing past it. Thus it is almost impossible to force the bolt open with a credit card or similar tool.

These secondary bolts are not very strong, however, and are easily bent out of the way or even sawed through with a hacksaw blade. In addition, they don't project very far into the strike-plate opening, so if the door fits loosely inside its frame, the burglar can use a pry bar to force the frame open enough so that the latch bolt slides out of its opening in the strike plate, thus permitting the door to swing open.

The best type of lock to offer full resistance to forcing or prying is the deadbolt or dead latch. This has a steel latch bolt that projects far enough into the door jamb to make prying difficult—a ½-inch projection is considered minimum, but 1 inch is even better. The bolt has a blunt end, not a sloping one like a spring latch, with a square or rectangular cross section. It should be at least ½ inch thick, and the best ones will have a round steel roller on the inside so that cutting through with a hacksaw blade becomes almost impossible.

A deadbolt may be incorporated as part of the basic door lock, or it may be installed as a separate auxiliary lock activated by a separate key. One of the best is the heavy-duty mortise-type lock that is recessed into the edge of the door and has both a deadbolt and a spring latch with an extra guardbolt behind it. With this type of lock the door latches and locks automatically when the door is slammed shut, but then an extra turn of the key throws the deadbolt for extra "double-locking" security. This may not be practical unless you are installing a new door, since it can require a lot of patching and redrilling on an old door. So for those who have older houses with a lock already installed, it is often easier to add a separate auxiliary deadbolt.

Auxiliary deadbolts are installed in one of two ways: by mounting on the inside face of the door or by recessing (mortising) into the edge of the door. Surface-mounted auxiliary locks are easier to install, but many people object to their appearance on the

Heavy-duty mortise-type entrance door lock has a separate deadbolt, in addition to the spring-latch lock.

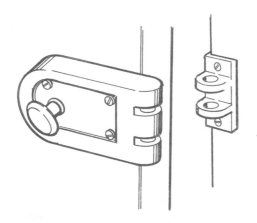

Auxiliary deadbolt, also called a night latch, can be added to provide additional security for entrance doors.

inside. Most auxiliary deadbolt locks have a knob on the inside for opening and closing, with a key tumbler on the outside. The better-quality ones will also have a special tapered ring around the cylinder on the outside so that a burglar cannot use a wrench to unscrew the cylinder.

Deadbolts that are recessed into the edge of the door are a feature of single-cylinder locks that use a key on the outside and a knob on the inside; or they come in double-cylinder locks that require a key on both sides for opening and locking. The latter type is recommended for doors that have glass panes in them or next to them, so that if the burglar breaks the glass, he still can't unlock the door. With this type of twin-cylinder deadbolt, however, a key should be left in the lock or hung close by when you are at home, so that in the event of a fire or other emergency no time will be lost in getting the door unlocked.

Since every door lock can only be as secure as the door itself, and the frame in which the door fits, attention should be paid to making certain that all entrance doors (back, side, and front) are secure and solid (hollow-core doors offer poor protection against break-ins). They should fit snugly in their frames with no large gaps between the jamb and the door, and they should be mounted so that the hinge pins are on the inside, not the outside.

An entrance door's frame should be mounted solidly against the studs. When installing door jambs, builders often leave a hollow space between the jamb and the 2×4 studs against which it is nailed, then fill this hollow space with shims in order to plumb up the jamb more easily. You can check for this by pushing hard against the door jamb—away from the opening—

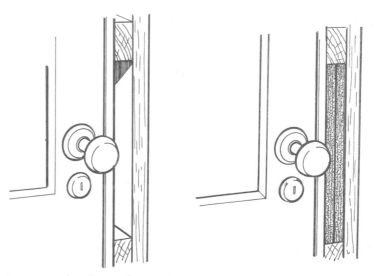

To prevent bending or forcing the door frame away from the door lock by using a heavy pry bar, fill the hollow spaces behind the door jamb with pieces of solid wood.

while the door is wide open. If the jamb seems to "give" or acts springy (as though it has no solid backing behind it), it would be worth the trouble to remove the jamb and fill in the spaces behind it with full-length strips of solid wood. This will make it much harder for a burglar to pry the door frame apart so that he can unlatch the lock without ever actually unlocking it, a common technique.

Equally important is making certain that the strike plate into which the latch bolt slides is solidly mounted with long screws that go into the studs behind the jamb or frame; short screws can be easily pried out when the door is given a hard kick. Hinges should also be mounted good and tight with long screws that go into the 2×4 studs behind the jamb, not just into the jamb frame. Loosely mounted hinge screws can make it easy to pry the whole door out without ever having to unlock it.

Remember that an entrance door that has glass panes in it (especially if it is a back door or side door) is a sure invitation to burglars—particularly if that door is not easily seen from the street or from neighboring homes. All a would-be thief has to do is break the glass and reach in to release the lock from the inside. He might hesitate to make this much noise if the door is in the front, but a back or side door is much more vulnerable to forced entry.

Incidentally, having side panels of glass next to a door is just as bad. However, if you have such panels within reach of the door, make sure they are glazed with a burglarproof (unbreakable) plastic such as Lexan, or have shatterproof glass installed.

Another point to keep in mind is that chain locks (or door chains, as they are most often called) that allow you to open the door a couple of inches while speaking to a caller really do not offer much protection. Regardless of whether they are the kind that must be unlocked with a key or by releasing the chain from the inside, these chain locks are almost always attached with relatively short wood screws. A strong kick from a grown man will usually pull these screws right out. Or the chain itself can be easily cut using an ordinary bolt cutter (which many burglars carry as "standard" equipment).

If you do install one, make sure the screws that go into the jamb are long enough to penetrate the jamb and go through into the solid wood stud behind it. For attaching the lock to the door, use bolts that go through the door, rather than wood screws or sheet-metal screws. The bolts should have the heads on the outside, and the heads should be rounded off with a file or ground down in such a way that they cannot be grabbed with a wrench or turned with a screwdriver.

PROTECTING SLIDING DOORS

Sliding glass patio doors that lead to an outside deck, patio, or screened terrace have become a popular feature in many condominiums and apartments. Desirable because of the amount of light and air they let in, sliding glass doors also make it easier for burglars to break in. The locks on these doors are usually small and easy to force, yet in spite of this many apartments and condominium units, even if located at street level, have little else to prevent forcible entry.

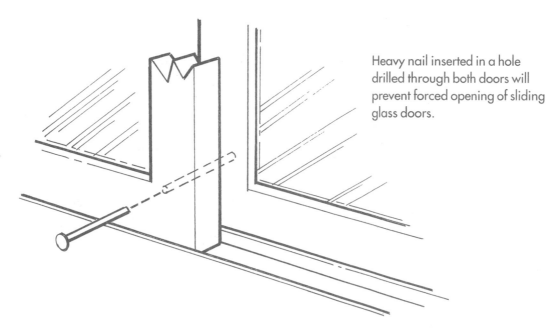

Heavy nail inserted in a hole drilled through both doors will prevent forced opening of sliding glass doors.

Fortunately there are a number of different types of auxiliary sliding door locks that you can buy and install yourself to make these doors more secure. Some bolt onto the frame of the door and have a bolt that goes through a hole in the track along the bottom. Some require a key to open, while others merely have a pin that you release from the inside.

There are also some simple methods you can use to secure a sliding glass door without having to buy any type of special lock. One simple but effective method is to close the door and then drill a hole through the frames where the doors overlap. Then insert a snug-fitting steel bolt, nail, or long screw through this hole to "pin" the two doors together. Now no one can slide either door open, yet the pin can be quickly pulled out from inside when need be.

Another positive means of protecting sliding doors against forcible entry is to close the door and then drop a length of pipe or a heavy wood stick into the inside

section of the sliding track. This stick or pipe should be just long enough to fit between the edge of the door and the vertical door frame when the door is closed (see below). With it in place, opening the door becomes impossible. Yet the stick or

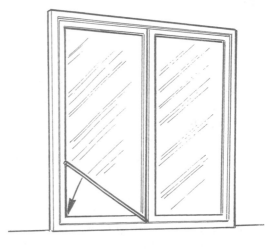

Another way to prevent forced entry through sliding glass doors is to drop a wood rod or length of metal pipe into the track at the bottom.

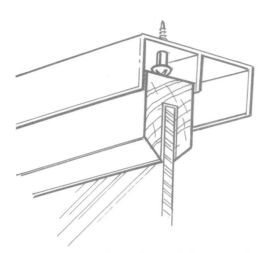

To keep burglars from lifting a sliding glass door out of its track, drive a screw partway up into the overhead track. Allow head to stick down just enough to clear the top of door while allowing it to slide easily.

pipe can be easily lifted out of the track on the inside.

Another point to consider is that most sliding doors can be removed by lifting them straight up until the bottom end clears the track. A simple way to protect against this possibility is to drive a couple of sheet-metal screws straight up into the top track (as shown), leaving the heads sticking down a fraction of an inch—just far enough to prevent lifting the door out of its track, but not far enough to interfere with the door sliding back and forth. The projecting screws will thus prevent anyone from prying or lifting the door up high enough to get it out of its track, yet you can still remove the door when necessary by sliding the door open and then taking out the screws.

WINDOW LOCKS

Although it is easy to get in through a window simply by breaking the glass, most burglars try to avoid this because of the noise it makes and because a broken window is a sure sign of forced entry if seen by anyone passing by. Most will opt for forcing or unlocking the window instead. The widely used butterfly type of sash catch that is found on most double-hung windows—a rotating catch that locks together to keep either sash from being opened—is actually of very little value when it comes to keeping out burglars. It can be opened easily from the outside by sliding a thin metal blade or screwdriver up between the sash frames and then pushing sideways to unlock the catch.

While even the best of window locks won't always prevent a break-in, it is par-

ticularly important that windows on the first floor or ground level have extra protection. Installing a rotating window lock that can be opened only with a key helps, because then even if the burglar breaks the glass, he still won't be able to open the catch so he can slide the window open and climb through.

Key-operated, wedge-type locks, similar to the one shown in the illustration, are also effective. These are screwed to the inside of the upper sash frame so that when the window is closed the foot or base of the metal "wedge" presses down on top of the lower sash frame, thus preventing anyone from opening either sash. A key enables you to remove the wedge from its mounting plate when you want to open the window. Most come with a sec-

One type of key-operated lock that can be installed on double-hung windows. The second mounting plate allows you to leave the window open slightly for ventilation, but prevents opening it any farther.

"Pinning" window sashes together with a heavy nail is one simple method for preventing forcible entry.

ond mounting plate that you can fasten to the upper sash a couple of inches above the lower one. With the wedge locked on to this plate you can leave the window open slightly for ventilation, yet the wedge will keep it from being opened any farther.

One of the simplest and most effective methods for securing a double-hung window against forcible entry is to use a heavy nail to "pin" the window shut, as shown in the illustration. With the window fully closed, drill a hole clear through the top rail of the lower sash and a little more than halfway through the lower rail of the upper sash.

The hole should slope downward slightly so the nail (or bolt) won't fall out after it is in place, and to prevent anyone from working it out simply by rattling the sash from the outside. The end of the nail or bolt should be cut off so that its head barely reaches the surface when it is inside the hole. Painting the head of the nail (or bolt) the same color as the window will make it almost invisible.

Special window locks that require a key are also available for sliding windows and casement windows—some that are bolted to the window, some that merely clamp on to the frame to keep the windows from opening. Sliding windows can also be secured like sliding glass patio doors by dropping a stick or length of pipe into the track at the bottom (see page 225).

BURGLAR ALARM SYSTEMS

Although the most sophisticated burglar alarm systems are those that are installed by professionals who specialize in this type of work, many alarm systems that are widely sold in local hardware stores, home centers, and electronic stores can be installed by the do-it-yourselfer. All are designed to set off a loud horn, bell, or siren when an intruder is detected. In addition to the horn or siren that is built into the central console, most systems also allow you to add a separate external siren or horn that can be mounted either inside or outside the house. Some will also turn on lights inside and outside the house when the alarm goes off—a further help in scaring off intruders.

Many of the more sophisticated systems also offer optional attachments that will activate your phone automatically and cause it to dial any number you have selected when the alarm goes off. You can set it to call a friend or neighbor who will alert the proper authorities, or you can have it dial the police directly in communities where this is still permitted (many police departments no longer allow this).

The most reliable and most effective type of phone alarm is the kind that automatically sends a signal—by telephone, radio, or cable TV—to a central security monitoring station when the alarm is activated. The central office (which may be located almost anywhere in the country) will then call your home to see if this is a false alarm. If you don't answer with the proper code, they will immediately call your local police department or sheriff's office to notify them of the break-in.

This type of system not only costs more to install, it also involves paying a monthly fee for the central monitoring service. In addition, it must be remembered that in a growing number of communities the police (and sometimes the fire department) may charge for coming out if the call turns out to be a false alarm (in most cases they will allow one or two "false" alarms before they start to charge for each subsequent one).

Most residential alarm systems can be roughly classified as falling into one of two broad categories: perimeter alarms and space alarms. The perimeter alarm system, as its name implies, is one that is designed to protect the perimeter of the dwelling—more specifically the windows and doors through which burglars normally enter. It will set off the alarm when an intruder tries to gain entry by forcing open a window or door—in other words, the alarm goes off *before* the intruder has actually entered the premises.

Space alarms, on the other hand, sound the alarm after an intruder has entered a protected area or zone—for example, an entrance hall, a bedroom, a garage, and so forth.

PERIMETER ALARM SYSTEMS

These usually consist of a centrally located console or control unit that is connected electrically to a series of sensors attached to each of the doors and windows that you want to protect. All these sensors or switches are linked together in a continuous loop through which a low-voltage current flows whenever the system is turned on. As long as the loop is unbroken nothing happens. However, if a window or door is opened, or a wire is cut, the alarm goes off.

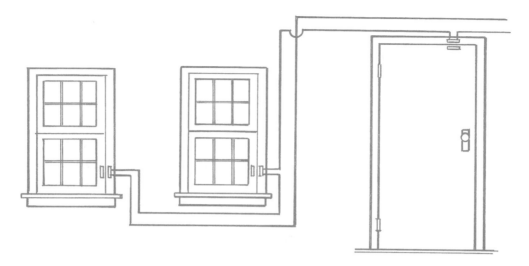

Wired perimeter alarm system has magnetic switch sensors mounted on doors and windows so that alarm will sound if one of these is opened or if the wire is cut.

The sensors most often used to protect doors and windows are two-piece magnetic switches that are installed so that one piece (a magnet) is fastened to the movable part of the window or door, while the other piece (a magnetic switch) is fastened to the frame. As long as the two pieces are in close proximity, the switch is closed and the circuit is unbroken. However, if one of the protected windows or doors is forced while the circuit is "armed" (the system is turned on), the magnet will be pulled away from its switch, the switch will open, breaking the circuit, and the alarm will go off.

In addition to magnetic switch sensors, the continuous electrical loop can also include magnetic foil tape that is applied to the glass on some large windows or on glass doors. If this glass shatters, the tape tears, thus breaking the continuous loop and setting off the alarm. Some companies also sell pressure-sensitive mats that can be wired into the system. If someone steps on the mat while the system is armed, this too will set off the alarm.

WIRELESS PERIMETER ALARM SYSTEMS

The hardest part of installing a perimeter alarm system is running wires throughout the house to connect up the central console with each of the switches and sensors mounted on the protected windows and doors. This wiring carries only a low voltage, so there is no danger of shock or fire while working, but installing all the wires so they won't be visible is a time-consuming and sometimes difficult job, especially when going from one floor to another. The job takes a great deal of time and effort if you try to do it yourself, and if you hire a professional to do the installation, his labor costs may actually equal or exceed the cost of the equipment involved.

High-tech wireless perimeter alarm systems eliminate the need for running wires

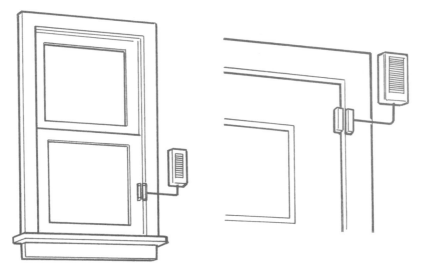

Wireless perimeter system uses the same type of magnetic switches on doors and windows. Small transmitter connected to these sensors will send a signal to the central console without need for wires.

all through the house. These are much simpler and easier to install, especially for the do-it-yourselfer, and they are widely sold in hardware stores, home centers, and department stores.

These wireless systems use the same kind of two-piece magnetic switches on windows and doors, but instead of being connected by wires to the central console each switch comes with its own little radio transmitter. This transmitter, which is connected to the stationary half of the switch with a short length of wire, is mounted on the wall near that switch.

When the switch is activated (when a door or window is opened while the system is armed), the transmitter sends a radio signal to a receiver that is built into the central control. This receiver then activates the alarm in the same way that most garage door openers are activated by a small hand-held transmitter from inside the car.

Instructions from the manufacturer will almost always recommend installing one transmitter for each two-piece magnetic

sensor switch, but in actual practice there is no reason you cannot connect more than one magnetic switch to a single transmitter, as long as the switches are close to each other—for example, when two windows are right next to each other or when a window is located next to a door. In each of these cases you can save money by installing one set of magnetic switches on

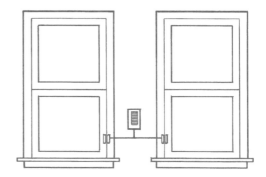

To keep down the costs of a wireless system, two or more magnetic sensor switches can be wired to a single transmitter when doors or windows are close to each other.

each of the windows or doors, then wiring both switches to a single transmitter (mounted between them).

You can buy wireless systems in kits that include a central console and anywhere from two to five door and window sensors, or you can buy the components separately. Additional switches and sensors can always be purchased separately so that you can add on to the original installation at any time.

All wireless alarm systems depend on small batteries that must be installed in each transmitter, so it is important to remember that batteries fail in time, even if not used. Some systems have a built-in testing circuit that allows you to check the condition of the batteries without sounding the alarm (a red indicator light on the transmitter will light up for the test). Others have "dead battery" indicators that show when batteries need replacing.

However, on some systems you have to actually set off the alarm each time you test the system. If that's the case in your home, buy an inexpensive battery tester sold in most hardware stores and electronic supply houses, and use it at least once a month to check each transmitter battery's condition.

SPACE ALARMS

Space alarms are set up inside the dwelling to detect an intruder who enters the area covered by that particular unit. Some units are infrared to detect body heat, but most use something like radar or ultrasound to detect movement within the zone of protection. This zone of protection is usually the cone-shaped pattern formed by the waves or radiation sent out by that particular unit.

Most space alarms are self-contained units that can be set up anywhere and simply aimed at the area you want to

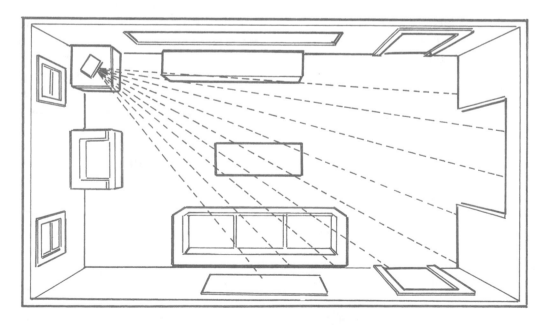

Self-contained space alarms sense motion or body heat inside a protected cone-shaped area.

protect—for example, an entrance door or entrance hall, a bedroom, or even a garage door. Anyone entering or passing through those areas would set off the alarm, even if nothing was touched.

The appeal offered by this type of alarm unit is that it is portable and can be carried with you when you travel or move. Also, these units require no installation and can be quickly set up almost anywhere. All you have to do is aim the unit at the area to be covered, then plug it into the nearest wall outlet. The alarm should be positioned so its zone of protection will cover the doors or windows through which a thief is likely to enter or to protect areas through which the intruder is most likely to pass.

There are several drawbacks to these units. First, they don't sound the alarm until *after* the burglar is inside. Second, they have to be located out in the open, where they can be easily spotted—in other words, where an intruder could get his hands on the unit and disable it quickly. Third, many are susceptible to false alarms—they can be set off by curtains waving or by a child or pet roaming around in the night.

OTHER WAYS TO DISCOURAGE BURGLARS

Police departments and other crime experts generally agree that a high percentage of burglars and break-ins are spur-of-the-moment crimes that are not planned ahead of time. More often than not the thief is simply cruising around looking for an easy "target"—preferably a house that looks unoccupied. To a burglar an unoccupied home means less chance of getting caught and more time to search for valuables.

The simplest way to hide the fact that no one is at home when you are away is to use several timers to turn on lights, radios, and television sets at different times of the day and night. The idea is to simulate the normal living patterns of the family when everyone is at home. Don't make the mistake of simply leaving a light on all the time. Burglars are quick to spot a light or lamp that is left on twenty-four hours a day—if they have been watching for several days. It is a sure sign that the family is away.

Timers for controlling lights and appliances are sold in practically all hardware stores, as well as in home centers and electrical supply houses. You plug the timer (or its extension cord) into a wall outlet, then you plug the light or appliance to be controlled into the timer.

There are also programmable wall switches that you can install to replace a standard wall switch. These can be set to turn lights and/or appliance receptacles on and off at different intervals during the day or night. When not used as a timer, they can still be used as a conventional manual switch to turn lights on or off.

When you are shopping for electrical timers, remember that they vary as to the number of on/off cycles that can be set up for each twenty-four hour period, as well as to the maximum and minimum "on" and "off" times that can be programmed into each cycle. The less expensive models may allow only for one on/off sequence per day; more expensive models may allow for as many as forty-eight separate on/off cycles per day. Once set, the same sequence will be repeated each day. Some

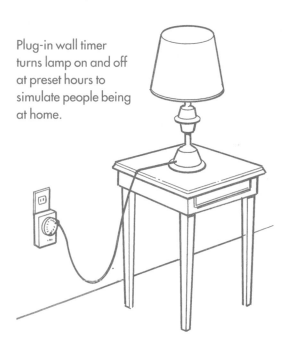

Plug-in wall timer turns lamp on and off at preset hours to simulate people being at home.

on at regular intervals by a timer, can make the potential intruder think that there are people talking on the inside—especially if the radio is left tuned to an all-talk station. But don't turn the volume too high. Set it just high enough so that one can hear voices when you listen from the outside, but not quite high enough to hear what is being said. Another timer should be used to turn on the TV set for those hours when you would normally turn it on if you were at home (the radio should go off during that period).

Another good "trick" is to use a tape recorder with prerecorded conversations, or even the sounds of a dog barking periodically, to make it seem as though the house is occupied. The recorder should be on a timer and should have either a long-playing tape that will last till your return or a means of repeating the same tape so it will run over and over again.

When setting up timers, don't forget front entrance lights if you normally turn them on each evening. Having them come on as it gets dark (if that's what you usually do when at home) will not only help make the dwelling look occupied, it will also help to discourage break-ins through that door, because burglars prefer to work in the dark.

When the house is to be empty for several days or weeks—while you are off on a trip, for example—there are also a number of other precautions that should be taken. These include the following:

• Stop all newspaper and mail deliveries so that they don't pile up in front of your entrance door or in your mailbox. Or ask a friend or neighbor to pick these up each day—and make sure they pick up packages that you don't expect.

• If you live in a condominium where

timers randomly vary the times slightly from one day to another (this is more effective in fooling someone who is watching the house).

For maximum protection several timers should be used to control different lights or appliances in various parts of the home to more closely duplicate the "lived in" effect of a typical family. For example, one or more lights can be turned on in the early evening in the kitchen and family room, while bedroom lights should come on later and stay on later. Living room or family room lights should go off earlier than bedroom lights, and so on.

Timers with short "on" intervals are also a good idea in bathrooms and bedrooms—again, to simulate people going in and out of rooms in a manner that would be typical of the family's normal living habits when everyone is at home.

Leaving on a radio, or having it turned

each family sets out their own garbage can for pickup, don't leave empty garbage cans standing around on the outside.

• If you can, leave a car in your driveway, or ask your neighbor to park his car in your driveway several times a week.

• Don't close all drapes, shades, or blinds, since this will signal that the house is not occupied. Try to leave them about half-drawn on most windows, or as you normally do when at home.

• Don't hide spare keys under the doormat, in the mailbox, inside a nearby planter, or in other obvious places. These are the first places most burglars will look.

• If you have an attached garage, make sure the garage door is locked and make sure the door connecting the garage to your apartment or condominium unit is bolted and has a strong frame. Many burglars favor breaking in through a connecting garage.

• If all precautions fail and your house is burglarized, remember that you can improve your chances of recovering stolen goods if all valuable items are marked with an engraving pen (this would include television sets, radio and stereo sets, cameras, power tools, and so on). Also, make a list of all valuable items, with serial numbers, model numbers, date purchased, price, and so forth, before you leave. Put this list in a safe-deposit box or other place outside the home.

Solving Storage Problems

No matter how large or spacious your new apartment or condominium home seemed to be when you first looked at it or moved in, chances are it didn't take long for you to realize that there is not as much storage space as you thought for everything you want to keep at home. It now seems that more closets, cabinets, or drawers are needed but, unlike the owner of a private house, you cannot add on another room or erect a storage shed in the yard behind your home.

However, this doesn't mean that you can't do something to increase—or at least improve—the storage space that you do have. In most cases you could make much more efficient use of the existing closets and cabinets simply by reorganizing them for greater efficiency. In addition,

there are ways that you can actually "create" additional storage space by making more efficient use of storage areas and spaces that are now being at least partly wasted.

One of the simplest ways to increase the amount of storage space available in any apartment or condominium unit is to select furniture with storage capabilities in mind. Where possible, buy functional pieces that include storage compartments or storage features. For example, there are beds you can buy that have drawers built in under the springs, and instead of ordinary end tables that have four legs with nothing between them you can select small chests or cabinets that have drawers or compartments for storing books, stereo tapes, party supplies, and so on.

REORGANIZE YOUR CLOSETS

Since closets are the principal storage spaces in most condominiums and apartments, this is obviously the place to start when trying to solve home storage problems. For most people the solution lies in remodeling the inside of existing closets to maximize the space that is already available. For more extreme cases where the closets you have are just too small, you may be able to build in an additional closet—for example, in an unused corner of a large bedroom or at one end of a long foyer or hallway where there is a vacant corner or an unused length of wall that can be converted.

However, before doing anything, you should empty all your closets and do a survey of what you have and what you need. Empty all the shelves and take everything off the closet floors, then spread everything out on the floor where you can see it. Now look over the contents of each closet carefully as it is spread out before you with two main thoughts in mind:

1. How many of these items do you really need? In other words, how much can you get rid of—either by throwing out some items, or perhaps by storing them outside of the apartment (for example, in a basement store room or in a rented public storage locker).

2. After you have decided what you are going to keep, start thinking about how to rearrange these items inside the closet so they will be easier to find and readily accessible when needed.

Luggage is one of the first items you should think about. In most families luggage is used only a few times a year, so plan on storing these pieces toward the back of the closet or on one of the highest and hardest-to-reach shelves. If those shelves are deep enough, try to store smaller items in front of the luggage, where they will be more visible and easier to reach.

When storing your luggage, don't forget to make use of the space available *inside* each piece. Suitcases that are empty most of the time can be filled with neatly folded out-of-season clothing or seldom-used items of sporting equipment. But be sure you hang a tag or put a label on the outside of each bag so that you will know what is inside without having to go through it every time you need something. Even small pieces of luggage can be used as storage containers when not traveling—if you place them on an easily reached closet shelf; they are ideal for storing gloves, scarves, or similar small items.

REMODELING THE INSIDE OF A CLOSET

Although rearranging the contents of a closet may often be adequate, at least for a while, a far more effective and more permanent way to solve closet storage problems is to remodel the inside completely in order to make maximum use of the space available. This usually means rearranging the existing shelves and closet poles, as well as possibly installing additional bins, racks, and drawer units for storing shoes, sweaters, scarves, hats, and so on. With proper planning, this type of closet remodeling project will have the effect of actually "creating" more storage space inside that closet.

"Standard" closet has only one shelf and one pole and is hard to keep neat.

Properly rearranged and reorganized, same closet has double-decked poles on one side to increase capacity and make it a lot neater.

For example, the "standard" clothes closet has one closet pole that is mounted under a single shelf. This pole is normally positioned about 5½ feet off the floor to allow room for hanging full-length garments. The single shelf above this pole goes from one side of the closet to the other and is most often used for storing hats, shoes, suitcases, sports equipment, and a variety of miscellaneous items.

There are several things wrong with this traditional arrangement. First of all, many of the garments that are hanging in the average closet are shorter than full length—especially in children's closets. As a result, a good deal of the space underneath these hanging garments is largely wasted.

Another thing wrong with this arrangement is that it greatly encourages clutter. People tend to pile things up on the floor under the shorter garments, and this in turn means that finding small items—shoes, boots, gloves, or hats that have been thrown in—is often a difficult and very frustrating chore. Furthermore, the single shelf above the closet pole is almost always hard to reach and awkward to get at, especially in the corners or at the far ends. Items stored there are often forgotten or simply "lost" as far as the family is concerned.

The most efficient way to rearrange the inside of such a clothes closet is to rip out the existing shelf and the single closet pole that is mounted beneath it. Then, in place of the single closet pole you install new poles in a "double-decked" arrangement similar to the illustration on page 239. This allows you to hang two rows of short garments, one over the other, in the same closet width that was previously taken up by a single row of hangers. And since most closets hold more short garments than long ones, only a small amount of pole space need be left in one part of the closet for longer items of clothing.

In some cases, it may be necessary to install such double-decked poles in only half the closet. To support the end of each closet pole in the middle of the closet, you will either have to install a vertical divider of some kind or you will have to mount special brackets against the back wall of the closet to support the pole ends.

When you are installing two poles one above the other in this manner, it is usually more efficient to mount the top pole a little higher than the original single pole. The lower pole should be mounted about halfway between this upper pole and the floor. In most closets this will still leave enough space for shoe racks or miscellaneous storage on the floor under the garments on the lower pole.

Depending on personal needs, chances are that you won't want all closet poles to be doubled up in this manner. You will still need at least one closet pole where long garments can be hung without touching the floor, so keep this in mind when planning your new closet layout. To avoid wasting space under these longer garments, install shallow drawer units or shelves to provide storage for many items. You can also lower that single pole a few inches so that the longest garment just clears the floor, then install extra shelves above that pole. In most such closet remodeling projects, it's also a good idea to include small shelves, drawers, or bins that can be used for neatly storing shoes, sweaters, gloves, and other items instead of having to pile them up on the floor or on one large shelf.

Of course, the quickest and easiest way to complete such a closet remodeling project is to call in one of the many professional contractors or closet accessory dealers (some can be hired through local department stores; others advertise in newspapers or in the Yellow Pages). These specialists will completely redesign the inside of your closets to meet your particular needs—often completing the job in a single day.

However, having the job done professionally is often quite costly. Doing the job yourself can cut the cost by more than half in most cases, and this is, fortunately, not a particularly difficult project—especially if you buy one of the many kits that are sold for just this purpose in large hardware stores, home centers, and department stores.

Consisting of precut, modular components, and packaged with complete instructions, these units can be installed by any do-it-yourselfer who can use a screwdriver and a drill. Each kit contains all the poles, shelves, and other hardware needed to remodel the inside of an existing closet, and they come in all sizes—from smaller packages that will fit single-door closets only 3 or 4 feet wide, to large, 9-foot closets that may have two or three doors.

Most manufacturers also sell a wide range of optional accessories that you can add to further increase the versatility and storage capacity of your new closet. This might include a choice of different-sized drawer units, small cabinets with hinged or sliding doors, and modular-size storage bins that are specially made for use in closets. All can sit either on the floor or on one of the shelves, and all serve to further eliminate clutter.

Careful planning is important before you go out and buy a closet kit or any of the materials you will need to remodel your closet. Measure the inside of the closet carefully and then use the manufacturer's literature and brochures as a guide to figure out how poles and shelves can best be arranged. Decide on how much space you will need for short garments, how much for long garments, for shoes, and for all of the other items stored in that closet. Figure out what shelves, poles, and modular units will fit, then play with different arrangements on paper to see which will work out best in your case.

Kits for larger closets often include shelves in the center, as well as double-decked closet poles for short garments, plus additional shelves across the top.

Other closet arrangements include drawers in the center for socks, underwear, and the like.

If you are planning to use a kit, remember that some kits are intended primarily for use in children's closets, where only short garments will be hung, while others are for closets that will hold mostly long garments (dresses, coats, and possibly slacks that are not folded over a hanger). Also, make sure you understand what each particular kit contains—some include only poles and shelves, plus the brackets and other hardware needed to install them. Others may also include bins, drawers, or narrow shelving units that can be mounted in a vertical row in the middle of the closet. (Most offer such accessories as options that can be purchased separately or added later on as your needs change.)

Bear in mind that with most of these kits the interior arrangement can be changed later on if desired simply by moving shelves, poles, and other components to form a different interior layout (this also holds true if you buy separate components instead of a kit).

For example, in a closet originally set up for children's clothes the poles could be rearranged to accommodate longer garments as a child grows older. In addition, if you move to another apartment or condominium in the future, most of the shelves, poles, racks, and bins you installed can be taken down and carried with you for installation in your new closets.

Although using a prepackaged kit will make the job of remodeling an old closet a lot simpler for most people because it does most of your planning for you, and because it eliminates the need for shopping for many separate components, these kits do have their limitations. Your kit will be designed to fit a particular plan for a particular-size closet. (It's true that some variations in the basic arrangement are usually possible, but these are limited in scope.) With maximum sales potential in mind, the manufacturer tries to include components for the most popular layout for a given size or type of closet—and that design may or may not coincide with your ideas, preferences, or needs.

That is why some people prefer to buy the various components separately and then design their own closet layout. If your dealer does not stock separate components, look up one of the specialty dealers who are usually listed in the Yellow Pages under "Closet Accessories" or simply "Closets."

The precut shelves furnished in most storage systems are made of either particle board (also called flake board) that is covered with a plastic veneer or of prefinished plywood. However, several of the more popular closet remodeling systems use shelves made of welded, vinyl-coated steel rods instead of wood. These "open" shelves, which are more like wire grates or the shelves found in many older refrigerators, are lighter in weight than solid shelves, and they allow air to circulate freely through and around them. Also, they do not collect dust in the corners.

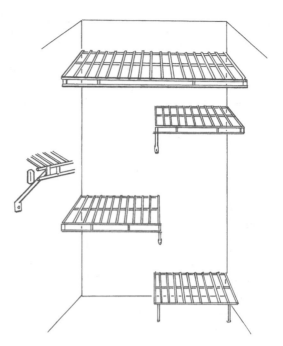

Vinyl-coated "open" wire shelving can go from wall to wall or only partway across. These eliminate the need for separate closet poles because the bar under the front of each shelf will support hangers.

Another advantage of this type of open shelving is that there is often no need for a separate closet pole; a reinforced vinyl-coated rod below the front edge of the shelving permits inserting hangers without need for a separate pole (see illustration).

Like most other closet systems, open wire shelving allows for the addition of all kinds of optional storage units, including narrow-shelf assemblies that will fit against one side of the closet or that can be installed down the center, bins and drawer units that sit on the floor, and all kinds of shoe racks, skirt racks, tie racks, and other accessories that will further help to organize the inside of your closet.

LARGER DOORS MAKE THE INSIDE OF THE CLOSET MORE ACCESSIBLE

In addition to remodeling the inside of a closet, you can also make the space inside most closets more accessible by replacing the existing door (or doors) with a door that is wider or taller or both. Here's why:

A typical clothes closet will have a single door that is anywhere from 24 to 36 inches wide, but the closet may be anywhere from 4 to 6 feet wide on the inside. This leaves "blind" corners and hard-to-reach areas at each end of that closet—space that is never used efficiently. In addition, garments hung at the end of the closet pole on each side of the door are very difficult to reach—or even to see.

To solve these problems and make such space more accessible, and thus more usable, the closet door can be removed and the opening enlarged so that a wider door—one that is the full width of the

closet—can be installed. This also makes it practical to install drawers or narrow shelves on each side in space that would have been almost impossible to reach through the original door.

Instead of a single wide door you can also install double doors that are hinged at each side and open in the center, or bifolding and sliding doors that fold back from the center to each side. Bypassing sliding doors that allow you to open only half of the closet is another possibility, but as a rule these are not as convenient as center-opening doors that allow access to the full width of the closet at one time.

When planning to enlarge the closet opening, you might also think of making the opening (and the doors) higher. Making the doors full height (almost up to the ceiling) will enable you to see what is

before

after

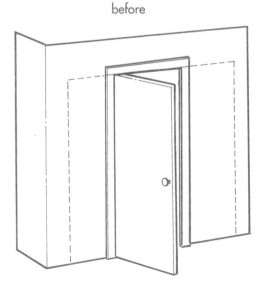 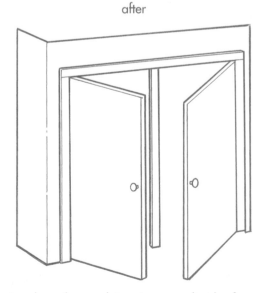

Most closets are wider than their door opening, making it awkward to reach interior on each side of door (left). Replacing the single door with a set of double doors that go across the full width of the closet eases access to increase storage capacity (right).

stored on shelves that are located at the top of the closet and allow you to add at least one more shelf at the top in most cases because that space was almost impossible to reach when the original door was in place.

BUILDING A NEW CLOSET

One sure way to solve the problem of not having enough closet space in your apartment or condominium is to build an additional closet—perhaps in an unused corner of a large bedroom or in the corner of almost any room that has extra space (even in a garage or basement, if your condominium has one).

This is really not as difficult, or as expensive, as it may seem, regardless of whether you hire a contractor to do the work or elect to build the closet yourself. If you build it into the corner of an existing room, you will be starting out with two walls already in place, plus the ceiling and the floor. So all you have to do is build one side wall and frame out the front of the closet where the door will go.

The illustration below shows how such a closet can be built into the corner of a

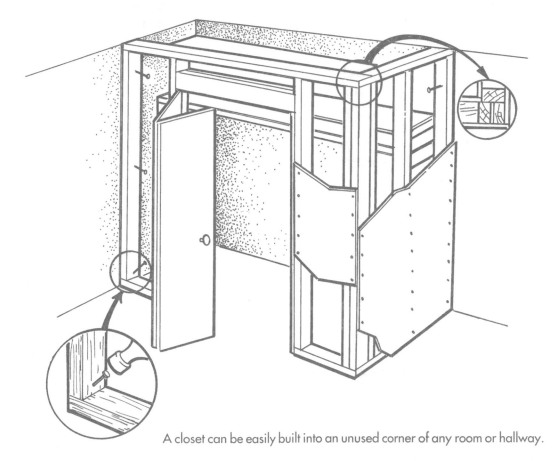

A closet can be easily built into an unused corner of any room or hallway.

room. The closet is framed out with 2×4s and is finished inside and outside with gypsum board (drywall) that is then painted or papered to match the existing walls in that room. To allow adequate room for clothes hangers, build the closet at least 24 inches deep on the inside (front to back).

The closet shown on page 243 has bifolding doors that are almost ceiling height to allow full use of storage space near the top of the closet. (To save on costs, use standard height doors instead; taller doors may have to be custom-made or special-ordered.) Buy the doors and have them on hand before you start to frame out the opening so you will be sure they fit when you install them.

Here are the steps to follow when building such a closet:

1. After deciding on the size, draw the outline of the outside of the closet on the floor, using chalk or masking tape. Then nail the 2×4 bottom plate flat against the floor to form the bottom of the new closet wall.

2. Install the two vertical 2×4s that go against the existing walls on each side. They should rest on top of the bottom plates just installed and should be a snug fit between these and the ceiling. Each vertical 2×4 must be absolutely plumb (vertical), so check with a level before nailing them in place. Fasten them in place by toenailing to the 2×4s along the top and bottom of the existing walls, as well as by toenailing to the new 2×4 you have just put down against the floor. (Toenailing calls for driving nails in through the face of the stud so they go in at a steep angle and thus will penetrate the horizontal 2×4 at the top or the bottom, as shown in the illustration on page 243.)

3. Install the 2×4s against the ceiling next (called the top plates). A plumb line should be used to accurately align these so they are directly above the bottom plates, with corners positioned directly above each other. The top plates can be fastened to the ceiling by nailing to overhead beams or joists in the ceiling or by using expansion anchors to fasten each piece securely through the plaster.

4. The corner post for the new closet consists of two 2×4s nailed flat against each other as shown. It should be just tall enough to be a snug fit between the top and bottom plates. Using doubled 2×4s minimizes the likelihood of warping later on and provides the rigidity needed for nailing on the drywall panels afterward. Secure this corner post by toenailing to the top and bottom plates, then nail a horizontal cross brace between it and the wall stud, positioning this about 30 inches up from the floor.

5. The header that goes across the top of the door opening is installed next. Consisting of doubled 2×4s placed on edge, this should be formed from two pieces of straight lumber. The track hardware for the bifolding doors will be mounted under this later on.

6. After framing is finished, the gypsum board (drywall) panels are nailed up and all seams taped (see chapter 3). Cove molding is installed to finish off the corner joints where the new closet walls meet the existing walls.

7. The bifolding doors are hung last, following the directions supplied by the manufacturer (these doors are usually sold complete with all necessary tracks and other hardware, plus instructions). The door frame is finished off with suitable moldings to match other moldings in that room.

SHELVES—THE ANSWER TO MANY STORAGE PROBLEMS

Broadly speaking, shelving can be classified in one of two overall categories: fixed shelves and adjustable shelves.

Fixed shelves are mounted on permanent brackets or cleats that cannot be easily moved or adjusted—the spacing between the shelves is always the same unless you rebuild that set of shelves or rip out the brackets or cleats that support them. Adjustable shelving, on the other hand, can be moved up or down without need for rebuilding. The shelves are usually supported by brackets that fit into slotted vertical standards fastened to the wall behind the shelves or by small clips that snap into matching standards that are mounted vertically at each end of the shelving (this type is most often found inside bookcases or closed cabinets).

Both types of shelving can be either open or closed. Open shelving is not enclosed at either end and is usually mounted on a wall. It is supported by brackets that stick out from the wall behind the shelves, and these brackets may be either adjustable or fixed. Closed shelving is usually installed inside a cabinet, bookcase, or similar enclosure. These shelves are most often supported at each end by cleats or grooves in the frame of that enclosure (fixed shelving) or by means of special movable clips or pins at the end of each shelf (closed shelving that is adjustable).

ADJUSTABLE OPEN WALL SHELVING

Wall-mounted, adjustable shelving is probably the most popular type to be installed where a group of shelves is needed. A set of these shelves is less expensive and not

Adjustable wall shelving that mounts on vertical standards comes in different styles and sizes.

as bulky as a bookcase, and since they are mounted on the wall they do not take up valuable floor space—often at a premium in smaller apartments and condominiums. Generally used for storing books, as well as for decorative items that people like to have on display, this type of shelving can also store many other items that you may not have room for in closets or chests.

For example, in a child's room such shelves are ideal for keeping toys off the floor or for storing gloves, hats, and similar objects that youngsters often have a hard time finding. In the kitchen a set of these wall-mounted shelves can hold small appliances, cups and mugs, cookbooks, spice racks, condiment jars, decorative platters, and cooking accessories. And in a bedroom these shelves may be the answer for neatly storing sporting equipment, hats, gloves, shoes, and even folded shirts, sweaters, or similar items.

Sold in almost all hardware stores, home centers, and lumberyards, these adjustable shelving systems come in a wide variety of colors, styles, sizes, and finishes. The finishes range from the least expensive models that are made of painted metal, to more decorative systems that may be made of prefinished hardwood, ornamental brass, or wrought iron. Each system consists of wood or metal pilasters (usually called standards) that are mounted vertically against the wall first. The standards have evenly spaced slots (1 inch apart) along their entire length to accept matching shelf brackets that snap into them (see illustrations).

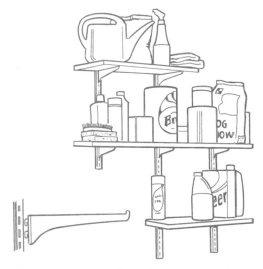

Adjustable shelving allows for an unlimited number of different arrangements. Each shelf rests on brackets that snap into slots in the vertical standards, and these can be rearranged at any time.

Matching shelves that are prefinished in a choice of colors and finishes are also available. Usually made of particle board covered with a plastic veneer, or of prefinished plywood, the shelves come in widths of 6, 8, 10, and 12 inches and in lengths of 24, 30, 36, and 48 inches. The supporting shelf brackets can be snapped out of the slots in each standard and the shelves moved up or down. All you have to do is lift off the shelf, move the bracket to its new position, and then replace the shelf on top.

At least two standards are needed to support each set of shelves, but for long shelves (over 3 or 4 feet in length), or for those that will support heavy loads, three standards may be required—one in the center and one a few inches from each end. For shelves that will support light to medium loads (15 to 20 pounds per lineal foot), supporting brackets should be spaced no more than 24 inches apart (which means that the slotted standards must be spaced about that distance apart on the wall). However, for heavier loads (30 to 40 pounds per foot), standards and brackets must be spaced closer together to keep shelves from bowing—usually no more than 16 to 18 inches apart.

Ideally each slotted vertical standard could be positioned directly over a wall stud so that you could fasten it in place with long screws that go clear through the wall and into the stud. However, this will seldom work out so conveniently, because studs never seem to be located just where you want to mount the shelf standards. That is why in most cases the standards are mounted on the wall with expansion-type hollow wall anchors, rather than with screws.

After deciding on the spacing and location for your shelf standards, start by

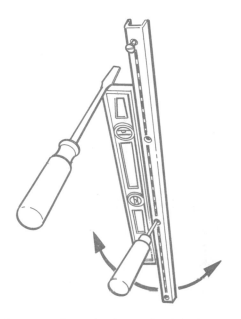

Make sure wall standards are plumb by hanging from top screw first. Then use a spirit level to check plumb before driving in the additional mounting screws.

inserting one screw at the top of the first standard, positioning this at the correct height for your shelving. Do not tighten this screw all the way yet—the idea is to let that standard swing back and forth until you make sure it is perfectly plumb (vertical).

Hold a spirit level against the side of the standard and swing the bottom end until the level shows you the standard is plumb (you can use a plumb line instead of a spirit level for this). Hold the standard in place against the wall while you use a long nail or ice pick to mark each of the mounting screw holes on the wall, then swing the standard out of the way and drill holes in the wall for the other anchors. Insert an anchor into each of these holes, then swing the standard back into position and insert the rest of the mounting screws and tighten all of them.

When installing the second standard for that set of shelves, you have to make certain that this standard is at exactly the same height as the first one so that when the shelf brackets are snapped into the slots they will be level with each other. In most homes and apartments you can't just measure up from the floor or down from the ceiling—very often the floors and ceilings are not level. However, here is a simple solution:

1. Insert a shelf bracket in the top slot of the standard you have just installed on the wall, then insert the matching bracket in the top slot of the second standard (the one you are about to install).

2. Hold this second standard temporarily in place against the wall with its shelf bracket in position at about the height it should be to match the first standard. Have someone place a level across the top of the two shelf brackets to check. Move the second standard (the one you are holding and about to install) up or down as

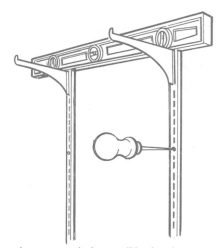

To make certain shelves will be level, use a spirit level placed across top row of standards. Then mark locations for the mounting screws for the second standard.

necessary until the bubble indicates that the shelf brackets are level, then use the ice pick to mark the location of the top hole on this second standard.

3. Now remove the level and set aside the second standard. Drill a hole at the spot you just marked on the wall for the screw, then insert an expansion anchor.

4. Mount the standard with the top screw only, just as you did the first one, then again use the level (or plumb line) to make sure this standard is plumb before marking the rest of the holes and inserting the rest of the anchors. Finish by driving in all the screws, just as you did on the first one.

You can now snap the shelf brackets into place and install all of the shelves.

ADJUSTABLE CLOSED SHELVING

When adjustable shelves are to be installed inside a bookcase, cabinet, or alcove of some kind, slotted standards and brackets of this type are seldom used. One reason is that the brackets under each shelf take up too much space—space that could be used for books or other items. Also, inside a bookcase the brackets are not particularly attractive looking. Instead, most experienced cabinetmakers

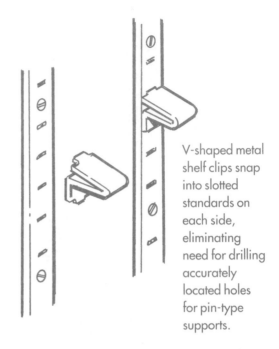

V-shaped metal shelf clips snap into slotted standards on each side, eliminating need for drilling accurately located holes for pin-type supports.

use small, movable clips to support adjustable shelves inside a case or cabinet. Each shelf rests on four of these clips, one in each corner. The clips fit into holes or tracks attached to the sides of the cabinet or enclosure, as shown in the illustrations.

These clips come in two basic types, both of which take up little or no room under the shelf. One type consists of small metal or plastic tabs that have a round pin or lug that projects out in the back. This pin fits snugly into any one of the (vertically aligned rows of) evenly spaced holes that have been drilled into the sides of the case or cabinet. You simply push them into the holes at the height desired, then drop the shelf on top. The vertical row of holes in each corner of the case or cabinet is also horizontally aligned so that when the four clips for each shelf are inserted, that shelf will sit evenly on top of the clips.

The other type of adjustable shelf clip is a V-shaped bent metal clip that snaps into

Two pin-type shelf supports often used to support adjustable shelving inside cabinets and bookcases.

one of the slots in a vertically mounted metal standard. Four standards are installed, two at each end, against the sides of the case or cabinet. These standards have slots, usually spaced 1 inch apart, for the V-shaped clips. Each shelf then rests on four clips—one in each corner. To ensure that shelves will be level when supporting clips are in place, install the standards so that the matching slots in all four strips are at exactly the same height (the same distance from the bottom or top of the cabinet). The clips can then be easily moved up or down as necessary to change the spacing between shelves.

FIXED SHELVING

Not all shelves have to be adjustable, and not always do you need a group of shelves—sometimes a single shelf is all that is required. Also, there are places where a single decorative shelf will be more attractive and/or more suitable for a particular location than a set of adjustable shelves would be—for example, in living rooms, dining rooms, and other places where appearance is important. For these installations you can buy beautifully prefinished wood brackets and matching shelves that will look almost like a piece of wall-mounted furniture. And in garages, utility rooms, and similar areas where appearance is secondary, a single large utility-type shelf may be all there is room for.

For maximum strength, where the shelf will have to support a heavy load, it is best to locate the brackets where they can be fastened with screws that can be driven directly into the wall studs; otherwise, you can mount them onto plaster or drywall with expansion anchors as described previously (see pages 34–36).

For utility shelves that will be erected where appearance is secondary, the least expensive shelf brackets you can use are the inexpensive steel ones that are sold in every hardware store and lumberyard. These L-shaped metal brackets are best

Inexpensive painted steel brackets are often used for utility shelving in garages, attics, and basements.

Where appearance is not important, shelves can be supported inside enclosure by wood cleats nailed or screwed to each side.

installed by fastening to wall studs or beams with wood screws, although expansion anchors could also be used. Just remember that anchors in drywall or plaster will not support as much of a load as screws will (however, if the anchors go into concrete or cement blocks, they may be just as strong if properly installed). Ordinary ¾-inch-thick lumber is usually used for the shelves, the width depending on the width shelf desired.

If you are installing fixed shelves inside a wall alcove or an enclosure—for example, inside a closet, wardrobe, or cabinet—the simplest way to support them is with wood cleats attached to the sides (see page 249). Although cleats are normally installed only under each end of the shelf, when loads are heavy it is a good idea to install a long cleat under the back edge of the shelf as well. In most cases it is best to fasten cleats in place with screws and glue rather than with nails.

USING PERFORATED HARDBOARD PANELS FOR STORAGE

Instead of shelves, another way to store things on a wall is to use sheets of perforated hardboard (usually called Peg-Board, although this is actually the brand name of the original manufacturer). These perforated panels can be mounted almost anywhere—on walls or doors, in garages or basements, and so on. Once in place, there are all types of hooks, brackets, clips, and other wire or plastic fixtures that can be fitted into the holes for hanging and storing tools, hobby supplies, sewing equipment, kitchen utensils, and all kinds of other items that would otherwise get thrown into boxes or drawers or simply piled up on a shelf. There are even shelf brackets available that enable you to quickly set up a shelf for storing jars, cans, and other small containers.

Perforated hardboard panels are sold in all lumberyards and home centers, as well as in many hardware stores. They come in two thicknesses—⅛ inch and ¼ inch—and usually measure 4 feet by 8 feet. However, most lumberyards will cut them down if you want a smaller piece, and many dealers also stock panels in other sizes. Unfinished

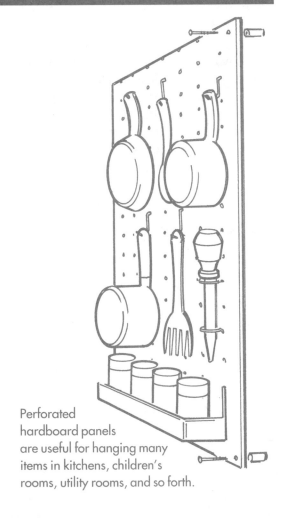

Perforated hardboard panels are useful for hanging many items in kitchens, children's rooms, utility rooms, and so forth.

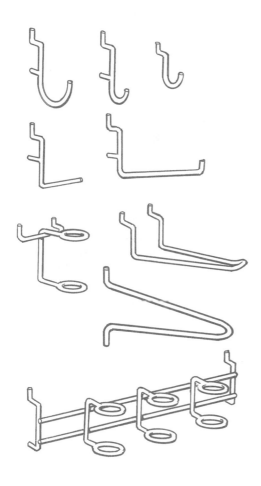

A wide variety of hooks, brackets, and other fixtures are available for use with perforated hardboard panels.

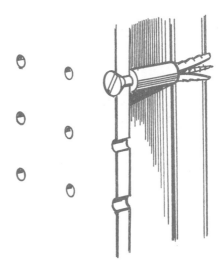

There should be at least ⅜ inch space behind each perforated hardboard panel to allow for hooks and brackets. Plastic or rubber spacers on each mounting screw provide this clearance.

Peg-Board is dark brown, but it can also be bought factory-finished in a choice of colors. The unfinished panels can be easily painted after applying a suitable undercoat. Painting these panels with a spray can or a short-nap roller is a lot faster and easier than painting them with a brush.

When installing perforated hardboard against a wall or other surface, remember that there must be at least ⅜ inch of space behind the panels in order to allow for the various hooks and other fixtures that will be inserted in the holes (they stick out slightly on the back side). Dealers sell small plastic or rubber spacers that have holes in the center for the mounting screws. These spacers go in the back of the panel so that the mounting screws go through them, as illustrated.

Instead of these spacers you can also make a frame behind the panel with strips of ½-inch-square lumber that will keep the Peg-Board away from the wall. Mounting screws (or wood strips) should be spaced no more than 16 to 18 inches apart (horizontally and vertically) to keep the hardboard panels from bowing or warping after they are installed.

If you are installing one of these perforated panels on the back of a closet or bedroom door (for hanging clothes, hats, sporting equipment, and the like), be certain you make the panel at least 2 inches narrower and 1 foot shorter than the door so the door can close properly. In the case of a closet door you also have to be sure that when the door is closed the hooks or racks that will be used will not get caught on clothes or other items inside the closet.

SOME ADDITIONAL WAYS TO "CREATE" STORAGE SPACE

The pages that follow outline some other ideas that apartment dwellers and condominium owners can use or adapt to increase storage capacity inside their home with major remodeling or extensive alterations.

1. Where appearance is not as important and utility is a primary concern, you can use free-standing modular drawer units made of vinyl-coated steel rods, similar to the "open" shelving described at the beginning of this chapter. These "ventilated" drawer units are available with and without wheels (or casters) and are often used in kitchens, laundry rooms, utility rooms, bathrooms, and children's rooms —as well as in closets.

Handy for storing small clothing items such as hats, gloves, and sweaters, they are also particularly useful for toys and miscellaneous items that are often hard to locate, because you can see the contents even when the drawers are closed. Since air can circulate freely, there is also much less likelihood of mildew problems. Modular storage units of this kind come in two-, three-, and four- drawer units that you assemble yourself.

2. You can mount all kinds of hooks and racks on walls to help with storage problems. For example, a row of upward-angled wood pegs, or a row of metal or plastic clothing hooks, can be attached to a 3- or 4-foot board that is about 8 inches wide, then this board can be fastened to a wall near the entrance door to hold coats, jackets, scarves, hats, and similar items. This is especially handy during wet weather to keep people from hanging wet clothes in the closet—or when visitors arrive and the hall closet is already full.

3. You can mount extra cabinets on a blank wall to provide added storage space in kitchens, laundry rooms, or utility rooms. For example, a couple of cabinets mounted over the washing machine or dryer can hold all kinds of hobby and recreational equipment, as well as laundry and cleaning supplies. A wall-mounted cabinet in the den or family room can be used to hold toys, games, spare paper goods, and sporting equipment.

4. If your bed is on legs, chances are the space under that bed serves only to collect dust. However, you can buy (or build) shallow "chests" or drawer units that are mounted on casters and can be slid under the bed. These are ideal for storing extra blankets, pillows, linens, or even out-of-season clothing. The casters make it easy to pull out the drawer or chest, then simply roll it back out of sight when not needed. If possible, these units should be no more than half the width of the bed so that you can fit two of them underneath—one that pulls out from each side.

5. For a nursery or infant's room, you can buy small stackable drawer units that will fit underneath the crib in the space that is normally wasted. The drawers will

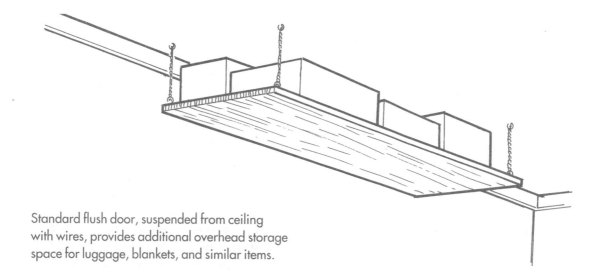

Standard flush door, suspended from ceiling with wires, provides additional overhead storage space for luggage, blankets, and similar items.

be handy for storing diapers, blankets, and clothing, as well as for bulky stuffed animals and other toys.

6. If your apartment or condominium has extra-high ceilings, you can create additional overhead storage space in a den or family room by hanging an overhead platform or miniature "storage loft" from the ceiling. This can be reached by using a short ladder that is stored out of the way when not needed, or you can build in a permanent set of stairs. An even simpler way to create such an overhead storage area is to suspend a flush door from the ceiling, as illustrated, using four short lengths of chain to hang it horizontally below the ceiling and at least 78 inches above the floor. The top end of each chain is attached to a sturdy eyebolt driven into the overhead ceiling beams, with the bottom end attached to the sides or edges of the door.

7. Space can be "created" on the back of most basement doors, closet doors, and utility room doors by adding racks, shelves, or small cabinets. Shallow shelving units made of vinyl-coated wire (similar to the "ventilated shelving" previ-

"Closet on a door" adds unseen storage to back of door for storage of canned goods, spray cans, and other small items.

ously mentioned) are designed for this purpose and sold in many home centers and department stores, as well as by dealers who specialize in closet accessories.

An even neater method to make use of a door is to build a shallow "closet on a door" similar to the one pictured. This cabinet has its own door to keep things from falling off the shelves and to keep all contents neatly out of sight (and out of reach of tiny hands). Easy to construct of plywood, such cabinets are ideal for storing a wide variety of small items such as canned goods, aerosol sprays, bottles of soda, insecticides, and cleaning supplies.

8. Since most interior walls are hollow and about 3½ inches deep (the thickness of the 2×4 studs), you can always build narrow shelves that are recessed *into* the wall, rather than being mounted on the surface of the wall—much as a bathroom medicine cabinet is set into the wall in most homes and apartments. All you have to do is cut away the plaster or drywall in order to expose the studs where you want the shelves to be. Then build narrow shelves between the studs. In a kitchen, such shelves are ideal for spices and condiments; in a bathroom they can hold cosmetics, small bottles of medicine, bottles of shampoo, and similar supplies. And in a den, family room, or teenager's room, these shelves can be used for storing audio- or videocassettes.

Noise Control Inside the Home

Noise can be defined as a series of unpleasant sounds or sounds that have been raised to an annoying and disruptive level. Of course opinions differ as to what sounds are annoying and what sounds are too loud—for example, loud music may sound pleasant to one person but may be decidedly unpleasant to another.

Often referred to as "noise pollution," this problem has been heightened by the fact that today's condominiums and apartments contain more TV sets, stereos, radios, and other noise-making appliances than ever before. Trying to cut down on the amount of sound transmitted between rooms, or between apartments, is never a simple matter because in most cases the building you are living in was really not built with acoustical considerations in mind.

However, by following the methods and procedures outlined in this chapter, you can reduce noise levels and cut down on the amount of noise that will travel from one room or apartment to another. Don't expect any of these measures to fully eliminate *all* your noise problems; to do so you would have to call in an architect and make extensive (and expensive) structural alterations.

Sound waves travel through the air as vibrations—actually tiny changes in air pressure that our ears hear as sound. These waves or vibrations radiate outward in all directions in much the same way ripples will travel through water when a stone is dropped into a pond. Besides traveling through the air, sound waves, or the vibrations caused by sound waves, can also travel through many solid materials, including wood beams, wall surfaces, floors, and the like.

When airborne sound waves strike a flat

surface such as a wall or a door, they tend to set that material to vibrating. These vibrations will then continue to travel along that material—the way the sound of someone tapping on one end of a long pipe can be easily heard at the other end (especially if you put your ear close to the pipe).

Sound vibrations in a solid object can also be created by impact—for example, when someone wearing hard-soled shoes walks on a wood floor or when doors and cabinet drawers are slammed. These impact sounds not only set up vibrations that actually travel through that object, they also create sound waves in the air around it, which then radiate outward in all directions.

This accounts for a large part of the noise that often seems to pass right through a typical interior wall or partition. But not all the sound waves that are transmitted to the other side of the wall will get there simply by passing through solid materials—some will pass through holes, cracks, or other openings. Most people do not realize that sound waves will travel through any crevice or opening where air can pass, and that is why sealing off openings is one of the most important measures you can take to block the passage of noise from one room or apartment to another.

Another point to keep in mind: When sound waves strike a wall or another smooth, hard, and rigid surface, a percentage of those sound waves will be reflected away, much the way light is reflected away by a shiny surface. These sound waves will then "bounce around" inside that room, going from one surface to another until all the energy is dissipated. Surfaces that are softer, more porous, or more textured and resilient will tend to absorb a high per-

centage of the sound waves that strike them. That is why a cork-lined room or a room with lots of heavy draperies on the walls will always seem to be quieter than one with bare plaster walls.

Normally, much of the noise that is generated inside a room—say, from a loud TV set—will be reflected off walls, ceilings, or floors. As these sound waves bounce around inside that room, two things will happen: some of the sound waves will be transmitted through the walls and other surfaces that line the room, and some of them will be reflected back to continue bouncing around until all their energy is dissipated.

In the fight to reduce noise pollution and the amount or intensity of the noise heard inside your condominium or apartment, heed the following:

1. Reduce, or better yet eliminate, the noise at its source whenever possible.

2. Use acoustical materials to absorb as much of the sound as possible near the point of origin and thus minimize the amount of noise trying to find its way out into adjoining rooms or apartments.

3. Use acoustical insulation to attenuate (block) the passage of sound waves as they try to travel from one room or apartment to another. This usually means using a combination of sound-absorbing and sound-blocking materials to at least minimize the transmission of noise.

When considering the effectiveness of any type of acoustical insulation, remember that the heavier, the bulkier, and the denser that material is, the more effective it will be as a sound barrier. That is why a thick masonry wall of solid brick or poured concrete will be more effective as a sound barrier than a wall of the same thickness made of hollow concrete blocks

—and why either will be a better sound barrier than a hollow wall of 2×4 studs covered with plaster or gypsum board.

This also explains why sheet lead is one of the best natural sound barrier materials available. It's very heavy and very dense, yet resilient enough not to reflect away sound waves. Unfortunately it is also very expensive—which is probably why it is almost never used in residential construction for acoustical insulation. (It is used in heavy-duty industrial and marine applica-tions, where noisy engines and machinery are a serious problem. Thin sheets of lead, or special lead-and-foam laminates, are often used to line rooms or spaces where such machinery is located.)

In most cases any serious effort to cut down on the transmission of noise from one room to another, or from one apart-ment or condominium unit to another, will almost always call for using a combination of several soundproofing or sound-block-ing methods.

REDUCING THE NOISE AT ITS SOURCE

Cutting down on the amount of noise at its point of origin is by far the most efficient way to solve any noise problem—if it can be done. For example, it's obviously easier and more effective to turn down the volume on a loud stereo set than it is to cut down on the amount of this sound that is transmitted to other rooms or to other apartments or condominiums in the same building.

Of course, eliminating, or even lower-ing, the noise level is not always possible, especially when the noise is coming from a neighbor's apartment or condominium. However, as long as the source of the noise is under your control, there are a number of measures you can take to lower the decibel rating:

• If your refrigerator or washing machine vibrates a great deal, it may need servicing. Call in a repairman to make needed adjustments or to replace worn belts, bearings, or other parts that may be causing the vibration. Also, check the "feet" or leveling pads under the machine to make certain it sits level.

• Many pieces of equipment that have moving parts will squeak or squeal simply because of a lack of lubrication. Included in this category might be fan motors, older vacuum cleaners, door hinges, and even cabinet doors and drawers. A few drops of oil, or a few squirts of silicone or Teflon lubricant, will do wonders.

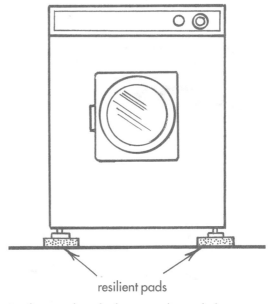

resilient pads

Resilient pads under large appliance help to absorb vibration, cutting down on the amount of noise created.

• If a large household appliance or piece of mechanical equipment such as an attic fan, room air conditioner, or furnace blower cannot be silenced by making normal repairs or adjustments, it is often possible to cut down on the amount of noise created by placing rubber mounts or acoustical pads under the motor or its housing. Any resilient material under the base will serve to absorb vibrations, thus diminishing the amount of noise that will be transmitted.

• Loud television sets, large stereo speakers, and radios that are mounted on shelves or inside a wall unit will often send sound waves along or through the wall to which they are attached, as well as out into the room. To minimize the amount of transmitted noise, place a resilient pad under or around each speaker housing. This won't lower the volume of the sound coming out of the speaker, but it will

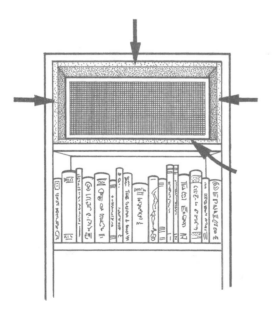

Surrounding stereo speakers with resilient padding will deaden sound transmission to adjoining rooms.

reduce the amount of throbbing or vibration that is transmitted through the cabinet or the shelf on which the speaker is mounted.

• In the same way, rubber coasters or resilient plastic cups placed under a piano will help muffle some of the sound generated when this instrument is in use, as will a rubber pad under a typewriter or computer printer.

• The sound of heels clicking against a hardwood or tile floor can be muffled or dampened by covering that floor with heavy carpet that has a thick pad of resilient open-core foam underneath. In kitchens or laundry rooms where vinyl tile or a sheet vinyl would be more practical than carpet, install a cushion-backed vinyl instead of a conventional unbacked vinyl. These measures will not only greatly reduce the sound of people walking on that floor, they will also minimize the amount of impact noise transmitted to other rooms through floor beams and structural members.

• Homes that have forced-air heating or central air-conditioning often have a problem with noise that is transmitted through the ducts that run from room to room. In many cases this can be minimized by wrapping ducts with insulation or by adding flexible sections where ducts connect with each other or with the furnace plenum. If one room is the source of a great deal of noise, you can even close off the duct openings that lead into that room—at least temporarily when heating or air-conditioning is not needed there.

• Water pipes that hammer or bang are another source of noise. In some cases the pipes are not properly secured or mounted—supporting straps may be loose or missing in various places. Adding more supports or replacing those that are loose may solve the problem. An even more frequent cause of noisy plumbing is a condition known as water hammer—caused by faucets or automatic valves inside appliances shutting off too quickly. Water is not compressible, and it slams to a stop, causing pipes to vibrate or rattle and to bang against studs, beams, or other structural members. To prevent this, you can install special "antihammer" devices for just this purpose that are widely sold in hardware stores and plumbing supply outlets (see page 191 for more information).

USING ACOUSTICAL MATERIALS TO ABSORB NOISE

If you have done all you can to eliminate or cut down on the amount of noise generated, the next step is to absorb as much of this noise as possible near or at its point of origin. This will leave less noise to travel out into other rooms or apartments.

The most effective way to do this is to make liberal use of acoustical materials such as cork or tiles or panels that are designed for this purpose. Such acoustical materials are often referred to as "soundproofing" materials, but this is really not accurate—they are actually sound-*absorbing* materials, not sound-*insulating* materials.

To put it another way, all of these sound-absorbing acoustical materials will do little to stop the *transmission* of sound waves that pass through them, but they will help deaden or absorb a high percentage of the sound waves that strike them. This not only helps to lower the decibel level of the noise that is generated inside that room, it also cuts down on the number and intensity of the sound waves that will be left to pass to the outside. (Bear in mind, however, that too much acoustical material can make a room seem "dead" because it will abnormally muffle normal sounds.)

It's important to understand that acoustical materials that absorb sound only help to lower noise levels when the noise is generated *inside* that room. They are not really efficient as sound insulators and thus are not very effective at blocking the transmission of sound passing through them from the *outside*. In other words, they won't help much to block out noise that originates in an adjoining room or apartment, nor will they be of much use in blocking out street noises that come in through walls, windows, and the like. (This explains why applying cork or acoustical panels to your side of the wall will not help much if you have a noisy neighbor.)

One exception to this is when the sound-absorbing material you use is also very bulky and/or very dense and heavy—then it can block a sizable percentage of the sound that tries to pass through it, in addition to absorbing a percentage of the sound waves that strike it. For example, multiple layers of thick drapes, large, deep pieces of upholstered furniture, bookcases filled with books, large cabinets and pieces of furniture filled with dishes or linens, closets full of clothing—all will help insulate against noise. The denser and heavier the material, the better a sound barrier it will be. However, this holds true only if there are no openings or holes that will let sound waves pass through. Remember that any opening through which light and/or air can pass will also allow sound waves to pass through to the other side and thus negate the effectiveness of the sound barrier.

USING ACOUSTICAL INSULATION TO BLOCK THE PASSAGE OF NOISE

Some of the most difficult noise problems involve the transmission of sound that travels through walls, ceilings, or floors. Although complete insulation against the passage of noise may not be possible, there are fortunately a number of steps that you can take to cut down on the amount of noise that gets transmitted from one room to another.

First, block off and seal up all openings that exist in the walls, ceiling, or floor. Look for holes or openings around water pipes, waste pipes, heating and air-conditioning ducts, and electric cables or conduits that go from one room to another.

Small openings can be sealed with a good grade of latex or acrylic caulking compound or, better yet, with one of the silicone rubber compounds. Don't forget to pay particular attention to the openings that are often found under a kitchen sink or bathroom vanity where various pipes pass through the wall, as well as around heating pipes that go through floors or ceilings. Holes that are too large for caulking alone should first be stuffed with wads of fiberglass insulation, then covered with caulking compound. Rope-type caulking materials that come in rolls and can be wadded up like putty are also very useful for filling holes that can't be easily plugged up with regular caulking or for places difficult to reach with a caulking gun.

Another place where noise often enters

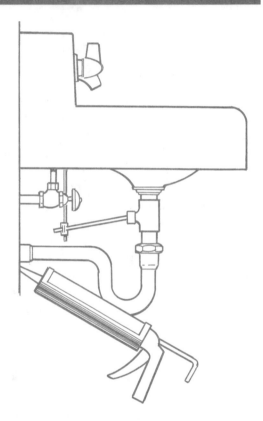

Sound waves travel through smallest openings, so sealing wall openings with caulking compound helps block passage of noise.

is through gaps along the base of the wall where baseboards or moldings do not fit tight against the floor. Removing the baseboard and then caulking along the bottom of the wall will usually cut down on the transmission of sound waves through these openings.

Openings around electric boxes that

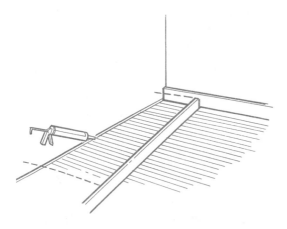

Removing baseboard and then caulking joint where wall meets floor will also help to block passage of sound waves.

contain outlets or wall switches can also serve as a passageway for noise to travel through walls, especially when these electric outlets are located directly opposite each other on the same wall. Take off the cover plate, then stuff wads of fiberglass insulation into the space around the outlet box. Before replacing the cover plate, place a rubber or foam gasket behind it, as

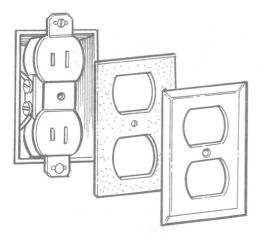

Foam-type gasket behind electric receptacle plate helps seal out sound waves from adjoining room.

illustrated (these gaskets are sold in most hardware stores to seal out cold drafts around electrical outlets that are located on an outside wall).

The soundproofing quality of a door that closes off one room from another will vary with the thickness and weight of that door. A solid door will block out more sound than a hollow core door, and a flush hollow-core door will block out more sound than a thin door that has only a single panel in the center (or even one that has several recessed thin panels), because the flush door actually consists of two thin panels (one on each side) plus a hollow core that helps deaden sound waves trying to pass through. However, the acoustical qualities of any door can be greatly improved by installing rubber or high-density foam weatherstripping around that door.

When doing this, don't forget also to seal the gap under the bottom of the door. Hardware stores and home centers sell "door bottom" weatherstripping that is normally used to seal out cold drafts, but any of these can also be used to seal out noise.

For maximum protection against sound transmission through a door opening, you can also follow a practice common in many psychiatrists' offices—install a second door in front of the existing one. The two doors will swing in opposite directions, one opening into each room. With this setup you not only end up with two separate doors that double the amount of sound blocked out, there will also be an air space between the doors that forms an additional acoustical barrier against noise transmission.

Sealing off noise that comes in from outside the building is a much more difficult

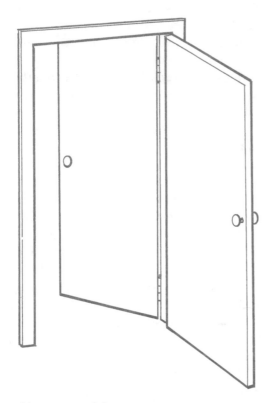

Adding a second door to an existing opening will greatly cut down on the amount of noise transmitted.

problem, one that can be only partially cured in most areas. Windows are probably the biggest culprit, so make sure all the windows are sealed with weatherstripping—preferably a high-density foam or rubber. A further barrier against sound transmission is the addition of storm windows on the outside of the existing windows.

Replacing old-style single-pane windows with new ones that have double- or triple-pane glass is another excellent choice—the new windows will not only help to conserve energy (with both heating and air-conditioning), they will be equally helpful in cutting down on noise transmission through those windows. If street noise is really a serious problem, installing shutters over the windows will help even more—especially if the shutters are made of solid wood or plywood and lined with plastic foam or foam-core insulating board. The shutters can be hinged so that you can close them to shut out noise only when desired. Heavy lined draperies on the inside will also help, especially if the lining is of heavyweight material.

INSULATING WALLS AGAINST SOUND TRANSMISSION

Many people mistakenly believe that simply filling the hollow spaces inside a wall with ordinary fiberglass insulation will provide an acceptable amount of acoustical insulation for that wall. However, thermal insulation alone will not really help much—unless it is also combined with some structural changes or modifications.

As explained earlier in this chapter, sound waves can travel through or along a wall so that sound vibrations on one side can be transmitted to the plaster or wall-

board on the other side. These vibrations will then generate airborne sound waves of their own in the next room. The best time to prevent this kind of sound transmission is during initial construction.

One of the most effective ways to build a wall that will serve as an effective sound barrier is to use two separate sets of vertical studs $(2 \times 4s)$, as shown in the illustration opposite. The studs on each side of the wall are staggered so that every other one is offset about 2 inches from the

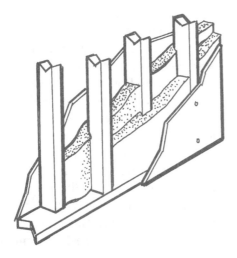

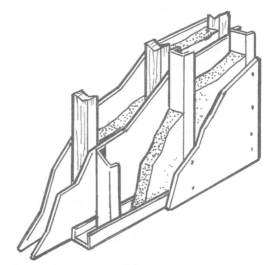

Most effective way to build a soundproof wall is by erecting it with two sets of studs that are staggered. Wall panels on each side are then nailed to different studs.

To avoid major remodeling, put up a separate wall with insulation between the studs in front of the existing wall.

one next to it. The wallboard on one side is then nailed to only one set of studs, while the wallboard on the other side of that wall is nailed to the other set of studs.

The two wall surfaces are thus isolated from each other so that any sound waves that strike one side of the wall will not be transferred immediately to the other side. Additional acoustical insulation can be added by filling the cavities between studs with thick batts of fiberglass.

Since installing this staggered-stud system in an existing wall would require major demolition and rebuilding, most apartment dwellers and condominium owners are not likely to try it. However, where space permits, there is an alternate method that is just as effective. This involves erecting an additional wall or partition immediately in front of the existing wall. This new wall should be constructed about 2 inches in front of the present wall and built so that no part of the new wall

touches any part of the original wall (as shown above).

Sound muting effectiveness can be further enhanced if the space between the two walls and the cavities between the studs are also filled with acoustical fiberglass insulation. And for maximum results when creating such a sound barrier, the new wall should be built with metal studs instead of wood 2×4s (metal studs are more resilient and thus less likely to transfer sound waves from one side to the other).

The top and bottom plates of the second wall (the horizontal 2×4s along the top and bottom) should be bedded in silicone rubber caulking compound before being nailed in place against the floor or ceiling—not only to seal any gaps that could allow sound waves to seep past, but also to help break the path of vibrations that could be transmitted from the wall to the floor or ceiling. Also use caulking in the corners where the framing for the new wall meets the existing walls.

Since putting up an extra wall or partition means losing anywhere from 5 to 6 inches of floor space inside that room, many people might be reluctant to go through an alteration of this type. However, there is another, simpler method that involves adding only slightly to the thickness of the existing wall so that you will lose less than 2 inches of floor space. This method, which calls for adding extra layers to the existing wall to increase its mass (and therefore its sound-absorbing qualities), is not as effective as building a separate wall, but it will help a lot in most cases.

The simplest way to accomplish this is to apply one or two additional layers of gypsum board to the surface of the wall or—better yet—one layer of sound-dead-ening acoustical board, followed by a layer of ⅝-inch-thick sound-deadening gypsum board (sold in many lumberyards and home centers). For best results, this should be done on both sides of the wall, but even if you do it on only one side, the reduction in noise transmission will be quite noticeable.

The new panels can be applied directly on top of the existing wallboard with drywall screws and panel adhesive (also called construction adhesive), but for maximum soundproofing the new layers should be applied over resilient metal channel strips similar to the ones illustrated. These resilient furring channels are made of a springy metal and are designed to be fastened to the wall along one edge only, using nails or drywall screws driven into the studs. The other edge of each strip

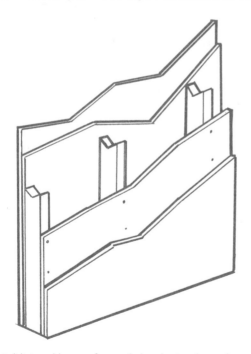

Additional layer of sound-deadening board or gypsum board will also help insulate against sound transmission.

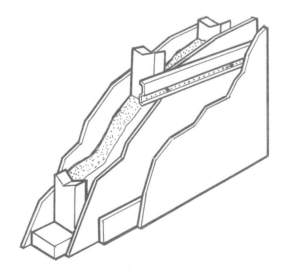

For best results, additional layer of gypsum board should be applied over resilient metal channels that have been nailed to existing surface first.

is left free so that it can move in and out slightly.

When the new layer of sound-deadening board or gypsum board is attached to these metal channels with drywall screws, you end up with a "floating" wall surface that can give in minute increments, thus acting as a "shock absorber" of vibrations without transmitting them from one side of the wall to the other.

Bear in mind when resurfacing a wall in this way that the baseboard molding must be removed before you start, then renailed after the new wall panels are installed. Any electric outlets or wall switches on that wall will have to be extended out so they won't be buried by the additional layers of wallboard. You can either add an extension collar to the front of the outlet box or simply move the outlet box farther forward so that its front edge is flush with the new wall surface (be sure you shut off all power before starting to work on any electric switch or receptacle box).

INSULATING FLOORS AND CEILINGS AGAINST SOUND TRANSMISSION

Cutting down on noise that comes down through the ceiling or up through the floor is usually much more difficult than trying to cut down on noise that comes through a wall, especially if the noise originates in someone else's apartment or condominium. Since you probably have no control over the occupants in that other apartment, you cannot do much about eliminating the noise or at least cutting down on the volume.

Noise that comes down through the ceiling is often impact noise—people walking or running, children jumping, or people dropping things on the floor above. This is one of the most difficult sound transmission problems to combat because the noise travels through the flooring, along the beams, and down into the walls below, as well as coming down through the ceiling itself and being airborne in the room below.

The best way to cut down on the amount of impact noise coming through the ceiling is to cover the floor above that ceiling with a sound-absorbing material

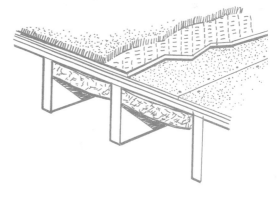

Installing layer of sound-deadening board under carpet pad and carpet will help cut down on noise going through to the floor below.

such as thick carpet with a dense foam pad underneath. If the room is part of your apartment or condominium, you can go much further to insulate against noise if you wish. For example, you might rip up the existing flooring and then cover the exposed subflooring with a resilient "blanket" of sound-deadening board before installing a new layer of finished flooring.

Obviously, in many cases you will not

have much to say about covering or rebuilding the floor above your ceiling, so all you can do is work from below. As pointed out earlier in this chapter, installing acoustical tile on your ceiling won't help much. However, if your room has high ceilings, you can obtain some relief by installing a suspended ceiling of acoustical panels that hangs beneath your existing ceiling (the new ceiling will have to be at least several inches below the present one).

A suspended ceiling consists of an aluminum grid formed of interlocking lightweight channels (T-shaped bars). The channels or T bars are suspended below the existing ceiling by tying them to lengths of wire that have been attached to screw eyes driven into the overhead joists. Acoustical panels, usually measuring about 24 by 48 inches in size, fit inside this gridlike framework and rest on the flanges of the metal T bars. For still more insulation against the transmission of noise from the room above, you can fill the space between the two ceilings with bulky fiberglass acoustical insulation. (For more details on putting up a suspended ceiling, see chapter 3.)

If there is not enough headroom to install a suspended ceiling, another technique can be used to create a "floating" ceiling that will help isolate sounds from the floor above. First nail resilient metal furring channels (similar to those described on page 264 for use on walls) to the existing ceiling, then attach a layer of

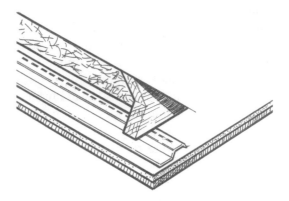

Sound-insulating qualities of ceiling can be improved by installing a "floating" ceiling that has gypsum board panels nailed to resilient metal channels, instead of directly to overhead beams.

sound-deadening board to these strips. This is then covered with an additional layer of gypsum wallboard. The layers of wallboard will add density and mass to help deaden impact noise from above, while also cutting down on the amount of noise that gets transmitted through that ceiling from the room above.

In addition to using resilient metal channels and additional layers of gypsum board or sound-deadening board on walls or ceilings, it also helps if fiberglass insulation is used to fill in the spaces left between the old and the new surfaces. As a rule, resilient channels will permit adding about ¾ inch of fiberglass between each strip and behind the first layer of wallboard or paneling.

*F*urniture Refinishing and Repair

With furniture prices higher than ever before, it is no surprise that more and more people are saving money by purchasing moderately priced unfinished furniture and then finishing it themselves. There are also many who like to shop for used, vintage pieces even if they show some signs of wear; this old furniture can be refinished at home for considerably less than the price of new pieces of equivalent quality and style. In addition, there are all those people who have basically solid furniture that they still value, even if it is a bit worn or in need of minor repairs and refinishing.

Having old furniture professionally refinished is obviously the best choice for those who can afford it, but in many cases this can cost as much as the original furniture, or at least more than some are willing—or able—to spend. With a little time and effort anyone can do a competent job of finishing or refinishing furniture at home. Here is how it is done.

RESTORING THE OLD FINISH

There are times when the finish on an old and valued piece of wood furniture gets so dull, dingy, and worn looking that it seems the only way to rejuvenate it is to strip off all the old finish and then refinish it completely from scratch. This also holds true when you buy (or inherit) some pieces that are still solid and basically sound, but badly in need of some restoration.

It's true that in some cases stripping and

refinishing may be the only solution, but there are a surprisingly large percentage of cases when there may actually be no need for going to such extremes.

The first step in any restoration job is cleaning the old surface in order to remove all the old wax, polish, and oil, as well as the years of grime that may have accumulated on the surface. As a rule, the simplest way to clean wood furniture without damaging the finish is to wipe it down with a rag moistened with paint thinner. Since the thinner is inflammable, work in a well-ventilated room and make sure there are no open flames nearby. Although paint thinner will not harm most furniture finishes, it's best to play safe and try it on an inconspicuous corner or side first to see what effect, if any, it has on the finish.

Assuming that this test shows no harm to the actual finish, proceed with your cleaning job by dipping a folded cloth into the thinner, squeezing out most of the excess, and then rubbing vigorously over a small section at a time. Immediately wipe with a dry cloth to absorb or pick up all dissolved wax, polish, and grime, then continue wiping with thinner. Turn the rag frequently as it becomes soiled and change the thinner in the pan as it becomes very discolored. The idea behind all this is to pick up and remove the softened wax and dirt instead of merely spreading it around on the surface.

After being cleaned in this manner, the finish will almost always look dull and may even be slightly cloudy in places. If the finish is otherwise sound with no outstanding blemishes or other defects, you may be able to restore it simply by applying one or two coats of a good-quality furniture polish or wax. Try one section as an experiment. Rub the wax or polish on

sparingly, then buff vigorously with a dry cloth. If this restores life to the finish, you can repeat the process on the entire piece.

Sometimes merely repolishing is not enough, because the old finish may be crazed or so dull that simple polishing will not restore it. In these cases it is sometimes possible to rejuvenate the finish by a process often referred to as reamalgamation. This involves using a solvent to soften up and partially dissolve the old finish so that it flows together and forms a new film that is free of surface blemishes. However, to do this you have to know the kind of finish on the furniture. The technique works best with shellac and lacquer finishes; it is seldom effective on varnish finishes. However, most commercially finished furniture is not varnished—unless it was custom-made and finished by hand.

To test for a shellac finish, dip a rag into some denatured alcohol and rub on an inconspicuous corner. If the finish is shellac, the thinner will soften or dissolve it. If the finish is not shellac, the alcohol will have little or no effect on it (other than perhaps to make it look cloudy).

To test for a lacquer finish, dip a rag in lacquer thinner and then rub one corner as just described above. If the finish is lacquer, the thinner will soften and dissolve it almost immediately. However, lacquer thinner will also break down a varnish finish—but the difference is that on varnish it will cause the finish to blister and wrinkle rather than merely softening it, and it will remove the finish entirely down to the bare wood.

To rejuvenate an old shellac finish with this reamalgamation technique, the simplest method is to rub denatured alcohol over a section at a time. Dip a pad of very fine (4/0) steel wool into the alcohol and wipe this on in straight lines. Allow it to soak for about a minute, then wipe the same area lightly with a cloth that has also been dampened in alcohol. The idea is to soften the top layer of shellac without actually removing it so that it flows together to form a uniform film.

To use this technique on a lacquer finish that is cracked, checked, or cloudy, the same basic technique is followed, except that lacquer thinner is used instead of denatured alcohol. Some experts prefer to apply the thinner with a brush, rather than with fine steel wool, so experimenting with both techniques may be advisable to see which one works better for you. If you use a brush, spread on the thinner in straight lines parallel to the grain and then wipe immediately with a soft cloth moistened with additional lacquer thinner. Here again, the idea is to do all wiping lightly so that you don't remove the finish—you merely soften it and spread it around so that it flows out to form a fresh film.

After using either of these techniques to restore the finish, let it harden overnight and then build up the luster by using an oil-base furniture polish or a good grade of furniture wax.

RX FOR WATER MARKS

One of the most frequent types of damage to an existing finish is a white ring that is left when a wet glass, dish, or similar container is left standing on the surface. Depending on how long the moisture was allowed to penetrate before it was wiped off, and depending on the shape of the container or spill, the white mark may be in the form of a definite ring, or it may consist merely of a series of spots or "blush marks" on the surface. As long as the spots are white, the moisture did not penetrate

White ring mark in finish can often be removed by rubbing with a rag dipped in toothpaste.

all the way through the finish into the wood. This means there is a good chance that it can be removed without completely stripping off the old finish. If the water marks are dark, the moisture has penetrated completely through the finish and into the wood. The only way to correct a condition of this kind is to take off all the old finish and then sand or bleach out the dark marks (see pages 281–282).

If a white water mark on the surface has not penetrated much, it can sometimes be removed by rubbing with a rag that has been moistened with either denatured alcohol, turpentine, or camphorated oil. Try the alcohol first, then the camphorated oil, then the turpentine. If none of these work, then polishing with a very mild abrasive is the next step. Start by rubbing with one of the toothpastes that are advertised as having "extra brighteners" in them—these actually contain a very mild abrasive. Spread a little paste over the white mark and rub with your finger or with a small pad of cloth. If possible, try to rub parallel to the grain only. If the stain starts to lighten, keep rubbing until you have it all out.

If this fails, try a slightly coarser abrasive. Use some ordinary table salt with a little lemon oil or mineral oil. Sprinkle on the salt first, then dip a cloth into the oil and rub with this. If this seems to be working, then repeat with salt and vinegar instead of salt and oil. (The vinegar acts as a mild bleach.)

If the stain persists, you'll have to use a paste made by mixing powdered rottenstone with lemon oil or mineral oil. This will remove the stain eventually, although a considerable amount of rubbing may be required. When you're done, the surface will be quite dull, but in most cases you can restore the luster by waxing or polishing. If much of the old finish has been removed, a thin coat of varnish or shellac may be required, but try to avoid this since blending in such a touch-up is often quite difficult.

REPAIRING SCRATCHES

Scratches and small nicks that are in the finish and don't go all the way through the wood can be repaired in one of three ways:

1. Touch up the scratch with a colored oil stain of the right shade or with one of the various "scratch-removing" liquids that are widely sold in hardware and houseware stores. This will not fill in or remove the scratch, but it will color or camouflage it so that it becomes scarcely noticeable—particularly after you apply a polish or wax over the touch-up.

2. If the scratch is a shallow one, you can often remove it by using the reamalgamation process (see page 268). A little solvent applied with an artist's pointed brush will dissolve the finish at that point so that it flows together, and the scratch becomes scarcely noticeable after it is polished or waxed.

3. Deeper scratches will have to be filled in and possibly colored in order to conceal them completely. The best material to use for this purpose is stick shellac. It comes in a range of different wood colors and is made specifically for patching wood finishes. Unfortunately it is seldom stocked in local paint and hardware stores anymore, but you can buy shellac sticks from dealers who specialize in furniture-finishing supplies, or you can order them from mail-order houses that cater to home craftsmen. You can buy an assortment with enough colors to match any furniture finish, or you can blend two or more colors to produce the exact shade needed.

To use a shellac stick for patching, you'll need an alcohol lamp or similar source of smokeless heat. A cigarette lighter can also be used, but a candle flame is too smoky to be useful. An artist's palette

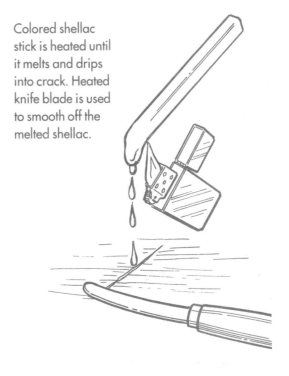

Colored shellac stick is heated until it melts and drips into crack. Heated knife blade is used to smooth off the melted shellac.

knife is a handy tool to use for applying the shellac because it has a thin flexible blade that is perfect for smoothing; special spatulas are also available.

After selecting the shellac stick that most closely matches the color you need, start by heating the blade of the knife until it is quite warm. Hold the end of the shellac stick over the flame until it starts to melt, positioning it in such a way that any molten shellac that drips will fall onto the area to be patched. If this is not practical, heat the shellac till it starts to soften and scrape some off with the heated knife blade. Use the warm blade to "butter" the shellac into and over the scratch to fill it completely. Actually it's better to build the patch up slightly higher than the surrounding surface and then reheat the knife blade to scrape off the excess and make it level. If the shellac starts to cool while you're working it, heat the blade again, then stroke it over the hardened shellac to soften it.

Instead of shellac sticks, there are also colored wax sticks that you can buy in most local paint and hardware stores. These wax sticks or pencils (some look like children's crayons, others look like wax-type marking pencils) are also available in a range of colors, and they can also be blended if necessary to achieve a specific shade.

The directions furnished with these usually state that all you need to do is rub them back and forth over the scratch until it fills in, but a much neater and smoother job will result if you use a heated spatula or knife blade as previously described for working with stick shellac. The heated blade will soften and partially melt the wax so it blends in more smoothly than is possible if you merely rub it on cold.

Although wax sticks are easier to use than shellac sticks, wax is not as permanent as shellac, and the repair is more noticeable and not as clear looking.

After the scratch has been filled in with either one of these methods, touching up with a very thin coat of shellac and then waxing or polishing will help to preserve and further conceal the repair.

REPAIRING BURN MARKS

Small burn marks or scorch marks, such as those caused by cigarettes and hot ashes, can usually be patched or repaired without need for completely refinishing the piece. The success of this treatment will depend to some extent on how large the burn mark is and on whether or not the scorch mark is only in the finish or goes clear through into the wood itself.

If only the finish has been scorched, you should be able to rub away the scorched material by wrapping a small piece of very fine steel wool around one fingertip and then rubbing carefully with this till all the blackened residue is gone. If the scorch mark is deep and shows some blistering in the center, a more drastic method will be required. Scrape back and forth carefully with a knife blade held at right angles to

Scorched material should be carefully scraped away with knife blade held as shown.

the surface. Keep scraping until all the blackened material has been removed. Then use a clean piece of steel wool to rub the spot smooth. Wipe all the dust away and examine the slight cavity that remains to see if the scraping has gone clear through the finish and down into the wood itself. If a good deal of finish still remains (even though it is dull), you can probably restore the luster simply by waxing and polishing.

However, if you have scraped away most of the finish down to the bare wood, you'll want to fill in and build up the slight cavity with several thin coats of varnish or shellac. Apply with a small artist's brush and allow each coat to dry before applying the next one. Use enough coats to build up the finish so that it matches the surrounding area, then polish with 4/0 steel wool that has been dipped into paste wax. Rubbing parallel to the grain will blend in the patch so that it's scarcely noticeable after you buff it.

REMOVING DENTS

When wood is dented, it means the fibers at that point have been severely compressed. In many cases you can restore the wood to its original shape by decompressing or swelling the fibers back to their normal size. The best way to do this is to use moisture and heat to create a mild steaming action. If the wood is unfinished, this is simple—the moisture can penetrate directly to the wood. However, if the wood is finished with varnish, shellac, lacquer, or a similar surface coating, in order to make this steaming process work you will have to either remove the finish over that spot or puncture the existing finish with small pinholes that will allow moisture to penetrate. (These tiny holes will be easy to

Metal bottle cap placed over damp cloth and heated with hot iron will often remove dent by swelling wood.

fill with dabs of varnish after the dented area has been repaired.)

Start by placing a wet cloth pad over the dent and then apply heat from a hot iron. The safest way to do this without damaging the surrounding area is to place a metal bottle cap, flat side down, on the cloth directly over the dent. Press down on this with your hot iron. The iron will heat the metal, and this will in turn heat the water in the damp cloth under the cap, causing it to steam. This steam will, if all goes well, cause the wood to swell back into its original shape so that the dent is no longer visible.

Although this technique is the most effective way of correcting small dents, it is apt to cause white spots or blushing of the finish because of the heat and moisture. If so, treat these as previously described, then restore the luster by waxing or polishing. In some cases you may have to fill in or touch up with several finish coats of clear shellac or varnish before polishing in the usual manner.

USING A REFINISHING LIQUID WITHOUT NEED FOR STRIPPING

When cleaning, polishing, and waxing alone is simply not enough to restore a dull, worn-looking finish, there is still one more method that can be used to rejuvenate most furniture finishes, and that is to use one of the various furniture refinishing liquids that are sold in almost all paint and hardware stores.

These refinishing liquids contain strong solvents that are similar to, but not nearly as strong as, those contained in a regular paint and varnish remover. When used according to directions they will actually remove a thin layer of the surface finish without taking all of it off down to the bare wood. In addition, they tend to partially dissolve what remains so that the finish flows together to form a relatively smooth, reconstituted coating that can then be touched up effectively with a clear finish recommended by the manufacturer. Using one of these refinishing liquids eliminates the need for complete stripping and restores much of the wood's original color and tone without having to do any scraping, sanding, bleaching, or staining.

Refinishing liquid scrubbed on with fine steel wool eliminates in many cases need for completely stripping off old finish.

To use one of these refinishing liquids, you start by pouring a small amount into a shallow metal or glass pan. Dip a pad of very fine steel wool into this and then scrub it on over the surface with a series of circular motions (wear rubber gloves to protect your hands). After you have covered a small area (about 1 square foot), dip the steel wool pad back into the liquid and squeeze it several times to flush it out. Then pick up more liquid and repeat the process on the next section.

Continue working in this manner until the entire piece has been scrubbed down, rinsing the steel wool repeatedly in the refinishing liquid. Use a fresh piece of steel wool as soon as the original one starts to shed or show signs of wear. When the liquid in the pan starts to thicken and get very dirty-looking, pour it into another container and add fresh liquid (the dirty liquid does not have to be discarded—you can allow the gummy residue to settle and then pour off the top portion to be saved for reuse).

After each panel or section has been scrubbed in this manner, go over it with a fresh pad of very fine steel wool and clean liquid—only this time rub in straight lines parallel to the grain in order to remove all of the swirl marks and circular streaks left by the original scrubbing. When finished, allow the wood to dry for about 30 minutes, then buff lightly with clean, dry steel wool (also very fine) to give the wood its final smoothing.

You're now ready to apply a fresh coat of clear new finish. You can use a regular varnish if you wish, but the most popular material to apply after this process (and the one recommended by the manufacturers of these various finishing liquids) is one or two coats of clear tung oil–base wood sealer. This penetrating oil is rubbed on with a pad or cloth and allowed to soak on the surface for 15 to 30 minutes. Then the excess is buffed off with a piece of clean dry cloth. A second coat can be applied in the same manner on the following day.

WHEN COMPLETE STRIPPING AND REFINISHING IS THE ONLY SOLUTION

There are times when no matter how hard you try, the old finish is simply beyond repair and past the point where treating with a refinishing liquid will help. And there are times when you want to give that piece a different look—for example, when you want to stain the wood a darker color or bleach it to get rid of dark blemishes that won't come out otherwise (in order to use a bleach, all of the old finish must be stripped off first).

In all such cases complete stripping, down to the bare wood, is the only solution. There are two ways you can do this: by removing the finish mechanically with scrapers and/or sandpaper or by removing it chemically with a paint and varnish remover. (There are also electric "heat guns" you can use to remove paint and varnish, but these are not advisable on furniture that is to be finished with a transparent or natural finish—too much chance of scorching the wood.)

Removing the finish by sanding and scraping is cheaper than using a chemical remover and is generally less of a mess, but it is a lot more work, takes more time, and requires more care in most cases. In addition, many experts frown on sanding as a stripping method, especially on older pieces that have delicate carvings or molded edges, because there is too much chance of damaging the original wood or design. Also, many have another objec-

tion: wood on old furniture ages and darkens in a certain way that most people find adds to its appeal and to its "feel" or to what is known as its "patina"—something that is almost impossible to duplicate once it is removed. When the wood is sanded enough to take off all the finish, you will almost always remove a thin layer of wood at the same time, and this is what kills the original "patina."

Theoretically it is possible to sand carefully with a fine-grit paper and with a gentle hand—the way it's done regularly when sanding between coats of varnish or enamel. However, removing multiple coats of paint or varnish with sandpaper is a job that calls for a heavier hand and a coarser abrasive—heavy enough, most experts agree, to mar fine or ornate carvings and molded edges and to round off square edges or corners on plain pieces.

Sanding with an electric sander is most effective when you are stripping off the finish on a relatively flat surface, so if you do have to strip a comparatively plain and inexpensive piece that is not old enough to have a patina, or one that is covered by some tough old paint, sanding may be the fastest and easiest way to proceed.

It is also possible to give wood a more aged look by staining and refinishing, so don't be afraid to get down to the bare wood—*if you have to*. Most times you will have to sand even after the finish has been removed chemically.

STRIPPING BY SANDING AND SCRAPING

Although we tend to refer to all abrasive papers as "sandpaper," they don't actually have any sand in them. The oldest type is flint paper, which is coated with grains of quartz, a natural mineral that looks very much like sand. It's the cheapest of all abrasive papers, but it dulls quickly, clogs easily, and wears out much more rapidly than other types. Ultimately it costs no less than the newer and better types, which are coated with synthetic minerals.

The most versatile and widely available type of flexible abrasive is aluminum oxide paper (also called production paper). Aluminum oxide is a synthetic mineral that is much harder, sharper, and longer-lasting than flint or quartz in normal use. In addition, aluminum oxide papers have a stronger, more tear-resistant backing than flint papers. Garnet paper is not quite so hard or long-wearing as aluminum oxide, but many finishers prefer it because it works particularly well on raw wood.

Sandpapers are also graded according to the size of the abrasive particles coating them. The lower the number, the coarser the grade—30 is very coarse and will leave deep scratches, while 600 is very fine and is used mainly for polishing. Sometimes papers are simply marked Very Coarse, Coarse, Medium, Fine, and so on, or simply M for medium, F for fine, and the like.

For stripping purposes, 80 is best. It's somewhere between coarse and medium and is rough enough to take off the finish without taking a lot of wood with it. On flat surfaces it's best to use a sanding block. You can apply more pressure without tearing the paper or having it clog, and it helps you to apply pressure more evenly so you're not sanding down one part more than another.

You can buy commercially made sanding blocks padded with foam rubber or felt in different sizes and shapes in most paint and hardware stores. Most experienced finishers, however, prefer to make their own. They simply cut blocks of wood to

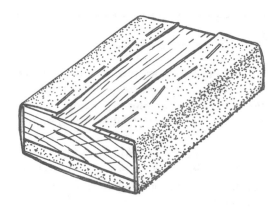

Wood sanding blocks can be made in any convenient size and shape.

the desired size and shape, then cover the working face with thick felt, foam, or sponge rubber.

Don't leave off the padding, A block without any resilient material between it and the paper can cause deep scratches—especially if the paper tears or if a large particle of abrasive grit gets caught between the block and the surface being sanded.

For sanding areas where a block is not convenient, tear a standard sheet of sandpaper in half, then fold each piece in half with the abrasive sides facing out. You can now hold each of these folded sheets comfortably in the palm of your hand and work with the double thickness. When one side becomes dull or clogged, simply flip the folded sheet over to expose the other side. The reason you tear the sheet in half before you fold it—instead of folding the large sheet four ways—is to keep the abrasive faces from rubbing against each other. That would only shorten their life by causing them to dull prematurely. Sand with the grain, where possible, and after sanding make sure you remove all dust by wiping with a tack cloth or tack rag (sold in most paint stores).

• •

Making a Tack Rag

If you cannot find tack rags in your local paint or hardware store, make your own out of a piece of cheesecloth. Start by folding the fabric into a pad and wetting it with water. Then squeeze almost dry.

Next, with the damp cloth still folded, pour a little turpentine over the fabric and work this into the cloth by squeezing or kneading it with your hands.

Now with the cloth still folded flat, pour a small amount of varnish over the fabric or sprinkle it through the folds. (Use about 1 ounce of varnish for a piece of fabric that's about a yard square when completely unfolded.)

Work this varnish through the pad, again by kneading the cloth with your hands, until the varnish has spread uniformly through the entire piece of cloth.

Unfold it to see if there are any dry spots remaining, and if so, sprinkle on a little more varnish and knead again. The cloth should be uniformly amber or light yellow in color and damp enough to feel kind of sticky. But it should not be so damp that it drips liquid when squeezed hard.

The tack rag is now ready for use. Store the rag in a tightly closed screw-top jar or airtight plastic bag to keep it from drying out.

• •

Sanding machines. Some purists still feel that the only way to do a proper job of smoothing fine wood is to do your sanding by hand. On some valuable antiques and heirlooms, this is probably the best way. However, for many projects with flat surfaces, sanding by machine is much faster and easier, but you must be careful to avoid cutting too deeply or accidentally scratching the surface.

Portable electric sanding machines gen-erally fall into one of three broad categories: disk sanders, orbital sanders (also called finishing sanders), and belt sanders.

To most do-it-yourselfers a disk sander is nothing more than an accessory sanding disk that one uses with an electric drill—it consists of a flexible rubber or elastic pad mounted on an arbor with an abrasive cemented to the face of the disk. Commercial disk sanders, such as those used by auto body finishing shops and other commercial finishers, have larger disks and more powerful motors, and they are designed specifically for sanding and grinding. Electric drills really are not designed for sanding; in fact, most light-duty drills could be damaged if used for any length of time in this manner.

Aside from this, any disk sander, especially in the hands of an amateur or do-it-yourself furniture finisher, is really not suited for use on furniture or paneling. It is suited only for rough work because the rotary action can easily damage the surface unless it is handled skillfully. The disk tends to dig in and create burn marks and is likely to leave gouges and swirls on the surface.

Orbital sanders, which are also called finishing sanders, have a flat pad that moves in an oval or orbital path to give a smooth finish similar to that achieved by hand sanding. They accept ordinary sheets of abrasive paper that have been cut into halves or thirds, depending on the size of the machine, but you cannot use ordinary flint paper (the least expensive type) in any electric sander. You must use either aluminum oxide paper (also called production paper) or silicon carbide abrasive papers, the kind often referred to as wet-or-dry sandpaper.

Orbital sanders are designed primarily

to do finish sanding (hence the name "finishing" sanders). They are not very fast when it comes to removing paint or varnish. The size of the sanding pad will vary with the size of the machine, so choose one that best fits your needs and pocketbook. Some models have an auxiliary handle on the front because they are designed for two-handle control, but the easiest ones to work with are the newer-style "palm sanders" (so-called because you hold them in the palm of one hand while working). These high-speed models leave an exceptionally smooth finish and permit easy one-hand operation and control. Because of their high-speed orbital action, they can be used across the grain as well as with the grain, and they leave no visible scratch marks on the surface.

Belt sanders are the fastest working of all portable electric sanding machines and do the fastest job of removing multiple coats of paint, varnish, and other finishes. Equipped with the proper abrasive belts, they are ideal for smoothing down rough surfaces, as well as for fine finishing—but only if handled carefully. Since they cut much faster than an orbital sander, they

Palm-type finishing sander is the most convenient power sander to use for most furniture finishing jobs.

cannot be held in one place while the belt is in motion—this will inevitably result in its digging in or removing more than you intended to. The sander must be kept moving at all times while the belt is in contact with the surface in order to avoid such accidents. Belt sanders cost more than finishing sanders in most cases, but for those who do a great deal of sanding on large surfaces, the extra cost may be worth it.

When using any power-driven sanding machine, never make the common mistake of bearing down hard while the machine is working in an effort to make it cut faster. Pressing hard does just the opposite: it tends to overload the motor and actually makes the machine cut slower. It can also result in scorching the sandpaper and overheating the motor.

You can press down lightly to ensure firm contact with the work, but never so hard that you slow down the machine. On horizontal surfaces the weight of the machine is almost enough—just press lightly. On vertical surfaces you'll have to compensate for the weight of the machine and thus will have to apply a little more pressure.

For safety's sake it is a good idea to wear goggles with any electric sander—especially when working overhead. If the dust bothers you, wear a spray mask similar to the kind sold for use with paint sprayers. (Inexpensive, disposable models are sold in almost all paint and hardware stores.)

Scrapers. Hook-type scrapers, of the kind illustrated, are useful for what finishers call "rough work"—taking off finishes. To use, hold the handle almost parallel to the surface with one hand, while you bear down on the blade end with the other hand. Then drag the tool toward you. Use this tool cautiously until you get the feel of

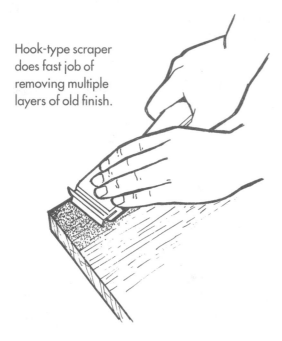

Hook-type scraper does fast job of removing multiple layers of old finish.

it, and don't try it with fine pieces—it's too easy to gouge the wood. Cabinetmakers' wood scrapers, available from mail-order houses, can also be useful, but some practice will be required before you learn how to use them.

Steel wool. This is a much finer abrasive than sandpaper, and you'll use a lot more elbow grease taking off a finish with it. It's likely to be more useful in the final smoothing operations and for getting into curves, carvings, and turnings you can't work with sandpaper. Like sandpaper, it's graded according to coarseness—3 is the coarsest, 1 is fine, and very fine grades go from 0 to 0000.

STRIPPING WITH CHEMICAL REMOVERS

When we talk about a "finish," what we're really referring to is the product that seals the wood—not the stain or the wood's color—and what chemical removers take

off is this finish. A wide variety of chemical removers are commonly available in paint and hardware stores, but all work in basically the same way. They contain special solvents and chemicals that soften and "lift" or blister up old finish so that it can easily be wiped, scraped, or washed away to expose bare wood.

Some removers are liquid, and some are creamy or semipaste in consistency. As a rule, the liquids cost less, but the thicker semipaste types are better for most furniture-stripping jobs. They "stay put," without running and dripping when used on vertical surfaces, and they don't evaporate or dry out as quickly. And a remover that stays wet longer keeps on working longer. The longer a remover stays wet and in contact with the old finish, the deeper and more thoroughly it will penetrate in a single application.

Another important difference between removers is their flammability. Many are highly inflammable and must be used with extreme caution when working indoors. Weather permitting, you should work outside or in the garage (with the door open). Others are nonflammable and cost only slightly more, so choose one of these when you must work indoors.

To keep paint removers from drying out or evaporating before they can completely penetrate and soften the old finish, manufacturers usually add special ingredients that retard evaporation by keeping air out. In many removers this is a waxlike compound, which leaves a residue that must be neutralized or washed away when the job is done. Otherwise a new finish will not adhere properly. However, many removers use a retardant that contains no wax, and these supposedly need no washing with solvent. Usually labeled "no-wash" or "self-neutralizing," these removers come in both liquid and semipaste forms, and they create fewer problems than those that contain wax. Nevertheless, it is best with either type to wipe down the surface with paint thinner or denatured alcohol after using the remover.

One of the easiest types of varnish remover you can use is a water-wash type. Most widely available in semipaste form, it is usually nonflammable. The advantage of using this remover is that after the old finish has been thoroughly softened with a heavy application, you can wash everything off simply by scrubbing with a brush or a piece of steel wool dipped in water. You can even take the piece outside and hose it down with water while you scrub the finish off with a stiff brush. But you do have to be careful about using water on old pieces of furniture. Many of them are assembled with glue that is not water-resistant. And *never* use water on a piece of furniture that is covered with veneer. The surface will almost always wrinkle or loosen, destroying the veneer.

When using remover, cover the floor and nearby areas to protect them. But don't depend on plastic drop cloths. Many chemical removers dissolve plastic. Put down a few layers of old newspaper, or use an old bedsheet or blanket covered with several layers of newspaper. Wear rubber gloves to protect your hands, and if you will be working on surfaces above eye level, wear goggles to protect your eyes.

Before starting to apply the remover, take off knobs, hinges, handles, and all other hardware. Stand the drawers up so the fronts are horizontal, and lay doors flat after the hinges have been removed.

Some repairs are done after stripping and some before, but now is the time to look for loose joints. If there are many that need repair, take them apart before stripping.

The easiest way to apply the remover is with an old paintbrush or an inexpensive brush that you can throw away afterward. Lay on the remover in thick layers with a minimum of back-and-forth brushing so that you don't disturb the film any more than necessary as you apply it.

Too much brushing only slows up the chemical action, because it allows air to enter the solution and speeds evaporation of the solvent. If you are outdoors, avoid working in direct sunlight, since this too hastens evaporation and shortens the working time.

As a rule, it is best to concentrate on one side or section at a time. Apply the remover to the area in a heavy layer, then wait about 15 to 20 minutes and test one

Paint remover should be brushed on in thick layers. Brush in one direction only and with no more strokes than necessary.

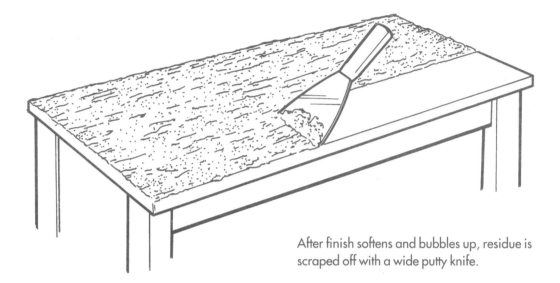

After finish softens and bubbles up, residue is scraped off with a wide putty knife.

corner with a putty knife to see if the old finish is softened all the way down to the bare wood. Ideally, all layers of finish should come off down to the bare wood with a single scraping. If your test indicates that the finish is not soft all the way down, and if the remover is still wet (and therefore not working), wait another 5 or 10 minutes and try again. If the remover has still not softened the finish all the way down to the raw wood, stop scraping and apply a second coat of the remover right on top of the original one. Allow this to work for another 10 or 15 minutes and then try again. Whatever you do, don't skimp on remover and don't wait longer than about 20 minutes before scraping off everything that you've put on thus far. It's too hard to scrape off otherwise.

On flat surfaces a putty knife is probably the quickest and easiest way to scrape off most of the softened material. In grooves or crevices, or where there are many carvings, you'll really appreciate the advantages of using a water-wash remover. All you do is dip a stiff-bristled brush into

water or a detergent solution and then simply scrub out the softened residue.

If you're not using a water-wash remover, you can accomplish the same thing with coarse steel wool and a wire brush. Read the label on your product carefully, and know what you're buying. Then you'll best know the most effective way to scrub up.

After the entire surface has been scraped clean, look over the piece carefully to make sure there are no spots where small patches of the old finish are still visible. Often these will show up as dark spots or as "glazed" spots that are still slightly glossy. Although barely noticeable on the raw wood, these will really stand out after the new finish is applied, especially if the refinishing process requires a penetrating type of wood stain. In those spots the stain will not soak in as much as it does on the rest of the wood—if at all. To prevent this, recoat the missed spots with remover and then scrub with steel wool or a wire brush.

When the wood has been stripped clean,

allow it to dry thoroughly, then sand lightly with 220 sandpaper. This not only gives the wood a final smoothing, it also removes any film or chemicals that may still be left on the surface and helps to open the pores of the wood so that the new finish will penetrate properly.

USING BLEACHES TO LIGHTEN WOOD

As mentioned earlier, paint and varnish removers take off only the finish—not the stain, or at least not very much of it. So if you are working on a pine or maple piece that has been stained to look like walnut or mahogany, and you want to lighten it to look more like oak, you may be able to do it with bleach. Or maybe you are hoping to get down to light wood so you can restain it to match the rest of the furniture in the living room.

Bleach is not only capable of lightening wood all over, it can be very effective in removing blemishes and discolored areas that have penetrated too deeply into the wood to be removed by sanding.

There are three types of bleach you can use on furniture: liquid laundry bleach, oxalic acid, or one of the two-solution wood bleaches that are sold specifically for this purpose. All are effective only on bare wood, so all the old finish must be taken off before bleaching—and there must be no skips or missed spots or the bleach will not soak in and you will wind up with a blotchy, uneven job.

For the same reason, it's important that close-grained woods, such as maple, be thoroughly sanded to open the wood's pores before bleaching. Otherwise you get an uneven job.

Of the three bleaches mentioned, laundry bleach is the weakest and hardest to con-trol. However, applying it several times is often convenient when you don't want to bleach an entire piece but just lighten some discolored areas. It's also good for taking out ink spots or watermarks that have darkened the wood in places.

Oxalic acid is stronger and easier to control than laundry bleach and comes in nonspillable crystal form. To use, dissolve as many crystals as you can in a container of hot (hot is important) water. Mop this solution over the piece while it's still hot, then allow the bleach to dry. Rinse off with plenty of clear water. Repeat the treatment if you want the wood even lighter.

If you're still not satisfied, try strengthening the action by combining oxalic acid with hyposulfite—ordinary photographer's hypo, available in any camera store. Apply the oxalic acid first. As it begins to dry, mop on the hypo solution (3 ounces of hypo in 1 quart of warm water). Let sit for about 15 to 20 minutes, then rinse off with plenty of clean water.

If even this is not light enough, you can try the two-solution chemical wood bleaches. These are the most expensive of the bleaches, but they're also the strongest, the most effective, and probably the fastest acting. You spread one solution on the piece first, then follow up with the second.

Pour the first solution into a plastic or glass bowl (not metal). Then take a synthetic nylon brush or rubber sponge, dip it into the solution, and spread the solution on the surface of your piece.

Allow the first solution to remain on the piece for the length of time recommended on the label or in the directions, usually 10 to 20 minutes. Then apply the second solution in much the same way. Again, let stand for the recommended amount of time, but this time keep your eye on the wood. If it looks as if it is getting lighter than you want it to, you can stop the action at any time by flooding the surface with ordinary household vinegar.

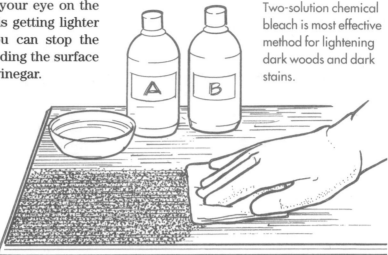

Two-solution chemical bleach is most effective method for lightening dark woods and dark stains.

When working with any bleach, wear rubber gloves and old clothes with long sleeves to protect hands and arms. If bleach spills on exposed skin, wash immediately with lots of water. After you've finished, throw out any bleach that remains in the bowl. Don't pour it back into the original bottle because it will ruin whatever's left for further use.

No matter what brand of bleach you use, or what it says on the label, it's always best to use a neutralizing rinse afterward. The simplest is ordinary white vinegar, and it works as well on two-solution bleaches as on laundry bleach.

First, rinse the bleached piece with plain water. Then pour on vinegar, full strength, and let stand for a few minutes. Wipe off with clean rags and rinse with more water.

Instead of vinegar, you can use a borax solution as a neutralizer. (This works as well on oxalic acid as on any of the others). Dissolve 1 cup borax in 1 cup of hot water, and apply to wood while still warm. Rinse off with clean water and allow wood to dry thoroughly before going ahead with any finish.

Since all bleaches have a water base, and since they have to be followed with a water rinse afterward, bleaching will almost always tend to raise the grain of the wood to some extent. This creates a slight fuzziness, which can be removed after the wood is dry by rubbing lightly with fine sandpaper. If several bleaching applications will be required, don't do any sanding until after the final rinse.

MAKING NEEDED REPAIRS

Although surface repairs—the filling and patching of dents and gouges, smoothing of uneven areas, and the like—should be done after the finish is off, loose joints— wobbly legs or spindles—should be repaired *before* stripping if you're going to use a chemical remover. Because removers are liquid, they inevitably seep into the open cracks of loose joints, and not even a strong flushing with water or solvent will get out all of the stuff. The slightest residue will keep the wood from drying or bonding properly.

You could take the joint completely

apart, without regluing, during the stripping process and have greater success flushing out residue. Sometimes the joint doesn't come apart until the stripping process, and that's what you have to do. But it's best and safest to do it all first.

If you're stripping mechanically by sanding and scraping, then it makes no difference when you glue.

Of course, if you're not going to strip at all—if you're going to paint or antique—your repair problems are just a little different. Wood with a transparent or translucent finish shows blemishes, so you've got to be very careful about filling and patching in terms of color and how fillers match the wood. But with an opaque finish only smoothness counts, since nothing else shows.

USING GLUE AND DOWELS

When chair or table legs or rungs work loose from the holes in which they were fitted, the only way to do a thorough, permanent repair job on these joints is to take them apart completely so that they can be reglued properly. This means all the joints, not just the loose ones, because it's just too hard to take one joint apart without cracking or splitting the others.

When taking joints apart, watch for concealed screws, nails, and other fasteners. They're sometimes driven in from the side or back or at such an angle that they're almost impossible to detect if you don't look carefully, and they can really damage a good piece of wood if you don't find and remove them first.

Pry the joints apart by hand if you can, but you may use a rubber or plastic mallet, which won't mar the wood, to tap the pieces apart if necessary.

Most of the glues that were used years

ago were not water-resistant and had an organic base, so if you find the joint difficult to take apart, you may be able to soften the old glue by wetting it with vinegar.

An even stronger solvent can be made by using glacial acetic acid (sold in photo supply stores), diluted with 3 or 4 parts of water. (When mixing acid with water, always pour the acid into the water rather than the water into the acid, and mix in a glass or plastic bowl. Concentrated acetic acid is very strong, so handle it with extreme care.)

After you have taken the joints completely apart, use a fine wood rasp or medium-grade sandpaper to clean the old glue off the ends of the rungs or legs, and use a pocketknife or similar tool to scrape all of the old glue out of the holes into which they fit. Sometimes hot water or vinegar will help clean out these recessed areas completely.

To reglue the joints you can use ordinary white glue that dries clear, but for a stronger bond and a "stickier" grip that will hold pieces in alignment more easily while you're setting them into position, use one of the pale yellow or beige aliphatic resin glues, which also come in plastic squeeze bottles and dry almost clear.

For some jobs, two-part epoxy glues are useful. They are exceptionally strong and completely waterproof, and they do not require clamping. All you have to do is keep the pieces in firm contact with each other while the adhesive sets. What's more, they have the ability to fill in voids when pieces fit loosely or when joints have decided gaps in them. However, they cost considerably more than other glues, and, worse, they form a dark-colored joint that is more noticeable when dry, so

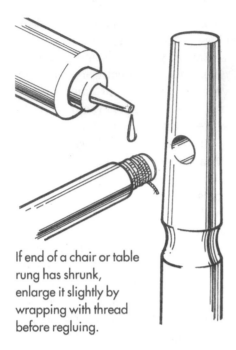

If end of a chair or table rung has shrunk, enlarge it slightly by wrapping with thread before regluing.

although they are okay for opaque finishes, they may not be suitable for transparent ones, on light woods.

When the end of a rung or leg has shrunk so much that it no longer fits snugly in its hole, there's no sense in merely pouring more wood glue into the joint. You have to take steps to make a snug fit first if you want to be sure the repair will be permanent and invisible. One easy method is to wrap the end of the loose-fitting member with fine cotton or linen thread to enlarge its diameter slightly. Then coat with glue and assemble in the usual manner.

Another way to do the job is to saw a slot in the end of the loose-fitting piece, then force a thin, wedge-shaped piece of wood into the slot. When the piece is hammered into place, the wedge will be forced in and will spread the end of the loose-fitting rung slightly, expanding it enough to ensure a tight fit.

When reassembling pieces, coat each surface with glue and then clamp or tie the parts together to apply the pressure required to achieve a permanent bond.

Bar clamps or pipe clamps are useful for this kind of project. So are C-clamps and other woodworking clamps. If you don't have any of these handy, there are several other ways you can apply the needed pressure.

Where practical, simple weights (books, buckets of sand or water, bricks) set on top of a piece will do the trick. In other cases, a rope tourniquet will serve almost as well as a professional web clamp. To make a rope tourniquet, wrap a piece of stout clothesline twice around the chair, drawer, or other piece being assembled. Then tie a knot to hold it in place. Pressure is applied by using a stick between the two turns of rope and then twisting. Before doing this, insert pieces of heavy cardboard or similar padding over each corner to protect against damaging the wood as

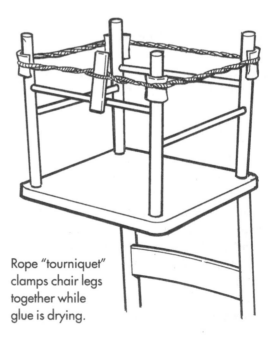

Rope "tourniquet" clamps chair legs together while glue is drying.

the rope tightens. Scrap pieces of cardboard or plywood should also be used under the jaws of all clamps to keep the metal from marring the wood.

There are many times when it is impractical to take loose joints apart in order to do a proper job of regluing. Sometimes taking them apart will cause too much damage. Or perhaps only one or two joints are loose and it is not worth taking apart all the other joints.

In these cases, first force the pieces apart as much as you can without actually disjointing them. Then use a thin blade to scrape out as much of the old glue as possible. One tool that is handy for this job is a small fingernail file; another is a stiff piece of wire with a very small hook bent at the end.

Blow out as much of the dust and scrapings as possible. Then work glue into the joint with a piece of wire or a flexible artist's palette knife.

It helps if you can turn the piece so that the joint is vertical, with the open end up, so that gravity will make the glue flow down into it.

After you have worked in as much glue as possible, open and close the joint a few times by pushing the loose pieces back and forth to spread the adhesive around on the inside. Then press the pieces together and clamp them to apply the needed pressure while the glue sets.

A very handy gadget for working glue into a loose joint is a syringe type of glue injector—a larger version of the syringe doctors use for hypodermic injections. Made of metal or plastic, and sold in many hardware stores as well as through mail-order houses that specialize in craftsmen's supplies, these tools have a narrow nozzle with a hole in the center. A plunger fits snugly inside the hollow barrel, which you fill with glue. Pushing on the plunger then forces the glue out through the nozzle.

To get the glue into the joint, drill a small hole where it will be least noticeable—the back of a leg on a chair, under the seat for bench slats. Inject the glue through the hole so that it penetrates the joint. Keep pumping in glue until it oozes out around the assembled pieces. Apply clamping pressure and wipe off excess glue afterward. The little hole that remains will be filled with a wood or plastic compound later on.

There is one other method you can use to tighten a loose rung or similar joint when simple regluing doesn't seem to work. Drill a small hole completely through the joint, again in a not too visible place, and just big enough to drive a small dowel through it. It's easiest to match the hole to the dowel—if you have a ¼-inch dowel, use a ¼-inch drill. Next, work glue into the loosened joint by one of the techniques just described. Then dip the dowel into more glue and drive it home with a wooden mallet.

The hole you drill for the dowel should be snug enough to ensure a tight fit, but not so tight that the dowel will be smashed when you try to drive it home. Your best bet is to drill trial holes in scrap material first to make sure you are using the right size bit for your particular dowel. To provide room for the glue, file a small flat area along the length of the dowel, using a rasp or piece of sandpaper. Cutting grooves lengthwise with a knife or fine saw is another method. Make the dowel longer than necessary and leave the excess sticking out until after the glue dries, then trim it off neatly with a hacksaw blade or coping saw and use sandpaper to contour the exposed part for a flush fit.

USING NAILS AND SCREWS WHEN NECESSARY

On some pieces where you can't use dowels and glue you may have to use small nails or screws. Drill small pilot holes before driving in the nails or screws, so that you don't split the wood. The nails or screws will be driven in through the side of a joint, where they are least visible, so that's where you can drill your holes. Again, try to work as much glue into the joint as you can before driving in the nails or screws.

Once a nail is in, countersink the head beneath the surface of the wood with a nail set and a hammer. To countersink screws, use a counterbore or drill bit that is the same diameter as the screw head. Drill a shallow hole just deep enough to permit recessing the screw's head beneath the wood's surface, but be careful to go no deeper than necessary. The holes left in each case will be filled later with matching wood plastic or a colored patching compound.

There are even times when this kind of invisibility isn't quite necessary. Chairs and tables that have aprons or skirts beneath the seat or top, for example, with legs that butt up against the underside will often get wobbly because the brace that goes across the corner joint has worked loose. The brace may be a piece of wood secured by screws driven into the frame on each side, or it may be a steel brace, with a threaded lag bolt going through the center to the inside corner of the leg.

In the latter case, tightening the wing nut will draw the assembly together more firmly. In the case of a wood brace, the screws may have worked loose and merely need tightening. If tightening the screws doesn't do the trick, or if the screws have gouged out oversize holes in the wood, you may be better off installing a new wood block, slightly oversize, and securing this with both glue and screws.

REPAIRING DAMAGED VENEER

Veneer is a thin layer of beautiful wood that is bonded to a lesser wood to make it richer-looking. In time the glue may come loose and the veneer may loosen and lift in spots. Blistering and lifting repairs are not very difficult, but replacing a missing piece of veneer can be tricky.

If the veneer is loose along one edge, pry it up carefully and slide a knife blade or fingernail file under it to scrape out as much of the old glue as you can. An emery board, the kind used on fingernails, is especially handy for jobs of this kind. Just be careful not to lift the veneer any more than necessary to avoid splitting or cracking it.

Use a soda straw to blow all dust and dried glue flakes out from under the veneer, then work fresh glue underneath by poking it in with a piece of wire or a knife blade. Ordinary white glue is probably the easiest material to use, since it dries clear and is virtually nonstaining.

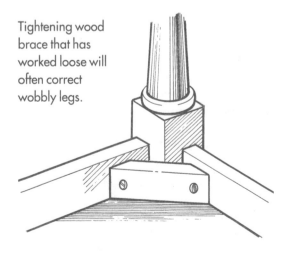

Tightening wood brace that has worked loose will often correct wobbly legs.

After the glue has been spread around as much as possible, move the loose veneer up and down a few times to make certain both surfaces are coated. Now press down hard and use clamps or weights to keep the two surfaces in contact until the glue dries. Be sure you wipe off excess glue that oozes out before it dries.

If the veneer is loose in the center of a panel, creating a noticeable blister, use a *very sharp* knife or razor blade to slit through the middle of the blister. Then press one half down while you work glue under the other half with a thin spatula or piece of wire. (An artist's palette knife, with a thin, long, flexible blade, is ideal for this job.)

After you have spread glue under one half of the blister, press that half down and work glue in under the other side.

Now press the entire blister up and down several times to spread the glue around and apply weights or clamps to hold both sides of the veneer in place while the glue hardens. To keep the weights or clamps from sticking to the surface (some glue will ooze up through the slit you made in the middle of the blister), cover the veneer with a piece of waxed paper, after wiping off as much as possible of the oozed-up glue with a damp cloth. There will be a barely visible slit, but on old pieces it sort of adds to the antique look.

When a piece of veneer is missing entirely, the only way to make a repair that won't be noticeable is to insert a patch of the same veneer. Very few lumberyards stock wood veneer these days, but it can be obtained from some mail-order houses that cater to home craftsmen, as well as from some dealers who specialize in cabinetmaker's supplies.

However, since wood is a natural prod-

To repair blister in veneer, slice through center with razor blade, then work glue under one half of blister at a time. Apply weights to hold veneer down until glue dries.

uct, even if you can find the veneer, chances are it won't match the tone and grain of your surface exactly, so in many cases you are better off trying to remove a small piece of veneer—enough to make the patch you need—from the same piece of furniture. You do this by cutting out a piece in a place where it is not easily visible. For example, the back of a piece may be covered with the same veneer, or there may be veneer on the inside of a door or drawer front. Sometimes you can even get away with cutting a piece out of one side of a large unit that stands in a corner or against another large piece. A small patch of veneer removed from the hidden side, near the back or near the floor, won't be noticeable.

The easiest way to "steal" such a piece is to cut it out near the edge. This will enable you to slide a knife or sharp chisel in from that edge in order to lift off a small piece of the veneer.

If this is not practical, you can use a sharp knife to cut out a rectangular or oblong piece that will be large enough to make the size patch needed. Use a metal straightedge to guide your knife and cut along each side three or four times to make certain the piece will lift out cleanly. Then carefully slide chisel or knife blade under this cut-out section to slice the glue away until you can lift it out neatly.

The next step is to trim this piece to a neat rectangle, square, or diamond shape, so that when laid over the area where the veneer is missing, the new piece will cover it fully.

If you have a choice, try for a diamond-shaped patch with the grain running in the long direction of the diamond. This shape tends to blend in more easily than a rectangle or square that has two edges running straight across the direction of the grain.

After the patch has been trimmed to a size slightly larger than the damaged area, lay it directly over the damage and trace its outline onto the existing veneer with the point of an awl or ice pick. Now lay the patch aside and carefully cut out the old veneer to match the pattern just outlined.

Don't cut on the outside of the line. If anything, cut slightly inside the line. You can always trim the patch slightly if needed to make a snug fit. Be particularly careful about matching the direction of the general grain pattern. If trimming is needed, use a single-edge razor blade until the patch drops neatly into the area where the damaged veneer has been cut out.

After the old veneer has been removed, scrape the dried glue out from underneath, blow all dust away, and glue the new patch in its place. Use weights or clamps to apply pressure until the glue sets, and wipe away any glue that may have oozed out. The hairline seam or joint will fill in when the new finish is applied and—if you have worked carefully—should be scarcely noticeable when the job is done.

PATCHING CRACKS, HOLES, DENTS, AND GOUGES

Some old pieces of furniture have "distress" marks that add to the character and appearance of the piece and should be left as is when refinishing. However, there are times when scratches, dents, gouges, and other defects are just plain unsightly and should be patched or smoothed over if you want the final finish to have a smooth, professional look.

Patching compounds for filling cracks, holes, and gouges in wood generally fall into two categories: ready-mixed plastic compounds that dry quickly, and powdered compounds that you mix with water to form a puttylike material for use on wood.

Generally, the powdered wood-putty compounds are available only in a kind of light tan or buff color that is fine for opaque finishes, while ready-mixed wood plastics come in a variety of wood-tone shades so you can blend them in better with different-colored woods and finishes.

These wood-patching compounds differ in porosity when hard—that is, in their ability to absorb stain. Some are fairly porous and will "take" stains to some degree, while others are extremely hard and dense and will not absorb any stain at all. This means you have to be very careful about using them on a piece that you plan eventually to treat with stain. The stain will not be absorbed uniformly, so that all the patch marks will stand out when the job is done, or the stain may not "take" on any of the patched areas.

For best results, it's smart to experiment beforehand with various brands and types. Make some gouges on a few pieces of scrap wood, then apply the patching material and let it dry hard. Sand smooth and apply stain over this to see how the patch absorbs the stain. Don't rely on a manufacturer's claims that its filler absorbs stain. Even if it does, it won't absorb it in exactly the same way as the wood around it.

The usual way to avoid this headache is to apply the stain to the wood first, then use a colored filler or patching compound that matches the stained wood when dry. If you can't find a patching compound to match the color of your stained wood, remember that colors can be intermixed or "doctored" by adding tinting colors, which you can buy in most paint stores. This will take some experimenting, especially since patching compounds dry to a different shade from their appearance in the can. But this is really the only way you can be sure what the final results will look like, and you'll learn a lot in the process.

Never try to fill a deep crack or gouge with a single application of patching compound. Although some of these materials are labeled "nonshrinking," most will contract to some degree when applied in heavy layers. Also, they may not dry properly if you put them on in thick layers. The compound dries at the surface first and remains soft underneath for quite a while. To prevent this, apply the material in layers, allowing each one to harden before applying the next one. The last layer should be slightly higher than the surrounding surface so that you can trim it flush by sanding or shaving carefully with a very sharp chisel or scraper.

When using any of these compounds to build up a chipped edge or corner, you can increase the strength of the patch by drilling a few small holes in the bottom of the recess or cavity before applying the first layer of patching material. As you press the compound into position, with a little extra pressure you'll force some of it into the holes, increasing the strength of the bond.

Another method is to drive a few small staples or brads into the cavity, allowing the heads to protrude slightly—but not high enough to interfere with the smoothing over of the final patch. When the wood plastic is packed around the staples or brads, the heads will firmly lock the patch into place and greatly reduce the chances of its being knocked or chipped away later on.

SANDING AND SMOOTHING

The last step before applying any finish is the final sanding and smoothing. This requires more care when refinishing an old piece than it does when applying any finish to a new piece. On new wood your only concern is to get the wood as smooth as possible—no matter how much sanding is required. On old pieces you want to retain that aged patina we've talked so much about.

On most small surfaces, and on older pieces that require special care, hand sanding is probably the safest and simplest procedure. Even if you use a finishing sander for preliminary smoothing, it's still advisable to switch to hand sanding for the final smoothing.

On curved, carved, or contoured surfaces, steel wool works better than sandpaper. It's less likely to leave scratch marks in the wood than sandpaper. It is slower working and takes more rubbing to do the same job, but it does give much better control.

For round pieces, such as legs or spindles, you can tear the steel wool in long strips and then use it shoe-shine style. Grab each end with one hand and pull back and forth, maintaining a steady pressure on each end.

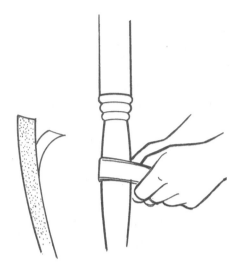

To sand round legs, back strips of sandpaper with tape, then use this strip shoe-shine style by pulling back and forth as shown.

You can do the same with fairly fine sandpaper. Simply cut the paper into long strips and follow the directions above. To keep the strips from tearing, reinforce the backs with strips of cellophane tape.

Start on the raw wood with 100 or 120 paper. Sand at a slight angle to the direction of the grain, but no more than necessary to level off any ridges or scratches left after stripping. Then switch to 200, this time working parallel to the grain wherever possible so no visible scratches remain.

The 220 paper will give you a satin-smooth finish, but you can go on to an even silkier surface with 280 or 320 paper. Before switching to this fine grade, wipe the surface clean with a rag moistened slightly with paint thinner to get rid of any grit left by the coarser papers, and once again go with the grain.

Check the surface frequently with your fingertips; you can feel rough spots more easily than you can see them. You can also hold a bright light behind the surface and almost parallel to it. This angular light will show up the slightest irregularities.

And remember, when hand sanding on a flat surface, it's best to use a sanding block.

On some types of wood, especially in the softer varieties, sanding with even the finest grit does not always leave the surface perfectly smooth, because the wood fibers tend to stand up along the grain. This creates a fuzzy surface that never really looks or feels smooth. Sometimes this isn't noticeable until the first coat of stain has been applied, while in other cases it can be seen clearly even on the raw wood. Here's an old preventive trick that many professional finishers use. Just before the final sanding, dampen the wood slightly by wiping with a sponge that has been moistened in water. The water will cause the wood fibers on the surface to swell slightly so that when they dry, these fibers will remain erect. The final sanding will remove this fuzz and leave the surface very smooth. It also minimizes the likelihood of more grain raising when the stain is applied.

If the wood is very soft and fuzzy, here's another method that works even better. Dilute 1 part 4-pound-cut shellac with 2 parts of denatured alcohol. Apply a very thin "wash" coat to the surface. Avoid overlapping strokes with a brush. You want to make sure the wood gets only one coat over its entire surface.

The shellac will not only raise fibers, which can be sanded down, it will also partially seal the surface and tend to stabilize the grain and make it uniform in porosity. Partially sealing the grain also helps ensure that a wood stain applied over it will "take" uniformly without blotchy spots where the stain soaks in more rapidly in some places than it does in others, a common problem with very soft woods such as pine or fir.

After sanding, it is important that you remove every bit of dust and grit before you apply the first coat of stain, sealer, or other finishing material. Slight specks and fine dust particles, which may be practically invisible on the raw wood, will stand out conspicuously after a finish has been applied.

Wiping down the surface with a dry cloth or brushing off the dust is not enough. Using a vacuum cleaner is better, but even this will not remove all of the dust.

The best thing to do is vacuum to remove the heaviest accumulations. Then wipe down the entire surface carefully with a tack rag.

Sold in most paint stores as well as in many hardware stores, and often referred to as a "tacky cloth," a tack rag is nothing more than a piece of coarse-mesh cotton or cheesecloth that has been impregnated with a varnish-and-oil mixture to make it sticky. It picks up dust without leaving any residue on the surface of the wood.

To use the tack rag, fold it to a convenient size and wipe it over the surface of the wood carefully. Don't skip any spots. As the exposed side of the cloth gets loaded with dust, keep folding it to expose a fresh surface.

CHOOSING AND USING WOOD STAINS

The true purpose of a wood stain is to change the color or tone of the wood without hiding its natural grain pattern or texture. A stain that is wisely selected and applied properly should enhance the appearance of the wood on which it is used, not detract from it. In many cases a stain can be used to completely change the character of a particular wood—in other words, to make it look like a different species or type of wood.

Many light woods, for example, have little character or tone when left in their natural color. But properly stained they gain life and color and therefore can become more interesting or richer-looking. The grain in most woods can be highlighted and accented with a suitable stain, and pieces that don't match can be made to blend in by first stripping off the old finish and then staining them to more closely blend in with other pieces.

However, it must be remembered that simply coloring the wood with a stain cannot always make it look like another type of wood—no stain can really do much about matching the grain pattern if the wood you are trying to match has a distinctive grain. That's why using a mahogany or walnut stain on pine, birch, or similar light wood won't make it look like real mahogany or walnut (or whatever wood you are trying to match). The grain will still look very different.

Also consider using a stain (again, after first stripping off the old finish) when the furniture is made with several different types or colors of wood. A dark- to medium-tone stain applied over the whole piece will often minimize the differences in shading and will thus help to give the piece a more uniform overall appearance.

In all cases where you are trying to match colors or change the colors of the wood, remember that a stain will "take" differently and look different on different types of wood. A walnut stain applied to a piece of pine won't come out the same as when that same stain is applied to walnut or some other wood. In fact, it may not look the same even when applied to another piece of pine—which is why testing or experimenting is always advisable before you go ahead with any staining project.

PRESEALING SOFT WOODS AND EDGES

Many hardwoods have a uniform density of grain that allows stain to soak in evenly over the entire surface—except where end grain is exposed (where the wood was cut across the grain—the ends of shelves, for example). End grain is very porous, so stain will soak into it quickly, penetrate deeply, and make it look much darker than the rest of the wood.

The same thing happens when staining some types of soft wood, like pine and fir, that have alternating layers of hard and soft grain and alternating areas of porosity. You wind up with a streaky, blotchy, "wild" grain effect, which is a lot less interesting than it sounds and definitely unattractive.

There is a cure. A thin coat of sealer is applied first—thin enough to seal the surface partially so that the stain doesn't soak in too deeply in porous areas. It's important *not* to seal the wood completely. You want to limit the stain's penetration, not prevent it entirely. If you're not sure whether a sealer is needed, test the stain first on a scrap piece of the same kind of wood or on the back or bottom of the piece.

The two products most often used to seal porous wood are thinned shellac and penetrating wood sealer.

Professionals generally prefer a "wash" coat of shellac. It dries very quickly, for one thing, and you can stain over it in about an hour. It's made by mixing 4 parts denatured alcohol with 1 part 4-pound-cut shellac. (See page 303 for more about various "pound cuts" of shellac.)

Brush the shellac wash on rapidly with a wide brush, making every effort not to overlap or cover any area more than once. Because shellac dries so quickly, if you overlap, or even brush back and forth too much, some spots may get two coats of shellac instead of one, which means some spots will be sealed more than others, and gone is that uniform staining job you've just taken this extra step to ensure. As a rule, a light rubdown with very fine steel wool, before the first coat of stain is applied, will help.

If all those precautions about overlapping have you feeling a bit nervous, here's another method that's much safer, although you'll have to wait a bit longer for it to dry. It's easier to control, and there's less likelihood of buildup.

Mix 1 part clear penetrating wood sealer with 2 parts thinner, and brush on over the surface. Wait a minute or so, then wipe down with a clean cloth to remove any excess still on the surface. Allow it to dry overnight before applying wood stain.

TYPES OF STAINS

The stains you're most likely to use fall into three broad categories: pigmented stains, sometimes called pigmented wiping stains; penetrating or dye-type stains; and powdered aniline stains designed to be mixed with water or alcohol.

Pigmented stains are made up of tiny particles of pigment suspended in either an oil or an emulsion-type latex base. The pigments never really dissolve, which means the stain has to be stirred frequently when you're using it, or the particles will settle to the bottom of the container and your stain will vary in both consistency and color. It's the easiest to use and the most forgiving of errors. If you think you've put too much on, you can usually wipe off as much as you want by rubbing promptly with a dry cloth or a rag saturated with paint thinner. Since pigmented stains don't penetrate as quickly as the dye types, there's little likelihood of streaking or lap marks, and if necessary, you can sand to take off some of the color even after the piece has dried.

There are drawbacks to stains that don't penetrate very deeply. They will fade more quickly if exposed to sunlight, for example, and they're not as transparent or clear as the penetrating dye-type stains. Therefore, color tends to be a bit "cloudier" when dry. The tiny particles of solid pigment will also partially conceal or "cloud" some of the grain, but this can be an advantage on poor-quality woods.

There's very little difference between oil-base pigmented stain (loosely referred to as an oil stain) and latex-base pigmented stain, except that the latter can be thinned with water (that means you can also clean your tools and hands with water).

Penetrating oil stains are more like true wood dyes. No pigments or other solid particles in suspension here. Colors are completely dissolved, which makes this type of stain much more transparent and brilliant in color than pigmented stains. No grain is hidden, and the dye penetrates deep into the wood, making it far more resistant to fading.

Most of the ready-mixed penetrating stains available from the local paint store have an oil base, and are labeled "penetrating" or "dye-type" so you can't mistake them for pigmented stains.

On really fine furniture made of good-quality wood, penetrating-type stains are always preferable to pigmented stains. They not only allow everything to show through, they're not as likely to mask a patina if used judiciously. However, they're not quite as foolproof as the pigmented stains. On the less expensive or softer woods, or pieces that have an uneven porosity because of surface damage of some sort, a preliminary sealer may be needed to avoid blotchiness. This type of stain will penetrate far more deeply in the softer parts of the grain than it will in the denser parts.

Powdered water stains are aniline-type wood dyes. You buy them in powder form and dissolve them in water or alcohol. Preferred by professionals because they dry very quickly and provide the clearest, purest color and deepest fiber penetration, they can be very tricky for the amateur. They're not widely available except from mail-order houses, and you have to do a lot of experimenting when you mix anything yourself. But there are more important objections:

1. They raise the grain of the wood, so you not only have to sponge with water and sand the wood before applying the stain, you also have to rub down with fine sandpaper after the stain has been applied.

2. They dry very quickly, so you have to be careful about lapping and streaking when putting them on with a brush (professionals prefer to spray them on);

amateurs find it difficult to achieve uniform results.

3. Most important, perhaps, water stains are not suitable for use on old wood that has been previously finished. Even if all the old finish has been carefully stripped off, water stains often will not penetrate properly and you'll wind up with a blotchy, uneven effect that's difficult to correct.

Powdered aniline-type stains that are designed for mixing with alcohol rather than water dry even faster. They have the advantage of not raising the grain the way a water stain will, but they are even harder to apply evenly, because they dry so quickly that it is almost impossible to brush them out smoothly—even on moderate-size surfaces. As a rule, amateur refinishers are better off staying away from them.

All the same, they can be important and are beautiful, so you may want to experiment. And there are certain finishes you may want to use that just won't work with any other stain—a French polish, for example (see page 304).

CHOOSING A COLOR

You can't simply wipe a stain entirely off the surface of wood and start from scratch if you don't like the color. You can come pretty close with pigmented stains, but some stain always soaks into the fibers, so it may take some sanding to get it all out. That's why it's important to go to the trouble of picking the right color to start with.

Manufacturers supply color cards and stores display samples, but you can't let them be your only guide. Unlike paint, which is opaque and looks the same on all surfaces, stain is very much affected by the color of the wood that shows through.

Stains also "take" differently on different pieces of wood—sometimes of the same kind.

Some manufacturers try to show you what several different stains look like on a variety of woods, but the variety is rarely broad enough, and the samples often don't look like real wood. The best way to be sure is to try the stain on the same type of wood as your piece or a very similar one. If you can't find any scrap pieces, try your stain on an inconspicuous part—back, bottom, or corner—where discoloration left over by the wrong stain won't be noticed.

Unfortunately there is no standardization of names to describe colors among different companies. One brand's black walnut may be very different from another's. In fact, the same colors by one manufacturer may vary from batch to batch.

The lesson to be learned here is that if you find a color you like, and you're planning to use it on a big piece or a whole suite of furniture, buy enough for the whole job. Then, before you begin, mix all the cans together. It's your only way to ensure a uniform color.

If you don't find a ready-mixed shade you like, don't be afraid to mix two or three colors together. In many cases, it's the only way to get a shade you want. Once you find it, don't forget to mix up a batch of it big enough to finish your project.

Don't forget, no wood, not even a freshly stained piece, looks the way it will with a clear finish on it, so if you've got scraps with stain tests on them, try the actual finishes over them. You'd be surprised what a finish with an amber or orange cast can do to a stain color. Even a supposedly perfectly clear finish makes a big difference.

STAINING TECHNIQUES

Except for some special preparation for water stains, methods of applying most stains are pretty much the same. They can be put on with a brush, rag, sponge, or one of the flat painting pads that are so popular today.

Generally, after a few minutes excess stain is wiped off with a rag. Most stains should be wiped for uniformity of color, but exactly how long you wait before wiping it off depends on the type of stain you're using, the porosity of the wood, and the depth of color you're after. A penetrating stain, for example, soaks into wood more rapidly than a pigmented product and should generally be wiped sooner.

There is no set rule that governs how long you should wait before wiping. Only experimentation and experience with similar stains and woods will tell you how

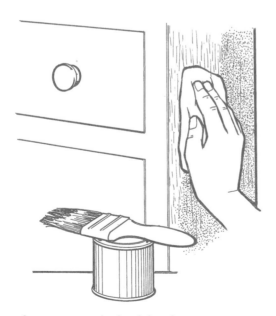

After stain is applied with brush, excess is wiped off with a rag to give a more uniform tone and in some cases to lighten the color.

long to wait. Just remember that it's easier to correct the effects of wiping off too soon—with another coat or a darker stain—than it is to sand, bleach, and otherwise strenuously lighten a piece on which the stain's been left too long.

Start by applying the stain to a small section of wood at a time, and begin wiping with a dry rag as soon as the wood looks dark enough. If you find yourself removing too much of the stain, wait a little longer. If this doesn't help, you may have to switch to a darker stain. Or you can darken your original stain by adding tinted pigments available in most paint stores.

When you're dealing with matching problems, like lighter and darker woods next to each other on the same piece, you can control the final effect to some extent by wiping the dark piece sooner or more vigorously than the other. Or you can first stain the lighter piece with a stain that will bring it closer to the darker wood in tone. After the stain dries, apply another coat over both pieces. This minimizes any differences in color that remain.

To prepare wood for aniline or water-stain dyes, follow the suggestions on page 292 for getting a soft wood smooth, with no fuzzy wood fibers sticking up. Only this time dampen the wood—all of it—with a sponge moistened in warm water. After the piece has dried, sand as you would for a final sanding. This will probably eliminate any grain raising after staining. If not, sand again. Since staining does not tend to be uniform with this type of dye, sanding may help you control color. You can always stain again for a darker color, but keeping an entirely even tone won't be easy.

Aniline stains can be dissolved in alcohol, too, as mentioned, and they don't raise the grain. But they dry so quickly that splotching becomes an even greater hazard. Investigate these only if you intend to spray.

USING A PIGMENTED PENETRATING SEALER AS A WOOD STAIN

Penetrating wood sealers come in clear as well as in wood tones, so it's possible to use them as stains as well as finishes. In fact, if you're going to use this kind of finish and your piece needs added color, this is the best way to stain it.

A penetrating sealer is not a surface finish; it is rubbed *into* the wood to penetrate its fibers and has little or no shine. The effect is more of an "oiled" look and bears a resemblance to the old beloved "rubbed" linseed-oil finish, which generally takes half a year to build up and an eternity to maintain.

The important thing here is that you can use this staining and finishing technique to take advantage of open-grained, beautifully textured wood, yet these penetrating sealers can look lovely on close-grained woods, too.

Clear sealers can also be used as a medium if you want to mix your own stain. Thin the sealer with about 25 percent paint thinner, then add tinting colors to get what you want.

Tinting colors are available at most paint stores and are called by such names as raw umber, burnt umber, sienna (also raw and burnt), Venetian red, ocher, black—in short, the basic colors that can be mixed to get a wood tone. You have to experiment a bit to get what you think is a rich oak or walnut or teak, but here are a few rule-of-thumb suggestions to get you going. Burnt umber and a touch of

Venetian red are mixed to get a mahogany tone. (*Caution:* A little red goes a long way.) You can use burnt umber with a little raw umber for walnut. Raw umber with a small amount of burnt sienna will give you oak. Here, testing on scrap wood is really a must, and bear in mind that your colors will often look considerably different dry than wet.

Whether you buy them ready-made or mix your own, the agents used to color the sealer are pigments, not dyes, and in most cases results will be very similar to what you get with pigmented oil- or latex-base wiping stains. Colors are not quite as clear or rich as they are with a true penetrating-type dye. However, grain shows through very well, and texture is marvelously emphasized; sealer finishes compare well in beauty with most other stains and finishes.

WHEN AND HOW TO USE PASTE WOOD FILLER

Although open-grained woods such as oak, teak, walnut, and mahogany are often finished with a penetrating sealer that does not fill in the pores of the wood, there are times when you will want to give wood pieces of this kind a smooth, built-up "piano-type" glossy finish. But to do this you will have to fill in the open pores first by using a paste wood filler. Otherwise it makes no difference how much sanding you do—you will never get a really smooth finish on the open-grained wood. This also holds true when you are refinishing older pieces that were originally treated with wood filler—if you used a chemical remover to strip off all of the old finish, you probably took off a good deal of the filler at the same time. So plan on reapplying filler when you start refinishing.

If your piece is to be stained, do it *before* applying the wood filler. Then the wood filler must be tinted to a tone slightly darker than your piece before you start working with it. The reason for this is that paste wood fillers come in a "natural" or "neutral" shade about the color of cashew butter—a bit lighter than peanut butter. If applied as is to raw wood, any subsequent stain will soak much more into the wood than it will into the filler, leaving lots of light spots and streaks just where you might want them a little bit darker.

One of the advantages of wood filler, aside from its smoothing qualities, is that, if colored, it allows you to darken the pores, giving the wood a more distinctive grain.

Several manufacturers make paste fillers in wood tones, but most stores stock them only in "neutral," so to get what you want you'll have to add tinting colors. Again, you'll have to experiment a bit, to get the shade or color you want.

To simplify mixing, dilute the tinting color with a little solvent first, then mix this in with the paste wood filler. This will, of course, thin the filler a little, but since you have to thin it anyway, no harm is done.

Another way to tint filler to the shade you want is to mix it with some of the actual stain you'll be using—but only if you're using an oil-base stain. Use the thickened sediment that settles to the bottom of the stain can after you've poured off some of the liquid on top.

When applying a tinted wood filler, you'll actually be staining the wood as well as filling the pores, since the wood will absorb the color contained in the solvent. It won't make much noticeable difference on an already stained piece, but it offers you another staining alternative for open-grained woods—you can tint your wood and fill its pores in one step.

Whether you're filling pores, staining, or both, before using any paste wood filler you have to thin it with turpentine or a similar solvent in order to reduce it to brushing consistency. The manufacturer's directions will usually suggest the amount of thinning required, but as a rule the filler should be about the consistency of a heavy-bodied interior flat wall paint.

Spread the filler on liberally with a brush, covering only a few square feet at a time. Brush across the grain to work it into the pores. Allow it to set for a few minutes until the filler starts to lose its wet look and begins to get slightly dull-looking, then take a folded pad of coarse cloth (burlap is excellent) to wipe off the excess. Rub vigorously with a circular motion and turn the cloth frequently as it becomes saturated.

For best results, switch to a second piece of clean cloth and rub hard *across* the grain to remove all excess from the surface before it dries. Finally, finish by wiping almost parallel to the grain, but this time don't rub hard. You don't want to

Paste wood filler is brushed on liberally, then wiped off with a coarse rag before it dries by rubbing hard across the grain.

wipe the filler out of the pores of the wood, just smooth it all down.

Actually, the wiping-off process is the most critical part of the whole operation, and it may take some experimenting before you learn how to do it correctly. If you start wiping too soon, you will rub most of the filler out of the pores, but if you wait too long, the filler will start to harden and become sticky and will be extremely difficult to remove. You may even have to sand it off.

After the entire surface has been filled and wiped, let it dry for at least 24 hours. Then sand lightly with very fine-grit paper. On flat surfaces, use a sanding block that has been faced with felt or sponge rubber.

On curved surfaces, use fine steel wool instead of sandpaper. Dust thoroughly with a tack rag before going any farther.

A SHORTCUT: FINISHING WITH VARNISH STAIN

Since varnish stains apply color and finish in one application, they are not something you'd use on your finest pieces, or where you want a good wood to show through, or on a piece that's going to take a lot of scrutiny. However, if you feel it isn't worth stripping and refinishing the inside of an old cabinet or the inside of a drawer or the bottoms of shelves that are not normally seen, but you want a decent, durable, cleanable surface there all the same, varnish stain may be the answer.

The very name *varnish stain* suggests that it allows you to stain the wood as you varnish. However, you're dealing with pigments, not wood dyes, and the effect is more like a thinned-down paint or translucent color wash.

Since varnish stain colors and finishes in one step, and can be applied over an old coat of shellac, varnish, or similar finish without stripping, it can be a time and work saver on those jobs where appearance is secondary or where you want to give some inexpensive furniture or cabinets a quick "once-over" without doing a lot of stripping and refinishing. You still have to do a thorough job of cleaning off all wax and polish first, and you must sand down the old finish to remove all gloss before the new coating is applied. Bear in mind that you really cannot apply a light-colored varnish stain over a dark finish—you have to go to a darker shade than the one that is on there now.

CHOOSING AND APPLYING CLEAR OR TRANSPARENT FINISHES

All furniture finishes can be roughly classified in one of two broad categories: surface coatings such as varnish, shellac, or lacquer that remain mostly on top of the wood, and penetrating-type finishes that soak into the pores of the wood so that they actually build up little or no surface coating (the so-called Danish oil finishes are typical of this type).

VARNISHES

Originally made of natural oils and resins, most varnishes today are based on man-made or synthetic resins and have either an alkyd, a phenolic, a vinyl, or a polyurethane base.

Alkyd-based varnish is the least expensive, but not the toughest. Varnishes with a phenolic base work better outdoors than indoors. In most cases they don't really dry hard enough for indoor use. (Most spar varnishes belong to this category of finish.)

Vinyl-based varnishes are the clearest in color. They dry more quickly and darken the wood less than any other varnish. They aren't as tough as most of the other types, but if clarity, trueness of color, and quick-drying capability are top priorities, this is a good choice.

Polyurethane, the newest type of varnish, is the most durable and expensive of all ready-mixed varnishes. It offers maximum protection on surfaces that take a lot of punishment, such as tabletops, serving bars, and other places where food and liquid spills are common, and can be very useful on floors and other surfaces.

The thing to remember about polyurethane is that it dries to an exceptionally hard finish. That means if you are varnishing over an old piece that already has a polyurethane finish, a thorough sanding is required between coats to ensure proper adhesion. If you miss any spots with this sanding, chances are in those areas the bond will be poor, and peeling or cracking is likely. If you're varnishing on raw or stained wood—with no finish—the rules are different. With some polyurethane and vinyl formulations, you will note that a second coat must be applied *within* a certain number of hours—usually a lot less time than other varnishes. If you follow those directions, you will eliminate the need for any sanding between coats. But if you wait too long, you will have to sand thoroughly, as above.

Other factors to consider when choosing a varnish are color—actually, lack of color, or clarity—and the amount of gloss.

As mentioned earlier, vinyls are the "clearest," and although all varnishes are labeled "clear," most of them do have a slight amber tone. On a dark wood it's not likely to make much of a difference and may even enhance some woods by "aging" and enriching them just a bit. But if it's a light finish you want, or if you're trying to retain the original color of the wood, then the degree of amber may become important. Then it's best to test on scraps of the wood you'll be using.

Many varnishes come in either a high-gloss, a semigloss, or a completely flat finish. Not every finish is available in all three choices, but you can probably find what you want among the various types available.

If you want a piece to have a built-up, highly polished, piano-type finish, use a high-gloss finish. But if you want the duller "rubbed" finish, you can choose the rich luster of one of the various semigloss or satin-finish varnishes.

Years ago, when all varnishes were glossy, the only way to achieve a low-luster finish was to apply many coats of varnish, then rub down the glossy finish with powdered pumice and rottenstone. Nowadays you can get much the same effect—with little or no rubbing—by using one of the low-luster varnishes. Most manufacturers differ in describing the amount of gloss their varnish provides; one company's semigloss may be duller or shinier than another company's satin gloss. Ask to see samples and experiment on scraps.

Regardless of the type of varnish you select, or whether you're going shiny or dull, if you want to achieve professional-looking results, you must make sure the surface of your piece is dust free. In addition to wiping the wood down carefully with a tack rag (see pages 276 and 291), try to work in a room that is as free of dust as possible. If you use a vacuum cleaner in that room, wait at least a few hours before varnishing in order to allow the airborne dust (blown around by the vacuum's exhaust) to settle.

As a rule, varnishes are ready for use in the can without need for additional thinning. However, it's generally advisable to slightly thin the first coat on raw wood so that it soaks in more and does a better job of sealing the surface. Consult the instructions on the label for the amount of thinning recommended, or experiment with a small amount of the varnish beforehand. Periodic thinning as you work may be required to maintain a consistency that works easily and flows out smoothly.

Never shake a can of varnish before opening it. It may cause air bubbles in the liquid that will be difficult to brush out later on. For the same reason, stir gently when adding thinner to varnish.

It's best not to work out of the full can. Pour what you expect to use in a single session into a separate container and work from this.

Dip the brush into the varnish by no more than one-third its bristle length, and remove excess by tapping the bristle tips lightly against the inside rim of the can above the level of the liquid. *Never* wipe the brush across the rim. That kind of action is another cause of tiny air bubbles that run back into the can.

Whenever possible, try to work on surfaces that are horizontal. If the piece is small enough, turn it on its side or back and remove as much hardware as you can.

On most pieces it's best to coat all hard-to-reach places and the least conspicuous areas first. For example, do the backs and legs of a chair, as well as the rungs, before

To remove excess varnish from brush after dipping it, tap lightly against the inside of the can above the level of the varnish. Never wipe bristles across rim.

you do the seat and arms. In the case of a cabinet or chest, do the insides of doors before you do the outsides. The idea is to work toward yourself so that you are not reaching over or dripping on previously coated areas in order to varnish an unfinished area.

Varnish is applied by "flowing" it on, rather than by "scrubbing" it on. Brush with light, rapid strokes *parallel* to the grain. Then immediately cross-stroke lightly, with just the bristle tips, using long strokes *across* the grain. Follow this by cross-stroking again, *parallel* to the grain. (Cross-stroking simply means brushing at right angles to the direction from which you just stroked.) For this the bristles should be almost dry, and the tips should be dragged along the entire length of the panel in one single stroke.

If it is impossible to go from one end of a panel to the other with a single stroke, touch the tips of the bristles to the surface at one end and then drag them about halfway across before curving gently up and away from the surface in an arc. The next stroke is then started at the opposite end of the panel and brought forward until it overlaps the end of the stroke just completed—again in an arc up and away from the surface with a gradual motion. The idea is never to touch the bristles to the surface in the middle of a panel when you're smoothing off, since this will leave a mark or blemish that will be clearly noticeable.

When varnishing recessed panels or doors that have carvings or moldings around the edges, always coat the molded or carved edges first, then complete the flat area in the center. Avoid dragging the brush across the edges of a piece or a door, as this will cause runs and dripping.

Although most varnishes specify the minimum drying time required between coats, it's usually best to wait a little longer. The only exceptions are some polyurethane and vinyl formulations. On some of these the manufacturer specifies that the second coat must go on within a predetermined number of hours in order to eliminate sanding between coats. If you wait longer, you'll have to sand.

Except for these special cases, you should sand lightly between coats with 220 or 320 paper. Always sand parallel to the grain, and never sand if the varnish feels the least bit gummy or soft. Use a sanding block to avoid rounding off edges and corners, and sand no more than necessary to dull the gloss and remove any dust specks, air bubbles, or other irregularities in the surface.

Dust is a perennial problem when varnishing, so no matter how careful you are, it is possible that your final coat will show a few dust specks on the surface. If you notice these while the varnish is still wet, the specks can be lifted off by using a finely tapered splinter of wood or a round wooden toothpick with a pointed end. If you do this carefully and promptly, the wet varnish will flow together to fill in the tiny hollow that remains when the speck is removed.

When it is not possible to go from one end of a panel to the other with a single brush stroke, work from each end toward the middle, allowing strokes to overlap slightly. Always curve the brush away from the surface with a gentle arc, rather than lifting it straight up from the surface.

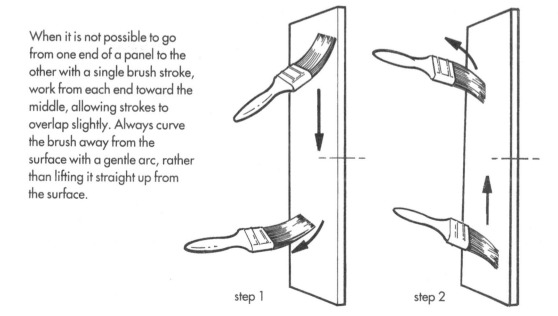

step 1   step 2

Despite precaution, a final surface may sometimes feel slightly gritty because of dust that settles on the surface as it dries. If desired, you can remove these blemishes by rubbing and polishing the final coat with powdered pumice after the varnish has hardened for several days. This will give a truly professional-looking rubbed finish that will be satiny smooth and as glossy or as dull as you like.

Though it's basically smoothness you're rubbing for, not luster, you can control the gloss by the amount of rubbing and polishing you do and by the grade of abrasive that you use for the final rubbing.

Start by mixing a creamy paste of powdered pumice (sold in all paint stores) and a lightweight oil such as lemon oil or mineral oil. Fold a piece of felt into a convenient-size pad, then pick up some of the pumice paste with this and spread it on over the surface. Press down with a moderate amount of pressure and start rubbing with long strokes parallel to the grain where possible. Overlap your strokes by at least half the width of the pad as you work your arm back and forth, but be careful to avoid bearing down hard along the edges or on corners of the piece to keep from cutting through the varnish.

Pick up the felt pad periodically to add more pumice paste as needed. If the paste shows signs of drying out, sprinkle a little more oil over the surface when necessary to maintain the original creamy consistency. After rubbing for several minutes in one place, examine the surface carefully by shining a light at an angle across a section that has been wiped clean with a separate piece of cloth. As an additional test, feel the surface, stroking lightly with your fingertips. You will know that you have rubbed long enough when the entire surface feels and looks perfectly smooth and when it has a uniformly dull satin luster after the pumice paste has been wiped off.

At this point some people may prefer to leave their dull luster as is. However, in most cases additional rubbing with a still finer abrasive—powdered rottenstone—is usually recommended.

Done properly, a final polishing with rottenstone will restore the gloss that the varnish had originally—either low luster or high shine, and in the latter case without that freshly wet look many people find objectionable.

Mix your rottenstone with oil, the same way you did with the powdered pumice. Now use another clean felt pad to pick up some rottenstone mixture and start rubbing, again with the grain, just the way you did with the pumice. Remember to periodically wipe a section clean and shine a light across it to determine when you have restored the amount of gloss you want.

If you want still more glow or gloss, finish by using a good-quality paste wax. However, if you decide to use wax, allow the varnish to harden for an extra three or four days before rubbing on the first coat of wax. Apply it sparingly and buff vigorously. Remember that a thin, hard coat of wax is more durable and actually provides better protection than a built-up heavy layer.

SHELLAC

Shellac is one of the oldest clear finishes around and still coats some of the finest antiques, since it predates the invention of what we now call varnish. Actually shellac is a spirit varnish made of a natural resin that comes from the lac bug, an insect native to India. The original flaky material is dissolved in denatured alcohol to form a sort of deep orange or amber-brown material commonly known as "orange shellac." "White" or clear shellac is made by bleaching the material before dissolving it in alcohol.

Orange shellac can give darker woods a beautiful finish. It's sometimes used on mahogany and walnut to give an aged look or to highlight the natural coloring. It's sometimes used even on lighter woods, like knotty pine, to give an "Early American" look. You can also mix orange and white together to mellow or "age" some of the whiter woods.

Shellac is fast-drying and easy to work with, and it dries to a beautiful clear finish when used properly. But it is seldom used as final finish on furniture these days because it does have a number of disadvantages.

For one thing, shellac discolors quickly when any liquid is spilled on it—and it's completely dissolved by liquids that contain alcohol. It turns white when subjected to dampness, so unless it's heavily protected with paste wax, it's not a very practical finish on most pieces of furniture.

However, it is still excellent for use on decorative pieces that get very little wear—picture frames, for example—and its quick-drying characteristics can be valuable when something has to be finished in a hurry.

Unlike varnish, unused shellac deteriorates in time, just from aging in the can, so you can't keep quantities of it on hand for more than a few months. Most manufacturers recommend that shellac be stored no longer than about six months.

Some manufacturers date their cans, but others don't, so you are better off buying shellac in small cans only as you need it. If the can is not dated, and you have any reason to doubt its freshness, open the can and look at it. If it's very dark or gummy-looking, don't use it. As a further test, smear a little onto a piece of wood and let it dry. It should get tacky in 5 or 10 minutes and be completely dry in about 30 minutes.

Shellac almost always has to be thinned with denatured alcohol before you can use it on furniture. It is sold in various consistencies, known as "cuts." The most widely sold is 4-pound-cut, although some stores stock 3-pound-cut and 5-pound-cut shellac. The cut refers to the amount of shellac that has been dissolved in a gallon of alcohol. For example, 4-pound-cut means that 4 pounds of flake shellac have been dissolved in 1 gallon of alcohol. To reduce 4-pound-cut shellac to 2-pound-cut, for example, you would simply add 3 quarts of alcohol to a gallon of the 4-pound-cut shellac.

When shellac is used primarily as a sealer under varnish—for example, to keep a stain from "bleeding" through the finish—the shellac should be no heavier than about 1-pound-cut or 2-pound-cut. However, for building up a regular shellac finish, 3-pound-cut is usually preferred, although some experts would rather use 2-pound-cut and apply additional coats. Building up a finish with several thin coats, rather than one or two heavy ones, is how you get the deep clear luster characteristic of a fine shellac finish.

When building up a shellac finish, sanding lightly between coats and then removing all of the sanding dust with a tack rag is essential for a fine finish. Use progressively finer grits of sandpaper. Start with 120 after the first coat; 220 after the second coat; and 320 or 400 after the third coat. The final coat can be left as is and waxed, or it can be rubbed down with pumice and rottenstone just as you would a varnish finish (see section on varnishes).

Brushes and other tools that have been used in shellac are best cleaned in denatured alcohol, because this is the thinner for shellac (never turpentine or other paint thinners). Or you can save money by washing a shellac brush with ammonia and water, if the shellac is reasonably fresh.

FRENCH POLISH FINISH

In the days when shellac was *the* finish for fine furniture, one of the most beautiful—and durable—finishes was achieved by a method known as French polishing. It takes lots of hand rubbing—hours, and sometimes days, of work—but it's also highly practical, since it can withstand years of wear and exposure and can be easily touched up or renewed when necessary.

Of course, craftsmen in bygone days did not have today's varnishes and sealers, which can give somewhat the same effect without all those hours of work, but some purists still feel that no modern finish can match the luster and beauty of a patiently applied French polish finish. Because of the amount of work involved, few craftsmen today still use this method, but for something really special, here's how:

1. If the wood has to be stained first, don't use a pigmented or oil-based stain. You must use only a powdered aniline-type dye stain that is mixed with water, the only stain over which a French polish will "take." New, unstained wood is good, too.

2. Pour some 1-pound-cut shellac into a shallow bowl or pan, and fold a clean piece of lint-free cloth into a thick pad. Grasp this with your fingers, then dip the pad into the shellac and start wiping it onto the wood with light rapid strokes, working parallel to the grain if possible.

3. Keep dipping and wiping in this manner until the entire surface is covered, then wait for the first coat to dry hard (usually 15 to 30 minutes).

4. Apply a second coat in the same manner and again wait for this to dry, then sand lightly with very fine sandpaper (400).

5. Remove all sanding dust, then keep on applying additional coats, rubbing each one on quickly and adding coats until you have built up enough of a finish to see a slight sheen over the entire surface.

6. At this point add a few drops of boiled linseed oil to the shellac in the pan and then continue applying more coats by dipping the pad into the oil-and-shellac mixture and rubbing it on. This time, however, use a series of rotary or circular motions instead of rubbing lengthwise.

7. Keep dipping and rubbing, adding a little more linseed oil to the mixture from time to time, until you have built up the depth of finish and the luster or gloss desired. You'll know it when you see it.

As rubbing progresses, you may find that you will have to rub harder and more vigorously to keep the pad from sticking to the surface. When this happens, add a little more shellac and alcohol to the mixture to keep it from piling up under the pad.

You can quit at any time and resume on the following day if you get tired, but when you do this, it's best to sand lightly before you get started again.

A little experimentation on scrap surfaces will give you an idea of how much oil, shellac, and alcohol you can use, although proportions really are not critical.

LACQUER

Lacquer has two advantages as a finish: it's very clear, and it's the quickest-drying of them all, which makes it popular with commercial finishers. But most home craftsmen will find it the most difficult of all finishes to work with. Lacquers dry so fast that they're almost impossible to brush out, which is why the pros almost always spray them on.

Although spraying is much faster than brushing, few home craftsmen have the right type of spraying equipment for use with fast-setting lacquers. In addition, a considerable amount of experience is required to handle this coating properly. Lacquer must be sprayed on in many coats because it forms a thinner film than varnish or shellac, and because of the solvents used lacquer cannot be applied over varnish, paint, oil stain, and many other finishes.

There are a few lacquers on the market that have been mixed with special slow-drying solvents so that they can be applied by brush. However, these are generally hard to find and offer only the advantages of drying more quickly than other finishes. They still do not give as fine a finish as you can achieve with many of today's quality varnishes.

PENETRATING SEALERS

These are the easiest to use and among the toughest-wearing. They give a beautiful finish, especially if you want a casual, informal look—or prefer a "natural" finish.

Penetrating wood sealers, which are often referred to as "Danish oil" finishes, are made of synthetic resin oils and are designed to give the type of "oiled" finish that once could be achieved only by repeated rubbing with linseed oil.

Unlike linseed oil, an organic material, modern penetrating sealers do not oxidize or turn dark in time. Nor are they subject to fungus or mildew growth, also a problem with linseed oil. Best of all, they are far easier to maintain and a snap to repair—when necessary.

This type of finish is meant to take advantage of a wood's texture—no perfectly smooth or high luster, no built-up finish; when you touch a piece of furniture finished this way, you know you're feeling wood.

Penetrating finishes are often used on contemporary pieces made of open-grained hardwoods—oak, walnut, teak. What's more, with these woods you're also eliminating a step for the glossier finish—applying paste wood filler. This type of finish is also perfect for today's "country" furniture, pieces beloved for their informal, almost no-finish look.

Unlike varnish and other surface coatings, penetrating sealers can be applied only over raw wood or wood that already has the same type of finish on it. It soaks into and bonds with the fibers of the wood to actually harden them so the finish is *inside* the wood and leaves no appreciable surface coating or film. Because of this, and because you wipe off the excess as each coat is applied, there is never a problem with brush marks, and you virtually eliminate the problem of dust settling on the surface to mar the finished appearance.

Because there is no surface film, the finish left by a penetrating sealer has very little gloss. It can be buffed (with very fine steel wool) to a pleasant satin luster, and additional gloss can be obtained by waxing and buffing.

One advantage in not having a glossy coating is that there is no surface finish that can get scratched. The finish is inside the wood. (You can scratch the wood itself, of course.) Most spilled liquids will not harm the finish if wiped up with reasonable promptness, but even if they do, touching up is quite simple. All you have to do is rub additional sealer on with fine steel wool and then buff off the excess.

Penetrating resin sealers come in clear as well as in various wood-tone shades. The colored sealers serve as stains that help to seal the wood in one application, although you can apply a clear sealer over them. Or you can use a regular wood stain first and then put two or three coats of sealer over it.

Generally speaking, penetrating sealers tend to darken wood more than varnish or shellac, but they will not obscure the grain or change the texture, so in most cases people do not find the added depth of color objectionable.

You can apply these finishes by brush or by wiping on with a rag. Application technique is relatively unimportant, since there is no need to worry about brush marks or lap marks. All you have to do is make sure you apply sealer liberally and work it into the fibers of the wood. The idea is to make certain it penetrates as much as possible—which is why having surfaces horizontal makes the job much easier when this is practical.

Allow the first coat to penetrate for anywhere from 15 to 30 minutes, depending on the manufacturer's recommendations, then use a lint-free cloth to wipe all excess liquid off the surface. Wipe with long parallel strokes, using a moderate amount of pressure, and make sure all excess oil has been removed from the surface before you go any farther.

After wiping the surface dry, allow the finish to harden for the recommended number of hours (usually from 4 to 24 hours, depending on the brand), then flow on a second coat and wipe off in the same manner.

Sanding between coats is generally not required, although some experts find that the finish will be smoother and more lustrous if you rub lightly with fine steel wool before the second coat of sealer is applied. This rubbing also helps to open the pores a bit more and thus enhances the penetrating qualities of the second coat.

As a rule, two coats are all that will be required. Tabletops, dresser tops, and other surfaces that can be expected to receive hard wear and more than average abuse should get a third coat.

After the last coat has dried hard, you can rub on a thin coat of paste wax for added protection. Buff vigorously with a soft cloth to achieve the luster desired.

Waxing is not essential, unless you want some luster and added protection. Just make sure you rub the wax on sparingly and buff vigorously after 10 to 15 minutes.

COLORED ENAMEL FINISHES

Although most people still think that all enamels dry to a high gloss, they actually come in a choice of finishes—high gloss, semigloss, and satin. However, since there is no standardization of these definitions from one manufacturer to another, the only way you can be sure of the exact gloss is to see a dried sample of the actual paint or test it yourself.

Bear in mind that the higher the gloss, the more noticeable will be any irregularities or defects in the smoothness of the surface, so if you intend to use a glossy finish, take extra care with the sanding, patching, and filling before any paint is applied.

Gloss also shows dents, nicks, and scrapes more than the duller finishes, so you might want to consider this factor if you're choosing enamel for a child's room.

If you can't find a ready-mixed enamel in the exact color you want, you can start with a color that is close and then doctor this up with tinting colors that you can add yourself. However, most well-stocked dealers have paint-mixing systems with hundreds of different-colored chips, which they can match exactly by using factory-measured formulas. You can almost always find the color you want via one of these systems. Once you select a color, the dealer can mix it in a matter of minutes, then duplicate it at any time in the future *as long as you have a record of the color number.*

Like any other finish, enamel can be no smoother than the surface over which it is applied, so don't stint on the sanding and smoothing. If you are painting over an old finish, be sure you "feather out" rough edges where the old finish may have chipped off by sanding till smooth. Remove any of the old finish that shows signs of chipping or not adhering firmly, and when you are finished sanding be sure to remove all dust by wiping carefully with a tack rag.

As a rule, to achieve an even gloss and color at least two coats of enamel will be required. However, if you are applying the enamel over raw wood, or over a badly worn finish, an enamel undercoat will also be needed for the first coat. The two coats of enamel go on after this.

Enamel is supposedly ready for use when the can is opened, but as a practical matter some slight thinning will almost always be required as you work in order to maintain a good working consistency. If you are apply-

ing two coats, thin the first coat slightly (5 to 10 percent) and don't try to make it cover completely. The second coat will cover up any "thin" areas that remain.

Brushing techniques for enamel are similar to those used in brushing varnish (see pages 300–301). Use a good-quality brush with lots of soft bristles. Brush marks and such are more noticeable in color than they are in a clear finish, so a good brush and patience are essential.

Like varnish, the enamel is flowed on with long strokes and with only a moderate amount of pressure. Never dip the bristles in by more than one-third their length, and whenever possible lay surfaces horizontal to help the finish flow out smoothly.

As a rule, it is best to paint across the narrower dimension of each panel first, then cross-stroke lightly with just the bris-

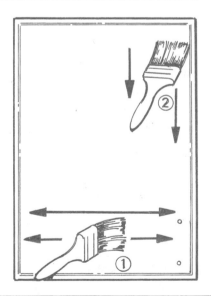

It's best to apply enamel across the narrow dimension of each panel first, then cross-stroke lightly by brushing lengthwise to smooth out brush strokes.

tle tips to eliminate brush marks and to smooth out uneven areas. As you work, keep checking for runs, sags, or drips, especially in the corners, and pick these up promptly with the tip of your brush to keep them from growing. However, once the paint starts to get tacky—thick and sticky—you won't be able to smooth out these irregularities, so just let them dry and then sand them out on the following day before the next coat of enamel is applied.

Sanding is not always necessary between coats of a semigloss or low-luster enamel, but it is essential when putting one coat of high gloss on top of another. Regardless of what the manufacturer's instructions say about drying time, always make sure each coat is completely hard before you sand it or start applying the next coat. If in doubt, test with a fingernail—the paint should be hard enough to resist easy indentation.

Then test sand one spot; the paint should not gum up or rub off. If it does, the paint is not hard enough for sanding or recoating.

It is possible, by the way, to get the same fine, built-up look with enamel as it is with varnish. Follow the directions for building up and sanding three to four coats of varnish and rubbing down with pumice and rottenstone (pages 300–302), and use either low-luster or high-gloss paint. Obviously this is a fine finish, meant for a good piece.

COLORED LACQUERS

Colored lacquers dry much faster than enamels, which is why they are almost always applied by spraying. Professionals who have the proper type of spray equipment and are familiar with the techniques involved in working with these fast-drying finishes prefer them for that reason: they can apply several coats in a single day. However, you have to have a fair amount of experience to get a really smooth finish.

Aside from its quicker-drying capabilities, lacquer offers no advantage over enamel. Contrary to what many amateurs seem to think, you can get just as high a gloss with an enamel, and the finish is usually more resistant to chipping and abrasion, because enamels tend to be more resilient and less brittle.

Lacquers also contain powerful solvents, which present more of an odor problem when working indoors. More important, perhaps, they generally cannot be applied over old enamel and other finishes, because the solvent in the lacquer will lift or soften the old finish.

Lacquers designed for brushing are available, but they are generally hard to find, and the color selection may be very limited. In addition, even though these lacquers have special solvents added to slow the drying, they are still harder than an enamel to brush out smoothly. And they still have all the disadvantages of spray-type lacquers.

ANTIQUE OR GLAZED FINISHES

This is one of the easiest of all finishes for the amateur to apply. It requires little skill, no stripping, and only enough sanding to make your surface smooth. Furthermore, you don't have to patch dents, gouges, and bruises unless you really want to. This finish actually looks good with a few marks.

And for all this, it's an attractive, sometimes even beautiful, finish. It's the perfect way to rejuvenate "junk" furniture that still has some wear in it and to give character and color to uninteresting pieces. It's also a way of rejuvenating a great old piece—even some fine furniture—with badly marred wood.

Although the terms *glazing* and *antiquing* are often used interchangeably, glazing is actually the process used to achieve an antique effect. It consists of a translucent or semiopaque colored liquid that is applied over a previously painted surface and then partially wiped off. The end result is a two-tone effect in which the top color (the glazing color) partially covers and changes the effect of the base color.

The glazing process can actually be used to create several other finishes when a two-tone, color-on-color effect is desired—such as an imitation wood-grain effect or a "limed" or "pickled" finish. In the last two cases a light-colored glaze is applied over a darker-colored base coat. Glazing, however, is most often associated with the application of an antique finish.

Applying an antique finish is basically a three-step process:

1. Paint the surface of your piece with the background color of your choice, and allow this to dry hard. The type of paint most frequently used for this background color—and the one that is easiest to glaze over—is a semigloss or satin-finish enamel.

2. After the base has dried hard, a colored glazing liquid, which you can buy ready-made or can mix yourself, is brushed on over the surface and then partially wiped off.

3. Although not essential on pieces that will get no handling, the finish is then protected with a clear coat of semigloss or low-luster varnish. This final coat of clear varnish is often omitted in the prepackaged kits, but it should be applied over any piece of furniture that gets normal han-

dling. Otherwise the glaze coat will start to rub off prematurely.

The base coat of enamel can be applied by brush, painting pad, or spray. A perfect job is not necessary, but a reasonable amount of care should be exercised to avoid skips, sags, runs, and drip marks. You should sand the old surface a bit to get it reasonably smooth, and remove all wax, grease, and dirt by scrubbing with a detergent or by wiping down with a paint thinner. One coat will generally be adequate for this base coat, but if a radically different color is being applied—very light over very dark, for example—you may require a second coat in order to ensure reasonably complete coverage.

Allow the base coat to dry until thoroughly hard (usually 24 hours). Even if the label says it dries in 4 hours, wait longer, because the process of rubbing on the glaze will soften paint that is not completely cured.

You can buy glazing liquid in ready-mixed colors in many paint stores, so if you can find the color you want, that is probably the simplest method. However, it is not difficult to mix your own glaze.

To mix your own you can either buy an untinted glazing liquid, which some paint stores carry, or you can use a clear penetrating wood sealer as a glazing liquid base. In either case you add color by mixing in regular tinting colors or by adding small amounts of dark-colored enamel in various shades.

Since it is hard to tell beforehand what effect the glazing color will have when it is rubbed on over the background color, some experimentation is essential. One trick that will save time is to paint the base coat onto several pieces of scrap wood while you are painting the actual piece of furniture. These scrap pieces will dry at the same time, so when you're ready to mix your glaze coat you can experiment on these scrap pieces first. This will not only help you decide on the color of the glaze coat, it will also help determine how much you want to wipe off and how hard you want to rub when wiping.

Since the glaze dries slowly, there is plenty of time to fool around with various wiping techniques. In fact, if you don't like the results, you can always wipe the glaze off completely with paint thinner and start all over again.

After the base coat of semigloss enamel has dried hard, start brushing on the glaze coat over one section of the furniture at a time. Smear it on liberally, using a brush or cloth, and don't miss any spots.

If you have coated some scrap pieces with the base color, as mentioned above, try your glaze on one of these first. Depending on the type of glazing material used, and on the amount of color it contains, you may want to start wiping immediately, or you may find it better to wait a few minutes.

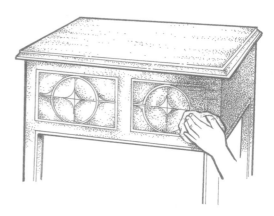

Glaze is partially wiped off with pad of cloth. Different effects can be achieved by wiping with steel wool, cheesecloth, or crumpled ball of tissue paper.

Wiping is most often done with a pad of cheesecloth or a piece of very soft, loose-weave cotton cloth. Experiment with the effects achieved by using the cloth while it's folded as against using it while wadded into a loose ball. Other effects can be achieved by wiping with steel wool, with crumpled tissue paper, or with a coarse cloth such as burlap. For antique finishes, cheesecloth is by far the most popular method.

The final result is controlled by how much you wipe off and how hard you rub. The more you wipe off, the more the base coat will show through, so if your background color is white or off-white, more wiping will result in a lighter overall tone and less wiping will result in a darker tone. By the same token, if your background color is a dark color and your glaze is a light shade, the reverse will be true. Bear in mind that the background color should generally be sharper or brighter than you think you want it to be, because the glaze color will ultimately dull or subdue it to some extent.

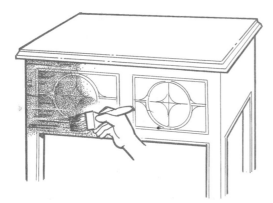

After base color (ground coat) has dried, brush on the colored glaze over one section at a time.

The final effect will vary with how you wipe off the glaze. It's probably the most important step in the whole process. The glaze should not be wiped off uniformly. Instead, allow more of the glaze coat to remain in the grooves and in the recesses, while rubbing more of it off on the high spots. On moldings, wipe parallel to the length of the molding and again wipe off more on the high spots and less in the grooves or recessed areas.

On flat surfaces such as doors or furniture tops, wipe off more of the glaze in the center of the panel and leave the panel darker around the edges and in the corners. This simulates the natural wear that a piece of old furniture would exhibit if the glaze had been worn off over the years.

Again, experiment with wiping techniques on some scrap pieces. In some cases wiping in a straight line is most appropriate, while in others the glaze will look better if wiped off with a circular or oval motion. Sometimes the most pleasing effect is achieved with little or no wiping and then stippling or patting lightly with cheesecloth.

Each wiping technique gives a different effect. If you don't like the results the first time you try, remember, you can always wipe off the glaze with a rag moistened in paint thinner and start all over again.

Another process that is often used to enhance the antique effect of a glazed finish is to spatter on a little of the concentrated glazing color after all wiping has been completed. The simplest way to do this is to use an old toothbrush. Dip the brush into the concentrated glazing color, then hold it a few inches away from the surface and flick the bristles with your thumb. This will spatter flecks of the concentrated color onto the freshly glazed

surface. You can vary the size of the flecks by varying both the distance between the toothbrush and the surface and the speed with which you move the brush along.

After the glazing color has dried completely (wait at least 48 hours), apply a clear coat of varnish. Although a gloss varnish is sometimes used, most experts agree that a satin-finish or low-luster varnish is far more appropriate for a finish of this kind.

The varnish can be applied by brush or spray, and one coat is usually sufficient. However, tabletops, children's pieces, and other surfaces that get hard wear will stand up better if two coats are applied. Keeping the surface waxed is also a good idea to protect against spills and staining.

IMITATION WOOD-GRAIN FINISHES

Sometimes you will want to refinish a piece of furniture or set of cabinets to make it look as if it has natural wood grain. The real wood underneath the paint may not be attractive enough to be worth stripping and finishing in the usual manner, or it may be so badly marred and mismatched that a "natural" wood finish is completely impractical. In such cases the same type of glazing process that is used for antiquing can often be used to achieve an imitation wood-grain effect. It's merely a matter of selecting the right glaze for the right background color and then varying the technique used to wipe off and streak the glaze.

The background color you select as a base coat should be in a beige or brownish tone that is similar to the lightest part of the grain in the wood you want to imitate. For woods such as mahogany or maple, the background should have a slightly more reddish cast, while for oak or pine it might have a creamier tone. Walnut is usually simulated by using a sand color or a light brown as a base.

The color of the glazing liquid will have to be quite a bit darker—something like the darkest streaks in the wood grain of the actual species being imitated. For example, you'll want a dark brown glaze for walnut, while a medium brown glaze will be more appropriate for pine or chestnut. For an oak grain the glaze should be more of a grayish or muddy brown. In each case, if you have painted a number of samples with the background color first, you will have pieces on which you can experiment until you achieve the color combination that looks right to you.

Actually, specific tones are not really critical in most cases, because all you want to achieve is the appearance of a wood grain—not necessarily to match a specific type or shade of wood. And as long as you don't place an imitation finish right next to a real piece of wood it's surprising how realistic the effect will be.

The most important step is the technique used in wiping off the glaze. The idea is to create streaks that will look like a natural wood grain. One popular method is to first wipe off part of the glaze with a coarse pad of steel wool dragged lightly along the surface. This will create a streaky effect without removing too much of the glaze color. As you finish each panel with the steel wool, go over it again by lightly dragging the tip of a dry paintbrush in the same direction over the same area. This will soften the coarse streaks left by the steel wool and will create a more natural-looking wood-grain effect.

Since no wood grain is ever perfectly straight, imitate a weaving pattern by twisting the brush slightly as you drag it over the surface and by weaving it slowly from side to side as you move it lengthwise along the panel. Study a piece of natural wood grain to note how it has streaks that weave in and out, and try to stroke your dry brush in such a way as to create this same appearance.

After you have achieved the effect you want, apply a protective coat of varnish to keep the finish from being rubbed off or damaged. You can use either a high-gloss or semigloss varnish for this purpose, but remember that the higher the gloss, the more it will show up irregularities and imperfections in the surface.

GILDING TECHNIQUES

Very often pieces of furniture with carved or molded edges will have these edges finished in gold. The traditional material used for applying a real gold finish is gold leaf, which is not a paint. As its name implies, gold leaf is exactly that—ultrathin leaves of 22-karat gold metal. These are cemented to the surface with a special tacky varnish (called gold size) that is made for the purpose. The leaves of gold are so thin (4 of them are equal to about 1/1,000 of an inch in thickness) that they cannot actually be handled with the fingers. They would fall apart. They must be picked up with a special brush by using static electricity to make them cling (you run the brush through your hair to build up a static charge). There is also a type that has a special tissue-paper backing for handling. This permits you to press the gold leaf into place and then peel off the tissue paper.

Gold leaf is extremely expensive, and many dealers no longer stock it. This, plus the fact that it requires considerable skill to use and apply, does not make it very popular with home furniture finishers.

Fortunately, there are a number of synthetic materials that, while not as long-lasting as real gold leaf, will stand up for some time in normal use. Most art supply stores and many paint stores sell synthetic gold paints that are far superior to the old-fashioned gilt paints used years ago. Better yet, these stores also sell paste-type, wax-base gilt finishes that are rubbed on much as you would shoe polish. These come in a variety of different colors or shades and build up to a beautiful gold luster if they are buffed after they have been rubbed on. You can also leave them as dull and as aged-looking as you like.

They are easy to use and often look as good as the real thing.

One good method for achieving a lustrous gold finish is to use a combination of both of these materials. Start by priming the area to be gilded with orange shellac and allow this to dry for 1 to 2 hours. Then brush on a coat of artist's-quality gold-leaf paint, using a soft camel's-hair brush. Allow this gold to dry overnight, then highlight the finish by rubbing on a coat of paste-type wax gilt. Spread it on uniformly with a folded pad of cloth, then buff lightly with a clean piece of cloth. When finished, the gold can be left as is, or it can be "antiqued" by wiping a glaze over the surface.

Dealing with Contractors

. . . .

Sooner or later even the most experienced and most willing do-it-yourselfer will come across a sizable remodeling project or a major maintenance job that calls for the services of an experienced professional contractor. It may be because the project is much too complex for you to tackle alone, or because it calls for the use of specialized tools and equipment that you don't have. Or it may simply be because the job is so large and so time-consuming that you couldn't complete it alone within a reasonable length of time.

Whatever the reason, it is wise not to get in "over your head" on any home repair or home remodeling project—if you have serious doubts about your ability to do the work, or about being able to finish the job in a reasonable amount of time, chances are you should seriously consider hiring a professional contractor who has the

equipment and the skills to do the job right.

Unfortunately, this is when things sometimes start to go wrong—all too often a condominium owner's dealings with a contractor can lead to unexpected and sometimes serious misunderstandings and unnecessary frustration that in more serious cases may even end up in court. However, things do not have to work out this way, in spite of the many home remodeling "horror" stories that we have all heard about. In a high percentage of cases the work does get completed properly and close to the date promised.

Of course, just as in any other business, there are some unreliable and unscrupulous contractors who think nothing of "ripping you off" with shoddy or incomplete work if they can get away with it. But these contractors are in the minority. Most are honest, hardworking businessmen who will try to satisfy their customers and make every effort to fulfill their contracts—*or at least what they believe is called for in their contract.* Unfortunately, this is where the trouble often occurs—all too often the contract is not as clear as it should be, making some type of misunderstanding almost inevitable.

The reason for this is that far too many contracts and estimates do not clearly spell out *in writing* exactly what work the contractor is to complete and what materials he is to supply, as well as what materials or appliances he expects the home owner to pay for separately. The written contract must be detailed and explicit enough so that both parties understand it clearly with no chance of different interpretations. Vague language or the omission of specific details in a contract can easily lead to the kind of argument that is the hardest to resolve— where each side thinks that he is right.

For example, if you understand the contractor's price to include all labor and all materials, then his contract should state this. If he will pay for appliances, cabinets, or other items only up to a certain price, then again, the contract should say so. On the other hand, if you are agreeing to pay for the appliance or cabinets separately, this too should be spelled out in the contract. Don't take anything for granted, even if someone tells you "that's how it's always done."

Never depend on any kind of oral promises or a handshake type of agreement, no matter how well you think you know that contractor or how highly recommended he comes to you. Putting everything in writing is the only way to make sure you are both talking about and agreeing on the same terms and conditions so there is no possibility of either one misunderstanding the other.

CHOOSING AND HIRING A CONTRACTOR

The best way to find a reliable contractor is through personal recommendations from friends, neighbors, relatives, or other people whose opinion you trust. Make sure the contractor recommended has had some experience doing work similar to what you need. Visit some of the people the contractor has worked for to get their opinions.

Were his men reasonably neat and clean while working? Did the crew show up when promised, and did the contractor complete his work approximately in the time promised? Were there substantial extra costs that had not been expected or agreed upon ahead of time? Was he reasonably easy to talk to and get along with,

especially when changes were required in the original contract (almost inevitable on most jobs)? Did he come back to fix things when necessary?

If possible, ask his customers these and other questions when the contractor, or his representative, is *not* present.

Since most people do not hire remodeling contractors often, it's not always easy to find one through personal recommendations—if you want more than one estimate (you should always try to get at least two or three bids so you can compare prices). Another good source for names in your area would be the local chapter of the National Association of the Remodeling Industry. If you contact their national office at 4301 N. Fairfax Dr., Suite 310, Arlington, Va. 22203 (703-276-7600), they will give you the address of a local branch, which will then refer you to its members in your area. Or you can contact the Remodelers Council, 15th and M streets NW, Washington, D.C. 20005 (202-822-0216). They too will refer you to a local branch, which will then furnish a list of members in your area. Another good source is the Home Owners Warranty Corp., 1110 N. Glebe Rd., Arlington, Va. 22201. Remodelers who belong to this organization offer a written warranty against defective materials and workmanship of up to five years after the job is completed, and this warranty is backed by an insurance company so you don't have to worry that the company may go out of business in the near future.

Getting estimates from contractors who belong to local chapters of these organizations is no guarantee of outstanding honesty, superior quality of work, or complete reliability, but it does indicate that the contractor is an established businessman with roots in the community and has at least agreed to abide by the organization's ethics and standards of accountability.

Other sources of recommendations in most communities are the local suppliers and dealers who sell to these contractors—lumberyards, paint stores, building supply outlets, wholesale plumbing and electrical supply houses, and the like. They usually are familiar with many of the local contractors in your area and will sometimes make recommendations, but don't accept these blindly. Remember, these dealers want to push their own customers over others who may be preferable, but you can get some clues that

will be helpful. For example, if several dealers recommend the same contractor, chances are that he has an excellent reputation in the area.

Reliable and successful contractors almost always have a good credit rating, so it's also a good idea to check with your local banks, supply houses, and various dealers to see what you can find out. If a contractor buys for cash only, or if you get other indications that his credit is shaky, beware—you may be better off dealing with others.

As you come across various names, check these with the local office of your Better Business Bureau. That organization doesn't make recommendations or give opinions as to qualifications, but they do keep track of complaints and will tell you if any complaints have been lodged against that contractor.

Once you have decided on several names, ask each one for a written estimate. Each estimate should specify, in addition to the price, exactly what work the contractor will do and what materials or supplies he will furnish. Make sure that all estimates are based on doing the same work and supplying the same materials (in quality as well as in quantity). For example, if you are contracting for a paint job, make sure each contractor specifies how many coats of paint will be applied to walls, woodwork, or other surfaces, what type of preparation there will be in each case, and what brand of paint he will be using (each should specify the same brand or a brand that is equal in price and quality). If you are remodeling a bathroom, make sure each estimate specifies the same brand fixtures to be installed and states whether or not the price includes supplying those fixtures and any accessories required. If plumbing must be replaced or removed, this should be spelled out, and in those cases where colors may affect the price, the colors also should be specified in writing.

When trying to decide which contractor to hire, don't be pressured into making a quick decision. Be wary of those who tell you that they can do the job cheaper because they happen to be working in your neighborhood at the time or those who insist that prices will be going up next week (or next month). Avoid those who want you to sign a contract immediately without giving you adequate time to study it or make comparisons, and be especially cautious of anyone who asks for a sizable deposit up front (from 10 to 25 percent may be reasonable in some cases, but only

if a substantial amount of material that cannot be easily returned must be purchased ahead of time in order to get the job started).

Don't automatically accept the estimate with the lowest price—do some further investigating first. That contractor's work may or may not be on a par with the others, so check his references more closely. Be very wary if one bid is a great deal lower than the others—he may have simply made a mistake and underestimated the job. If so, then he could try to cut corners to make up for his mistake later on.

An exceptionally low price may also be deliberate—that contractor may be overly anxious to get the job, but then intends to cut corners or shortchange you on some of the materials when doing the work.

WHAT THE CONTRACT SHOULD INCLUDE TO AVOID DISPUTES

Once you have decided on a particular contractor and accepted his estimate, use that estimate as the basis for the contract you will draw up; don't just sign the original estimate and assume that it is adequate to cover all facets of your agreement. To avoid future arguments and frustrating misunderstandings, a number of stipulations and specifications should be clearly spelled out:

• The contract should give an approximate starting date and an expected completion date—although this will always be subject to delays caused by bad weather, strikes, and other conditions beyond the contractor's control. The idea is to avoid having him drag out the job forever while he stalls for various reasons—for example, while he takes men off

your job and then spreads them around on other jobs.

• Plans and specifications should be made part of the contract, and the contract should state that the contractor will file for all necessary permits and will call for all required inspections and then procure all necessary approvals as work progresses. It's best not to get permits yourself because you could then be liable if the work doesn't comply with the building codes. The contract should also stipulate that the work will comply with all applicable codes and regulations that govern that type of work in your community.

• Insist on seeing proof of adequate liability and casualty insurance, as well as compensation insurance that covers all his workers (otherwise if they get hurt in your home, they could sue you). If in doubt as to whether or not you are adequately protected, show these insurance certificates to your own insurance broker.

• Where applicable, the contract should call for specific brands or grades of material. If you are remodeling a bathroom, it should not just say "new tub and vanity," but should give the brand and model number or style of the fixture you have selected. Be careful about the words *or equal* and *or equivalent* if inserted right after this. Although these terms are normally acceptable and often used in such contracts, they should be qualified with the understanding that you will have the right to accept or reject the product that is being substituted if you don't feel it is "equal" to the one specified.

• Many remodeling jobs involve some tearing down and considerable creation of dust and debris. If you expect the contractor to clean this up and remove all trash or old appliances at his expense, the contract should say so. In addition to stipulating who pays for cleaning and trash removal, and who is responsible for arranging this, it should also say if this will be done at the end of each working day, at the end of each week, or only after all work is completed.

• The contractor should be required to issue a "waiver of liens" before you give him his final payment in order to ensure that no suppliers or subcontractors can put a lien against your property if he failed to pay them in full.

• Terms of payment should be clearly spelled out, including how much money will be paid at each stage of the job and how these "stages" are defined. Under no circumstances should you ever pay more than the value of the work actually completed. This not only protects you if the contractor decides to quit before the job is over, it also provides him with added incentive to get the work finished—especially when it comes to the finishing touches at the end of the job. Then when it comes time for the final payment you should hold back at least 10 percent for a few days after all work is completed. This gives you time to check everything that he has done to make sure it meets with your approval before making that last payment or signing any kind of release.

• The contract should also specify how any change orders will be handled. Changes that you request, or that may be agreed upon by both parties after the contract is signed, should be put down in writing, along with the cost of these changes, if any. All such change orders should be signed by both parties.

Index

• • • •

ABOUT THE AUTHOR

Bernard Gladstone was the home improvement editor of *The New York Times* for more than thirty years, during which he also wrote two columns per week. He is the author of over a dozen books on home repair, maintenance, and improvement, including the best-selling *The New York Times Complete Manual of Home Repair* and *The Simon & Schuster Complete Guide to Home Repair and Maintenance*.

Today, Bernard Gladstone writes a column about home improvement that is syndicated to various newspapers throughout the U.S. and Canada, and is a contributing editor to *Motor Boating & Sailing* magazine. He lives in Sarasota, Florida.